GLOBAL INTERNET LAW

IN A NUTSHELL

SECOND EDITION

By

MICHAEL L. RUSTAD

Thomas F. Lambert Jr. Professor of Law &
Co-Director Intellectual Property Law Concentration
Suffolk University Law School

WEST®

Mat #41313632

Nutshell Series, In a Nutshell and the Nutshell Logo are trademarks registered in the U.S. Patent and Trademark Office.

© 2009 Thomson Reuters
© 2013 LEG, Inc. d/b/a West Academic Publishing

      610 Opperman Drive
      St. Paul, MN 55123
      1-800-313-9378

West, West Academic Publishing, and West Academic are trademarks of West Publishing Corporation, used under license.

Printed in the United States of America

ISBN: 978–0–314–28330–6

PREFACE

This book distills the main contours of settled Internet law as well as areas that are still evolving. The goal is to provide the reader a succinct exposition of basic concepts and methods in diverse Internet law topics as well as multiple perspectives on what shape the law should take. This second edition of the Nutshell expands the scope to include global developments as well as U.S. Internet law because, since the previous edition, Internet law is less U.S. centric. One of the central themes of the book is that lawyers of the twenty-first century must master global Internet law developments to represent online businesses in a cross-border legal environment.

As e-businesses use the border-defying Internet, they will increasingly become subject to foreign procedural and substantive law. The U.S. business community, for example, needs legal audits for its websites sales and services whenever it targets European consumers. Websites that collect personally identifiable information need to comply with the Data Protection Directive even if they are not physically located in Europe.

In contrast, foreign websites may be dragged into U.S. courts where they infringe the rights of U.S. users. The Internet is interconnected and transnational, challenging traditional sovereignty based upon geographic borders. No transnational sovereign devises uniform rules for Internet jurisdiction and the enforcement of online judgments. The lack of certainty about the law of cyberspace requires cross-border treaties and conventions. To date, the countries connected to the Internet have not agreed to cede their sovereignty in order to harmonize cyberjurisdictional rules. Instead, courts adapt their own national rules to determine jurisdiction. In numerous places, I address European Commission regulations, directives and conventions as well as Internet law from other foreign jurisdictions. The organization of the book summarizes many of the cases and statutes taught in e-commerce, Internet law, or cyberspace law courses.

This book will be helpful to business lawyers as well as litigators confronted with Internet-related legal issues. I have provided a concise yet systematic examination of UCITA, the Principles of the Law of Software Contracts, and other projects to reform online contracting law. This nutshell is comprehensive in its coverage of global Internet issues that practitioners and students will encounter but will also serve as a useful introduction for non-lawyers and students in diverse disciplines such as computer science, business, nursing, sociology, law and society and criminology.

MICHAEL L. RUSTAD

June 14, 2013

ACKNOWLEDGMENTS

Great thanks are due to Suffolk University Law School's reference librarians Diane D'Angelo and Rick Buckingham. I appreciate the help of Stetson University College of Law librarians Sally Waters and Ashley Krenelka. I have had an experienced and gifted team of research assistants working on this project. I would like to thank Senior Research Assistants Alex Chiulli, Jesse Gag at Suffolk and Paris Tsangaris at Stetson for their hard work editing and commenting on numerous drafts. Alex Chiulli co-authored a practice pointer on the admissibility of evidence of text messages with me.

I would also like to thank Suffolk University Law School students Colin Barrett, Borana Hajanj, Jason Collettis, J. Daniel Duval, Brian Lynch, Jack Lindsay, Stefan Martinez, Brooke Perrone, Nate Rice, and Wystan Umland for their sure-footed editorial work.

Vit Svejkovsky, a 2010 Magistr graduate of Prague's Charles University Faculty of Law and a LL.M. graduate of Suffolk University Law School, co-authored the section comparing U.S. to European consumer law. My Suffolk University Law School colleagues Andrew Beckerman Rodau, Stephen McJohn, and Gabe Tenenbaum gave me useful examples and editorial suggestions for several chapters. Komal Hayat, a 2009 LL.B. graduate of University of the Punjab and a LL.M. graduate of

Suffolk University Law School, edited many chapters. Tom Koenig edited a number of the chapters while he was traveling and working in India.

During the fall of 2012, Borana Hajanj and Vit Svejkovsky edited every chapter often providing foreign cases and statutory references. My son James Knowles Rustad, M.D., edited Chapter 6 on Internet torts and provided me with contemporary examples. My daughter Erica Rustad Ferreira, Esq., also provided fresh and interesting Internet law examples and explanations throughout the book. Kara Ryan, Jessica Fehr and Shannon Edgar provided me with excellent secretarial and administrative support. Dr. Vittoria Onufrio and Dr. Patrik Lindskoug assisted me with European Internet law developments. Professors Thomas H. Koenig, Marshall Shapo, Gabe Tenenbaum, and Darryl Wilson also provided me with useful research and editorial suggestions. Finally, as always, I appreciate the editorial work and good company of my wife, Chryss J. Knowles.

OUTLINE

TABLE OF CASES

References are to Pages

TABLE OF STATUTES

References are to Pages

TABLE OF AUTHORITIES

References are to Pages

GLOBAL INTERNET LAW

SECOND EDITION

CHAPTER 1

OVERVIEW OF THE GLOBAL INTERNET

You must imagine at the eventual heart of things to come, linked or integrated systems or networks of computers capable of storing faithful simulacra of the entire treasure of the accumulated knowledge and artistic production of past ages and of taking into the store new intelligence of all sorts as produced. Lasers [and] satellites [among others] will operate as ganglions to extend the reach of the systems to the ultimate users.

Benjamin Kaplan, An Unhurried View of Copyright Law (1967).

Where to begin in explaining a topic as vast as global Internet law? There is an inherent problem in writing about the omnipresent Internet, which is continuously in the process of becoming—a moving stream, not a stagnant pond. Courts and legislatures must continually update the law as the Internet creates new legal dilemmas. Writing about Global Internet Law is like trying to hold back the ocean with a broom. Benjamin Kaplan's prediction of a vast computer network storing all accumulated knowledge is close to fruition in less than two decades. How much content is on the Internet? The scale of information on the Internet is difficult to fathom. Wikipedia is the largest encyclopedia in the world, consisting of sixteen million articles in over 260 languages, created and maintained by more than 100,000 contributors from around the world.

Each month, contributors add four million entries to Wikipedia and edit a vast amount of its existing text. Jimmy Wales, Wikipedia's founder, asks us to imagine a world where everyone has free access to the treasure trove of human knowledge. Flickr users add five million images each day or sixty photographs a second.

There is an inherent problem in writing about the omnipresent Internet, which is continuously in the process of becoming—a moving stream, not a stagnant pond. Where to begin in explaining a topic as vast as global Internet law? The scale of information on the Internet is difficult to fathom. Courts and legislatures must continually update the law as the Internet creates legal lag in all procedural and substantive fields. Google Book, alone, is the equivalent of Benjamin Kaplan's treasure trove of information with its colossal collection of digitalized books from library collections all over the world. Google estimates that there are fifteen billion web pages and by the time you are reading this, it will be even greater as 60,000 new websites go online each day.

Flickr users add five million images each day or sixty photographs a second. Google estimates that there are fifteen billion web pages and by the time you are reading this, it will be even greater as 60,000 new websites go online each day. Netflix announced that it had streamed two billion hours of content in the fourth quarter of 2011 alone. Google Book is a colossal collection of digitalized books from library collections all over the world. The next chapter explores the legal implications of this ocean of data for the path of Internet governance.

The unique legal issues arising from an ocean of data on an international computer network of interoperable packet switched data networks is the subject of Internet law. Internet law is more than applying traditional principles of procedural and substantive law to the web or old wine in new bottles. Internet law was predominately U.S. law during the first fifteen years of the World Wide Web. U.S. courts and legislatures led the way in developing specialized statutes and cases to accommodate traditional principles of law to the global Internet.

The Internet is a cross-border transnational legal environment. Increasingly, national legislatures attempt to regulate conduct by defendants outside their borders. Trademark infringement, copyright infringement, patent law, privacy issues, Internet fraud, cybertorts and crimes are increasingly cross-border and transnational. The globalized Internet is a new realm governed by many nations but without a transnational sovereign, international treaty, specialized court system, or virtual alternative dispute system. While once the Internet was governed exclusively by the U.S. government, other countries are pressing for a greater role in transnational governance.

U.S. mobile application developers, for example, will need to comply with data protection regulations in the twenty-seven countries of the European Union. Foreign providers will need to provide users with notice about a specific application's collection and use of personal information and obtain the user's consent to those terms and conditions under a proposed U.S. statute.

These examples illustrate the necessity for casting Internet law as a global legal environment. Counsel advising a buyer or seller in a cross-border transaction will need to comply with foreign as well as domestic law to protect its rights and to avoid infringing upon the rights of others. For example, Microsoft was charged with anticompetitive conduct in its licensing practices in Europe. EU competition law does not permit the restriction of passive sales. One of the difficult issues in assessing competition law is to extend the concept of vertical guidelines to the Internet. Most Internet law or cyberspace law classes focus exclusively on U.S. cases and statutory developments. In contrast, each chapter of this treatise includes an analysis of foreign law developments, often comparing approaches to U.S. law.

Daily headlines confirm the transnational nature of Internet law. Increasingly, national legislatures attempt to regulate conduct by defendants outside their borders. Trademark infringement, copyright infringement, patent law, privacy issues, Internet fraud, cybertorts and crimes are increasingly cross-border and transnational. The Deter Cyber Theft Act of 2013, for example would require the Director of National Intelligence with creating a list identifying foreign countries that engage in the cyber theft of trade secrets from U.S. companies. An example of a global Internet dispute is the trade war between Antigua and the United States. Congress enacted the Unlawful Internet Gambling Enforcement Act ("UIGEA") of 2013 that ratcheted up criminal penalties for online gambling businesses that accept payment through credit cards, checks, or fund transfers.

The globalized Internet is a new realm governed by many nations but without a transnational sovereign, international treaty, specialized court system, or virtual alternative dispute system. While once the Internet was governed exclusively by the U.S. government, other countries are pressing for a greater role in transnational governance. Laura DiNardis writes how:

> The Internet has transformed the manner in which information is exchanged and business is conducted, arguably more than any other communication development in the past century. Despite its wide reach and powerful global influence, it is a medium uncontrolled by any one centralized system, organization, or governing body, a reality that has given rise to all manner of free-speech issues and cybersecurity concerns. The conflicts surrounding Internet governance are the new spaces where political and economic power is unfolding in the twenty-first century.
>
> LAURA DINARDIS, THE GLOBAL WAR FOR INTERNET GOVERNANCE 1 (2014).

Cyberspace is the fastest growing free-trade zone. Internet business is multi-hemispheric, as the sun never sets on a Web site that stands ready to communicate with customers 24 hours a day, seven days a week in all countries connected to the World Wide Web. Cyberspace is a new realm without a transnational sovereign, international treaty, specialized court system, or virtual dispute resolution system. National differences among the regimes of different countries connected to the Internet will inevitably lead to conflicts of law. The Internet has made it necessary to rework every branch of the law, and these ongoing changes will be examined throughout this nutshell.

The remainder of this introductory chapter focuses on the technology, history, and the distributed geography of the Internet in order to provide context for understanding Internet law. Designing legal solutions for the networked information society requires a clear conception of what is technologically possible as well as an understanding of the cultural and business context of Internet law disputes.

The Internet affects every aspect of society. The more limited the connections, the more likely country-wide Internet shutdowns will occur. In 2011, an elderly woman in the Republic of Georgia shut down the Internet in Armenia for five hours when she sliced through a fiber optic cable while scavenging for copper. Since the World Wide Web, the Internet has never gone done.

What would happen if the Internet suddenly collapsed and shut down worldwide? Business operations have grown dependent upon the Internet. Businesses already suffer interruptions in supply chains and operations from malicious code and defective software design; but attacks on

Internet hubs could result in a breakdown of critical information infrastructure.

Cell phones would shut down as well as desktop computers, laptops, and GPS devices. Financial institutions would face a frenzied payments crisis that would quickly dwarf what occurred in Cyprus in 2013 if electronic financial systems suddenly went offline.

Cloud computing would halt, leaving countless businesses without access to key data, software applications, and other operational software. Governments around the world would suffer dislocations because of interruptions in key business, banking, military, fiscal, and governmental infrastructure. Medical records, shipment and aircraft tracking systems, and numerous other vital communications would become unavailable. A world without text messages, Twitter (2006), Skype (2003), or Facebook (2004) is difficult to imagine, but these Internet-based inventions have only been a part of mass culture for the past decade.

How might law and society be different if the U.S. government never invented the Internet? The Internet is of overarching importance to post-industrial societies. In less than two decades, we have come to take the Web for granted when we book flights, communicate with each other, contribute to social media sites, purchase e-books, shop in virtual bookstores, listen to music, and explore trending videos. Netflix, an on-line entertainment service providing movies and television programming to subscribers by streaming content through the Internet, has driven Blockbuster and other brick and mortar video stores out of business, while bookstores are being forced to revise their business models. Dick Tracy used revolutionary technologies such as the two-way wrist radio and later the two-way wrist television. At the time, these devices were futuristic, but now seem almost quaint with the ceaseless innovation and technological advances in smartphones and iPads.

Carl Sagan famously said, "We live in a society exquisitely dependent on science and technology, in which hardly anyone knows anything about science and technology." Lawyers need a rudimentary understanding of Internet technology in order to frame arguments about such topics as cross-border jurisdiction, deep linking, framing, metatags, or domain names. This chapter only scratches the surface of the mechanics that govern the Internet, but it will provide enough understanding as to what is technologically possible.

§ 1-1. The History of the Internet

(A) HISTORY OF THE WORLD WIDE WEB

No one even used the term, "Internet," prior to the early 1980s. The word, "cyberspace," was coined by William Gibson in his 1984 science fiction classic, *Neuromancer*, which was the story of a computer hacker for hire planning the ultimate computer intrusion. The Internet was not assimilated into the mass culture until the mid-1990s when the World

Wide Web went mainstream. The Internet evolved in the 1970s and 1980s as a product of a joint private and public partnership that networked university and government computers enabling computer-to-computer communications. The World Wide Web, as we know it today, was prefigured by the Internet created by the U.S. Department of Defense's Advanced Research Projects Agency ("ARPA") in 1969.

(B) NSFNET

The National Science Foundation ("NSF") received a grant from the federal government and assumed control of the T1 backbone from ARPA in the mid-1980s. NSFNET originally limited the Internet to education, military, and other governmental purposes, prohibiting commercial uses. By the mid-1980s, the NSF employed packet switching to develop the major backbone communications service for the Internet. Scientists at ARPANET developed TCP/IP to enable computers to communicate with each other across the United States. It was not until the mid-1980s that computer scientists at most U.S. universities had Internet access. Several other governmental agencies also developed computer networks so their researchers could communicate and share data.

The privatization of the Internet began in the early 1990s when NSF opened the Internet up to businesses. In 1990, the NSF held the first workshop on "The Commercialization of the Internet" at Harvard University. The NSF lifted the ban on commercial traffic in 1991, jumpstarting the

24/7 virtual marketplace we know today. Non-state actors including companies and non-governmental organizations began to play an increasingly important role beginning in the mid-1990s.

In cooperation with NSF, private companies developed a T3 backbone, connecting the networks of major companies. By September 1995, the demand for Internet registration had become largely commercial (97 percent) and began to expand exponentially. The commercialized Internet created new legal dilemmas, such as the conflict between domain names and trademarks, the enforceability of online contracts, and how to protect copyrights in the new digital marketplace. Courts began to resolve Internet-related jurisdictional disputes between business entities selling products and services on the Internet.

The federal government appointed the NSF to supervise the domain name registration system until May 1993 when Network Solutions, Inc., ("NSI") was charged with administering of the domain name registry under a sub-contract with the U.S. Defense Information Systems Agency ("DISA"). The Internet Corporation for Assigned Names and Numbers ("ICANN") currently controls the "domain name system" ("DNS"), formerly regulated by the U.S. Government. ICANN is a quasi-governmental nonprofit responsible for Internet infrastructure such as IP address space, domain name management, and root server functions.

In September 1998, when NSF's agreement with NSI expired, the number of registered domain names surpassed 2 million. Today, there are over 2.5 billion Internet users. The current "Internet Protocol version 4" ("IPv4") has the capacity to support 4.2 billion addresses. Each computer assigned to the Internet has a unique IPv4 address and thus it is a critically important element of Internet infrastructure. This address space will be greatly expanded by IPv6 to space for an estimated trillion addresses. Veni Markovski describes the differences between IPv4 and IPv6 as comparing a tennis ball to the sun. Veni Markovski, ICANN, Vice President for Russia, CIS and Eastern Europe, Remarks at The Geopolitics of Internet Governance, Center for Strategic & International Studies (May 23, 2013).

Within a decade, the computer scientists of the U.S. Department of Defense's ("DoD") Advanced Research Projects Agency Network ("ARPANET") used "Transmission Control Protocol/Internet Protocol" ("TCP/IP") to network computers across the United States. The TCP/IP protocol is the most widely used communication system within the Internet, and functions to enable file transfers, e-mail, remote terminal access, and other vital essential tools of the World Wide Web. The TCP is the data packeting protocol whereas IP is the protocol for routine packets. Each packet has a header containing its source and destination, a block of data content, and an error checking code.

"Internet Protocol Numbers" ("IP") encompass four groups of digits separated by periods, such as "192.215.247.50," pinpointing the location of a specific computer connected to the Internet. The domain name system ("DNS") protocol replaces strings of numbers with easier to remember words. Increasingly, copyright owners are using this information to catch infringers. Service providers collect this data for administrative purposes to improve system performance.

The first four computers connected to the Internet were located at the University of California-Santa Barbara, Stanford University, UCLA, and in Utah. By 1977, ARPANET's network of interconnected computers spanned the continent but not yet the world. In 1981, the Internet consisted of 300 computers and by 1985; the Internet consisted of 2,000 connected computers. As late as 1989, that number stood at fewer than 90,000 computers. ARPANET and U.S. Department of Defense contractors developed the Tier One ("T1") backbone for the Internet, which were the principal data routes in the Internet's formative period.

Few persons outside the military and educational institutions used e-mail or electronic bulletin boards during this period. A turning point occurred when computer scientists at the University of Minnesota created Gopher, the first user-friendly interface in 1991. The Gopher search engine enabled users to search, distribute, and retrieve documents from the Internet, prefiguring the World Wide Web's friendly user interfaces. The National Center for Supercomputing Applications at the University of Illinois launched "Mosaic", the first graphical web browser in 1993.

Tim Berners-Lee is the George Washington of the World Wide Web as well as the Internet's Thomas Jefferson and Benjamin Franklin all rolled into one person. He developed the first "Graphic User Interface" (GUI) browser, named the "World Wide Web," and launched the first web page on August 6, 1991. Berners-Lee's life work reflects the saying: "The best way to predict the future is to invent it." Berners-Lee also developed a new tool for sharing information on the Internet using "hypertext transfer protocol" or HTTP, which allowed real time communications graphics and text processing.

(C) FTP & HTTP

Users send requests to access websites employing the File Transfer Protocol ("FTP"), a standard that permits data and images to be copied and transmitted from one machine to another over TCP/IP networks. HTTP is a high-level protocol that enables the user to transfer files from one machine to another over TCP/IP networks. HTTP interprets and classifies metadata in files, which in turn, enables browsers to exhibit hypertext files as web pages in HTML. HTML5 is the latest format, which is especially well suited for mobile game apps because it functions like a highly advanced walky-talky system. Since 9/11, the federal government requires companies and contractors to support Simple File Transfer Protocol ("SFTP"), which is a secure FTP implementation providing secure file management functionality over any data stream. A growing number of states are also requiring vendors to implement *secure FTP* or Virtual Private Networks.

(D) MICROFORMATS & XML

Extensible Markup Language ("XML"), like HTML, is a micro format to transport and store data. XML is text based and used to represent any structured information such as a book or other document. XML was derived from an older standard format called SGML (ISO 8879). XML, unlike HTML, allows users to create their own formatting tags and converts data into indexed data. Home electronics incorporate XML in IUniversal Plug and Play ("UPnP").

(E) MPEG & MP3

The Motion Picture Expert Group ("MPEG") sets standards for compressing and storing video, audio, and animation in digital form. MPEG developed the MP3 and MP4 highly compressed formats. MPEG1 is a standard for CDBROM video whereas MPEG2 is a standard for full screen, broadcast quality video MPEG4 is the standard for video telephony. MPEG1 Audio Layer 3 ("MP3") is a digital audio encoding format. MP3 does not signify the borderland between MPEG2 and MPEG4, but is short for MPEG1, Layer 3 Audio. A MP3 is able to compress WAV audio making audio files easily downloadable.

(F) XML'S METALANGUAGE

XML is a markup language for documents, enabling users to create custom-made tags that organize and deliver content more efficiently. XML is a metalanguage, prefiguring ever more sophisticated markup languages. Today, the researchers continue to upgrade XML as well as other WWW standards.

§ 1-2. Internet Technologies Demystified

The five types of hardware comprising key Internet technology infrastructure are: (1) hubs, (2) bridges, (3) gateways, (4) repeaters, and (5) routers. Routers and bridges transmit information from one network area to another. A switch is a network device that selects how data gets to its next destination. These devices may be used to transmit data from the Internet to LAN destinations and vice versa. Companies may connect their personal computers to a Wide Area Network ("WAN"), which utilizes routers to transmit data between LANs.

(A) HUBS OR IXPS

The Internet's major hubs or network access points are physical entities that connect computers around the world. The Internet Exchange ("IX") acts as a junction between multiple points of Internet presence. Here, peers are able to connect to each other in order to exchange local Internet traffic. An oppressive regime can use their hubs as a kill switch without affecting the Internet in other nations. China, for example, creates temporary blackouts of its Internet to stifle the political opposition, a policy sarcastically referred to as "The Great Firewall of China." The United States Congress is debating installing a kill switch that could shut down the Internet in the event of a national emergency. The proposed "kill switch" is opposed by many academics and policymakers who note that Hoshni Mubarak, the then Egyptian President caused the Internet to go dark to stymie massive demonstrations against his regime during the Arab Spring in 2012. "Today you can run an approximation of *1984* out of a couple of rooms filled with server racks." Matthieu Aikins, *Jamming Tripoli*, WIRED, (June 2012), at 146, 176. The supporters of the "Kill Switch" contend that it will only be used in a true emergency against cybercriminals that threaten America's information infrastructure.

(B) BRIDGES

A bridge is an intelligent connectivity device connecting computers on a Local Area Network ("LAN") and World Area Network ("WANS"). A bridge examines each message on a LAN, sorting and forwarding messages between LANS and WANS.

(C) GATEWAYS

A gateway is the network point that acts as an entrance into another network. A gateway typically includes a firewall designed to block out unrecognized Internet protocols. These firewalls authenticate data and identify users, preventing intruders from intercepting data or planting viruses. The proxy server, or application gateway, runs on the firewall. Application gateways employ authentication and logging tailored for high security businesses or the military. A company or individual will typically install anti-virus software at its gateway.

(D) ROUTERS

The Internet is essentially a collection of communication networks interconnected by bridges and/or routers. A router is a piece of hardware that essentially routes, or guides, computer traffic along a network. Cisco Systems is a leading producer of routers, which are intelligent devices conjoining routed data over many networks. Information is exchanged in the form of "packets," which do not travel along predestined routes. The packet switching system allows efficient traffic control.

(E) REPEATERS

Wireless repeaters amplify a signal once it loses strength or is attenuated as it is transmitted along a cable network. This repeater takes a signal from a router or access point and rebroadcasts it, creating what is, in effect, a second network. Repeaters remove noise and solve the problem of attenuation caused by cable loss. Wireless repeaters are frequently used in "hot spots" to improve signal range and strength. In a home wireless network, repeaters help extend a signal across a wider area.

(F) CABLE MODEMS

By the early 1990s, telephone access to the Internet was largely displaced by DSL and broadband. Today Internet users access the Internet using three methods: (1) by smartphones, (2) Wi-Fi, and (3) a broadband connection. Smartphones enable consumers to make phone calls, send text messages, send e-mails, surf the Internet, navigate using GPS, and play media files. In 1999, the Internet was able to transmit at a speed of 2.5 Gbps. Less than a decade later, software engineers beta tested transmission speeds of more than 10 billion bits per second (10 Gbps).

(G) BANDWIDTH

Broadband is a much-expanded pipeline for the transmission of digital data. High bandwidth is required for fast transmission on the Internet. The basic measurement unit for bandwidth is bits per second ("bps"). To place bandwidth in perspective, the first modems developed in 1958 had a capacity of only 300 bps. Modern modems, using standard telephone lines, have the capacity to transmit data at up to 56 thousand bits per second, or 56 Kbps. In contrast, the Federal Communication Commission ("FCC") classifies broadband speeds as ranging from 200 Kbps, or 200,000 bits per second, to six Mbps, or 6,000,000 bits per second.

(H) DSL

Digital Subscriber Lines ("DSL") enable high-speed data transmission of digital data over traditional copper telephone wire. DSL incorporates an uninterrupted, high-speed connection directly to an Internet Service Provider ("ISP"). Asymmetrical Digital Subscriber Line ("ADSL") is broadband used principally for residential users. ADSL allows faster downstream data transmission over the same line used to provide voice service without disrupting regular telephone calls using that line. Symmetrical Digital Subscriber Line ("SDSL") is a broadband application with equal downstream and upstream traffic speed used by many businesses. "Downstream" refers to data sent from the ISP "down" to the PC; conversely, "upstream" means data transmission from the PC to the ISP.

(I) SEARCH ENGINES

An Internet search engine categorizes and indexes information or websites. When I want to listen to my son's music, I can find it by typing the keywords, "James Rustad music" and "music." into a search engine to locate all web pages on the Internet containing these keywords. Users can download and listen to James' original songs and learn about his latest gigs at www.jamesrustad.com. Search engines such as Google create lists of websites corresponding to the searched term, "James Rustad." Google, Bing, Yahoo!, Ask, America Online, and MyWebSearch are the most popular U.S. search engines according to an eBiz/MBA survey assessing Alexa Global Traffic rankings.

Google is by far the leading U.S. Internet search engine with an estimated 900 million monthly users. Some search engines index each discernible word on every web page, while others index by invisible metatags. Metatags are HTML tags that provide information describing the content of the web pages a user will be viewing. Search engines allow website owners and administrators to control their positioning in search engine results. The browser wars are largely between Microsoft's Internet

Explorer, Google's Chrome, Mozilla's Firefox4, Apple's Safari, and Opera. Microsoft's IE6, once accounted for more than three of four browsers, is nearly extinct in the U.S. although still a popular browser in Europe.

(J) MOBILE DEVICES

Mobile devices are handheld computers—e.g. smartphones and tablets—that enable consumers to surf the Internet, answer e-mail, take photographs, and run hundreds of thousands of software applications ("Apps"). Akin to miniature personal computers, mobile devices have operating systems that come with apps preloaded by the manufacturer. New apps can be downloaded and installed on the system. These operating systems include Google's Android, Apple's iOS, and Blackberry OS, just to name a few.

(K) MOBILE APPS

Facebook's $1 billion purchase of Instagram in 2012 evidences the growing impact of mobile apps as a gateway for Internet access. Instagram, which was designed specifically for mobile applications, enables Facebook to capture a larger segment of the ever-increasing population of Internet users accessing the Internet via smartphones or other mobile devices. Users download Mobile applications through various distribution platforms, such as Apple's iTunes App Store for the Apple iPhone and iPod. A patent is a grant by the U.S. government that entitles the owner (e.g., an individual inventor or a company like Apple or Samsung) to exclude others from making, using, selling, or importing patented inventions. Samsung and Apple, the leading contenders in the smartphone market, are currently embroiled in patent litigation, which will be covered in Chapter 13.

§ 1-3. Web 1.0, 2.0 & 3.0

(A) THE ASYNCHRONOUS INTERNET

Web 1.0 describes the "passive" Internet, where forums and bulletin boards were the exclusive way to post information. Web 1.0 offered little by way of interactivity, aside from users sharing files, writing in guest books, and posting comment forms. Under Web 1.0, the owner of the website was the one and only publisher and communications were asynchronous, meaning that it is independent of time and place. Chapter Three explains how U.S. courts are using tests for personal jurisdiction that tacitly assume that the Internet is still largely asynchronous.

(B) THE SYNCHRONOUS INTERNET

The Internet is no longer primarily about listservs or non-interactive bulletin board for posting information. Web 2.0 is the current Internet, which is interactive, individuated, and user generated. Web 2.0 users connect through blogs and social media. Wikis are an example of a Web 2.0 platform that allows users to work collaboratively. Web 2.0 increases the scope of synchronous communications, such as online chats, audio, and video. Personal jurisdiction tests based upon Web 1.0 or Web 2.0 are doomed to devolve into legal fossils.

(C) WEB 3.0's ONTOLOGY

The World Wide Web Consortium ("W3C") is working on standards for a more interactive Web 3.0. The W3C led "semantic web" employs groundbreaking languages such as the Resource Description Framework ("RDF") and the Web Ontology Language ("OWL"). RDF is a standardized language of the web, which enables computer systems to infer or extrapolate relationships between databases and computer users. The Web 3.0 language fashions the multi-tier representation behind a web page using Universal Resource Identifiers.

The semantic web is beginning to evolve out of Web 2.0 formats of XML tagging, folksonomies, and microformats to the computer readable format of RDF and OWL. The RDF is layered on top of the HTML and other WWW protocols. Web 3.0 will continue to evolve but it will not entirely displace Web 2.0. Web 3.0 creates a need to update personal jurisdiction tests and the meaning of purposeful availment in cyberspace, a topic addressed in Chapter 3.

§ 1-4. Setting Standards Through Voluntary Organizations

Yochai Benkler conceptualized three layers of Internet governance: the "physical infrastructure" layer, the "content" layer, and the "logical" layer. No one country has control over the three layers of Internet governance especially for conduct occurring outside their territory. Chapter 2 examines the problems of Internet governance in the virtual world in the absence of a sovereign or international convention. Voluntary organizations bridge the governance gap by establishing standards and protocols.

(A) OPEN SYSTEMS INITIATIVE

The International Standards Organization's Open Systems Initiative Model ("OSI") conceptualized networking as an assembly line composed of seven different layers or stages. OSI's aim is to create an open networking environment in which all systems can interconnect and are interoperable worldwide so that computer systems made by different vendors can communicate with each other. The seven-layer model processes the data after the web browsers or other applications make requests. Each of the seven generalized layers performs precise functions to ensure that data travels seamlessly across the network. The OSI converts data into packets that consist of zeroes and ones, and are transferable over the network. When a computer receives one of these packets, it runs through the assembly line backwards. After this "disassembly," the OSI reassembles the data into the order sent.

(B) WORLD WIDE WEB CONSORTIUM

The World Wide Web Consortium ("W3C"), an international voluntary organization, develops open standards to ensure the long-term growth of the

Web through standard protocols, ensuring interoperability. The originators of the Internet worked collaboratively as the W3C developing specifications for writing eXtensible Markup Language ("XML") code, as well as the template for Web 3.0 languages.

(C) INTERNET ENGINEERING TASK FORCE

The Internet Engineering Task Force ("IETF") and the Internet Architecture Board ("IAB") are two of the most important global standards-setters for the Internet. The IETF identifies and proposes solutions for technical problems on the Internet. The IETF is an example of the generativity of collaborative community described by Jonathan Zittrain in his 2009 book, *The Future of the Internet and How to Stop It*. The public Internet is a generative technology because it allows individuals and voluntary organizations to improve it. In contrast, digital rights management ("DRM") to prevent unauthorized use of copyrighted works is emblematic of the closed, walled Internet. The IETF, like Zittrain, favors an open, generative Internet as opposed to a "walled garden" without significant user input.

(D) ISOC

The Internet Society ("ISOC") is a "cause-driven voluntary organization that supports the IETF and the IAB to ensure that the Internet remains open and transparent." Internet Society (ISOC), https://www.arin.net/participate/governance/isoc.ht ml. "ISOC is the organizational home of the Internet

Engineering Task Force ("IETF"), the Internet standards body responsible for developing the Internet's technical foundations through its open global forum." Id. The Internet evolved rapidly in large part because of the role of nonhierarchical, open standards-setting organizations such as ISOC. "ISOC was founded in 1992 by a small group of Internet pioneers who came together to promote principals of Internet design openness. ISOC's focus is on connecting the world, collaborating with others, and advocating for equal access to the Internet." Id. ISOC works on issues such as access, privacy, Internet exchange points or hubs, children and the Internet, net neutrality, spam, domain names, and open network standards. The organization provides insurance coverage for those involved in the IETF standards-setting groups.

§ 1-5. The Commercial Internet

Today's Internet is a virtual network that connects hundreds of millions of potential buyers and sellers. Mobile phones are displacing browsers to access the Internet in Generation "C" ("Connected"). Canada ranks first in the world with 108.6 computers per 100 of its population followed by the Netherlands with 103 and Sweden with 102. The United Arab Emirates had 232.1 mobile phone subscribers per 100 people in 2009. Russia had 164 mobile phones per 100 in its population. YouTube visitors upload approximately ten hours of new content every minute. Still only one in three persons in the world has Internet access: There are 2.4 billion users out of an estimated 7.1 billion in the world population.   In evaluating the theories of Internet governance, it is unclear who represents those that are not yet part of the Global Internet. Internet World Stats, Internet Users in the World (2012, Q2).

CHAPTER 2

PERSPECTIVES ON GLOBAL INTERNET GOVERNANCE

§ 2-1. Overview of Cyberlaw

Modern philosophers such as Martin Heidegger describe society as a moving stream rather than a stagnant pond. The Internet is not a timeless essence but rather the fastest growing information technology in world history; its governance structure is continually in the process of becoming. In 1897, Nikola Tesla invented telegraphing without wires, which made it possible to transmit electrical signals the unfathomable distance of twenty miles. By the beginning of the twentieth century, torts were beginning to address automobile, streetcar, and railway accidents. The Internet enables a remarkable variety of new crimes, torts, and ways to infringe patents, trademarks, and copyrights as well as its many positive functions. The U.S. government no longer controls the Internet and multistakeholder solutions are needed to resolve problems of spam, cybercrime, multilingualism, and connectivity for the two-thirds of the world still not online.

The remainder of this chapter explores contemporary debates regarding who should govern the Internet and under what model. This chapter summarizes the leading theories of governance and helps the reader recognize when courts and legislatures have adopted these perspectives in topics covered in other chapters. After providing a theoretical overview of the case for and against a specialized Internet law, this chapter concludes with the leading theories for Internet governance.

(A) AGAINST INTERNET LAW

The development of Internet law has inspired many theoretical debates among academics, practitioners, and the judiciary. In 1996, Judge Frank Easterbrook, a Seventh Circuit U.S. Court of Appeals judge, spoke at a University of Chicago academic conference on cyberspace law. He argued that Internet law deserved no more standing in a law school than an elective on the law of horses. Judge Easterbrook saw no urgency in harmonizing either the procedural or substantive Internet law, arguing that Internet law is nothing more than everyday cases whose only common element is the incidental use of a new technology.

In Judge Easterbrook's opinion, devoting time and effort to studying "the law of the Internet" makes as much (or as little) sense as studying "the law of the horse." He explains that: "Lots of cases deal with sales of horses; others deal with people kicked by horses; still more deal with the licensing and racing of horses, or with the care veterinarians give to horses, or with prizes at horse shows. Any effort to collect these strands into a course on "The Law of the Horse" is doomed to be shallow and to miss unifying principles." He thought it was better for law students interested in horse law to take overarching subjects such as property, torts, contract law, and intellectual property and stretch these principles to cases that involved horses. Judge

Easterbrook's broader observation is that the law of cyberspace requires no reworking of basic property law and there is no need to develop a specialized Internet law.

Internet jurisdiction, discussed further in Chapter 3, illustrates how courts have stretched the minimum contacts framework to cyberspace without creating special rules. Similarly, in Chapter 6, discussing torts, also confirms Judge Easterbrook's point because many cybertorts are simply "new wine in old bottles." However, contrary to those who oppose the study of cyberlaw as a distinct subject, a unique Internet law has emerged over the past two decades. For example, the dynamic development of cyberlaw has led to a complete reworking of many basic principles of copyright law, trademark law, trade secrets, and patent law.

(B) DEFENSE OF INTERNET LAW

Scholars such as Lawrence Lessig strongly disagree with Judge Easterbrook, arguing that there is a compelling reason to focus on the unique intersection between law and cyberspace. Lessig, a founding father of the Berkman Center at Harvard University, contends that Internet law illuminates the entire legal landscape, offering new perspectives on topics such as intellectual property, globalization, private regulation, and Internet governance. Cyberlaw is not just about statutes or cases but also encompasses the architecture of the Internet, informal norms, as well as industry standards.

Lessig identified four modalities of Internet regulation: law, norms, markets, and software architecture. LAWRENCE LESSIG, CODE AND OTHER LAWS OF CYBERSPACE (1999). The functions of architecture or real-space code are not a matter of technological necessity but rather a human-created mechanism for controlling the Internet. In Lessig's view, the software code infrastructure is a form of law "We can build, or *architect,* or code cyberspace to protect values that we believe are fundamental." The Internet, for example, creates new copyright wars that influence the future of the public domain of ideas because of conscious decisions to encrypt or protect code.

§ 2-2. Models of Global Internet Governance

Internet theories of governance generally fall into five camps: (1) self-governance or libertarian, (2) global transnational, (3) code and Internet Architecture, (4) national governments and law, and (5) market-based or economic-based regulation. The chart below provides the basic attributes of the five models identified by Lawrence Solum in Models of Internet Governance, Chapter 2 in MODELS OF INTERNET GOVERNANCE INFRASTRUCTURE AND INSTITUTIONS 48-55 (Lee A Bygrave ed. 2009).

Five Models of Internet Governance	Domain Assumptions
(1) Self-Governance or Libertarian	The Internet is beyond the reach of governmental control and is an independent legal space.
(2) Global Transnational	Transnational multi-stakeholder institutions need to evolve to address Internet governance since this information technology transcends national borders.
(3) Code and Internet Architecture	Voluntary organizations make regulatory decisions when they construct protocols and develop software dictating how it operates. Code is law.
(4) National Governments and Law	National governments have had little difficulty stretching laws and regulations to the Internet. Only governments through trade agreements and conventions can cope

	with governance.
(5) Market-Based or Economic-Based Regulation	Market forces, private ordering and industry practices should largely determine Internet governance to ensure efficiencies. Since the mid-1990s, private ordering has played a critically important role in Internet governance.

§ 2-3. Self-Governing or Libertarian Governance

(A) LIBERTARIAN MANIFESTO

The Internet is the functional equivalent of a global village, first anticipated by Canadian philosopher Marshall McLuhan, who coined the phrase, "The media is the message." From the libertarian perspective, this new media of communication creates an entirely new "global village," that is beyond the reach of law. John Perry Barlow, in his 1996 essay, "A Declaration of Independence for Cyberspace," argued that governments have no business repressing content in the flattened world of the Internet: "In our world, all the sentiments and expressions of humanity, from the debasing to the angelic, are parts of a seamless whole, the global conversation of bits." Barlow stated, "On behalf of the future, I ask you of the past to leave us alone."

His utopian vision was an Internet free from government censorship: "Governments of the Industrial World, you weary giants of flesh and steel, I come from Cyberspace, the new home of Mind." He famously thundered, "The First Amendment is a local ordinance, where is the consent from Netizens for any country imposing its laws on the Internet?" By what authority does the U.S. impose its First Amendment on the rest of the world?

This argument brings to mind a *Seinfeld* episode, "The Pothole," which featured Kramer complaining about a poorly maintained highway outside of New York City after he ran over an abandoned sewing machine. Kramer proceeded to repaint the four-lane highway creating two extra-wide lanes with the intent to transform it into a "two lane comfort cruise." By what authority did Cosmos Kramer have the right to repaint the lines on the highway converting it to a two-lane comfort zone? When can a given nation state legitimately impose its sovereignty on the borderless Internet?

John Perry Barlow's insight is that legitimacy must ultimately come from the consent of Internet users in hundreds of countries. Barlow's Manifesto was written shortly after a German government's prosecution of a Bavarian Internet service provider that enabled German users to access objectionable content such as Nazi memorabilia or hateful commentary posted by third parties. By what authority can a Bavarian court order a U.S. service provider to block content to German citizens? Under this same argument, what gives the European Union the right to demand that U.S. companies get the consent of users before dropping cookies that capture consumer information?

Barlow's concern about widespread censorship on the Internet has materialized. China, Syria, Saudi Arabia and many other countries censor Internet content because their regimes do not value free speech or expression. China's "great firewall" screens out information threatening to the regime. Libertarians fear that an alliance of authoritarian governments will use the United Nations as an instrumentality of control over free expression on the Internet. By what authority can Internet visitors demand that the degrading portrayal of Mohammed in the Innocence of Muslims film trailer be stricken from the cyberspace landscape? The legitimation crisis for cyberspace governance is the byproduct of an Internet binding countries with radically different cultural and legal traditions. The Innocence of Muslims debacle illustrates the mismatch between the permissive Internet and the values of countries not committed to freedom of expression. A large number of authoritarian regimes view the Internet as an "existential threat." Phil Verveer, Remarks at the Geopolitics of Internet Governance. Center for Strategic and International Studies (May 23, 2013). Countries such as Brazil and India know that they need the Internet but are concerned that they have less influence in Internet governance. Id. Brazil calls for a greater participation of governments and an enhanced role for the United Nations' International Telecommunication Union (ITU). Daniel Pruzin, U.S. Satisfied With Internet Forum Has Concern on Brazil Proposal, BLOOMBERG

BNA, ELECTRONIC COMMERCE & LAW REPORT (May 21, 2013).

Privacy advocates such as the Electronic Freedom Foundation worry about the potential for widespread surveillance and the emergence of a new form of Jeremy Bentham's Panopticon, where anyone and everyone can be seen without being able to tell when they are being watched. As Lawrence Lessig notes, libertarians appear somewhat naive: "Cyberspace, it is said, cannot be regulated. It 'cannot be governed;' its 'innate ability' is to resist regulation. In its essence, cyberspace is a space of no control." LAWRENCE LESSIG, CODE AND OTHER LAWS OF CYBERSPACE 24 (1999).

In fact, a change in the architecture of the Internet can radically restrict the freedoms of users. ISPs and broadband providers historically only examined the header section of packets for routing purposes but message content can also be scanned to increase social control or to target potential customers. Internet protocols permit the easy identification of individual users and their preferences by their IP address but changing the architecture of the Internet could increase anonymity. For example, the World Wide Web Consortium's P3P protocol enables individuals to control their preferences about the exchange of private information.

(B) DECENTRALIZED GOVERNANCE

David Johnson and David Post's article portray the sovereign Internet as a separate realm beyond the ability of individual nation states to govern. David R. Johnson & David Post, *Law and Borders—The Rise of Law in Cyberspace*, 48 STAN. L. REV. 1367, 1367-75 (1996). Cyberspace, in their view, is beyond the control of any nation state because it transcends the law's central assumption of reliance on territorial borders. Johnson and Post describe a sovereign legal space bounded by screens, access controls, and passwords, rather than territorial boundaries.

Their approach to Internet law calls for displacing territorially based law with customary law tailored to cross-border transactions while protecting intellectual property rights. Owners of trademarks, copyrights, and patents must satisfy the hundreds of different intellectual property regimes' procedural, substantive, and jurisdictional requirements and still be unable to protect their rights in cyberspace.

The argument that cyberspace is a distinct place, beyond the rule of territorial sovereigns, is refuted by two decades of Internet law developments in the U.S. and other countries. "For a long time, the Internet's enthusiasts have believed that it would be largely immune from state regulation. The theory was not so much that nation states would not want to regulate the Internet, it was that they would be unable to do so, forestalled by the technology of the medium, the geographical distribution of its users, and the nature of its content." James Boyle, *Foucault in Cyberspace: Surveillance, Sovereignty and Hardwired Censors*, 66 U. CIN. L. REV. 177, 178 (1997). Still, private ordering has played an even greater role than governments in many Internet governance functions.

§ 2-4. Global Transnational Governance

By 2013, there were 2.4 billion Internet users out of the 7.1 billion world population. The Internet is reshaping every aspect of human social existence, creating legal dilemmas in every procedural and substantive field of law. Radically different legal cultures encounter each other on a 24/7 basis for the first time in history. United States Supreme Court Justice Benjamin Cardozo's description of judicial process applies equally well to the Internet: "Nothing is stable. Nothing absolute. All is fluid and changeable." Courts and legislatures are increasingly scrambling to update the law to account for the global Internet.

(A) CO-REGULATION OF THE INTERNET

Co-regulation of the Internet by civil society envisions governance by diverse stakeholders from hundreds of nation states agreeing to core procedural and substantive principles. This model is often described as multistakeholder governance. The United Nations Secretariat established the Working Group on Internet Governance ("WGIG") to propose governance solutions for the information society at the World Summit on the Information Society ("WSIS"). Transnational Internet Governance is a counter-hegemonic alternative to top-down governance by any one nation state. In its Final Report, the WSIS concluded that the international management of the Internet should be multilateral, transparent, and democratic. Shared governance and meaningful participation by diverse stakeholders is WSIS's ideal organizational form.

(B) UN-ANCHORED WGIG MODELS

(1) Global Internet Council

WGIG posited four alternatives for international Internet governance that illustrate Lawrence Solum's second model of evolving transnational institutions. Each governance alternative performs necessary coordinating functions such as audit, arbitration, policy setting, regulation, and day-to-day operational management but has a different organizational structure. The UN-anchored Global Internet Council ("GIC") would consist of representatives of national governments, which would replace the Internet Corporation for Assigned Names and Numbers ("ICANN").

The GIC would first identify public policy issues relevant to Internet governance and work with existing organizations, much like the civil society process overseen by the WGIG. The proposal is that GIC would displace ICANN and create policies more transparently and with greater public participation because of the role of the UN. The GIC would synchronize cyberspace public policies and oversee Internet resource management for intellectual property, domain names, Internet security, cybercrime, as well as development issues. The GIC, for example, would supervise IP addresses, introduce new TLDs, and delegate country code top-level domains ("ccTLDs"). Examples of ccTLDs include .us (United States) and .de (Germany). The GIC would also establish public polices as to spam, privacy, cybersecurity, and cybercrime that are currently not addressed by other intergovernmental organizations. Most significantly, this new transnational entity would oversee all Internet public policy issues including trade and intellectual property protection.

In 2013, ICANN launched a controversial expansion of global top-level domains ("gTLDS"), charging hundreds of thousands of dollars to applicants competing for this new domain space. The WGIG might have approached this differently. With a truly representative WGIG, Islamic or Christian fundamentalists would oppose the creation of .xxx domains zoned for pornography.

(2) No Specific Oversight

The "no specific oversight" alternative is a second UN-anchored governance model that would create a more democratic oversight of ICANN to resolve current domain name management issues in a more inclusive way. This minimalist model suggests the participation of a wider spectrum of stakeholders to allay the concerns that governmental power will be used to undermine Internet freedom.

(3) International Internet Council

WGIG's third alternative is a multilateral International Internet Council ("IIC") that displaces ICANN's Government Advisory Committee ("GAC"). The IIC will spearhead public policy issues such as

Internet resource management and universal access. The IIC will resolve Internet resource management issues and institute transparent and democratic decision-making in a coordinated way. Eurozone governance, for example, stresses the need to have an open, transparent and regular dialogue between the European Union and diverse sectors of civil society.

(4) Mixed Model

The mixed or hybrid model conceptualizes government as leading public policy development with oversight by a Global Internet Policy Council ("GIPC"). The hypothetical GIPC calls for governance that is supplemented by participation of civil society and the private sector, but only as passive observers, not active participants. The World Internet Corporation for Assigned Names and Numbers ("WICANN") would theoretically displace ICANN as well as the preeminent role performed by the U.S. Government's Commerce Department. WICANN has not gained traction as a mechanism to displace today's piecemeal and decentralized Internet governance.

§ 2-5. Law, Code, Markets, & Norms

Internet law, Lawrence Lessig argues, consists of interrelated conceptual layers with four interrelated modalities: (1) laws or legal sanctions, (2) social norms, (3) the market, and (4) code or architecture depicted in the chart below. Under Lessig's model of "code as law," digital rights management or access controls is a form of architecture useful for social control. Software code constrains what Internet users can do and is legal, which threatens the Internet freedoms.

Four Modalities Comprising Internet Law: Code as Law

Law: "Norms constrain through the stigma that a community imposes; markets constrain through the price that they exact; architectures constrain through the physical burdens they impose; and law constrains through the punishment it threatens." LAWRENCE LESSIG, CODE: VERSION 2.0 124 (2006).	*Architecture*: (computer software and hardware): "The code or software or architecture or protocols set these features, which are selected by code writers. They constrain some behavior by making other behavior possible or impossible. The code embeds certain values or makes certain values impossible. In this sense, it too is regulation, just as the architectures of real-space codes are regulations." *Id*. at 25.
Market Forces: "Market forces encourage architectures of identity to facilitate online commerce. Government needs to do very little— indeed, nothing at all—	*Norms:* (collectively determined social norms): "Talk about Democratic politics in the alt.knitting newsgroup, and you open yourself to

to induce just this sort of development. The market forces are too powerful; the potential here is too great." *Id.* at 77.	flaming; "spoof" someone's identity in a MUD, and you may find yourself . . . "toaded" [take off and die] filter. Id. at 208.

Law shapes and is shaped by norms, architecture, and the market in Lessig's model of Internet governance. Homeland Security's omniscient eye is an example of Lessig's architecture of control. In December of 2011, The Electronic Privacy Information Center ("EPIC") filed suit against the Department of Homeland Security to require it to disclose how it utilizes social networks for secret surveillance. Anti-circumvention software constrains fair use and has the potential to chill speech. Open source architecture, on the other hand, enables a culture of collaboration and sharing.

(A) INTERNET-RELATED STATUTES AND CASES

While Lessig is correct that code is law, Internet law is also composed of federal and state cases, administrative rulings, statutes, regulations, and local ordinances. Cyberspace raises inevitable jurisdictional issues because, by its very definition, the Internet involves transborder communications across hundreds of countries. Cyberlaw lacks comprehensive international conventions, codes, or directives covering diverse topics such as computer security, electronic contracts, cybertorts, cybercrimes, online privacy, intellectual property, content regulation or cross-border jurisdictional rules.

Policymakers need to be creating specialized cyberspace law and stretch brick and mortar doctrines to fit the new realities of cyberspace. They must consider how Internet architecture, norms, and markets interact with legal principles. The ever-expanding copyright law, trademark law, and patent law are attempts by powerful stakeholders to enlarge their rights at the expense of the Internet commons. Private fences combine with the civil and criminal law to comprise Internet law and governance. The evolving architecture of the Internet codetermines laws, norms, and markets.

(B) CODE AS INTERNET LAW

Cyberlaw is not just about statutes or cases but also encompasses the architecture of the Internet, informal norms, as well as industry standards. In his book *Code and Other Laws of Cyberspace*, Lawrence Lessig took issue with libertarians and others who argued that the Internet was not regulable. Lessig describes how the architecture of Paris with its broad boulevards limited the ability of revolutionaries to challenge state power. LAWRENCE LESSIG, ARCHITECTING FOR CONTROL: VERSION 1.0, at 3. The strategic location of the German Constitutional Court in Karlsruhe, a six hours drive from the Bundestag in Berlin, was a geographic constraint against urban-based dissident groups.

In the words of Winston Churchill: "We shape our buildings, and afterwards our buildings shape us."

The Internet is "layered architecture" which enables "specialized efficiency, organizational coherency, and future flexibility." Tim Wu, *Application-Centered Internet Analysis*, 85 VA. L. REV. 1163, 1189 (1999). Encryption or digital locks also illustrate how code is law. Digital locks prevent unauthorized users from accessing materials and are thus an instrumentality for access control as well as cabining conduct. An online company's failure to encrypt data may constitute a breach of the duty to protect the intangible assets of third parties. The functions of architecture or real-space code are not a matter of technological necessity but rather a human-created mechanism for controlling the Internet. In Lessig's view, the software code infrastructure is a form of law. The Internet, for example, creates new copyright wars that influence the future of the public domain of ideas because of conscious decisions to encrypt or protect code.

(C) NORMS AS INTERNET LAW

Sociologists divide norms into mores (socially important) and folkways (customary ways of doing things that are more easily changed). Communities, rather than the government, determine which norms constitute mores and punish breaches regardless of the formal legal rules. "*Sexting—the* texting of sexually explicit pictures—is a modern form of risqué love notes that has become controversial because it can violate mores. Overzealous prosecutors charged three Pennsylvania teenage girls with child pornography for sending photographs of themselves wearing training bras or baring their breasts to boyfriends and other peer group members. The legislators who drafted the child pornography statute never anticipated this stretching of a criminal law statute enacted to punish adult distributors of child pornography.

In the early years of the Internet, users would stigmatize conduct that violated social mores such as spamming, online ads, or other commercial misconduct on professional forums through "flaming" and other forms of vigilante justice. Posting inappropriate posts or pictures on Facebook is an example of norms as informal law. It is a violation of informal norms to engage in incendiary exchanges with Facebook posters. Social norms are enforced by informal norms such as "defriending" objectionable individuals or screening messages they can transmit.

Daniel Solove tells the story of how Internet users punished an individual who overused the free Wi-Fi available in a San Francisco Apple store. Vigilantes posted a YouTube video of the moocher who overused free Internet access at this flagship store. This video is an example of how informal sanctions are used by user communities to establish norms and informally sanction those that break them. Vigilantes stigmatize violations of norms by reposting obnoxious spam, political diatribes, or racist rantings with critical commentary. Internet hackers engage in vigilante justice against child pornographers, vendors who publicly brag that their security products cannot be breached, and other cyberspace actors that they find offensive.

The Internet has created new norms about the meaning of intellectual property and whether young people think it is wrong to violate the exclusive rights of copyright owners by copying and distributing infringing content. The Sociology of Law Department at Sweden's Lund University is conducting long-range studies of the gap between legal statutes and social norms arising on the Internet, which have uncovered a gap between the copyright law and evolving informal norms in favor of free sharing of content. Seventy-five percent of young Swedes "did not regard the file sharing of copyright protected material to be illegal," or as a normative reason to stop downloading illegal content. This rapidly evolving norm of free sharing among users is creating increasingly serious enforcement problems for content creators.

(D) MARKETS AS INTERNET LAW

The Cato Institute contends that self-regulation is a sufficient mechanism for Internet governance, maintaining that policymakers should refrain from imposing needless costs and unintended negative consequences by policing cyberspace. Regulators and other government entities should get out of the way and allow the Internet to develop in response to Internet service provider policies, consumer desires, and other market forces.

Opponents of this perspective argue for government oversight in order to guarantee net neutrality. Consumer advocates point to the need for government to enact mandatory minimum protection for Internet users because the marketplace for

privacy and consumer rights has failed. The free
market allows telecomm providers such as AT&T,
Verizon, and Comcast to create different tiers of
online service with differential pricing. Google, for
example, has been criticized for directing their
searches toward companies that pay for keyword
advertising. The U.S. follows a market-based
approach to consumer protection as compared to the
mandatory protections found in Europe and many
other countries connected to the Internet.

(E) THE GENERATIVE INTERNET

Jonathan Zittrain's work illustrates Solum's third
model by stressing the ways that software code and
Internet architecture interact. JONATHAN ZITTRAIN,
THE FUTURE OF THE INTERNET AND HOW TO STOP IT 2
(2008). The strength of the Internet is in its users'
collective collaboration, resulting in improvements, a
process he calls the "generativity." The generative
Internet is comprised of tens of millions of Internet
users collaborating to produce code and content. The
Apple II Computer was the "quintessentially
generative technology" because it invited tinkering
by users. The appliance-like platform of Apple's
iPhone and iPod, in contrast, is completely
controlled by the manufacturer, making it difficult
for the community users to modify or improve
applications. Apple counters widespread security
threats through digital certificates, passwords,
secure socket layer protocols, and other security
devices. Apple's iPhones and iPods are reliable and
easy to use but have chilling effects on user
innovation. DRM systems that control access to

copyrighted works discourage innovation in the user community.

§ 2-6. Why National Regulation Still Matters

(A) LOCAL GOVERNANCE

Lawrence Solum's fourth model of Internet governance is local regulation by individual governments. All over the world, local governments are imposing domestic laws on the Internet. Online companies such as Google, Microsoft, and eBay have capitulated to domestic regulations of various countries under the threat of being forced to abandon lucrative national markets. In March of 2012, for example, a court in India issued rulings that will require Internet Service Providers to block access to music-hosting websites because of massive copyright infringement.

(B) NATIONAL REGULATION

National governments frequently impose their extraterritorial will on cyberspace activities through directives and regulations. The European Community's Data Protection Directive, for example, prohibits the transfer of personal information across national borders unless the receiving country has implemented an adequate level of protection. The European Commission in 1995 granted all European citizens a fundamental right to control the collection, transmission, or use of personal information. (Council Directive 95/46/EC).

The twenty-seven member states of the European Union are signatories of the European Convention on Human Rights, which guarantees respect for one's "private and family life, his home, and his correspondence," subject to certain restrictions. The European Court of Human Rights gives this article a very broad interpretation, making privacy functionally equivalent to a fundamental EU-wide constitutional right.

§ 2-7. The Wealth of Networks

(A) ECONOMICS-BASED GOVERNANCE

Yochai Benkler of Harvard University's Berkman Center describes the shift from durable goods to an information-based economy as "the wealth of networks." YOCHAI BENKLER, THE WEALTH OF NETWORKS: HOW SOCIAL PRODUCTION TRANSFORMS MARKETS AND FREEDOM (2006). Karl Marx predicted class conflict between the bourgeoisie who controlled the means of production and the proletariat who were wage slaves. The rise of the Internet can be viewed as democratizing because it grants greater access to knowledge, which is the information age's means of production. The battle over control of the Internet pits a pro-capitalist proprietary paradigm against a collaborative community of users.

Yochai Benkler's concept of Networked Information Economics ("NIE") considers commons-generated content as decoupling physical constraints on production. Benkler's thesis about shared infrastructure of the Internet brings to mind Sly and the Family Stone's *Everybody is a Star*.

Where there were once walls preventing ordinary persons from access to mass media distribution, now the free-flowing information superhighway is available to build an "open, diverse, liberal equilibrium." Law is both a means of oppression and a means of resistance in Benkler's theory of networked society. Free and open source software, for example, is generative—controlled by those who produce it—whereas proprietary software reflects an oppressive model where the software publishers own the code.

(B) COPYRIGHT COMMONS

Yochai Benkler contends that Hollywood and the recording industry are systematically undermining the innovations of the collaborative-networked economy. He concludes that we should not let "yesterday's winners dictate the terms of tomorrow's economic competition." Urs Gasser, Benkler's Berkman Center colleague, describes the Internet as an information ecosystem that dramatically reduces the cost of production, which can potentially lead to a more participatory and egalitarian society with a broader governing class.

There is no inexorable logic driving us toward a more open, diverse, liberal equilibrium. Practicing attorneys often describe their work as "one damn case after another," without appreciating that law reflects wider social and technological developments. The broader theories of Internet governance discussed in this chapter are the backdrop for understanding procedural and substantive topics in the following chapters.

CHAPTER 3

GLOBAL INTERNET JURISDICTION

Traditional concepts of jurisdiction and enforcement of judgment need to be adapted to the Internet. In the United States, personal jurisdiction is the issue of whether a court can decide a case involving this specific defendant. Plaintiffs must demonstrate that defendants have sufficient 'minimum contacts' with the forum such that finding personal jurisdiction will not offend 'traditional notions of fair play and substantial justice,' *International Shoe v. Washington*, 326 U.S. 310, 66 S.Ct. 154 (S.Ct. 1945). A U.S. plaintiff has the burden of demonstrating that the defendant has minimum contacts with the forum by either general jurisdiction (pervasive contacts) or specific jurisdiction (nexus between conduct and minimum contacts).

This chapter asks the fundamental questions whether the *International Shoe* case can be accommodated to cyberspace. The borderless Internet challenges uniquely U.S. concepts such as the long arm statute, due process, and minimum contacts. U.S. courts have mechanically stretched the parochial minimum contacts approach to personal jurisdiction into cyberspace, creating jurisdictional dilemmas. The European Union's Brussels Regulation creates very different jurisdictional rules in civil and commercial disputes. This chapter focuses primarily on the U.S. due process approach to cyberspace jurisdiction but also addresses European Union and other foreign rules.

§ 3-1. International Shoe in Cyberspace: An Overview

(A) LONG-ARM STATUTES

Once a court determines a defendant's conduct is subject to a forum's long-arm statute, it must next consider whether asserting personal jurisdiction over a nonresident defendant comports with the Due Process Clause of the Fourteenth Amendment. A threshold question is, "Has the plaintiff demonstrated that the defendant's conduct falls within the long-arm statute of the state where the case is filed?" States have enacted one of two broad types of long arm statutes: (1) statutes asserting jurisdiction over the person to the extent allowable by the Fourteenth Amendment in the U.S. Constitution (due process clause) or (2) statutes limited to specified activities such as transacting business or causing tortious injuries.

A growing number of state long-arm statutes assert control over the defendant's activities to the limit of due process. Pennsylvania's long-arm statute, for example, claims jurisdiction to the fullest extent allowed under the due process clause. Assuming that a state's long-arm statute is satisfied, the next question is whether the plaintiff can prove that the defendant has sufficient minimum contacts with the forum to satisfy due process. If so, state courts may exercise personal jurisdiction over the defendant.

(B) GENERAL PERSONAL JURISDICTION

General personal jurisdiction exists when the defendant's contacts with the forum state are "substantial" and "continuous and systematic," such that the state may exercise personal jurisdiction over the defendant, even if the action does not relate to the defendant's contacts with the state. If minimum contacts are sufficient to establish general jurisdiction, the out of state defendant may be sued in the forum state for any cause arising in any place. The threshold for general jurisdiction is high; the contacts must be sufficiently extensive and pervasive to approximate physical presence.

With general jurisdiction, the defendant's contacts are so extensive in the foreign forum that the defendant becomes functionally present. "Systematic and continuous" activities in the forum state are required for a finding of general jurisdiction. After seven decades of U.S. Supreme Court jurisprudence, the Court has found general jurisdiction in only one case, *Perkins v. Benquet Consolidated Mining Co.*, 342 U.S. 437 (S.Ct. 1952). In 2011, in *Goodyear Dunlop Tires Operations v. Brown*, 131 S. Ct. 2846 (S.Ct. 2011), the U.S. Supreme Court strongly implied that general jurisdiction is even more limited than federal and state courts have previously asserted. In *Goodyear*, the Court held that a corporation is subject to general jurisdiction only in a "home" state, defined as the state of incorporation and principal place of business. The Court's decision sends a signal to lower federal and state courts that the threshold for a finding of general jurisdiction is extremely high.

To date, the Supreme Court has not rendered an Internet-related general jurisdiction opinion.

The only U.S. court to find general jurisdiction in an Internet-related dispute was *Gator.Com Corp. v. L.L. Bean, Inc.*, 398 F.3d 1125 (9th Cir. 2005), where the court found general jurisdiction based upon L.L. Bean's millions of dollars of sales to California consumers. The *L.L. Bean* court noted that direct e-mail solicitations and millions of catalog sales spurred this revenue stream. Gator.com Corp. filed suit against the outdoor outfitter in a California federal court, seeking a declaratory judgment that its pop-up ads did not infringe L.L. Bean's trademarks or constitute an unfair business practice. L.L. Bean is a Maine corporation with its principal place of business in Maine.

Because L.L. Bean had neither property nor employees in California, the district court granted L.L. Bean's motion to dismiss for lack of personal jurisdiction. The Ninth Circuit reversed this decision, holding there was a basis for general jurisdiction over the Maine outfitter. The *L.L. Bean* court premised its finding of general jurisdiction in part upon L.L. Bean's extensive marketing and sales targeting California consumers and contacts with California vendors. In addition, the L.L. Bean website created a virtual California store. Nevertheless, this finding of general jurisdiction predicated upon a highly interactive website was vacated after the parties settled before the Ninth Circuit's rehearing *en banc*. Few Internet cases will satisfy the rigorous general jurisdiction test after the *Goodyear* decision.

(C) SPECIFIC JURISDICTION

Assuming a court finds no general jurisdiction, the question becomes whether there is a basis for specific jurisdiction. Specific jurisdiction depends upon the plaintiff showing a relationship between the underlying controversy and the forum. Internet cases, like bricks and mortar lawsuits, always turn on whether the defendant targets the forum in some meaningful way. Beyond simply operating an interactive website that is accessible from the forum state, a defendant must expressly target the forum state's market to satisfy personal jurisdiction under "something more" tests discussed later in this chapter.

If the defendant merely operates a website, even a highly interactive website, that is accessible from, but does not target the forum state, then the defendant may not be summoned into court in that state. Posting allegedly defamatory comments or information on an internet site does not, without more, subject the poster to personal jurisdiction wherever the posting could be read, and the subject of the posting may reside. Courts typically use the three-pronged test of *Burger King Corp. v. Rudzewicz*, 471 U.S. 462 (S.Ct. 1985) to determine whether specific personal jurisdiction over a non-resident defendant is appropriate.

The *Burger King* test is as follows: (1) the defendant must have sufficient minimum contacts with the forum state, (2) the claim asserted against the defendant must arise out of those contacts, and (3) the exercise of jurisdiction must be reasonable.

The minimum contacts test for specific jurisdiction encompasses two distinct requirements: first, that the out-of-state defendant must have purposefully directed its activities at residents of the forum state, and second, that the plaintiff's injuries must arise out of defendant's forum-related activities.

Courts use a three-part test to evaluate whether specific jurisdiction exists in a particular case: (1) the defendant must either purposefully direct its activities at the forum or purposefully avail itself of the of the privilege of doing business there, (2) the claim must arise from the defendant's forum-related activities, and (3) the exercise of jurisdiction must be reasonable. *Lake v. Lake*, 817 F.2d 1421 (9th Cir. 1987).

This judicial test ensures that a defendant will not be subject to personal jurisdiction solely because of random, fortuitous, or attenuated contacts or of the unilateral activity of another party or a third person. Therefore, the issue becomes whether the specific activity or occurrence giving rise to the claim took place in the forum state and is subject to the state's regulation. A website's notice that it will not accept orders from a given forum is insufficient to shield it from a finding of purposeful availment. The fact that a defendant's postings were available over the Internet is not enough to establish purposeful direction toward a forum. "This is especially true where the alleged victims of the postings are not residents of the forum state." *Stevo Design, Inc. v. SBR Mktg., Ltd.*, 2013 U.S. Dist. LEXIS 10975 (D. Nev. 2013).

(D) INTERNET PERSONAL JURISDICTION

(1) Zippo.com Sliding Scale

No Jurisdiction	Gray Area	Jurisdiction Recognized
Passive websites with little commercial activity	Depends upon degree of interactivity of website	Interactive websites that permit online orders

The *Zippo Mfg. Co. v. Zippo Dot Com, Inc.*, 952 F. Supp. 1119 (W.D. Pa. 1997) interactive/passive website test is the gold standard for courts to determine personal jurisdiction. Under *Zippo.com's* sliding scale, websites range from "passive" ones, which merely post information and generally do not provide the contacts required to support jurisdiction, to "interactive" ones that enable contract formation. *Zippo.com's* three-part continuum divides websites into: (1) interactive, (2) passive, and (3) a "gray area" in the borderland between the passive and active website.

Passive websites, where courts find no personal jurisdiction, are asynchronous as companies (or individuals) merely post information and there is no interaction with visitors. At the other end of the spectrum, interactive websites often give rise to a finding of personal jurisdiction. In "gray area," middle-ground cases, the court will assess the level of interactivity in order to determine whether the exchanges are commercial.

Zippo.com's principal place of business is in California whereas the plaintiff, Zippo Manufacturing ("Zippo Mfg.") filed its trademark complaint in its home state of Pennsylvania. Zippo Mfg., a computer news service, alleged that the Internet company infringed and diluted its famous trademark. Zippo.com moved to dismiss the Pennsylvania trademark infringement complaint, citing a lack of personal jurisdiction. In upholding personal jurisdiction, the court posited a sliding scale test classifying Internet sites by the nature and quality of the online commercial activity. In the wake of *Zippo.com,* courts continue to deny personal jurisdiction to passive websites. However, this decision is becoming less relevant as website design increasingly emphasizes interactivity.

(2) Passive Jurisdiction

Bensusan Restaurant Corp. v. King, 937 F. Supp. 295 (S.D. N.Y. 1996) is the emblematic example of the passive website, where the court found no specific jurisdiction. The operator of "The Blue Note," a jazz club in New York City, filed a trademark infringement suit against "The Blue Note," a jazz club in Columbia, Missouri owned by Richard B. King ("King"). King created a web page for his club, posting a calendar of events and ticket information, as well as a disclaimer reputing any affiliation with the New York-based club of the same name, but did not permit the online purchasing of tickets. The district court reasoned that King did not purposefully avail himself of jurisdiction in New York by merely posting information on a website without interactivity or otherwise directing commercial activity in that forum.

In *Cybersell Inc. v. Cybersell, Inc.*, 130 F.3d 414 (9th Cir. 1997), Cybersell Incorporate ("Cybersell AZ") registered its service mark with the U.S. Trademark Office in 1994. In 1995, a Florida father and son formed a family business to conduct website consulting services also under the trade name of Cybersell ("Cybersell FL"). The Cybersell AZ plaintiffs, Laurence Canter and Martha Siegel, were infamous spam e-mailers who then filed a lawsuit for trademark infringement against Cybersell FL. The Arizona federal court dismissed the action, finding that it had no personal jurisdiction over the Cybersell FL website because it was neither interactive nor conducting commercial transactions.

The federal appeals court found that Cybersell FL did not purposefully avail itself of the privilege of doing business in Arizona, ruling the defendant must do something akin to specifically targeting the forum, rather than merely posting a website accessible in the forum state. Under *Cybersell*, mere operation of a passive website was insufficient to establish personal jurisdiction over a defendant, while operation of an interactive, commercial website often is sufficient. The greater the commercial activity, the more likely a court will exercise jurisdiction.

(3) The Gray Zone or Borderline

Courts closely inspect the gray region or the borderland between passive and interactive websites to determine whether a website targeted the forum with advertising, solicitation of orders, or other emblems of the defendant's presence in a forum. The middle ground is the borderland between interactive and passive websites. In *Cambria Co. v. Pental Granite & Marble Co.*, No. 0:12-cv-00228-JRT-AJB (D. Minn. 2013), a Washington company's website enabled Minnesota website visitors to pay bills online, which was a key factor in the court finding specific jurisdiction. Pental's website's was in the middle ground in having email and payment functions. In addition, visitors could "like" the website on Facebook and follow it on Twitter. In these cases, the exercise of jurisdiction is determined by examining the level of interactivity and the commercial nature of the exchange of information that occurs on the website.

The court found the website to be in the borderland between passive and active websites. A key factor in favor of jurisdiction was that the website advertised infringing products targeting Minnesota residents even though it had no agents, operations, or facilities in Minnesota. A growing number of courts recognize that Zippo's interactivity test has been outgrown and needs to consider factors beyond interactivity such as the *Cambria* court's mention of a defendant's presence on social media. Too many U.S. courts are engaging in mechanical jurisprudence by applying an outmoded interactivity test to determine specific jurisdiction in cyberspace.

Nevertheless, in GOFIT LLC v. GoFIT LLC, 2013 U.S. Dist. LEXIS 5284 (N.D. Oka. 2013), the federal court held that a minimally interactive fitness website did not satisfy minimum contacts. The plaintiff, GOFIT LLC, an Oklahoma fitness equipment company, sued the defendant GoFit LLC, a Delaware company for trademark infringement in an Oklahoma federal court. The court found that the only basis for minimum contacts in Oklahoma was the defendant's nationwide policy of giving free passes to its fitness centers. The federal appeals court reasoned that the defendant did not intend to do business in Oklahoma and found no personal jurisdiction.

(E) THE EFFECTS TEST

The focus of minimum contacts in cybertort cases: is the "effects" or "brunt of the harm" test first articulated in *Calder v. Jones*, 465 U.S. 783 (S.Ct. 1984). In *Calder,* television star Shirley Jones filed suit in California, where she lived, against the author and editor of a National Enquirer story that stated she was an alcoholic. The allegedly libelous story concerned the activities of Jones centered in California. The article was drawn from California sources, and the brunt of the harm, in terms both of respondent's emotional distress and the injury to her professional reputation, was suffered in California. In sum, California was the focal point both of the story and the harm suffered. The Supreme Court unanimously found that the defendants were "primary participants in an alleged wrongdoing intentionally directed at a California resident, and jurisdiction over them is proper on that basis."

The *Calder* effects test requires the plaintiff to show that (1) the defendant committed an intentional act, (2) that was expressly aimed at the forum, and (3) that caused harm, the brunt of which is suffered and which the defendant knows is likely to be suffered in the forum. In *Calder*, the U.S. Supreme Court upheld a California state court's finding that it had personal jurisdiction over The National Enquirer, which had offices in Florida.

The U.S. Supreme Court reasoned the publisher of the tabloid knew the brunt of the harm would occur in California, a state where The National Enquirer had its largest circulation. The *Calder* Court reasoned that California was the focal point for the brunt of the harm because Ms. Jones worked and lived there and that The National Enquirer story about Jones's alcoholism would be felt the most there—the home of the movie and television industries.

An appellate court typically does not require that the brunt of the harm be suffered in the forum. Instead, the foreseeable-harm element is satisfied when defendant's intentional act has foreseeable effects in the forum. If a jurisdictionally sufficient amount of harm is suffered in the forum state, it does not matter that even more harm might have been suffered in another state. The *Calder* effects test is ill suited for the Internet because it is overly inclusive. A federal court found that Asian-based websites hosting Korean pop songs copyrighted in the United States were expressly targeting California residents when they incorporated third party advertisements in their online messages. *Kollective Co. v. Yang*, No. 4:11-cv-01051-CW (N.D. Cal. 2013).

California's personal jurisdiction distinguishes between jurisdiction based upon purposeful direction in tort or infringement cases and purposeful availment, where the underlying cause of action arises out of contract. Courts have ruled that something more than email is necessary to pass the effects test. *Johnson v. Mitchell*, No. 10-1968 (E. D. Cal. 2013). The court in Mitchell stated that, "personal jurisdiction would be boundless" if sending an email was enough to satisfy due process. Jurisdiction is proper under the effects test if the defendant (1) committed an intentional act, which was (2) expressly aimed at the forum state, and (3) caused harm, the brunt of which is suffered and which the defendant knows is likely to be suffered in the forum state.

(F) "SOMETHING MORE" TEST

(1) GTE New Media Services

U.S. federal courts have adopted an effects test for torts and intellectual property infringement actions, but are beginning to demand "something more" in addition to website interactivity to support a finding of minimum contacts. *GTE New Media Services Inc. v. BellSouth Corp.*, 199 F.3d 1343 (D.C. 2000) was one of the first courts to articulate a "something more" test in addition to interactivity to satisfy personal jurisdiction. GTE New Media ("GTE") filed a Sherman Antitrust Act complaint against Bell South ("Bell") alleging they were in a conspiracy to dominate the Internet directories market in the Washington, D.C. metropolitan area by diverting Internet users from the GTE website to the defendant's websites.

The D.C. Circuit Court of Appeals found Bell lacked minimum contacts with the District of Columbia based solely upon the fact its residents could access its Internet Yellow Pages from within the city. The court ruled that GTE could conduct discovery in order to seek proof of whether Bell had sufficient contacts with the forum. The district court applied the *Zippo* "sliding scale" test, finding that BellSouth's websites fell into the uncertain gray zone and that jurisdiction existed based on the highly interactive nature and commercial quality of the sites. The federal appeals court reversed, finding no personal jurisdiction because accessing an Internet Yellow Page site was no different than searching a telephone book.

The court found that consumers did not pay to use this search tool and any resulting commercial transactions were between the consumer and the businesses found in the Yellow Pages. The lack of any commercial relationship between the consumer and the provider of the Yellow Pages failed to meet the "something more" test. The *GTE* court brought common sense to the common law in updating personal jurisdictional rules for changes in Internet web technologies and practices.

(2) ALS Scan

The court in *ALS Scan v. Digital Services Consultants, Inc.*, 293 F.3d 707 (4th Cir. 2002) held that an Internet service provider was not subject to personal jurisdiction based solely upon a third party's copyright infringement occurring on its website. ALS Scan, a Maryland based adult entertainment website, filed suit against a Georgia ISP for enabling a third parties' misappropriation of its copyrighted photographs. The plaintiff argued that Digital Services enabled Alternative Products' publication of the infringing photographs on the Internet, which caused ALS Scan to suffer an injury in Maryland.

The *ALS Scan* court found no personal jurisdiction because the ISP did not engage in continuous and systematic activities within the forum. The court's approach was that a state may exercise judicial power over a person outside of the state when they: (1) direct electronic activity into the state, (2) with the manifested intent of engaging in business or other interactions within the state, and (3) the activity creates in a person within the state, a potential cause of action cognizable in the state's courts. The Ninth Circuit reasoned that satisfying *Zippo's* interactivity test was not enough to support a finding of general jurisdiction because it is possible for a website to be interactive, but to have no meaningful quantity of contacts. In other words, the contacts would be continuous, but could also not be meaningful or substantial.

(3) Dudnikov

In *Dudnikov v. Chalk & Vermillion Fine Arts Inc.*, 514 F.3d 1063 (10th Cir. 2008), the Tenth Circuit reversed a district court's dismissal of a complaint for lack of personal jurisdiction. In *Dudnikov,* a Connecticut-based company notified the online auction host eBay, based in California, that a line of prints featured in an eBay auction infringed its copyright. EBay responded by cancelling the auction for the prints. The online sellers of the prints lived and operated their business in Colorado.

Dudnikov, a Colorado company, auctioned various products through eBay. In October 2005, Ms. Dudnikov and Mr. Meador launched an auction on eBay, offering fabric for sale with the imprint of the cartoon character Betty Boop wearing various gowns. One of these gowns closely resembled a famous Erte gown. Erte was a twentieth century Russian-born French artist and fashion designer celebrated for his iconic depictions of Parisian high fashion. "In Erte's original works, *Symphony In Black* and *Ebony On White,* a tall, slender woman is pictured wearing a floor length form-fitting dress that trails her feet, and holding the leash of a thin, regal dog."

Ms. Dudnikov and Mr. Meador modified the iconic images using Betty Boop and her pet dog. EBay suspended Dudnikov's account when Chalk asserted that Betty Boop's image infringed its client's intellectual property rights. Dudnikov filed suit in Colorado district court, and the court dismissed the case upon the defendant's motion, claiming lack of personal jurisdiction. The Tenth Circuit reversed, reasoning that while the Connecticut company's conduct originated outside of Colorado and was technically directed at eBay in California, its express goal was to halt sales of an online auction item originating in Colorado. This factor alone satisfied *Calder's* "express aiming" requirement and was sufficient to establish personal jurisdiction over the Connecticut company in Colorado.

(G) *IN REM* JURISDICTION

Technically, *in rem* jurisdiction relates to the determination of title to, or the status of, property located within the court's territorial limits. A *quasi in rem* judgment affects the interests of particular persons in designated property. Neither *in rem*, nor *quasi in rem* jurisdiction will typically apply to intangible Internet assets. Nevertheless, the Anticybersquatting Consumer Protection Act ("ACPA") recognizes *in rem* jurisdiction over domain names where personal jurisdiction over defendant infringers or cyberpirates is unavailing.

The plaintiff in an *in rem* action under ACPA is the trademark owner, while the defendant is the infringing domain name. Courts will not permit a trademark owner to proceed *in rem* absent proof that the identity and address of the registrant of defendant domain name cannot be been found and that *in personam* jurisdiction was not possible. Chapter 11 explains the mechanics of how the ACPA *in rem* provisions operate in domain name/trademark lawsuits, an *in rem* action that is now rarely deployed to transfer or extinguish a domain name.

§ 3-2. Global Internet Jurisdiction

An Internet presence automatically creates an international presence, triggering the potential for cross-border litigation. Clearly, Internet law requires harmonized jurisdictional rules, as there is no sovereign or any international treaty establishing rules for cyberspace. It is theoretically possible for a U.S. business to be sued in hundreds of foreign countries for the same course of online conduct, but this has not yet happened due to the jurisdictional barriers to filing cross-border lawsuits—a topic explored throughout this Nutshell.

To date, there is no international convention that addresses Internet jurisdiction, the choice of law, or the enforcement of judgments. A growing number of U.S. courts are exercising jurisdiction over website activity occurring outside of the country's territorial boundaries. Conversely, U.S. companies are increasingly being sued in foreign venues for activities occurring on Web servers located in the United States. Clearly, global Internet law requires harmonization. Presently, almost no case law covers international Internet jurisdiction, and no statutory solutions exist to answer the question of cross-border Internet jurisdiction.

As companies use the border-defying Internet, they will increasingly become subject to foreign procedural and substantive law. Foreign websites may be subject to personal jurisdiction in state and federal courts if they target U.S. users. The chronic lack of certainty about the law of cyberspace requires cross-border treaties and conventions. To date, countries connected to the Internet have not agreed to cede their sovereignty in order to harmonize cyber-jurisdictional rules. Instead, courts adapt their own national rules to determine jurisdiction.

(A) FRENCH YAHOO! CASE

The French Government enacted laws against the expression of pro-Nazi and anti-Semitic views. In 2000, two French cultural organizations, *La Ligue Contre Le Racisme Et L'Antisemitisme* (*"LICRA")* and *L'Union Des Etudiants Juifs De France* ("UEJF"), after sending a cease and desist letter, filed a complaint against Yahoo! because users could access Nazi materials on Yahoo!'s French service. The *Tribunal de Grande Instance* ("TGI") in Paris convicted Yahoo! of making Nazi materials available to French citizens through the yahoo.com website as well as yahoo.fr. Yahoo! filed a declaratory judgment action in the Northern District of California, praying the French court order be deemed not enforceable in the United States. A declaratory remedy, as its name suggests, is to seek a court's declaration of the rights of parties.

The fundamental basis of declaratory relief for Yahoo! was to determine whether the French court order violated America's First Amendment. The *Yahoo!* case is emblematic of the Internet as a speech medium where national regulators may have different conceptions of free expression. American courts generally enforce foreign judgments and honor the doctrine of international comity. However, U.S. courts will not enforce judgments contrary to the First Amendment, which prohibits the government from restraining political expression, no matter how distasteful. Expression protected in the United States is criminalized in France, Germany, and other European countries. French authorities were able to impose their national will on Yahoo! France when it enabled sales of Nazi memorabilia on its auction website because the sales had detrimental effects in France.

The French court concluded that Yahoo! violated laws against the expression of pro-Nazi and anti-Semitic views by enabling its citizens to have access to Nazi materials on its service. The French court did not conceive of cyberspace as a separate place beyond its jurisdictional reach. The Paris court charged Yahoo! with giving French citizens access to swastika armbands, SS daggers, concentration camp photos, and even replicas of Zyklon B, the cyanide-based pesticide, used in gas chambers to kill human beings. Judge Gomez, a Paris judge, ruled Yahoo!'s auction website violated French law and ordered the Internet service provider to immediately take all necessary measures to block access to Nazi materials for French web surfers. Yahoo! eventually agreed to remove the Nazi materials from its Yahoo! French website, thus complying with a local governmental order.

A Paris court ruled that messages about Nazis and the sale of Third Reich memorabilia violated the French Criminal Code. Even though Yahoo!'s French subsidiary removed Nazi-related material and images, French users could still easily access this material by searching the American Yahoo! website. The French court issued an order, fining Yahoo! 100,000 francs per day until the provider blocked access to French citizens to all Nazi-related material.

(1) The Federal District Court's Decision

Yahoo! initially refused to honor the French court's order to block access to Nazi materials, filing a declaratory judgment motion in the Northern District of California, requesting a declaration that the French court's order was unenforceable since it was in conflict with the First Amendment of the U.S. Constitution. The California federal court found no basis for "international abstention" and reasoned that its obligation to uphold the First Amendment outweighed any consideration of international comity. Abstention is closely related to the doctrine of international comity, which gives respect for court proceedings in foreign countries.

In this case, the abstention doctrine, reinforced by comity, was at play in a declaratory judgment action concerning a foreign criminal action against Yahoo! The district court granted Yahoo's motion for summary judgment. The trial court held that the exercise of personal jurisdiction over LICRA and UEJF was proper, that the dispute was ripe, that abstention was unnecessary and that the French orders are not enforceable in the United States because such enforcement would violate the First Amendment.

(2) Three Judge Panel's Decision

Nevertheless, the Ninth Circuit U.S. Court of Appeals issued several opaque decisions and ultimately disagreed with the federal district court. Initially, a three-judge Ninth Circuit panel reversed the district court's decision and remanded with instructions to dismiss the action without prejudice. The three-judge panel found both the presence of personal jurisdiction and ripeness, but noted it was a close decision. The court acknowledged it was difficult to know whether enforcement of the French court's interim orders would have been repugnant to California public policy. Additionally, the appeals court refused to decide whether or to what degree the First Amendment may have been violated by enforcement of the French court's orders, and whether such enforcement would be repugnant to California public policy.

(3) *En banc* Decision

A majority of the Ninth Circuit U.S. Court of Appeals sitting *en banc* in *Yahoo! Inc. v. La Ligue Contre Le Racisme Et L'Antisemitisme*, 433 F.3d 1199 (9th Cir. 2006) found that the district court had personal jurisdiction over the French entities but dismissed the case on technical grounds, rather than the First Amendment. Of the majority of the *en banc* panel, three judges concluded that the action should be dismissed for lack of ripeness. Five judges concluded that the case was ripe for adjudication. Three other judges thought that Yahoo!'s action should be dismissed because the court lacked personal jurisdiction over the defendants.

Some members of the *en banc* panel questioned whether minimum contacts were present to support the exercise of personal jurisdiction against the French organization. The fundamental basis of declaratory relief is the existence of an actual, present controversy over a proper subject, which is also emblematic of the ripeness doctrine. The Ninth Circuit's three-judge panel found it a close question but concluded that the district court had personal jurisdiction over the French entities to decide the declaratory judgment.

After the Ninth Circuit's dismissal, Yahoo! agreed to comply with the French court's order to block access of the Nazi materials to French citizens. What was at play in the *Yahoo!* case was whether the federal court should defer to the French court order by way of international comity. The lesson of Yahoo! is that countries are not reticent to enforce local laws arising out of Internet conduct. See James Boyle *Foucault in Cyberspace: Surveillance, Sovereignty and Hardwired Censors*, 66 U. CIN. L. REV. 177, 179 (1997) (quoting John Perry Barlow that "In Cyberspace, the First Amendment is a local ordinance.").

(B) *DOW JONES & CO. V. GUTNICK*

Any entity doing business on the Internet may be subject to divergent jurisdictional rules in multiple dominions. Just as U.S. federal courts apply U.S. style minimum contacts test to foreign defendants, U.S. companies are subject to the jurisdictional rules of other countries when they engage in E-Commerce. In December of 2002, the Australian

High Court held that an executive could sue both Barron's Online and Dow Jones, for libel in the state of Victoria based on evidence that several hundred people in that state accessed the Dow Jones website.

In *Dow Jones & Company Inc. v. Gutnick*, HCA 56 (Austl. 2002), executive Joseph Gutnick sued Dow Jones, the publisher of *Barron's Online*. *Barron's* published an allegedly defamatory article about Gutnick's illegal stock transactions on the *Wall Street Journal* website. The allegedly libelous article was stored on a computer server located in New Jersey and uploaded to the Dow Jones website where paid subscribers downloaded the article. Dow Jones' argument was that if any tort was committed it would have been in New Jersey not Australia. The Australian High Court considered whether Gutnick's defamation action could be filed in Victoria, given that the claim stemmed from an online article posted on the Internet by a U.S. based web server.

The court held Gutnick's claim could be tried in Victoria since the allegedly defamatory article was downloaded and read there—the place where Gutnick suffered the brunt of the harm. The *Gutnick* court also refused to adopt the American single publication rule in which a single edition of a newspaper, magazine, or television program gives rise to only one cause of action.

Most U.S. jurisdictions follow the "single publication rule," which states that the statute of limitations period begins to toll when a defamatory statement is first published. Nevertheless, in

Gutnick, the High Court exercised jurisdiction over Dow Jones for simply posting material on a website. Dow Jones submitted that it was preferable that the publisher of material on the World Wide Web be able to govern its conduct according only to the law of the place where it maintained its web servers, unless that place was merely opportunistic.

The High Court rejected Dow Jones' theory, reasoning that the defendant knew its website would have a worldwide reach when it made its publishing available there, and therefore the law of Australia applies because that is where the harm resulting from the tort occurred. Cyberspace will not fulfill its promise if websites continue to be subject to hundreds of conflicting procedural and substantive rules solely because the material can be accessed in every nation of the globe.

(C) BRUSSELS REGULATION

The European Union ("EU") updated its cross-border jurisdiction rules in March 2002 when it replaced the 1968 Brussels Convention with the Brussels Regulation. The European Union ("EU") updated its cross-border jurisdiction rules in March 2002 when it replaced the 1968 Brussels Convention with the Brussels Regulation. The Brussels Regulation provides uniform rules for jurisdiction and enforcement of judgments throughout the European Union. This cross-national agreement is a possible model for developing global Internet jurisdiction solutions. The purpose of the EU is to create a seamless body of consumer protection, providing certainty for consumers and predictability for the business community.

European courts and legislatures view U.S. style terms of service agreement with one-sided terms in favor of the dominant party with suspicion. The EU's harmonized approach to consumer protection aims to provide all citizens of the Eurozone the same protection in each of the twenty-seven Member States. Europe's like-minded system of cross-border jurisdiction, a possible model for transnational Internet jurisdiction, has its roots in the unifying principles of the 1957 Rome Treaty. The founding treaty established the European Commission that is the only legal institution independent of national governments representing the entire European Union. The EU enshrines freedom for the parties to choose the applicable law as cornerstone of business-to-business ("B2B") transactions. In contrast, the EU protects consumers with conflict rules favorable to the weaker party in business-to-consumer ("B2C") transactions. See generally, Michael L. Rustad & Vittoria Maria Onufrio, The Exportability of the Principles of Software: Lost in Translation?, 2 HASTINGS SCI. & TECH. L.J. 25, 51-52 (2010).

The principal EU legislations addressing private international law ("PIL") are the Brussels Regulation, which governs jurisdiction and the enforcement of judgment; and the Rome I Regulation, which displaces the 1980 Rome Convention on the law applicable to contractual obligations. The Brussels Regulation governs jurisdiction and the enforcement of judgments, while the Rome I Regulation governs courts' choice of law in cross-border transactions.

EU's Brussels Regulation	Purpose
Brussels Regulation on Jurisdiction and the Recognition and Enforcement of Judgments, Council Reg. (EC) 44/2001	Covers two topics, jurisdiction and the free movement of judgments; Jurisdiction is based upon domicile; Business to business ("B2B") parties may agree to a choice of forum clause. Consumers have a non-waivable right in business to contract ("B2C") contracts to litigate disputes in their home court. The mandatory B2C rules for jurisdiction apply to most civil and commercial matters with statutorily prescribed exceptions.

(1) Defendant's Domicile

The Brussels Regulation is broadly applicable to civil and commercial matters with delineated exceptions. It does not apply to issues such as revenue, customs or administrative matters. The basic principle is that jurisdiction is to be exercised based on domicile rather than nationality. In the case of legal persons or corporations, domicile is determined by the country where they have their statutory seat, central administration, or principal place of business.

(2) Where Defendants May be Sued

Under the Brussels Regulation, domicile is determined in accordance with the domestic law of the EU country where the matter is brought before a court. If a party is not domiciled in the EU country of the court considering the matter, the court is to apply the law of another EU country to determine where the party is domiciled. In the case of legal persons or firms, domicile is determined by the country where they have their statutory seat, central administration or principal place of business. In the case of trusts, domicile is defined by the court that is considering the case by applying its own rules of private international law. For business-to-business ("B2B") transactions, the parties are free to choose what jurisdiction applies in advance.

Persons domiciled in an EU Member State may be sued in the courts of any other Member State. Article 2(1) states that courts are to determine domicile in accordance with the domestic law of the Member State where the matter is brought before a court. The Brussels Regulation approach to choice of forum clauses for B2B contracts is similar to the U.S. approach in honoring freedom of contract. However, if the parties do not include a choice of forum clause in their terms of service or other online contract, the Brussels Regulation supplies the default rule.

(3) Special Jurisdictional Rules

The Brussels Regulation forges special rules for determining jurisdiction for contracts where the offeror and offeree are located in different EU signatory countries. Article 5 of the Brussels Regulation provides that in most contracts where the parties are from different signatory states, the jurisdictional country is where performance took place. The EC devised a specialized rule for determining jurisdiction in sales of goods transactions. European courts base jurisdiction in sale of goods cases by the place of delivery as specified in the contract. Article 5(1) dictates that the place of delivery will frequently turn on shipping terms or other contractual provisions. For services, courts determine jurisdiction at the place where services are rendered. To date, the "place of performance" test has not been adapted to Internet-related contracts by any European court.

Perhaps the most significant development that the Brussels Regulation, with implications for all websites selling goods or rendering services to European consumers is that this EU Regulation imposes mandatory consumer rules. Under Articles 15-17, consumers in the Eurozone are entitled to have their disputes settled in their home court or the country where they reside. Article 15 defines consumer as someone who is acting outside her trade or profession.

Additionally, Article 17 of the Regulation prevents the parties to a consumer contract from agreeing to waive their right to jurisdiction in their home court except the parties may agree to allow a consumer to have the option of bringing their jurisdiction in another jurisdiction. Companies cannot compel European consumers to waive the benefit of Brussels Regulation's mandatory home court rule. Thus, an online business has no ability to enforce a contractual term in which a consumer waives her right to sue in her own country or home court. While the Brussels Regulation does not explicitly address electronic commerce related contracts, European courts will have little difficulty extending mandatory consumer rules for jurisdiction and the enforcement of judgments to cyberspace.

(4) Extraterritorial Impact

The principle of territoriality is that laws addressing problems within the boundaries of the European Union should not be enforceable outside their boundaries. The Internet combined with increased cross-border trade means that U.S. companies may be subject to the Regulation's mandatory consumer rules. The Brussels Regulation does not have an express extraterritorial provision like the Rome I Regulation that governs choice of law. Nevertheless, a U.S. federal district court interpreted the Brussels Regulation as being applicable even though the plaintiff was a domiciliary residing outside the EU.

Any company directing its activities to a European consumer's home country will automatically be subject to jurisdiction because it has directed activities to that forum under Article 15 of the Brussels Regulation. In *Air Canada v. United Kingdom*, (1995) 20 EHRR 150, the European Court of Human Rights held that the seizure of an aircraft carrying illegal drugs belonging to the Canadian applicant had not infringed Article 1 of the First Protocol of the European Convention on Human Rights. The court did not find it persuasive the applicant was a resident in Canada but nevertheless applied the European law of human rights.

It is likely that European courts will extend the mandatory consumer rules to U.S. companies with subsidiaries in Europe. Similarly, European courts will apply mandatory consumer rules such as the "home court rule" if a European consumer files a lawsuit against a U.S. company. U.S. companies that include one-sided choice of law and forum clauses in their terms of service cannot be confident that European courts will respect them outside of business-to-business contracts. The Rome I Regulation provides mandatory B2C rules for determining choice of law. As with jurisdiction, the parties are free to choose the law in B2B transactions.

CHAPTER 4

INTERNET-RELATED CONTRACT LAW

Internet business is multi-hemispheric, as the sun never sets on a Web site that stands ready to communicate with customers 24 hours a day, seven days a week in all countries connected to the World Wide Web. During the past two decades, the Internet evolved as a business tool. Internet contract law is also rapidly evolving as industry groups, governments, and international organizations formulate new standards, usages of trade, regulatory initiatives, statutes, and court decisions.

The rapid evolution of the Internet has created a problem of "legal lag." For instance, the law governing end user license agreements suffers legal lag where the law of contracts "is in the rear and limping a little." The timeworn doctrines of contract law are continually being eroded, fractured, and shattered by the Internet's rapid evolution. Website development service providers, for example, are bound by legal restrictions placed upon content. The chapter focuses on the concepts and methods of licensing, which is the chief means of transferring value in an information-based economy.

Courts and legislatures must update Internet law as it limps along far behind technological developments. With the advent of the World Wide

Web, much commerce is now conducted over the Internet. The timeworn doctrines of contract law are continually being eroded, fractured, and shattered by the Internet's rapid evolution. Website development service providers, for example, are bound by legal restrictions placed upon content. This chapter examines many of these developments including the rise of shrinkwrap, clickwrap and browsewrap. The chapter focuses on the concepts and methods of licensing, which is the chief means of transferring value in an information-based economy. Licensing software permits software publishers to commodify their intellectual property assets, while retaining control of its uses.

Unlike toasters, rental cars, or other tangible personal property, software can be reproduced at the click of a download button at almost no cost, resulting in contracting practices primarily based upon the licensing of information. Many Internet-related contracts are mass-market agreements such as terms of service agreements or software license agreements. Many Internet-related contracts are mass-market agreements such as terms of service agreements or software license agreements. As software companies go global, online contracts will be subject to radically different legal traditions. U.S. style terms of use widely enforced in the United States are unenforceable in the European Union. A new legal paradigm is necessary to facilitate E-Commerce, which may soon eclipse brick-and-mortar commerce. Paper-based signatures are rapidly giving way to digital signature in E-Commerce. Electronic agents with or without human review are increasingly forming contracts. Trading partner agreements form rules in advance for protocols for the ordering of goods and payment through electronic messages.

Businesses around the world as well as consumers are entering into "service level agreements" with cloud computing providers. The term, cloud computing, is a metaphor that describes public as well as private providers of software access or storage. The National Institute of Standards and Technology (NIST) definition of cloud computing consists of five essential characteristics: On-demand self-service, Broad network access, Resource pooling, Rapid elasticity, Measured Service); three service models (Cloud Software as a Service (SaaS), Cloud Platform as a Service (PaaS), Cloud Infrastructure as a Service (IaaS)); and, four deployment models (Private cloud, Community cloud, Public cloud, Hybrid cloud)." National Institute of Standards, NIST Cloud Computing Program (2013).

Cloud providers have developed the next generation of IT services, storing data and running applications and permitting users access data and collaborate on any device, from any location 24/7. Ideally, data or software can be accessed, edited, and shared securely from any location on any device. To date, cloud-computing providers have adopted a services paradigm. A typical provision, for example, makes a term of service automatically renewable in perpetuity, subject only to written cancellation by the customer. The fees are generally in form of monthly service fees with upgrades.

Service credits are issued to customer accounts to offset future billable services. Service credits are not typically transferable to other account holders.

§ 4-1. Licensing & the Internet

(A) DEFINITION OF LICENSING

Licenses are ubiquitous in the Internet-based economy. Software licenses impose duties that survive termination such as the duty to keep the other party's trade secrets confidential. A license is first a contract, generally between two parties—the licensor and the licensee—although licenses may also be assigned or sublicensed. Like a lease for personal property, a license agreement gives the licensee the right to use property under stated guidelines. For leases, it is the right to use personal property as opposed to intangible assets. Internet licenses may include computer software, website content, databases or other digital information. The licensor is the party that agrees to transfer software or to grant access to other computer information. The licensee's duty is to pay the licensing fee to the licensor in order to obtain access to or use of information under the terms and conditions specified in the agreement. While a consumer may have unconditional title to the tangible copy of the software (i.e., the purchased CD-ROM), it does not follow that she owns the intellectual property rights protecting the intangible digital data comprising software.

Internet licenses may include computer software, website content, databases or other digital information. The licensor is the party that agrees to transfer software or to grant access to other computer information. The licensee's duty is to pay the licensing fee to the licensor in order to obtain access to or use of information under the terms and conditions specified in the agreement. Typically, content that is downloaded from the Internet is subject to a license agreement. Software license agreements come in a mélange of affiliations ranging from the simple bipartite relationship between the licensor to licensee to complex development contracts providing for sublicensing or affiliates. See Michael J. Madison, Reconstructing the Software License, 35 LOY. U. CHI. L. J. 275, 316 (2003).

Calling an agreement a license does not make it so; courts have the duty to go beyond the labels to examine the economic realities in determining whether an agreement is a license or a sale. The elements of a breach of a license agreement are: (1) the existence of a valid contract; (2) performance or tendered performance by the plaintiff; (3) breach of the contract by the defendant; and (4) resulting damages to the plaintiff. A software license is, in effect, a waiver of the copyright owner's right to sue for copyright or patent infringement. Nevertheless, a software license is also a complex form of contracting with an array of conditions, covenants, and affirmative duties that sometimes survive beyond the term of the agreement.

(B) GRANTING CLAUSE

The granting clause is the "action section" of any license agreement. This clause determines what rights are conferred and under what conditions. Oracle, Adobe, and Microsoft, for example, make it clear in their license agreement that they are only granting a right to use software rather than selling it. Granting clauses may address the question of whether the licensee has a right to sub-license or assign rights to a third party. An example of a broad granting clause in a license agreement is "of all possible rights and all media even media yet to be developed." A narrow license agreement would grant the licensee a right to only use the software in consumer transactions in Montenegro for a three-month period. Licensing agreements are either "Perpetual" or "Non-Perpetual." "Perpetual" means that the agreement has no expiration date unless the licensee violates the terms of use or other condition specified in the agreement.

Software publishers and content creators typically use licensing as the chief method of transferring value for mass-market software products. Comparable to the creation of the corporation or the limited liability company, the invention of the software license agreement is equally significant. Licensing enables the software developer to prohibit assignments or transfers of their product so the initial purchaser may not resell or reproduce the copy. The legal invention of licensing makes it possible for a software publisher to retain title to its information-based product and impose significant transfer restrictions. Licensing enables the software publisher to slice and dice pricing based upon a complex array of variables. Software publishers have different fee schedules for databases depending upon whether the user is a large corporation, a community library, a small business, or a noncommercial user.

(C) FIRST SALE DOCTRINE

Generally, if the software publisher grants only a license to the copy of software and imposes significant restrictions on the purchaser's ability to redistribute or transfer that copy, the purchaser is considered a licensee, not an owner, of the software. Software publishers are far more likely to license information-based products than to sell or lease them. The first sale doctrine applies in all fields of intellectual property law. The patent owner cedes the right to file suit for patent infringement for the patented article that they have sold. Similarly, the first sale doctrine of trademark law permits the purchaser of trademarked goods to resell them without infringing the owner's marks. The common result is that an intellectual property owner cannot place conditions on goods once they are sold—an undesirable result from the perspective of the intellectual property owner.

The first sale doctrine gives the purchaser of a copyrighted work the right to "sell or otherwise dispose of the possession of that copy" without interference by the copyright owner. *Bobbs-Merrell Co. v. Straus*, 210 U.S. 339 (S.Ct. 1908). The first sale doctrine applies in all fields of intellectual property law. In *Kirtsaeng v. John Wiley & Sons,*

Inc., 2013 U.S. LEXIS 2371 (S.Ct. 2013), Supap Kirtsaeng, a citizen of Thailand, asked his friends and family to buy copies of foreign edition English-language textbooks at Thai bookshops, where they sold at low prices, and mail them to him in the United States. Kirtsaeng would then sell them, reimburse his family and friends, and keep the profit. The U.S. Supreme Court held the "first sale" doctrine—which permits lawfully acquired copies of copyrighted works to be resold by their owners—also applies to works such as the books manufactured in Thailand.

With licensing, there is a "first license," but not a "first sale." Software licenses, unlike sales of goods, enable the licensor to retain control of intellectual property rights underlying the code or digital data. In *Microsoft Corp. v. Harmony Computers & Electronic, Inc.*, 846 F. Supp. 208 (E.D. N.Y. 1994), Harmony sold Microsoft products, including Microsoft MS-DOS and Microsoft Windows, as stand-alone products installing them on their customers' hard drives despite not having a license to redistribute or copy these products. Microsoft sought declaratory relief, injunctive relief, and treble damages because of Harmony's unbundling of Microsoft suite of products.

Harmony's defense was that it had purchased the Windows products and had a right to resell their copies under the first sale doctrine of the Copyright Act. Microsoft contended that Harmony's unbundling both breached their licensing agreement and constitutes copyright infringement by exceeding the scope of the number of users' term. The court found that the Microsoft products were, in fact, subject to a single-user license agreement and therefore Harmony violated the license agreement and infringed the software company's copyright by unbundling these products. Because the defendants had purchased software from authorized Microsoft licensees, they are subject to the same terms and conditions as the original licensees.

In *Vernor v. Autodesk, Inc.*, 621 F.3d 1102 (9th Cir. 2010), a first sale dispute arose out of Timothy Vernor's purchase of Autodesk software at a garage sales and other secondhand sales. Architects, engineers, and manufacturers used this high-priced software for design purposes. EBay suspended Vernor's account when it received Digital Millennium Copyright Act takedown notices from Autodesk, protesting Vernor's eBay sales of used Autodesk software. Vernor filed suit against Autodesk, seeking a declaratory judgment to establish that he was a lawful owner of the software and had a right to resell it because of the first sale doctrine.

The Ninth Circuit rejected Vernor's argument, ruling that the design software was licensed, not sold, and therefore subject to the transfer and user restrictions that accompanied the product. The court developed a three-part test to determine whether a software user was a licensee or owner of a copy where the copyright owner: (1) specifies that the user is granted a license, (2) significantly restricts the user's ability to transfer the software, and (3) imposes notable use restrictions.

(D) MASS-MARKET LICENSES

Mass-market licenses are standard form contracts marketed to consumers with identical terms and no likelihood of individual negotiation. Typically, mass-market licenses are one-sided contracts that eliminate warranties and remedies. They are presented to the customer on a "take-it or leave it" basis with identical, non-negotiable terms for all licensees. They are generally single-user licenses but may be bundled in multi-pack license, which delineates the number of users. Symantec, a leading anti-virus licensor, for example, parcels out different bundles of rights depending on whether the user is a business or a consumer entity.

When an end-user of software downloads a Symantec product, they are given a legal notice that the software is licensed, not sold, and that they are subject to the terms of the licensing agreement, which is a presented in the login screen. In a typical standard-form end user licensing agreement ("EULA"), the licensee is not permitted to download the software until they have clicked "I agree" to the terms of service or other license agreement. Academics use imaginative terms such as shrinkwrap, installwrap, clickstream, or browsewrap to refer to mass-market licenses. The chart below depicts the major form of mass license agreements in wide currency on the Internet. Each mass-market form is an adhesive contract where the licensee adheres to the terms of the licensor and there is no semblance of balanced terms.

The vast majority of Internet contracts are standard form licenses defined in UCITA as transactions targeting a broad market. UCITA §101(61) provides: " 'Standard form' means a record or a group of related records containing terms prepared for repeated use in transactions and so used in a transaction in which there was no negotiated change of terms by individuals except to set the price, quantity, method of payment, selection among standard options, or time or method of delivery." Mass-market licenses are standard form contracts marketed to consumers with identical terms and no likelihood of individual negotiation. Typically, mass-market licenses eliminate warranties and remedies in order to spread allocate the risk of software failure to the user community.

In the 1980s until the mid-1990s, there was a swirl of uncertainty over the enforceability of shrinkwrap licenses as courts routinely struck them down on diverse contractual grounds. Mass-market licenses are standard form contracts marketed to consumers with identical terms and no likelihood of individual negotiation. Typically, mass-market licenses are one-sided contracts that eliminate warranties and remedies. They are presented to the customer on a "take-it or leave it" basis with identical, non-negotiable terms for all licensees. The Chart below depicts the leading forms widely used in Internet-related contracts.

Types of Mass-Market License Agreements

Types	Formation Principle	Controversial Aspects
Shrinkwrap License	Manifestation of assent evidenced by the customer opening plastic wrapping surrounding software package	Consumers may not be able to review or even learn of one-sided terms before being bound.
Clickwrap	By clicking on an icon or radio button, the user manifests assent.	Links to clickwrap agreements are sometimes below the fold of a web page, or presented inconspicuously.
Browsewrap	Binds consumers who browse or access a website without other affirmative acts.	Consumers may be bound even though they neither read the terms of use nor affirmatively manifested assent.

Terms of Use of a Website	Binds consumers by either browsing or clicking agreement.	One-sided terms of use often disclaim all warranties and meaningful remedies.

(E) TYPES OF MASS-MARKET LICENSES

(1) Shrinkwrap Agreements

Software makers used shrinkwrap licenses in the early 1980s, prior to the development of the World Wide Web. Shrinkwrap contracts are license agreements or other terms and conditions of a putatively contractual nature, which can only be read and accepted by the consumer after they break open the plastic wrapping surrounding the boxed software. Shrinkwrap is cynically referred as "sneakwrap" as captured in a well-known *Dilbert* cartoon. Dilbert states: "I didn't read all of the shrinkwrap license agreement on my new software until after I opened it,"—and concludes with Dilbert lamenting: "Apparently, I agreed to spend the rest of my life as a towel boy in Bill Gates' new mansion."

The first paragraph of a shrinkwrap license typically provides that the opening of the package indicates acceptance of the license terms because a licensor needs to reference the fact that the software is licensed. Internet related shrinkwrap rarely provides meaningful warranties and limits remedies by choice of forum clauses that often require the user to litigate in their licensor's home court. Installwrap is a closely related practice where the license terms appear on the screen when the user installs the software. Under this form of login screen contracts, the user must click the "I accept" button before the software will begin downloading.

(2) Clickwrap Agreements

The clickwrap agreement requires the user to click "yes" or take some other affirmative action to signify acceptance to the license agreement. The clickwrap license displays terms electronically and the user manifests assent by clicking the acceptance button. Like shrinkwrap, the clickwrap spells out permitted and restricted uses by licensees. U.S. courts will enforce clickwrap agreements so long as the user has an opportunity to review the terms and manifest assent, even though most users fail to read the terms before clicking the "I agree" button.

(3) Browsewrap

A defining feature of a browsewrap license is that it does not require the user to manifest assent to the terms and conditions expressly—the user need not sign a document or click on an "accept" or "I agree" button to be bound by the agreement. Facebook, for example, structures its terms of use as a browsewrap with the following introductory clause: "By using or accessing Facebook, you agree to this Statement."

(4) Terms of Service

U.S. courts enforce browsewrap agreements so long as the website developer places the terms of use conspicuously on the home page. In *Register.com, Inc. v. Verio*, Inc., 835 N.E.2d 113 (Ill. App. 5th Dist. 2005). the domain name database's terms of service ("TOS") stated that the user was agreeing to the terms and conditions merely by sending its search robots to query Register's online database of domain names called WHOIS. Verio contended that it did not click agreement to Register.com's TOS and thus was not bound by its provisions. The Second Circuit upheld the browsewrap agreement, ruling that Verio had manifested assent by merely submitting queries to Register's WHOIS database. Register.com was entitled to injunctive relief because it demonstrated a likelihood of success on the merits based upon a trespass to chattels claim as well as violation of the Computer Fraud Abuse Act and federal trademark claims.

The court's order enjoined Verio from: (1) using Register's trademarks; (2) representing or otherwise suggesting to third parties that Verio's services have the sponsorship, endorsement, or approval of Register; (3) accessing Register's computers by use of automated software programs performing multiple successive queries; and (4) using data obtained from Register's database of contact information of registrants of Internet domain names to solicit the registrants for the sale of web site development services by electronic mail, telephone calls, or direct mail.

In *Kwan v. Clearwire Corp.*, No. C09–1392JLR, 2012 WL 32380 (W.D. Wash., 2012), a federal court refused to enforce an Internet service provider's arbitral clause, finding it to be inconspicuous. The court ruled that mere access to a term of service agreement was insufficient to meet the conspicuousness test. The court ordered discovery to determine whether Clearwire's customers agreed to the TOS and to class action waivers. The lesson of this case is that location and conspicuousness matter. To date, only a single court has invalidated a terms of use or terms of service agreement on unconscionability grounds. *Bragg v. Linden Research*, 487 F. Supp. 2d 593 (E.D. Pa., 2007).

§ 4-2. Contract Formation in Cyberspace

In the 1980s, there was a swirl of uncertainty over the enforceability of mass-market licenses as courts routinely struck them down on diverse contractual grounds. However, the recent trend is for U.S. courts to enforce mass-market licenses in contrast to the more consumer-friendly laws of Europe.

(A) ENFORCEABILITY ISSUES

In *Specht v. Netscape Communications Corp.*, 306 F.3d 17 (2d Cir. 2002), the Second Circuit refused to enforce a mass-market license agreement with a predispute mandatory arbitration clause in a website contract because it was unclear whether a consumer had an opportunity to review the terms of a clickwrap agreement prior to manifesting assent. In *Specht*, Netscape urged users to download Netscape's free software with an immediate click of a button with only a reference to the existence of a license located on a submerged screen. Netscape's reference stated: "Please review and agree to the terms of the Netscape SmartDownload software license agreement before downloading and using the software."

As the representative of a class action of Netscape users, Specht contended that the SmartDownload contained cookies and keys that identified and tracked users, violating their privacy. The Computer Fraud & Abuse Act and Electronic Communications Privacy Act claims charged Netscape with secretly monitoring their online activities without the users' awareness or permission. In a rare consumer licensing victory, the Second Circuit refused to enforce a predispute mandatory arbitration clause that precluded the class action from being filed in court, finding that users did not have reasonable notice of the license terms or an opportunity to manifest assent prior to downloading this plug-in program. In addition, Netscape had not requested that the consumer click agreement to the SmartDownload license, only for Netscape's Communicator. In *Scherillo v. Dun & Bradstreet Inc.*, 684 F.Supp.2d 313 (E.D. N.Y. 2010), a more typical court decision, the federal judge upheld a click-wrap forum selection clause finding it to be reasonably communicated to the plaintiff, even though the user had to scroll down the page to view the "terms of use."

The court gave no credence to the plaintiff's argument that he "checked" the terms and conditions box inadvertently and therefore had not assented to the agreement. In general, a software licensor can create a "safe harbor" for proving manifestation of assent by using a "double assent procedure" that requires the user to reaffirm assent. A licensor must give the licensee a right to a refund if the licensee has not had an opportunity to review the terms and manifest assent prior to payment.

(B) ROLLING CONTRACTS

Courts have recognized a "layered" or "rolling" system of electronic contract formation, which is an extension of the layered contract formation industry practice in durable goods sales. With a layered contract, licensors structure their agreements so that a customer will manifest assent to different terms at different points in time. For example, a cell phone contract may introduce new terms after the initial monthly agreement by posting them on a website. Terms of service agreements for social media sites may reserve the right to modify unilaterally the terms of use or service such as changing a privacy policy.

Instagram, for example, altered its position as to the intellectual property rights of photographs posted on its service, creating a firestorm in the user community. The recent trend in judicial decisions is that courts enforce "cash now, terms later" licenses so long as the licensor gives reasonable notice to the user and an opportunity to decline the terms.

(1) ProCD, Inc. v. Zeidenberg: A Game-Changer

In *ProCD, Inc. v. Zeidenberg*, 86 F.3d 1447 (7th Cir. 1996), the Seventh Circuit upheld a shrinkwrap agreement in which the licensee paid for boxed software that included a software license inside the box. ProCD's software consisted of a CD-ROM containing a computer database consisting of more than 3,000 telephone directories called Select Phone compiled at the cost of $10 million. Matthew Zeidenberg purchased a single copy of ProCD's software at a cost of $150 and formed a company to resell access to the software over the Internet.

ProCD filed a copyright infringement lawsuit, seeking an injunction against Zeidenberg that would restrain him from further sales of its software. The federal district court held ProCD's license agreement was unenforceable since its terms did not appear on the outside of the package and a customer could not be bound by terms that were secret at the time of sale. The Seventh Circuit disagreed, ruling that ProCD's license agreements were enforceable under a "pay now, terms later" contract paradigm. The Seventh Circuit applied U.C.C. Article 2 to the license agreement, noting contract formation may be manifested in any manner sufficient to show agreement.

The *ProCD* court held that terms presented inside of a box of software bind consumers because they have an opportunity to read the license agreement and to reject it by returning the product. The court also rejected Zeidenberg's argument that shrinkwrap license agreements must be conspicuous to be enforced. The court also rejected the argument that the Copyright Act preempts software licenses because the rights created by ProCD's license agreement were not found to be equivalent to any of the exclusive rights of the Copyright Act. A copyright holder has exclusive rights to use and to authorize the use of his work in five qualified ways: (1) to reproduce the work; (2) to prepare derivative works; (3) to distribute copies of the work to the public; (4) to perform the work publicly; and (5) to display the work publicly.

(2) Hill v. Gateway 2000, Inc.

In *Hill v. Gateway 2000, Inc.*, 105 F.3d 1147 (7th Cir. 1997), a consumer ordered and paid for a Gateway personal computer during a telephone conversation with a company representative. Gateway's standard business practice was to send its computer system—with a software license agreement included inside the box—through the mail to the customer. The license agreement stated that the consumer must submit any dispute to mandatory arbitration unless they returned the personal computer within 30 days. Under classical contract law, silence or inaction by a party generally does not constitute assent.

Nevertheless, the Seventh Circuit upheld Gateway's delayed contract formation policy, including the arbitration clause, finding that the failure of a consumer to return the computer to Gateway within 30 days constituted a manifestation of assent. Hill was found to be the offeree and

Gateway the offeror who had the power to specify the manner of acceptance. The Seventh Circuit ruled that the "terms inside Gateway's box stand or fall together." UCC § 2–207, the battle of the forms, was inapplicable, since there was not an exchange of forms at all but a single form drafted by Gateway.

Judge Easterbrook's interpretation of the battle of the forms conflicts with Official Comment #1 to UCC § 2–207 that makes it clear that the battle of the forms also applies to a written confirmation of an earlier oral agreement as in this case. UCC § 2–207 would apply because Gateway's form could be construed as a written confirmation of the earlier oral agreement made between Hill and the company's authorized representative on the telephone.

UCC § 2–207(2) would construe the additional or different terms as "proposals for addition to the contract" since the transaction was not between merchants. The consumer would need to agree specifically to the arbitration term in order for it to be part of the contract. The contract had already been completed by the time Gateway placed the license agreement inside the box. Despite the court's incorrect reading of UCC Article 2, U.S. courts continue to cite the *Hill* decision, another example of the pro-industry trend.

§ 4-3. Uniform Electronic Transactions Act

The Uniform Electronic Transactions Act ("UETA") is a model state law proposed by the National Conference of Commissioners on Uniform State Laws ("NCCUSL") to create more uniformity for electronic transactions. UETA is not a substantive contract law statute, but rather has the purpose of validating records and e-signatures as the functional equivalents of writings and pen signatures. UETA substitutes the "record" for a paper-based writing and treats signatures in electronic form as the equivalent of signatures made by pen. As of September 15, 2012, eighty U.S. courts have mentioned EUTA in legal decisions. The UETA is law in forty-seven of the fifty states and the District of Columbia, as well as by the territories of Puerto Rico and the Virgin Islands. The purpose of UETA is to remove barriers to E-Commerce, implement reasonable practices, and harmonize contracting procedural rules by enabling the electronic retention and transmission of digital information.

§ 4-4. The Electronic Signatures in Global and National Commerce Act

The Electronic Signatures in Global and National Commerce Act ("E-Sign") is a federal statute that overlaps with UETA by also legitimating digital signatures and electronic records. E-Sign insures that courts may not deny the legal effect or the enforceability of contracts solely because the parties formed the contract through electronic signatures or electronic records. E-Sign establishes the ground rules for validating electronic signatures, authenticating the identity of the sender of a message or the signer of a document, and ultimately ensuring electronic documents are not modified.

E-SIGN § 101(C) requires that consumers affirmatively consent before an electronic communication or record can be sent in lieu of a physical writing. Consumers also have the right to withdraw consent at any time. Consumers are entitled to disclosures if an electronic record is substituted for a paper-based record. Section 101(C) gives consumers the right to demand that sellers or services providers make a record available on paper or in another electronic form. Congress took the unusual step of incorporating a saving clause, which defers to UETA where there is a conflict with E-SIGN. The vast majority of states already enacted UETA by the time Congress passed E-Sign in June of 2000. The legal significance of E-Sign and UETA is that it legitimated digital signatures and records as the functional equivalent for paper-based signatures and writings.

§ 4-5. Uniform Computer Information Transactions Act

(A) STATUTORY PURPOSE

The Uniform Computer Information Transactions Act ("UCITA") is a state statute that develops the ground rules for contracting in cyberspace. UCITA harmonizes legal infrastructure for Web-site linking agreements, affiliate agreements, legal notices, license agreements, access contracts, clickwrap agreements, end-user agreements, online shopping, auction bidding agreements, terms of services agreements, and online licenses of all kinds. The concepts and methods for attribution procedures, authentication, computer information, electronic agents, electronic events, electronic messages, and online contracting update contract law for the age of the Internet.

Maryland and Virginia are the only states to have enacted UCITA, a useful template for a wide array of software licensing transactions. UCITA is divided into nine parts: (1) General Provisions, (2) Formation and Terms, (3) Construction, (4) Warranties, (5) Transfer of Interests and Rights, (6) Performance, (7) Breach of Contract, (8) Remedies and (9) Miscellaneous Provisions. Lawyers frequently import UCITA provisions into their mass-market license agreement because of their flexibility.

(B) GENERAL PROVISIONS

Section 102 defines key terms such as access contracts, attribution procedures, authentication, computer information, electronic agents, electronic events, electronic messages, mass-market licenses, receipt, and record. This section also defines electronic agents to mean "a computer program, or electronic or other automated means, used independently to initiate an action, or to respond to electronic messages or performances, on the person's behalf without review or action by an individual at the time of the action or response to the message or performance."

(C) FORMATION RULES

(1) Statute of Frauds

UCITA's concept of a "record" enables the parties of an e-contract to satisfy the moth-eaten Statute of Frauds. Out of the hundreds of global nations conducting Internet commerce, the U.S. is the only country to require a Statute of Frauds for the sale of goods or the licensing of information. UCITA and U.C.C. Article 2 continue to require a signed writing by the party against whom enforcement is sought unless there is an exception. UCITA updates the Statute of Frauds for online contracts by treating a "record" as a functional equivalent of "pen and paper" signatures. UCITA defines "records" to mean information inscribed on a tangible medium. Records may also be stored in an electronic library or other medium, permitting it to be retrievable in perceivable form.

(2) Opportunity to Review

UCITA § 114 requires that the licensor of the terms of service give the potential customer an opportunity to review the terms of a standard-form license. UCITA § 114 is fulfilled so long as the licensor gives the customer an opportunity to review the terms of the license before the software maker delivers the software and the customer is bound to pay. Under Section 209(B), a licensor must give the licensee a right to a refund if the licensee has not had an opportunity to review the terms and manifest assent prior to payment. If the licensee returns mass-market software, the licensor bears the shipping and related costs. UCITA's drafters are cognizant of the importance of proximity because the statute requires the terms must be either close to the description of the computer or available by clicking on a hyperlink to another site.

(3) Manifestation of Assent

Section 209(A) of UCITA validates mass-market or standard form agreements "only if the party agrees to the license, such as by manifesting assent, before or during the party's initial performance or use of or access to the information." UCITA § 208(1) also states, "A party adopts the terms of a record, including a standard form, as the terms of the contract if the party agrees to the record, such as by manifesting assent." Assent is not conditioned on whether a consumer read or understood the terms of the agreement. The concept of manifesting assent is based solely upon an objective standard rather than a subjective "meeting of the minds."

Mass-market contracts are enforced if three conditions are met: (1) the user has an opportunity to review the terms of the license, (2) the user manifests assent after having an opportunity to review the terms, and (3) the actions are "attributable in law" to the user. UCITA rejects the doctrine of acceptance by silence for standard form licenses, which is a criticism of browsewrap.

(4) Rolling Contracts

UCITA also validates "rolling contracts," permitting a content provider or software publisher to add, delete, or change terms after the licensee has paid royalties for access. The trend in recent judicial decisions is that courts enforce "cash now, terms later" software agreements so long as the licensor gives reasonable notice to the user and provides an opportunity to decline the terms.

(5) Attributable to Licensee

UCITA's provisions closely track both E-Sign and UETA's concept of attribution. Section 107 of UCITA provides that "a record or authentication may not be denied legal effect or enforceability solely because it is in electronic form." UCITA spells out substantive rules needed for online transactions that provide safeguards and safe harbors against a user's inadvertent assent or attribution. Section 212(A) states that electronic events are attributable to either the person or their electronic agent. Trading partner agreements often specify the protocols used in computer-to-computer transactions.

Under UCITA, § 102(A)(5), for example, attribution procedure is defined as any electronic authentication or performance of a particular person that enables tracking of changes or the identification of errors in e-communications. UCITA considers "the use of algorithms or other codes, identifying words or numbers, encryption, or callback or other acknowledgement" to be attribution procedures. UCITA validates the use of electronic agents, automated means of initiating action, and responding to electronic records without review by human beings. Under UCITA § 206, the parties may use electronic agents to enter into contracts without review.

(D) UNCONSCIONABLE TRANSFERS

Section 111 of UCITA gives courts the power to police contracts or any one-sided or oppressive term. A court may refuse to enforce the entire software license or the remainder of the contract without the unconscionable term. The court has broad equitable powers to limit the application of any unconscionable term to avoid any unconscionable result. The issue of unconscionability is always a matter of law and one for the trial judge rather than a determination by the jury.

(E) CONSTRUCTION OF LICENSES

Part 3 of UCITA covers diverse topics such as the parol evidence rule, modification, changes in terms, and the interpretation of information-based contracts. UCITA's parol evidence rule substitutes the term "record" for a writing but is otherwise parallel to UCC § 2–202. Like Article 2, UCITA permits integrated writings to be supplemented by course of performance and by course of dealing and usage of trade. UCITA § 301 permits a party to introduce evidence of consistent additional terms unless the record states that it is a "complete and exclusive" statement of the terms of the license.

(F) INFORMATION-BASED WARRANTIES

UCITA divides warranties into two broad categories: warranties of non-infringement and warranties of quality. Common software licensing warranties include those of non-infringement, express warranties, the implied warranty of merchantability of a computer program, information content, fitness for licensee's purpose, and the warranty of system integration.

(1) Express Warranties

UCITA's express warranty provisions include both affirmations of fact and promises that the software publisher or other licensor makes to its customer relating to the software, which is the "basis of the bargain" test. Internet merchants create express warranties whenever they make definite statements about the software's performance in product packaging, banner advertisements, pop-up advertisements, and sales representations or demonstrations, whether on or off line. Website promotional materials, product descriptions, samples, or advertisements will also create express warranties.

An express warranty is breached when claims are not supported or product fails to live to affirmative statements about its performance. UCITA's express warranty provisions for computer information transactions borrows extensively from UCC § 2–313. Express warranties are not disclaimable because it would be fraud to make a statement about a digital product's performance and then later to disclaim it.

(2) Implied Warranty of Merchantability

Merchantability in software contracts are minimal quality standards with a reference to quality standards in the industry. The implied warranty of merchantability means that the software quality standards must be fit for its ordinary purpose. Software must be non-objectionable in the trade, be at least fair average, and be adequately packaged. Software vendors typically disclaim this warranty because of uncertainty as to the meaning of merchantability for software or digital products.

Software is rarely, if ever, bug-free, so vendors do not want to be held accountable for minor errors. The concept of merchantability requires the software to perform at a level that is at least fair, average, and not objectionable in the software industry. Information, software, or data, must have the minimal quality of similar code in the industry, which tolerates a certain amount of bugs without objection. The mere fact that there are problems with the software's performance does not render it unmerchantable. Software or data need not be the best, but cannot be the worst either to satisfy the merchantability standard.

(3) Fitness for a Particular Purpose

Courts subdivide implied warranties of quality into the implied warranty of merchantability and the systems integration warranty or fitness-type warranty. The concept of merchantability applies to the ordinary purposes of software, data, or information, whereas fitness or systems integration warranties signify interoperability standards or whether a given software application works on a specific computer system. The fitness for a particular purpose warranty has its genesis in UCC

§ 2–315. Section 405 of UCITA recognizes two fitness-type warranties: (A) the fitness for particular purpose (Section 405(A)) and (B) the systems integration warranty (Section 405(C)).

UCITA's fitness for a particular purpose warranty, Section 405(A), requires proof that the licensor knew or had reason to know of a particular purpose for which the information is required. The licensee must demonstrate that it was relying upon the licensor, and that the computer software or other information was fit for a particular purpose. The fitness warranty is disclaimable and modifiable, arising whenever a licensee relies upon a "licensor's skill or judgment to select, develop, or furnish" software or other information. This implied warranty is that the software delivered is fit for the licensee's purpose and is thus a contextual warranty. Subsection 405(A)(2) applies a reasonable effort standard for service-like obligations. The software fitness standard is less rigorous than that for the sale of durable goods that recognizes no period of acceptance testing.

The fitness warranty is contextualized, which means that software may pass the merchantability hurdle, but still not be suitable for a licensee's needs. In an illustrative case, a computer vendor delivered a computed topographer scan machine ("CT Scan") that was merchantable but still not suitable for the customer's particular purpose. The medical equipment met the standard of fair average quality but failed to pass the contextual fitness test, as it was not suitable for the radiologists' practice, which used x-rays to create pictures of cross-sections of the entire body.

The fitness warranty issue arose because the radiologists had informed the vendor that they needed software for full body scans, not just head scans, therefore the fitness warranty was breached because the CT Scan software delivered could only accommodate head scans. The fitness for a particular purpose warranty has its genesis in U.C.C. §2–315, which is Article 2 of the U.C.C.'s fitness warranty. Section 405 of UCITA recognizes two fitness-type warranties: (A) the fitness for particular purpose (Section 405(A)) and (b) the systems integration warranty (Section 405(c)).

(4) Systems Integration Warranty

UCITA § 405(C) creates an implied warranty of system integration for software that performs as part of a complex computer system. The systems integration warranty is a representation that a given component will interoperate with other components of a system. The systems integration warranty often arises when a customer relies upon the expertise of the vendor who represents that a given component or program will work on a given system. For example, an online company could be making a systems integration warranty if it told a customer its software would perform on a Windows 8 platform. Systems integration warranties are more important in the business-to-business context than in consumer transactions.

(5) Information Content Warranties

UCITA recognizes an implied warranty for informational content that is unlike those found in either Article 2 or 2A of the U.C.C. Section 404, the information content warranty, is given only by merchant/licensors with a special relationship of reliance with the licensee that "collects, compiles, processes, provides or transmits informational content." The merchant-licensor's duty according to § 404(A) as to information content is limited to inaccuracies "caused by the merchant's failure to perform with reasonable care." UCITA § 404(B) (1) does not extend this warranty to encompass published content nor is it applicable to the subjective qualities of information. The information content warranty is inapplicable to published conduits or where licensor is simply a conduit, which does not provide editorial services.

UCITA's information content warranty is negligence-based, not predicated upon strict liability like the other warranties. Section 404, cmt. 2 states that: "Reasonable efforts, not perfect results, provide the appropriate standard in the absence of express terms to the contrary." Section 404(B) does not warrant the accuracy of published information. Licensors frequently limit any warranty representation to what they contributed to a database, software or other digital information to avoid being held legally responsible for the shortcomings of the entire system.

This warranty is more appropriate to database access agreements than to software licensing.

Section 404(A) limits the warranty to merchant/licensors that have a special relationship of reliance with the licensee. This information-content warranty is limited to the statement that the content was not inaccurate due to anything that the licensor did in its processing. It is the information content creator, not the licensor, who would create inaccuracies in informational content. Therefore, this warranty gives little protection to the licensee against inaccuracies.

The warranty for informational content does not apply to subjective aspects of the informational content, published content or when the licensor is merely acting as an information transfer conduit without providing editorial services. This warranty is disclaimable despite UCITA's general prohibition against disclaiming reasonableness and care. The information content warranty does not extend to aesthetics, subjective quality, or marketability. No court has construed the meaning of the implied warranty for information content but presumably, the general standard for services applies.

(6) Warranty Disclaimers & Limitations

UCITA allows the parties to disclaim or modify all implied warranties by words or conduct. UCITA requires that disclaimers of the implied warranty of non-infringement and quiet enjoyment must be evidenced by specific language, although it may sometimes be disclaimed by circumstances. As with U.C.C. Article 2, the implied warranty of merchantability is sufficient to disclaim the implied warranty of informational content. In addition, the use of "as is" or like expressions may disclaim warranties but not the specific warranties of quiet enjoyment or non-infringement under UCITA § 401 or UCITA § 404. Both warranties are only disclaimable by specific language.

UCITA's legal infrastructure legitimates the software industry's practice of eliminating the implied warranty; licensors often follow Amazon.com's practice of offering its services on an "as-is" basis. In order to exclude the implied warranty of merchantability, the exclusionary language must mention the word "merchantability;" must be in writing; and must be conspicuous. Warranty limitations must not be unconscionable nor violate fundamental public policies. Fifty-three out of fifty-four prominent Internet websites in sampled one study eliminated all consumer warranty protection. Robert Hillman & Ibrahim Barakat, *Warranties and Disclaimers in the Electronic Age*, 11 YALE J. L. TECH. 1, 3 (2009).

(7) Non-Infringement Warranty

Section 401, UCITA's non-infringement warranty, is a licensor warranty that software does not infringe a third party's patents, copyrights, trademarks, or other intellectual property. The essence of this warranty is that the licensor represents that it has the intellectual property rights necessary to license the software or digital data. Most licensors are not willing to provide this broad non-infringement warranty and instead give a warranty that they have no knowledge of infringement. Under this provision, a licensor that knowingly delivers infringing software or interferes with its customer's right to use software will be required to indemnify its customer.

Any disclaimer of the implied warranty of non-infringement and quiet enjoyment must be done with specific language. UCITA adapts the warranty of quiet possession of information transfers from the law of real property. The essence of the quiet enjoyment warranty is the right of a licensee to use information for the duration of the license without interference by a licensor or a third party. The quiet enjoyment warranty applies only to the acts or omissions of the licensor, not to third parties. A licensee receives "peace of mind" that it is not purchasing an intellectual property lawsuit along with the software code. The licensor is accountable if the software or other information product infringes title or intellectual property rights of others.

(G) PERFORMANCE

Part 6 of UCITA extends commercial law concepts and methods to information performance standards. Section 605 applies a "material breach" standard in business-to-business transactions rather than the perfect tender rule, which is reserved for business-to-consumer transactions. UCITA's § 701 gives an aggrieved party the right to refuse a performance that is a material breach. Under this section, a material breach is first determined by examining the agreement. UCITA adopts a substantial performance or material breach standard versus Article 2's parochial and unrealistic perfect tender rule for performance, which is followed by no other country.

Examples of breach would be repudiation of a contract, failure to perform a contractual obligation in a timely way, exceeding the scope of use, or failing to comply with other conditions expressed in the contract. As with U.C.C. Article 2, it is a breach to repudiate a contract before the date of performance (anticipatory repudiation). UCITA's performance rules are functionally equivalent to U.C.C. Article 2 except for its articulation of a material breach standard for non-mass-market transactions.

Section 703, for example, imports U.C.C. § 2–508's concept of a cure. Section 704 adopts the material breach standard for defective tender of software. Section 707 imports the concept of revocation of acceptance from Article 2. Section 708 gives parties a right to an adequate assurance of performance, while Section 709 adopts the concept of anticipatory repudiation with similar provisions to U.C.C. Article 2, whereas retraction of anticipatory repudiation is found in Section 710. In contrast, the UCC § 2-601, the perfect tender rule, permits a buyer to obtain substitute goods if the goods fail "in any respect to conform to the contract."

The material breach standard adopted by UCITA parallels the fundamental breach of Article 25 of the Convention for the International Sale of Goods ("CISG"). UCITA imports a large number of performance-related concepts such as tender, acceptance, rejection, revocation, cure repudiation, and retraction from U.C.C. Article 2, with minor adaptations. UCITA's concept of tender is that a licensor transmits a copy of software or otherwise enables use or access to software, databases, or other information.

UCITA § 601(B)(1) excludes the material breach standard for copies of software or other information in a mass-market transaction. UCITA adopts the perfect tender rule for mass-transactions but this rule does not extend to business-to-business or custom licenses. UCITA § 102(a)(45) defines a "mass-market" transaction to include "consumer contracts" but also any other license where the end-user licensee receives software on the same terms. Mass-market end-user licenses are offered by the licensor on the same terms for the same rights without the possibility of individual negotiation.

Part 6 of UCITA also sets forth the procedure for terminating a license agreement. UCITA § 617 requires that the terminating party to give the other party a "reasonable notice of termination." Section 102(a)(64) defines termination to mean "the ending of a contract by a party pursuant to a power created by agreement or law. . ." Nevertheless, in software license agreements, a licensee may have continuing obligations that survive termination unlike sales or leases of goods.

(H) REMEDIES FOR BREACH

Part 7 of UCITA sets forth the basic rules that govern breach of computer information transaction agreements. Even if a licensor tenders software with a substantial defect, it will have an opportunity to cure—a concept UCITA imports from UCC § 2–508. A customer's failure to notify the vendor that it is rejecting software serves as a waiver of all remedies. Part 8 of UCITA imports remedies from U.C.C. Article 2 but adapted to computer information transactions. Section 816 of UCITA limits licensor's ability to electronically repossess information or disable software.

UCITA imports many of the U.C.C. Article 2's remedies by adapting provisions to licensing. Part 8 of UCITA addresses remedies for licensors and licensees. As with most UCITA provisions, the parties to a license agreement have the freedom of contract to forge their own contract remedies. UCITA gives the aggrieved party the right to seek a remedy for nonmaterial breaches as well as for material breaches. However, rescinding a software license agreement does not preclude the aggrieved party from pursuing other remedies. An aggrieved party may cancel a license agreement if there is an uncured material breach, but the breaching party has a right to notice before the nonbreaching party cancels a software contract.

UCITA tailored buyer and seller remedies to software transactions. UCITA § 804 is a carbon copy of UCC § 2–718, the doctrine of liquidated damages, which defers to the parties' compensation clauses. Parties may specify liquidated damages in advance so long as they not amount to a penalty clause. A compensation clause in a license agreement may set both a floor and a ceiling for recovery (minimum and maximum recovery).

Section 803(B) permits an aggrieved licensee to have all UCITA remedies if the vendor's sole and exclusive remedy "fails of its essential purpose." The result of a failure of essential purpose is that the licensee has the full panoply of remedies available under UCITA. A licensor should negotiate for a consequential damages clause that will survive a court's finding that a limited remedy fails of its essential purpose. UCITA's Reporter refused to accept the doctrine of the "minimum adequate remedy." For example, Section 803 reasons that an agreed limited remedy provision is enforceable even if it does not afford a consumer (or other licensee) a "minimum adequate remedy." UCITA does not adopt mandatory rules protecting consumers.

The licensee can only change limited remedies on the narrow grounds of unconscionability, fundamental public policy, or the issue of mutuality of obligation. None of these tools are promising for addressing consumer protection problems such as one-sided choice of law, predispute mandatory arbitration, and limited but exclusive remedies. Section 803(B) adopts the doctrine of "sole and exclusive" remedy from U.C.C. Article 2. If a licensee can prove that "performance of an exclusive or limited remedy causes the remedy to fail of its essential purpose," the licensee may pursue any other UCITA remedy. UCITA's doctrine of the failure of essential purpose is the functional equivalent of UCC § 2–719(2). UCITA § 803, which permits an aggrieved licensee to have all UCITA remedies if the vendor's sole and exclusive remedy "fails of its essential purpose." UCITA is the law in only two jurisdictions, Maryland and Virginia, but serves as an industry standard for the software industry embodied in mass-market license agreements and terms of service.

§ 4-6. Principles of the Law of Software Contracts

The ALI proposed the Principles of the Law of Software Contracts (Principles) because of the failure of UCITA to be widely adopted by state legislatures. The Reporters of the Principles concluded: "Perhaps no other commercial subject matter is in greater need of harmonization and clarification" than software contracts. The goal of the Principles is similar to a Restatement in providing guidance for courts and legislatures when addressing software contracting issues. The Principles, like Restatements, give courts guidance in applying existing software law principles. The Principles seek to present clear formations of the law as it stands or the path of the law as might plausibly be sketched out by a court. In the absence of a software contracting law, courts stretch U.C.C. Article 2 and other bricks and mortar principles to digital information. To date, only a single court has cited the Principles in a judicial opinion and no court has relied upon any of its provisions. *Conwell v. Gray Loon Outdoor Mktg. Group*, 906 N.E.2d 805 (Ind. Sup. Ct. 2009).

(A) SPHERE OF APPLICATION

The Principles apply to the transfer of any software as long as it is supported by consideration, which includes sales, leases, and licenses. Open source licenses without licensing fees or other consideration, are outside the scope of the Principles. These Restatement-like Principles address legal issues for transferring software for consideration, whether by lease, license or sale. The Reporters address four issues: (1) the nature of software transactions, (2) contract formation and how industry practices govern terms, (3) the juncture between federal intellectual property rights and software contract law, and (4) software contracting terms such as warranties, remedies, and transfer rules.

The Principles are inapplicable to physical media on which software is stored or transferred such as a CD-ROM, or firmware. Software contracts may be hybrid transactions consisting of sales, leases, and licenses. Section 107 applies a "predominant purpose" test, which asks whether the transaction is predominately goods or software. If goods are the predominant part, U.C.C. Article 2 applies. Otherwise, the Principles should be extended.

(B) PRELIMINARY CONCERNS

The prefatory Principles (Chapter 1) provide a legal infrastructure including definitions, scope, and general terms, digital content, record, software, choice of forum, choice of law and unconscionability. The Principles' Reporter makes it clear that the parties' choice of law must give way to federal intellectual property rules to the contrary. A software contract is unenforceable if it "(A) conflicts with a mandatory rule of federal intellectual property law, or (B) conflicts impermissibly with the purposes and policies of federal intellectual property law, or (C) would constitute federal intellectual property misuse in an infringement proceeding." Principles of the Law of Software Contracts, § 1.09.

There is little case law on what kinds of software contracting terms would violate a fundamental public policy. The Principles guide courts in policing unfair or unconscionable license agreements. Section 1.09, illus. #8 for example, would invalidate a provision in a license agreement where a transferee of a spreadsheet software program is asked to agree not to implement ideas or develop a competing program for 99 years. A few software licensors prohibit licensees from publicly criticizing software, a practice that is also challengeable under Section 109.

(C) FORMATION

(1) Liberal Formation Rules

The Principles adopt the liberal contract formation rules from U.C.C. Article 2. Section 2.01 covers standard form as well as customized software licenses. Software license agreements or other transfers may be made in any method as long as it shows the parties have reached an agreement. The Principles also validate "rolling contracts" even if presented to the consumer in a take-it-or-leave-it standard form. With a rolling contract, manifestation of assent does not occur at a single point in time.

Under webwrap contracts, a party will manifest assent to different terms at different points in time. Terms of service agreements, for example, reserve the right to unilaterally modify the terms of use or service. The licensor or buyer requires payment first and provides terms later. The recent trend in judicial decisions is that courts enforce "cash now, terms later" licenses so long as the licensor gives reasonable notice to the user and an opportunity to decline the terms. The Principles validate electronic records as the functional equivalent of a physical writing to satisfy the Statute of Frauds.

(2) Battle of the Forms Provision

The Principles also adopt a simple battle of the forms provision in which the contract consists in terms found in both terms and gap-fillers. The Reporters substitute electronic records for physical forms, thus updating UCC § 2–207 to the Internet. Section 2.02 applies special rules for standard or mass-market transfers of generally available software. The transferee will be deemed to have adopted a standard form if the standard form is reasonable accessible before the transfer and they must have access to the standard form before notice of payment. Section 2.02 addresses standard form transfers of generally available software. The contract rules for electronic and prepackaged software adopt an objective theory of contract formation in Section 2.01(B) where a transferee is deemed to have adopted a standard form where a reasonable transferor would believe that the other party intends to be bound.

(3) Formation Safe Harbors

As with UCITA, the Principles validate mass-market license agreements such as clickwrap, shrinkwrap but not browsewrap. The Principles adopt the "opportunity to review" test in UCITA, which gives the licensee reasonable accessibility to terms prior to the transfer. Clickwrap, for example, should be structured so that the "I accept" radio button appears either at the end of, or adjacent to, the license to pass the "opportunity to review" test. Under § 2.02(D), a transferor of software must give the transferee the capacity to store and reproduce the license or other standard form.

(4) Parol Evidence Rule

Section 3.08 adopts a parol evidence rule within the rules of admissibility to reduce fraudulent assertions of the existence of license agreements and other transfers. A license agreement does not fail for indefiniteness merely because the licensor does not specify all of the key terms; the Principles adopt a simple battle of the forms provision where the contract exists in terms found in both definitions and gap fillers. Section 3.08's parol evidence rule distinguishes between fully integrated and partially integrated records. The parties intend that fully integrated agreements be a complete and exclusive statement of their software contract arrangement.

In contrast, a partially integrated record or records are a complete and exclusive statement of one or more terms of their software contract. It is the court's role to determine whether a given software contract is integrated or not. Under Section 3.08(F) of the Principles states, "unambiguous terms set forth in a fully integrated record may not be contradicted by evidence of any prior agreement or of a contemporaneous oral agreement." The Principles import a liberal rule from U.C.C. Article 2 that calls for the broad admissibility of evidence as to course of performance, course of dealing, and usage of trade. This broad admissibility of supplemental terms also applies to fully integrated agreements.

(5) Contract Modification

Under the Principles, as with UCITA, modifications of software contracts require no consideration to be binding. Section 2.03 validates no-oral-modifications clauses unless waived by both parties. Section 2.03 also provides that contractual modifications require no particular form; they "may be formed in any manner sufficient to show an agreement." For electronic transfers of software, e-notices of modification are enforceable provided the transferee receives a reasonable electronic notice of the modification and the transferee electronically signifies agreement.

(6) General Principles of Integration

The Principles recognize a hierarchy of contract terms, which begins with the language of the entire agreement but also considers the parties course of performance, course of dealing and usage of trade in that order. If there is a disagreement over meaning of a term in a record, courts are to apply the standard of reasonable integration. Section 3.10 articulates two exceptions to 3.09(A)'s objective interpretation rule. The first exception arises if the parties to a software contract disagree over the meaning of words or conduct. The court will determine that the meaning intended by one of them should be enforced if, at the time the parties made the agreement, the other party did not know or have reason to know of any different meaning intended by the other party. The second exception occurs when parties disagree over the meaning of an ambiguous fundamental term or terms.

(D) SOFTWARE CONTRACTING WARRANTIES

Section 3.01 gives licensees and other transferees a lesser infringement warranty than what buyers receive under UCC § 2-312. Sections 3.02 through 3.07 in the Principles import warranties concepts from U.C.C. Article 2 and UCITA with some significant differences.

(1) Express Warranties

The quality warranties outlined in Chapter 3 of the Principles closely track U.C.C. Article 2, while accommodating them to software commercial realities. Section 3.02 of the Principles makes the transferor liable for express warranties to any transferee in the distribution chain, including all intermediate parties and end users. The creation of an express warranty is not dependent upon whether a transferor uses formal words such as "warrant" or "guarantee" or that it has a specific intention to make a warranty. A licensor's affirmation of the value of software is mere puffery and does not constitute an express warranty. The Principles replace the "basis of the bargain" test with an objective test focusing on whether the representations made by the licensor about software are sufficiently definite so a licensee or other transferee can reasonably rely upon them.

If the transferor makes a statement constituting an affirmation of fact, promise, or description, the statement constitutes an express warranty, so long as a licensee, assignee, or licensee can reasonably rely on the statement. As with U.C.C. Article 2, express warranties in software contracts survive unexpected disclaimers; the only way to disclaim them is not to make them.

The Reporters import Section 3.02 of the Principles from both UCITA and Article 2 of the U.C.C. This section creates a cause of action for the licensee if the delivered software fails to conform to the description in advertising or packaging. If an employee of the software licensor demonstrates the software to a licensee, the software must conform to the demonstration. A licensor is potentially liable for express warranties to any transferee in the distributional chain, including intermediaries and end users.

(2) Implied Warranty of Merchantability

The Principles downsize U.C.C. Article 2's six-part test for merchantability to three quality standards in Section 3.01(B) for merchant transferors. Merchantable software, at a minimum, must (1) pass without objection in the trade under the software contract, (2) be fit for the ordinary purposes for which such software is used, and (3) be adequately packaged and labeled. The Principles draw upon software industry standards in determining the minimal standards of merchantability. Section 3.04 of the Principles is drawn from UCC § 2–312 and UCITA § 405. The Principles do not extend the implied warranty of merchantability to open source software because software developers will frequently little control over quality.

(3) Systems Integration & Fitness Warranties

The Reporters imported Section 3.04 of the Principles from UCC § 2–312 and UCITA § 405. Section 3.04 of the Principles requires the licensor know, or have a reason to know, of the particular purpose of the licensee to make a fitness type warranty. If a software developer warrants its software will function with a given computer system, the company will be liable for the warranty of fitness for a particular purpose under § 3.04. A licensor violates a fitness warranty when it selects software for the particular purpose of the licensee.

Fitness warranties may be created in part by product advertising or sales representations. Companies claiming that they are systems integration specialists may create fitness warranties. Vendors frequently must address system integration tasks to make hardware and software compatible. For example, systems integration is required to link a given firewall system with other security systems such as surveillance products. Systems integration is a software engineering term meaning an engineer's ability to combine software components so they work as an integrated whole, which is also known as interoperability. Like the fitness warranty, systems integration depends upon a showing of reliance of the customer on the licensor's representation that software will work or is integrated with a given computer system. For example, if a software developer warrants that their software will function with Microsoft's Word 8 the license will be liable the systems integration warranty.

(4) Non-Infringement Warranties

The Principles generally follow the contours of warranties set forth in Article 2 of the U.C.C.— except for the non-infringement warranty. Under the Principles, a licensor is not liable for unknowingly transferring software that infringes the patent claims of others. Similarly, Section 3.02 creates a nondisclaimable warranty that its software or product does not have hidden defects of which it is aware at the time of transfer.

The U.C.C.'s non-infringement warranty does not depend upon the seller's knowledge because it is a strict liability-like obligation. Article 2 of the U.C.C. imposes a strict liability regime for transferring goods infringing the patents or other intellectual property rights of third parties, while the Principles adopt a negligence standard. Section 3.01 gives licensees and other transferees a lesser infringement warranty than U.C.C. Article 2 does. Like U.C.C.

Article 2, Section 3.01 permits software vendors to disclaim their implied indemnification obligations. Licensors routinely disclaim non-infringement warranties because of the uncertainty in patent law, which is a topic discussed in Chapter 13. Section 3.01(A) states that unless the parties otherwise agree, a transferor that deals in software of the kind and receives payment, agrees to "indemnify and hold the transferee harmless against any claim of a third party based on infringement of an intellectual property or like right."

(5) Nondisclaimable Warranty for Hidden Defects

Section 3.05(A) creates a nondisclaimable warranty that its software does not have hidden defects of which it is aware at the time of transfer; "The ALI Principles include three kinds of disclosure: disclosure of facts (concerning the quality of software), disclosure of terms (of standard forms), and disclosure of post-contract intentions (to pursue remote disablement of software)." Robert A. Hillman & Maureen O'Rourke, *Defending Disclosure in Software Licensing*, 78 U. CHI. L. REV. 95, 95 (2011).

Section 3.05(B) provides that a party that transfers software by sale, license, or otherwise, and receives money or a monetary obligation warrants that they are unaware of any material hidden defects at the time of transfer. This provision created a firestorm of protest because it prohibits software vendors from disclaiming liability for known software defects. Developmental software projects frequently contain known bugs that are slowly remedied by patches in their environment of use.

(E) SOFTWARE PERFORMANCE STANDARDS

(1) Breach and Material Breach

"A breach occurs if a party without legal excuse fails to perform an obligation as required by the agreement." Id. at § 3.11(a). The Reporters of the Principles import concepts such as tender, acceptance, rejection, repudiation, anticipatory repudiation, adequate assurance of performance, or other performance-related topics such as inspection from U.C.C. Article 2 and the common law without substantial reworking.

(2) Material Breach

The Principles import the concept of material breach from the Restatement (Second) of Contracts § 241 and UCITA § 701 in determining what constitutes a material breach. Section 3.11 defines a material breach as an electronic agent that allows the nonbreaching party to declare the end of the contract. A material breach occurs where transferors breach the warranty of § 3.05(B) (duty to disclose material hidden defects), a limited remedy fails of its essential purpose (§ 4.01), or the transferor breaches the contract by failing to comply with § 4.03, which is the provision for automatic disablement. Courts are to determine the following factors in determining whether a breach is material:

In determining whether a breach is material, significant factors include:

(1) the terms of the agreement;

(2) usage of trade, course of dealing, and course of performance;

(3) the extent to which the aggrieved party will be deprived of the benefit reasonably expected;

(4) the extent to which the aggrieved party can be adequately compensated for the part of the benefit deprived;

(5) the degree of harm or likely harm to the aggrieved party; and

(6) the extent to which the behavior of the party failing to perform or to offer to perform departs from standards of good faith and fair dealing.

Principles of the Law of Software Contracts § 3.11(c) (2010).

In addition to these six factors, it is a material breach, if a licensor breaches the warranty of not disclosing a hidden material defect, when a contract fails of its essential purpose, and "the transferor breaches the agreement to comply with §4.03." Principles of the Law of Software Contracts § 3.11(d) (2010). Section 4.03 is the provision dealing with the automated disablement of software. A licensor that programs a "time bomb" into the software that disables its operation at the end of that limited period is an example of an automated disablement. Id. at § 3.11, cmt. a. "Section 4.03 places meaningful limitations on the right to disable software by automated means as a remedial matter, and these protections may not be waived by agreement. Transferors may not disable software in the non-negotiated context of the standard-form transfer of generally available software or against consumers in any context. Automated disablement is a viable option only in other agreements in which the transferee is on notice of the provision and on notice of the particular breach for which the transferor plans to use automated disablement." § 3.11, cmt. b. Either party proving a material breach may cancel the contract.

(3) Right to Cure

The Principles of the Law of Software Contracts imported the concept of cure from UCITA, which essentially gives software licensors a second chance to get things right. "It provides a breaching party with a right to cure under certain circumstances. Certainly, the agreement itself can prohibit cure or otherwise limit it. Indeed, many, if not most, software agreements address a breaching party's right to cure in the agreement." Principles of the Law of Software Contracts § 3.12, cmt. a (2010). Breaching parties have the right to cure at their own expense where the time for performance has not yet expired or there are reasonable grounds to believe the nonconforming software would be acceptable to the licensee. Software licensors also often give licensees a period of acceptance testing in addition to the cure.

(4) Cancellation

"An aggrieved party may cancel a contract on a material breach of the whole contract if the breach has not been cured under § 3.12 or waived." Principles of the Law of Software Contracts § 4.04(a) (2010). This section "gives the aggrieved party the option to cancel the contract in the event of a material breach of the whole contract if the breach has not been cured or waived. The concept of material breach of the whole contract may be relevant when the agreement calls for repeated performance." § 4.04, cmt. a.

(F) REMEDIES FOR BREACH

(1) Expectation Interest

Chapter 4 of the Principles "addresses the issue of the appropriate remedies for breach of an agreement governed by the Principles. Remedial issues are, of course, central to contract law and in software agreements as in other contracts, expectation damages are appropriate." Principles of the Law of Software Contracts 4 Overview (2010). When the parties have not concluded an enforceable agreement on remedies, but one of them has breached, § 4.05 of the Principles calls for the award of expectancy damages.

The Principles of Software Contracts validate the parties' agreements as to what the remedies should be much like UCITA and U.C.C. Article 2. The Reporters assume parties to software contracts will adapt well-established principles from sales such resale, market price, specific performance, and liquidated damages to software contracts. In the absence of agreement, the drafters adopted the expectation theory of damages. The nonbreaching party is entitled to remedies for breach where the software fails to perform according to contract specifications. A single-user licensee that makes multiple copies of the code infringes copyright and breaches the agreement.

(2) Use of Automated Disablement to Impair Use

The Principles of the Law of Software Contracts limit the ability of a software licensor to remotely remove or disable software. Electronic self-help is always a controversial provision because of the unbridled power it gives licensors over software essential to the customer's business. For example, the electronic repossession of a business's billing software might deprive business of the ability to collect accounts. The fear of the licensee is that a licensor may repossess mission-critical software where there is a *bona fide* dispute over a term in a software contract.

Section 4.03 balances the interests of licensors and licensees by permitting automated disablement under certain limited circumstances, but strictly prohibiting disablement as a self-help remedy. Electronic disablement is strictly prohibited in standard form transfers of generally available software and all consumer transactions. Licensors using electronic disablement contrary to the

Principles are subject to liability for direct, incidental, and consequential damages.

(3) Liquidated Damages

Section 4.02 provides for liquidated damages but these clauses may not be penal provisions. The guideposts in UCC § 2–718 were imported to the Principles. If the court strikes compensation or liquated damages clauses, the remedies are available as if the clause not been included. The Reporters decline to develop precise formulas for measuring damages in software contracts, but direct courts to U.C.C. Article for guidance.

As with UCITA and U.C.C. Article 2, "[l]iquidated-damages provisions are enforceable if reasonable. As with amended U.C.C. Article 2, § 4.02 does not explicitly state, "A term fixing unreasonably large liquidated damages is void as a penalty." . . . It is unnecessary because it is redundant with the reasonableness requirement for enforcement, and misleading because it focuses only on unreasonably large damages—a liquidated-damages provision calling for unreasonably small damages would likewise be unenforceable." Principles of the Law of Software Contracts § 4.02, cmt. a. (2010).

(4) Cancellation & Expectancy Damages

Cancellation of the software contract is appropriate by the nonbreaching party who provides that the other party committed a material breach under § 4.04. As with U.C.C. Article 2, there is no right to cancel absent notice to the breaching party, which triggers their right to cure. Section 4.05 draws upon the common law of contract in recognizing that the aggrieved party has the right to expectation damages. Damages for lost expectancy include incidental and consequential damages less expenses saved that stem from the breach.

(5) Specific Performance

Section 4.06 recognizes the equitable remedy of specific performance where software is unique or the licensee proves other proper circumstances. Specific performance is not available for computer contracts that are predominately personal services as opposed to software or information transfers.

(6) Limitations of Remedies

Section 4.01 adopts the concepts of a minimum adequate remedy. "Section 4.01 "balances contractual freedom to limit remedies with safeguards should the exclusive or limited remedy fail of its essential purpose. Contractual freedom, however, is inappropriate in the cases of: (i) the implied warranty of no hidden material defects (§ 3.05(b)); and (ii) unauthorized automated disablement (§ 4.03(e)). Sections 4.01(a)(1) and 4.01(c) therefore do not permit limitation or alteration of damages in those cases." Id. Section 4.01 imports the concept of a minimally adequate remedy.

(7) Failure of Essential Purpose.

"The focus of § 4.01(b) is not on the bargaining process that produced the remedial term, but on application of the exclusive or limited remedy if the software is defective. An exclusive or limited remedy fails of its essential purpose when the transferor is unable or unwilling to provide the transferee with conforming software within a reasonable time regardless of the transferor's best or good-faith efforts." Id at § 4.01, cmt. c. "For example, when the exclusive remedy calls for repair of the software, if the transferor attempts in good faith to repair and is willing to continue attempting repair, the remedy nevertheless fails of its essential purpose after a commercially reasonable time." Id.

§ 4-7. International Internet Contracts

(A) SOURCES OF E-CONTRACT LAW

The Internet, by its very nature, is international, yet there is no uniform legal infrastructure for commercial transactions harmonized for the global marketplace. In the absence of international conventions, domestic law applies to license agreements and terms of service. There is great uncertainty as to whose law will govern online commerce, which knows no international borders. Uniform rules for safeguarding commercial information transfers would be a desirable international development. Contract law in cyberspace must take into account radically different social, economic, and legal systems. A growing number of companies are engaged in cross-border electronic commerce. The movement to devise uniform rules to be used in private international law has evolved rapidly over the past century.

The United Nations Commission for International Trade ("UNCITRAL"); the International Institute for the Unification of Private Law ("UNIDROIT"); the Council on Europe (Council); and the International Chamber of Commerce ("ICC") have all spearheaded past efforts to create international commercial law. The European Commission contends that E-Commerce will increase only if consumers are convinced they have a minimal adequate remedy when entering into cross-border sales and services. UNCITRAL's Model Law on Electronic Commerce is consistent with UCITA's E-Commerce infrastructure in addressing business-to-business but not business-to-consumer rules.

(B) UNCITRAL'S DIGITAL SIGNATURE

UNCITRAL's Model Law, like UCITA, validates the digital signature as the functional equivalent of the "pen and paper" signature. Article 7 of the UNCITRAL's model law on Electronic Commerce defines a signature as follows: "The only significant difference between a domestic contract and an international contract is that in the former all the relevant elements of the contract in question are connected with one country only." The parties to an international contract law will need to consider jurisdictional choice of law and conflicts of law issues that arise when radically different legal cultures converge.

(C) CONSUMER SOFTWARE LICENSING

Software licensing is increasingly a global enterprise, which creates new complications for an E-Commerce company. Lawyers representing E-Commerce companies must tailor cross-border licensing to consider different consumer protection and contracting rules, as well as linguistic and cultural differences. Internet companies targeting European consumers must comply with the Unfair Contracts Term Directive ("UCTD"); European courts will not enforce contractual provisions determined to be unfair under the Directive. The Annex to the UCTD classifies many terms in standard-form TOUs as unfair and this includes disclaimers of warranties, limitations of licensor's liability, unilateral modifications to contract terms, and the acceptance of the license agreement by performance.

If a given term in a license agreement is not addressed in the Annex of Suspect Terms, a European court may refuse to enforce it under a more general test of unfairness. Article 8 of the UCTD provides that Member States have the discretion to adopt provisions that are more stringent. In Europe, the EU Commission has launched a quiet revolution giving European consumers rights across the Continent. During the past decade, the EC has approved Internet regulations such as the E-Commerce Directive; E-Signatures Directive; Distance Selling Directive; Data Protection Directive; Database Protection Directive; and the Copyright Directive. The right to protection of personal data is established by Article 8 of the Charter, and in Article 8 of the European Convention of Human Rights. The EU recognizes E-Commerce does not flourish without mandatory consumer protection across national borders. Reverse engineering is a right guaranteed European licensees under the Software Directive for purposes of interoperability. Counsel representing U.S. companies will need to consider foreign law where they are marketing their digital products.

(D) E-COMMERCE DIRECTIVE

Article 9 of the E-Commerce Directive requires providers to recognize the validation of electronic or digital signatures. Id. at Art. 9(1). Article 9(2)'s list of exceptions for electronic contracts is similar to the U.S. approach in UETA and E-SIGN. As in the United States, Internet service providers have no affirmative duty to monitor illegal or infringing content in the European Union. Id. at art. 15(2). Article 9 provides: "Member States shall ensure that their legal system allows contracts to be concluded by electronic means.

Member States shall in particular ensure that the legal requirements applicable to the contractual process neither create obstacles for the use of electronic contracts nor result in such contracts being deprived of legal effectiveness and validity on account of their having been made by electronic means." Id. at art. 9(1).

Article 9 contains functionally equivalent provisions to EUTA and the E-Sign Act. Like these U.S. statutes, the European E-Commerce Directive provides that certain categories of contracts may not be concluded electronically: (a) real estate contracts except rental agreements, (b) contracts required to be in writing by courts or statutes, (c) contracts of suretyship or security agreements, and (d) contracts for family law or trusts/estates. Id. at art 9(2).

(E) DUTY TO REPORT ILLEGAL ACTIVITIES

Article 15(2) gives Member States the option of establishing a duty of service providers to "inform the competent public authorities of alleged illegal activities undertaken or information provided by recipients of their service or obligations to communicate to the competent authorities, at their request." Id. at art. 15(2). This role is similar to U.S. service providers who have a duty to report illegal activities such as the distribution of child pornography and respond to subpoenas of courts of competent jurisdiction.

The Directive requires seller to give consumers disclosures before electronic contracting on how to conclude online contracts, as well as the means of correcting errors. Article 10 gives consumers the right to store and retrieve contracts or they are unenforceable. Article 12 essentially immunizes ISPs for conduit activities much like the U.S. Digital Millennium Copyright Act's Section 512 discussed in Chapter 10. There are a number of requirements that must be met for a service provider to receive 17 U.S.C. §512(c) safe harbor protection.

(F) LIABILITY OF SERVICE PROVIDERS

The liability limitation for European service providers applies only if the service provider does not initiate or modify the transmission. Articles 13 and 14 of the Directive immunize a service provider's caching and hosting activities. Article 16 imposes no duty of providers to monitor their websites for illegal activities like the DMCA. Member States must develop legislation to inform the authorities of illegal activities. Member States are to develop legislation to encourage out of court settlements of disputes under Article 17.

CHAPTER 5

CONSUMER LAW IN CYBERSPACE

In the online marketplace, consumers can transact business without the constraints of time or distance. One can log on to the Internet day or night and purchase almost anything one desires, and advances in mobile technology allow advertisers to reach consumers nearly anywhere they go. Nevertheless, cyberspace is not without boundaries, and deception is unlawful no matter what the medium

Federal Trade Commission, *On-Line Disclosures* (2013)

This chapter provides an overview of consumer protection regulation of Internet business activities. The dark side of Internet advertising is the proliferation of deceptive and fraudulent online lotteries, pyramid schemes, e-mail swindles, spam emails, and Trojan horse programs that choke electronic commerce and bilk unwary consumers. During 2011, an estimated 10.8 percent of U.S. adults—25.6 million people—were victims of one or more of the frauds included in the 2011 FTC Consumer Fraud Survey. In a single year, there were an estimated 37.8 million incidents of these frauds were perpetrated.

The FTC takes the position that the same consumer protection laws that apply to commercial activities in other media apply to the Internet and the mobile marketplace. This chapter examines the difficulties of protecting consumers from fraudulent trade practices on the global Internet.

§ 5-1. FTC as Cyberspace Constable

Congress created the Federal Trade Commission ("FTC") in 1914 to prevent unfair methods of competition in commerce. The Federal Trade Commission Act ("FTCA") expanded the FTC's authority to include policing unfair and deceptive acts or practices. The FTC administers diverse laws applicable to cyberspace activities including The Undertaking Spam, Spyware, and Fraud Enforcement With Enforcers Beyond Borders Act of 2006 ("Safe Web"). Safe Web amended Section 5's "unfair or deceptive acts or practices" to include "such acts or practices involving foreign commerce" causing reasonably foreseeable injury within the United States. The Safe Web statute immunizes Internet Service Providers and consumer reporting agencies from liability for voluntary disclosures to the Commission about suspected online fraud or deception. The FTC takes the position that the Fair Credit Reporting Act, 15 U.S.C. § 1681 et seq. is applicable to those who aggregate information from social media sites.

Most U.S. states have enacted deceptive trade practices acts, sometimes referred to as "little FTC acts." For example, Section 2 of Massachusetts' Chapter 93A makes it unlawful to engage in "unfair methods of competition and unfair or deceptive acts or practices." Massachusetts' Chapter 93A provides double or treble damages and attorneys' fees for unfair and deceptive trade practices. In April 2013, the FTC issued guidelines that required marketers advertising product claims on mobile devices follow truth-in-advertising rules. Marketers must render disclosures to any claim in clear and conspicuous language across all user platforms

The Bureau of Consumer Protection is the primary unit within the FTC that polices unfair and deceptive Internet-related activities pursuant to Section 5 of the FTCA. The FTC considers three factors in determining whether a practice is unfair or deceptive under Section 5: (1) Does the practice injure consumers? (2) Does it violate public policy? and (3) Is the practice unethical? Section 13(B) of the FTCA authorizes the Commission to file suit in any U.S. federal district court to enjoin an Internet act or practice that violates Section 5.

(A) FRAUDULENT TRADE PRACTICES

(1) Fraudulent Internet Businesses

Beginning in the mid-1990s, the FTC has vigilantly patrolled websites to ensure that they do not contain unfair or deceptive advertisements. FTC's enforcers have identified the top ten dot cons: (1) Internet Auctions, (2) Internet Access Services, (3) Credit Card Fraud, (4) International Modem Dialing, (5) Web Cramming, (6) Multilevel Marketing Plans/Pyramids, (7) Travel and Vacation Schemes, (8) Business Opportunities, (9) Investments, and (10) Health Care Products/Services. In addition, social media sites must comply with Section 5 and other consumer laws governing Internet advertisements, sales of securities, taxation, unfair and deceptive trade practices, pricing laws, and general state and federal consumer statutes.

These policies apply in the "clicks" world just as in the brick-and-mortar world. In *FTC v. Fortuna Alliance, L.L.C., et al.*, Civ. No. C96–799M (W.D. Wash. 1996), the FTC shut down a pyramid scheme marketed on the Internet that defrauded 25,000 consumers. The fraudulent scheme was not a legitimate investment opportunity; it was "nothing but a high-tech chain letter, with certain losses for the great majority of investors and tremendous profits for the defendants." This particular Ponzi scheme yielded $11 million from consumers and the defendants transferred millions to an offshore bank account in Antigua. The FTC and the U.S. Department of Justice were able to freeze the defendant's Antigua accounts and recoup some of the illicit gains. In *FTC v. PCCare247 Inc.*, 2013 WL 841037 (S.D.N.Y. 2013), the FTC sought injunctive relief and damages against individual defendants in India that tricked American consumers into spending money to fix non-existent problems with their computers. The court approved the FTC's serving process through the defendants' Facebook accounts. Nevertheless, the FTC also transmitted the summons and complaint to the Indian central authority for service under Article 5 of the Hague Service Convention. In addition, the FTC attorneys attempted process by email, by FedEx, and by personal service.

(2) Deceptive Advertising Claims

The FTC takes the position that the FTCA prohibition on unfair or deceptive acts or practices applies equally well to cyberspace considering three basic principles: (1) online advertisements must be truthful and not misleading, (2) online advertisers must have evidence to back up their claims ("substantiation"), and (3) they cannot be unfair. The FTC has filed hundreds of Section 5 actions to enjoin fraud and deception on the Internet. The FTC looks for deception and unfairness in banner ads, pop ups, social media reviews, blogger endorsements, Geotagging offers, online targeted ads, and even in-game advertising.

In *FTC v. Corzine*, CIV–S–94–1446 (E.D. Cal. 1994), Corzine ran online advertisements, offering a $99 credit repair kit, on America Online. He represented that purchasers of his credit repair kit could legally establish a clean credit record. The FTC filed a complaint, charging Corzine with misrepresentations in violation of Section 5. The court entered an *ex parte* Temporary Restraining Order, freezing all of Corzine's assets. The court entered a Consent Decree, enjoining Corzine from making future misrepresentations and requiring him to reimburse defrauded customers.

(3) Online Endorsements

False or deceptive endorsements in a social media site or website also violate Section 5 of the FTCA. In December of 2009, the FTC issued new guidelines for online endorsements, prohibiting statements by bloggers and other online reviewers that would be deceptive if made by advertisers. 16 C.F.R. § 255(1)(A). The FTC guideposts include illustrations such as new marketing campaigns where paid bloggers fail to disclose material connections to the endorsed products or services. Both advertisers and bloggers are subject to liability for misleading or unsubstantiated statements made in social media or website endorsements. The FTC used the example of a blogger promoting a skin care product.

If an advertiser requests that a blogger try a new body lotion and writes a review of the product on her blog, she has an affirmative duty to disclose any financial remuneration or connection that may have influenced her endorsement. In *Legacy Learning Systems, Inc.*, Federal Trade Commission, C–4323 (FTC 2011), the Commission entered into a consent order for $250,000 to settle charges that the company deceptively used online affiliate marketers that masqueraded as ordinary consumers, when they were paid representatives.

(4) FTC Mandatory Website Disclosures

The FTC requires online advertisers "to ensure that consumers receive material information about the terms of a transaction . . . [and they] must be clear and conspicuous." FTC, DOT.COM DISCLOSURES 1 (2012). The FTC's rules on disclosure and proximity extend to advertisements on social media or other websites. The FTC also requires Internet advertisers to consider the prominence of disclosures and whether audio messages are in adequate volume and cadence to reach consumers. The FTC requires that visual disclosures appear for a sufficient duration and in a language understandable to the intended audience.

(B) PROTECTING CONSUMER PRIVACY

The FTC has initiated a formal enforcement actions against well-known companies. The FTC asked Microsoft, Google, Mozilla, and other browser designers to incorporate a "do not track" option so consumers can opt out of tracking software. In early 2012, the FTC joined European agencies in launching an investigation into Google for alleged privacy violations. The FTC filed suit to enjoin Toysmart.com's proposed sale of customer lists and profiles as Section 5 violation of consumer privacy. Toysmart.com had represented that it would "never" disclose, sell, or offer for sale customers' personal information. Before the federal bankruptcy court's distribution of assets, Toysmart.com entered into a settlement agreement with the FTC to protect the privacy of its customer list.

The Children's Online Privacy Protection Act ("COPPA") (15 U.S.C. § 6501) makes it illegal for companies to harvest personally identifiable information from children aged 13 and under without their parents' consent." The COPPA Rule applies to operators of commercial Web sites and online services (including mobile apps) directed to children under 13 that collect, use, or disclose personal information from children, and operators of general audience Web sites or online services with actual knowledge that they are collecting, using, or disclosing personal information from children under 13." FTC, *Complying with COPPA* (Apr. 13, 2013).

The FTC's COPPA regulation mandates that the site operator obtain verifiable parental consent and give conspicuous notice of their information practices. A website may not condition a child's use of the website in its terms of service on disclosing personal information. The FTC requires that a website give a child's parents the opportunity to restrain further use or collection of information. A website must have reasonable security to protect the confidentiality, security, and integrity of personal information collected from children.

The FTC's COPPA Rule provides websites with safe harbor if they comply with approved self-regulatory guidelines formulated by marketing or online industries. Self-regulatory guidelines must subject operators to the same or greater protections for children as contained in Sections 312.2 through 312.9 of the FTC's COPPA Rule. All websites are required to conduct periodic reviews of subject operators' information practices. The FTC states the website must comply with COPPA if the operator has a "general audience web site and actual knowledge that they are collecting personal information" from children aged 13 or under. 16 C.F.R. § 312.

The FTC developed a multi-factorial test to determine whether a given website targets children. The most important factors include the subject matter (visual or audio content), the age of models on the site, the age of the actual or intended audience and "whether a site uses animated characters or other child oriented features." 15 U.S.C. § 6101. The FTC requires the link to be clear and prominent. Personal information is defined to include: (1) an individuals' first and last name, (2) home or other physical address, (3) an e-mail address or other online contact information, (4) a telephone number, (5) a Social Security number, (6) a persistent identifier such as a code, and (7) any other information concerning the child or the parents of that child the operator collects online from the child.

The Commission issued an amended Rule on December 19, 2012. The amended Rule will become effective on July 1, 2013. In 2013, the FTC issued guidance on the updated definitions of personal information to include geolocation, screen names, audio files, thus accommodating COPPA to social media. FTC, *Complying with COPPA* (Apr. 13, 2013). "The amended Rule, which goes into effect on July 1, 2013, added four new categories of information to the definition of personal information. The amended Rule of course applies to any personal information that is collected after the effective date of the Rule." Websites that have collected geolocation information and have not obtained parental consent must do so immediately.

The Commission defines an entity as an "operator" if it owns, controls, and pays for the collection of personally identifiable information. If COPPA applies to the website, its operator must link to a notice of its information practices on the homepage of the website or online service. This notice must extend to each area where it collects personal information from children. Personal information may be collected directly from a child or passively through devices such as cookies. In May 2008, the Texas Attorney General settled that state's first COPPA action.

The Texas attorney general charged DollPalace.com, a site for cartoon dolls, with violating COPPA in unlawfully collecting personal information from children without obtaining parental consent. DollPalace.com conditioned website access on children completing a ten page questionnaires about themselves and their friends. The Texas Attorney General found that COPPA was violated because third parties could easily circumvent the parental consent feature of the sites.

Social media sites such as Facebook must also comply with COPPA by not signing up members under the age of 13. Still, children below the age of 13 will inevitably misrepresent their age to evade sign-up restriction. In May of 2011, 7.5 million Facebook users were below the minimum COPPA age 13 threshold. Courts can hold operators who violate the Rule liable for civil penalties of up to $16,000 per violation. Courts tailor civil penalties based upon a large number of factors, "including the egregiousness of the violations, whether the operator has previously violated the Rule, the number of children involved, the amount and type of personal information collected, how the information was used, whether it was shared with third parties, and the size of the company. FTC, *Complying with COPPA* (Apr. 13, 2013).

In March of 2012, the FTC announced that it had settled a COPPA case with RockYou Inc. where the privacy of 32 million children was at stake. The FTC's complaint charged the social media site with violating the COPPA rule by not spelling out its disclosure policy, not obtaining verifiable parental consent prior to data collection, and not implementing reasonable security to protect children's privacy. The FTC settlement required RockYou to implement and maintain a data security program and pay a $250,000 civil penalty to settle all COPPA charges.

§ 5-2. Regulation of Online Spam

Spam is defined as unsolicited bulk e-mail ("UBE"), or, unsolicited commercial e-mail ("UCE"). The term spam was inspired from a 1970 Monty Python Flying Circus sketch where a waiter recited a menu where every breakfast dish included spam. In a typical day, the average consumer has an e-mail inbox full of virtual offers to make fast money. A self-proclaimed spam king bragged: "When you're sending out 250 million e-mails, even a blind squirrel will find a nut." The Telephone Consumer Protection Act of 1991 ("TCPA") has been stretched to Internet telemarketing. 47 U.S.C. § 227.

The mobile social network provider, Path, was targeted by an Illinois class action in April 2013 for sending unsolicited text ads. The class action contends that Path violated the TCPA by using automated services to transmit SMS messages without the recipient's consent. The Federal Communications Commission ("FCC") is the chief agency that enforces the TCPA although private attorneys general can also file suit. The FTC needs to update its anti-spam guideposts to address the growing problem of junk messages on mobile devices and in cloud computing.

(A) CAN-SPAM

Congress enacted the Controlling the Assault of Non-Solicited Pornography and Marketing Act of 2003 ("CAN-SPAM"), 15 U.S.C. § 7701–§ 7713. CAN-SPAM prohibits fraudulent, abusive and deceptive commercial e-mail. The federal anti-spam statute provides for enforcement of the Act by the FTC as well as by Internet service providers ("ISPs"). CAN-SPAM requires that the commercial e-mailer to include a functioning return e-mail address and a method for opting out of future messages.

E-mailers must honor consumers' requests for removal made using e-mail or websites mechanisms within 10 business days. CAN-SPAM is less effective than it might be because Congress limited enforcement to federal agencies, states, and Internet Service providers. Victims of spam e-mail have no standing file suit against e-mailers and the federal statute preempts state anti-spam measures.

To state a claim under the CAN-SPAM Act, the government or a service provider must allege that the spammer sent e-mail containing "materially false or materially misleading" header information. CAN-SPAM defines false or materially misleading headers to includes a false and fraudulent electronic mail address, domain name, or Internet Protocol address: CAN-SPAM prohibits false or misleading transmission information, deceptive headers, and requires e-mail to give an easy to use opt out method.

CAN-SPAM is a cause of action normally pursued by FTC enforcers. Service providers do not have standing to file CAN-SPAM lawsuits unless they prove they were "adversely affected" by spam. Adverse effects include spam-related network crashes, a higher bandwidth utilization because of the flood of messages, and increased costs for hardware and software upgrades, network expansion, as well as the costs of additional people responding to complaints.

Section 7 of the CAN-SPAM Act provides for exclusive enforcement by the FTC and the Department of Justice. The FTC does not permit state attorneys general to file anti-spam lawsuits if there is a pending federal civil or administrative enforcement action. Furthermore, the new federal anti-spam statute preempts all state anti-spam legislation, even those providing consumers with a cause of action against commercial e-mailers. For text messages, CAN-SPAM needs consumers to give "prior express authorization" prior to transmittal. Commercial messages must identify the company and include an opt-out mechanism functioning for at least 30 days. If the consumer elects to unsubscribe from receiving more messages, the company must stop sending any other promotional messages within 10 days. CAN-SPAM does not authorize private lawsuits by aggrieved consumers.

(1) Constitutional Issues of CAN-SPAM

The CAN-SPAM Act regulates the manner in which commercial e-mail transmits, and regulates the various activities related to commercial e-mail, such as prohibiting the use of false, misleading, or deceptive information, prohibiting the use of automated bots to create multiple e-mail accounts, and requiring certain contact information in commercial electronic mail messages. In *White Buffalo Ventures v. University of Texas at Austin*, 420 F.3d 366 (5th Cir. 2005), the Fifth Circuit considered a challenge by an online dating site alleging the University of Texas anti-spam policy violated the First Amendment. White Buffalo operated several online dating services, including one, called "longhornsingles.com" that targeted university students.

The court reviewed three questions. First, did the University of Texas violate the First Amendment when it blocked delivery of unsolicited commercial e-mail or spam from White Buffalo? Second, did the University of Texas violate the Constitution of the United States when it blocked access from its on-campus network to White Buffalo? Third, did the CAN-SPAM Act preemption provision preempt the University of Texas at Austin's anti-spam policy? The question presented is whether the Texas anti-spam policy was preempted by the federal statute.

Commercial speech, defined broadly as expression relating to the economic interests of the speaker or audience, is entitled to less protection than non-commercial speech. The *White Buffalo* court applied *Central Hudson's* four-part test to evaluate the legality of the University's commercial speech regulation: (1) whether the speech is unlawful or misleading, (2) whether the government's expressed interest is substantial, (3) whether the state action directly promotes that interest, and (4) whether the state action is more extensive than necessary to promote that interest.

The *White Buffalo* court found that the dating service's commercial solicitations were legal, contained factually accurate information, and therefore passed the first part of the *Central Hudson* test. The court also found that the University's interest in stopping spam from clogging up its servers to be a substantial interest. The third part of the *Central Hudson* test asks whether the speech restriction directly and materially advances the asserted governmental interest. The court also found the university anti-spam regulations passed the third prong because they promoted a substantial interest. Finally, the *White Buffalo* court stated the University of Texas' policy in blocking e-mail was no more restrictive than what was necessary to secure the state's substantial interest in blocking unwanted spam. The court rejected the commercial e-mailers claim that their e-mail messages were protected as commercial speech under the *Central Hudson Gas & Electric Corp. v. Public Service Comm'n*, 447 U.S. 557 (S.Ct. 1980) test.

(2) Emblematic CAN-SPAM Awards

A federal court in *Yahoo! Inc. v. XYZ Companies*, No. 08–4581 (S.D. N.Y. 2011), imposed a $600 million damage award against a spam e-mailer that used Yahoo!'s marks in over eleven million fraudulent e-mails. The court awarded half of the maximum statutory damages, "$50 per wrongful communication," declining to award treble damages under the Lanham Act given the size of the CAN-SPAM award. 15 U.S.C. § 7704(A)(1). Facebook was awarded $711 million in damages against Sanford

Wallace, "the King of Spam." In December 2011, Yahoo! was awarded $610 million against Nigerian scammer that misused its trademarks in a massive spam attack. The CAN-SPAM verdict arising out of the Nigerian Advance Free Fraud is likely not collectible.

§ 5-3. Federal Communications Commission

(A) THE COMMUNICATIONS ACT OF 1934

The Federal Communications Commission ("FCC") is an independent United States government agency established by the Communications Act of 1934, 47 U.S.C. § 151. The FCC regulates interstate and international communications through radio, television, wire, satellite, and cable. The FCC jurisdiction covers the fifty states, the District of Columbia, and unincorporated territories. The 1934 Act combined previous statutes governing telephone voice service and radio broadcasting. The Telecommunications Act of 1996 amended and updated the 1934 Act with the goal of promoting competition in all communications sectors. The FCC is responsible for enforcing the Telecommunications Act of 1996 ("TCA"), which has been stretched to Internet communications. In 2013, the FCC repealed approximately 150 regulations, many of which were rendered legal fossils because of the Internet.

In *National Cable & Telecommunications Association v. Brand X Internet Services*, 545 U.S. 967 (S.Ct. 2005), the United States Supreme Court upheld the FCC's authority to classify methods of broadband Internet access into pre-existing definitions of the TCA. In that case, the Court upheld the FCC's classification of broadband cable Internet service as an "information service," and the FCC's conclusion that broadband cable Internet service was not a telecommunications service.

(B) NET NEUTRALITY

The policy debate over "net neutrality" concerns what role the government should have in regulating broadband Internet providers transmitting and delivering Internet traffic over their networks. A telecommunications carrier violated network neutrality when they block Web traffic over their networks. The major policy issue centers on what types and degrees of control the government should impose on broadband providers. The consumer interest in net neutrality is to prevent broadband providers from blocking or slowing traffic based upon content or the type of customer.

(C) CROSS-BORDER CYBERFRAUD

The FCC has limited jurisdiction over cross-border Internet fraud. For example, Nigerian 419 e-mail swindles, named after Section 419 of the Nigerian criminal code, typically begin with an e-mail offer to transfer millions of dollars into the victim's bank account. In these e-mail frauds, a purported third world official or business representative typically offers to share his family's fortune with an Internet user in return for supposedly circumventing his country's currency restrictions by moving assets outside his country to a safe banking haven.

One ongoing Internet swindle is the Nigerian letter fraud scheme, in which an e-mail message appearing to come from the Nigerian Government promises the potential victim a share of a substantial amount of money in exchange for the use of the victim's bank account. The U.S. Department of Justice filed a lawsuit against AT&T in 2012 alleging that it knew that its government-subsidized service for the hearing-impaired was "a haven for Nigerian swindles artists." The IP Relay Service enables the hearing impaired to place telephone calls by typing messages over the Internet that are read aloud to the person on the other end of the line by corrupt call-center employees.

These scammers used the IP relay service to purchase goods and services using stolen credit cards. The U.S. Justice Department filed suit shortly after a study found that ten out of twelve users of the service were foreign—mostly from Lagos, Nigeria. The FCC charged AT&T with billing the government $16 million for hearing-impaired calls, when 90% or more of these calls were attempts to defraud American citizens. AT&T's role in the fraud is one of negligent enablement by not taking measures to reduce the fraud.

§ 5-4. Securities & Exchange Rules for the Internet

The Securities and Exchange Commission ("SEC") regulates the sale of securities subject to the registration requirements of the Securities Act of 1933. The SEC Office of Internet Enforcement ("OIE") administers the SEC Enforcement Division's Internet program. Internet "road shows" or webcasts must comply with SEC regulations. The SEC, for example, protects consumers by policing websites offering securities, soliciting securities transactions, or advertising investment services offshore.

The SEC formulated proxy rules under the Securities Exchange Act of 1934 permitting issuers and other persons to furnish proxy materials to shareholders by posting them on an Internet website—provided that shareholders receive notice of the hard copy availability of the proxy materials. Issuers must make copies of the proxy materials available to shareholders for free, upon request. One of the unsettled issues is whether companies have a duty to disclose cyber-attacks. The SEC issued a voluntary disclosure plan, which is creating a de facto standard that companies disclose cyber-attacks in their SEC filings. A *Bloomberg Report* noted:

> Google, the world's biggest search engine, agreed in May to put its previously disclosed cyber-assault in an earnings report. American International Group Inc., Hartford Financial Services Group Inc., Eastman Chemical Co. and Quest Diagnostics Inc. were also prodded to improve disclosures of cyber-risks, according to SEC letters available on the regulator's website.

The Securities and Exchange Commission entered into an agreement with "Nasdaq Stock Market LLC agreed to pay a record $10 million penalty to settle administrative charges stemming from its 'poor systems and decision-making' during the initial public offering and secondary market trading of Facebook Inc." BLOOMBERG BNA, ELECTRONIC COMMERCE & LAW REPORT (May 31, 2013). In February of 2012, the Commodity Futures Trading Commission ("CFTC") and the SEC proposed Identity Theft Red Flags Rules requiring financial institutions to "develop and implement an identity theft prevention program that is designed to detect, prevent and mitigate identify theft." The obligation to develop identity theft programs applies to "certain existing accounts or the opening of new accounts. The Identity Theft Red Flag Rules will amend section 615(E) of the Fair Credit Reporting Act ("FCRA").

The SEC Commission proposes guidelines to assist entities in tailoring Red Flags to the size and complexity of their organization. In February of 2012, the SEC ruled that publicly owned wireless providers must allow resolutions on network neutrality to be included on their annual shareholder ballots and proxy statements.

In 2012, the SEC "issued guidelines that require public companies to disclose the risk of cyber incidents if they materially affect a registrant's products, services, relationships with customers or suppliers, or competitive conditions, or if they make an investment in the company speculative or risky." JODY R. WESBY, GOVERNANCE OF ENTERPRISE SECURITY, CY-LAB (2012) at 1. Regulation FD and Section 13(a) of the Exchange Act prohibit public companies, or persons acting on their behalf, from selectively disclosing material, nonpublic information to certain securities professionals, or shareholders where it is reasonably foreseeable that they will trade on that information, before it is made available to the general public.

An April 2013 SEC Report confirms that the Commission believes that Regulation FD applies equally well to social media as to any other public website. "The ways in which companies may use these social media channels, however, are not fundamentally different from the ways in which the web sites, blogs, and RSS feeds addressed by the 2008 Guidance" [given by the Commission]. SEC, REPORT OF INVESTIGATION PURSUANT TO SECTION 21(A) OF THE SECURITIES EXCHANGE ACT OF 1934: NETFLIX, INC., AND REED HASTINGS, Release No. 69279 / April 2, 2013

§ 5-5. Internet Taxation

(A) FEDERAL TAX LAW

Consumer taxation is an unsettled issue on the Internet. The Internet Tax Freedom Act imposed a "temporary moratorium on Internet specific taxes" by states and localities to avoid "stunt[ing] the growth of electronic commerce." S. Rep. No. 105-184 (1998). This statute does not create "tax freedom" for transactions on the Internet but instead forbids multiple or discriminatory taxes on electronic commerce. "Section 1105(6) says that a multiple tax means two states taxing the same thing without a tax credit." *City of Chicago v. StubHub! Inc.*, 624 F.3d 363 (7th Cir. 2010). Section 1106(C) makes it clear that sales and use taxes on tangible personal property are valid even if they otherwise would be called multiple taxes. Congress prohibited: (1) all state and local taxes on "Internet access" (unless grandfathered) and (2) all discriminatory taxes on electronic commerce.

(B) STATE INTERNET TAXES

In *Nat'l Bellas Hess v. Dept. of Revenue of State of Ill.*, 386 U.S. 753 (S.Ct. 1967) the U.S. Supreme Court held it was a violation of the Due Process Clause to require a mail order retailer, without offices or sales agents in Illinois, to pay a use tax. In this pre-World Wide Web case, the Court expressed concern that local tax collectors could restrain interstate commerce if the mail order retailer was subject to a tax. A quarter century later, the U.S. Supreme Court ruled states could not compel businesses to pay a sales tax unless the company had a physical presence in the state.

In *Quill Corporation v. North Dakota*, 504 U.S. 298 (S.Ct. 1992), Quill, a Delaware corporation with a physical presence in Illinois, California, and Georgia, sold $1 million in mail order office supplies to 3,000 customers in North Dakota. North Dakota wanted to charge sales tax on this income. The Supreme Court held that such a tax would not violate the Due Process Clause of the Constitution because Quill purposefully directed its activities at North Dakota residents sufficient for due process.

The Court, however, held the Commerce Clause does not allow individual states to interfere with interstate commerce when the only connection to the taxing state is by mail. The Court ruled that North Dakota could not impose its sales tax on Quill. The Court's decision means that states may not require retailers to collect sales taxes unless they have a physical presence in that state.

The Streamlined Sales and Use Tax Agreement ("SSUTA") joins twenty-four states to simplify and make more uniform sales and use tax collection and administration by retailers and states. The SSUTA was a legislative initiative of the National Conference of State Legislatures ("NCCUSL") intended to reduce the cost and administrative burdens on retailers that collect the sales tax, particularly retailers operating in multiple states. SSUTA changes local sales taxes from an origin-based system to one based upon destination with amnesty for remote sellers who voluntarily began collecting sales taxes.

Under SSUTA, Internet businesses that deliver products to customers, either directly from their stores or from warehouses have a duty to determine the local sales tax to that of the destination city or unincorporated county. One of the gaps in SSUTA is that it has been enacted in roughly half of all U.S. jurisdictions. This failure to harmonize state tax law obligations creates significant costs for online retailers. With cloud computing, there are questions of where the sites for taxable presence should be determined. In 2012, Amazon.com entered into a contract with the state of Nevada to collect sales tax revenues on the online bookstore sales to Nevada customers.

Internet retailers, like Amazon.com or Overstock.com have no obligation to collect state sales taxes absent proof of a physical presence. An Internet tax collection system is currently being discussed in Congress. The New York State Department of Taxation and Finance ruled in April 2013 that an out-of-state internet retailer with no business activity in New York State is not subject to the state's corporate income tax. Advisory Opinion, N.Y. Department of Taxation and Finance, No. TSB-A-13(6) C, Apr. 11, 2013).

§ 5-6. State Consumer Protection

A state deceptive trade practice act has three elements: (1) the business is engaged in trade or commerce, (2) the business has committed unfair or deceptive acts or practices in the trade or commerce in which they are engaged, and (3) the consumer proves a financial injury and is seeking damages. The phrase "unfair or deceptive practices" applies to a wide range of practices in online sales or services. The Washington State Attorney General filed a claim against Movieland.com for its abusive use of pop-up ads. The consumer was given a trial period to use the service and then was bombarded with pop-up ads appearing hourly.

The consumer could not delete these persistent messages without paying a fee ranging from $19.95 to $100.00. The court ruled Movieland.com's scheme was an unfair and deceptive method of generating online revenue. Washington is one of the few states to have an anti-spyware amendment to its computer crime statute. Washington imposes fines up to $2 million for deceptive practices such as planting software appearing whenever a consumer launches an Internet browser. This anti-spyware statute also makes it unlawful to use deceptive means to harvest personally identifiable information or to record keystrokes made by a consumer and transfer information to a business.

§ 5-7. Commerce Clause Challenges

(A) AMERICAN LIBRARIES ASSOC. v. PATAKI

The Internet raises difficult issues in determining the power of a state to prescribe conduct outside its borders. In these state regulatory cases, the court must determine whether the burden on interstate commerce outweighs the benefit of protecting state consumers. The Commerce Clause of the U.S. Constitution contains an express authorization for Congress to "regulate Commerce with foreign Nations, and among the several States." The Dormant Commerce Clause prevents states from regulating or taxing to discriminate, or materially burden interstate commerce. This constitutional provision limits the power of states to erect artificial barriers against interstate trade to protect local businesses. The idea behind the "negative" Dormant Commerce Clause is to prevent local authorities from burdening Interstate commerce activities.

The court in *American Libraries Association v. Pataki*, 969 F. Supp. 160 (S.D.N.Y. 1997), traced the Dormant Commerce Clause back to Justice Johnson's 1824 concurring opinion in *Gibbons v. Ogden*, 22 U.S. 1 (S.Ct. 1824), where the issue was whether New

York could restrain the navigation of out-of-state steamboats in its territorial waters. The Commerce Clause prohibits state regulations that discriminate or unduly burden interstate commerce, even if they are facially nondiscriminatory. In contrast, the Dormant Commerce Clause is the negative aspect of this grant of power that unduly impinges on interstate commerce.

In *Pataki*, a number of libraries challenged the constitutionality of a New York state statute attempting to screen out material harmful to minors via the Internet. The librarians filed a lawsuit seeking declaratory and injunctive relief contending the software filters violate the First Amendment as well as the Commerce Clause. The trial court granted a preliminary injunction finding that the librarians proved a likelihood of success on the merits based upon the Commerce Clause violation. This influential decision compared the blocking of websites to erecting barriers against trade on highways and railroads.

Courts typically evaluate Commerce Clause challenges to state regulations under a balancing test, requiring them to uphold a state regulation serving an important public interest—unless the benefits of the regulation outweigh the burden placed on interstate commerce. In *Pataki*, the burden on interstate commerce exceeded the benefits of preventing indecent materials from being available to minors.

(B) HEALY V. BEER INSTITUTE, INC.

In *Healy v. Beer Institute*, Inc. 491 U.S. 324 (S.Ct. 1989), the U.S. Supreme Court ruled the Commerce Clause prohibits state regulations attempting to govern conduct "that takes place wholly outside of the state's borders, whether or not the commerce has effects within the state." In *Beer Institute*, Connecticut enacted a statute requiring out-of-state beer shippers to affirm that their posted prices for products sold to Connecticut wholesalers are no higher than the prices charged in bordering New England states. A brewers' trade association, as well as major producers and importers of beer, challenged the statute under the Commerce Clause. The trial court upheld the Connecticut pricing statute, but the second circuit reversed, holding the statute violated the commerce clause by discriminating against out-of-state sellers. The U.S. Supreme Court ruled that the Connecticut statute violated the Commerce Clause.

(C) GRANHOLM V. HEALD

In the 2005 case of *Granholm v. Heald*, 544 U.S. 460 (S.Ct. 2005), the U.S. Supreme Court struck down Michigan and New York statutes that permitted in-state wineries, but not out-of-state wineries, from shipping alcohol to Internet customers. Michigan and New York argued their statutes were valid exercises of state power under the Twenty First Amendment that ended federal Prohibition.

The U.S. Supreme Court accepted certiorari because of a split between the Sixth and Second Circuits as to whether the respective statutes violated the Commerce Clause of the U.S. Constitution. The Court held both states' laws violated the Dormant Commerce Clause because the regulations favored in-state wineries at the expense of out-of-state wineries and that the Twenty First Amendment did not authorize discrimination against out of state shippers where the states did not establish a legitimate purpose to justify their discriminatory treatment.

(D) WASHINGTON V. HECKEL

The Washington Supreme Court held that Washington's Anti-Spam Act did not violate the Commerce Clause in *Washington v. Heckel*, 143 Wn.2d 824, 24 P. 3d 404 (Wash. 2001)—reversing a lower court's decision that the statute was unconstitutional. The trial court held that Washington's anti-spam statute unconstitutionally burdened interstate commerce and dismissed the suit. The Washington Supreme Court reversed, holding that the anti-spam act was sufficiently limited by reaching only those spam e-mail messages directed to Washington residents, or initiated from a computer located in the State of Washington.

This state statute did not impose liability for messages merely routed through Washington. The *Heckel* court ruled that the local benefits of the Act far outweighed any burdens placed upon those sending commercial e-mail messages. This discriminatory pricing statute had the practical effect of controlling commercial activity wholly outside of Connecticut thus violating the Commerce Clause on its face.

§ 5-8. Global Consumer Law[1]

Counsel representing U.S. companies need to conduct audits to determine whether standard mass-market licenses comply with consumer law in radically different cultures. For example, the following table demonstrates how U.S. style standard form contracts used in Internet transactions violate mandatory European consumer directives and regulations. The illustrative clauses in the table highlight diametrically opposed mass-market licensing paradigms between the United States and Europe.

The U.S. market-based approach is antithetical to European consumer law, which provides consumers with uniform procedural and substantive rights across borders. Chapter Three introduced the Brussels Regulation governing cross-border transactions in the EU. Chapter Four examined the substantive provisions of mass-market licenses. The table below demonstrates the U.S. style mass-market licenses will frequently violate multiple provision of EU consumer law. Provisions in consumer transactions such as choice of law, choice of forum, mandatory arbitration clauses and the

---

[1] The section on Global Consumer Law was co-authored with Vit Svejkovsky, a 2012 LL.M. graduate of Suffolk University Law School.

elimination of warranties and meaningful remedies violate the Unfair Contract Terms Directive as well as other national law throughout the European Union. The lesson for Internet businesses is that they must adjust their contracting practices to comply with mandatory, non-waivable consumer protection.

U.S. v. European Consumer Regimes

U.S. Standard Form Clauses	EU Mandatory Consumer Provisions Invalidating Provisions
<u>Compulsory Jurisdiction or Choice of Forum Clause:</u> You will resolve any claim, cause of action or dispute (claim) you have with us arising out of or relating to this [terms of service, shrinkwrap, clickwrap agreement, or browsewrap agreement] exclusively in a state or federal court located [in a U.S. city county]. You agree to submit to the personal jurisdiction of	European Consumers Home Court Rule Adopted by Articles 15-17 of the Brussels Regulation. (Regulation (EC) No 44/2201). Consumer home court rules applies, "In matters relating to a contract concluded by a person, the consumer, for a purpose which can

the courts located [in a U.S. county and state] for litigating all such claims.	be regarded as being outside his trade or profession." *Id.* at art. 15(1)(C) The consumer home court rules applies to contracts "concluded with a person who pursues commercial or professional activities in the Member State of the consumer's domicile or, by any means, directs such activities to that Member State or to several States." Article 17 makes this provision nonwaivable.
Choice of Law: The laws of the State of ___ will govern this Statement, as well as any claim that might arise between you and us, without regard to conflict of law provisions.	Prohibited by Article 6 of the Rome I Regulation governing choice of law. The governing law has to be the law of the member state where the consumer is

	domiciled. Regulation (*EC*) No 593/2008.
Elimination of All Warranties: WE ARE PROVIDING [content, software etc.] WITHOUT ANY EXPRESS OR IMPLIED WARRANTIES	The Unfair Contract Terms Directive ("UCTD") prohibits consumer contracts where: . . . there is a "significant imbalance in the rights and obligations of consumers on the one hand and sellers and suppliers on the other hand." Directive *93/13/EEC* of 5 April 1993 "A contractual term which has not been individually negotiated shall be regarded as unfair if, contrary to the requirement of good faith, it causes a significant imbalance in the

	parties' rights and obligations arising under the contract, to the detriment of the consumer." *Id.* at art. 3 (1).
	Term (B) in the Annex to the UCTD provides: "1. A contractual term which has not been individually negotiated shall be regarded as unfair if, contrary to the requirement of good faith, it causes a significant imbalance in the parties' rights and obligations arising under the contract, to the detriment of the consumer." *Id.* at annex at Term B.
<u>Browsewrap Agreement:</u> By using the Products and Services, you agree, without limitation or qualification, to be bound by, and to comply with, these Terms and	Browsewrap-type contracts also likely violate term (I) to the annex which provides that terms are unenforceable where they

Conditions and any other posted guidelines or rules applicable to [website] or any Product or Service.	"irrevocably binding the consumer to terms with which he had no real opportunity of becoming acquainted before the conclusion of the contract." *Id.* at annex at term (I)
<u>Rolling Contracts or Asserting the Dominant Party's Unilateral Right to Change Terms After the Conclusion of the Consumer Contract:</u> We can change [terms of use, shrinkwrap, clickwrap or browsewrap] if we provide you notice (by posting the change on our website). Your continued use of [our website] following changes to our terms constitutes your acceptance of our amended terms.	Term (C) in the annex to the UCTD prohibits making agreements "binding on the consumer whereas provision of services by the seller or supplier is subject to a condition whose realization depends on his own will alone." Term (J) prohibits sellers or suppliers from altering "the terms of the contract unilaterally without a valid reason which is specified in the contract." *Id.* at annex at term (J) Rolling contracts also violate term (I)

	to the annex which provides that terms are unenforceable where they "irrevocably binding the consumer to terms with which he had no real opportunity of becoming acquainted before the conclusion of the contract." Rolling contracts also violate term (k) to the annex.
<u>Pre-Dispute Mandatory Arbitration Clauses:</u> Any controversy or claim arising out of or relating to these Terms and Conditions or any user's use of the Products and Services shall be settled by binding arbitration in accordance with the commercial arbitration rules of the [arbitral provider].	Predispute mandatory arbitration provision violates the Brussels Regulation's mandatory home court rules for consumers found in Articles 15-17. Term (q) of the annex to the UCTD prohibits the dominant party from: excluding or hindering the consumer's right to

	take legal action or exercise any other legal remedy, particularly by requiring the consumer to take disputes exclusively to arbitration.
<u>Anti-Class Action Waivers:</u> You are prohibited from entering into disputes that are the subject of purported class action litigation.	European consumers with identical complaints against a company may join in a class suit or representative action in U.S. or European courts recognizing the aggregation of cases. Anti-class action waivers do not permit the consolidation of complaints into a single proceeding. This provision is significantly imbalanced in favor of the dominant party. Anti-class action waivers likely

	violate term (B) of the annex to the UCTD. Directive *93/13/EEC* of 5 April 1993 .
<u>Limitations of Remedy;</u> <u>No Minimum Adequate</u> <u>Remedy:</u> UNDER NO CIRCUM STANCES SHALL [provider] BE LIABLE ON ACCOUNT OF MEMBER'S USE OR MISUSE OF THE [. . . .] WEBSITE OR THE SERVICES, WHETHER THE DAMAGES ARISE FROM USE OR MISUSE OF THE [. . . .] WEBSITE OR THE SERVICES, FROM INABILITY TO USE THE WEBSITE OR THE SERVICES, OR THE INTERRUPTION, SUSPENSION, MODIFICATION, ALTERATION, OR TERMINATION OF THE WEBSITE OR THE SERVICES. SUCH	Limitations of remedies common in U.S. style standard term agreements are significantly imbalanced in favor of the dominant party and thus violate the UCTD.

LIMITATION SHALL ALSO APPLY WITH RESPECT TO DAMAGES INCURRED.	

As the table above confirms, many provisions in standard Internet contracts violate European mandatory consumer law. European courts take the position that even if a consumer assents to an abusive term, it is unenforceable as a matter of law and European consumers, unlike their American counterparts, cannot be hauled into distant forums and be divested of mandatory consumer protection. The purpose of the EU was to create a seamless body of consumer protection, providing certainty for consumers and predictability for the business community. U.S. companies targeting foreign countries on the Internet must localize their contracts to avoid enforcement actions by public regulators. The lessons from European consumer rule may also apply to other countries around the globe.

CHAPTER 6
GLOBAL INTERNET TORTS

§ 6-1. Overview of Cybertorts

(A) WHAT CYBERTORTS ARE

In this chapter, the term "cybertort" is used to describe civil litigation arising out of e-mail, social media sites, and other computer related injuries. Among the subjects covered in this chapter are intentional torts, personal property torts, information-based torts, privacy, negligent security, information products liability, foreign Internet torts or *delicts*, common law defenses, and Section 230 of the Communications Decency Act ("CDA"). Internet-related torts arise out of Twitter postings, blogs, e-mail transmissions, website postings, the misappropriation of trade secrets, and many other Internet contexts. The potential for Internet-related lawsuits in the blogosphere is staggering. Virtual torts—such as the invasion of privacy, or defamation—are frequently difficult to expunge once they go into a viral spiral. It is difficult to expunge or correct defamatory postings that have been reposted.

Since the mid-1990s, most Internet tort cases have been business or publication torts, filed by companies to protect their intangible assets, reputation, and e-market share. Relatively few consumers have been able to recover for virtual injuries arising out of Internet publication torts. For most Internet-related torts against individuals, the preferred remedy is to mitigate the damage to the plaintiff's reputation or peace of mind; obtaining a monetary settlement is of secondary importance.

(B) CYBERLIABILITY INSURANCE

Risk adverse companies will seek indemnification or insurance to reallocate the risks of cybertort liability but the vast majority of cybertorts are intentional torts, which are not insurable. Many U.S. states take the position that insuring against punitive damages creates a moral hazard and therefore should not be permitted on public policy grounds. Insurance policy options include coverage for information-based torts such as defamation, Internet security breaches, theft of consumer data, property damage, errors and omissions (such as professional liability for computer programming errors), directors' and officers' liability, extortion coverage, and group personal liability. Insurers have not yet offered business interruption policies because they have too little data on the risk factors.

(C) SECTION 230 OF THE CDA

Internet torts have been slow to evolve because websites are largely protected from liability for third party postings by Section 230 of the Communications Decency Act of 1996. The CDA sought to preserve the "vibrant and competitive free market" of ideas on the Internet. This broad shield from tort liability was originally restricted to publisher's liability for defamation but federal courts have stretched it to include a variety of other torts such as the intentional infliction of emotional distress, distributor's liability, and right of publicity.

Information service providers have prevailed in nearly every cybertort related case in the last decade and a half.

Section 230 of the CDA precludes plaintiffs from making interactive computer service providers liable for the publication of information created by third parties. Subsection (c)(1) of the Communications Decency Act states: "No provider or user of an interactive computer service shall be treated as the publisher or speaker of any information provided by another information content provider." 47 U.S.C. § 230(c)(1). Subsection (1)(3) of the CDA defines "information content provider" as "any person or entity that is responsible . . . for the creation or development of information provided through the internet. . . ." 47 U.S.C. § 230(1)(3). Subsection (e)(3) of Section 230 states, "no cause of action may be brought and no liability may be imposed under any State or local law that is inconsistent with this section." 47 U.S.C. § 230(e)(3).

The CDA shields any information service, system, or access software provider that provides or enables computer access by multiple users to a computer server, specifically including a service or system that provides access to the Internet. Because of the CDA, U.S. websites have no duty to remove third party postings even if they constitute ongoing torts or crimes; a rule that varies sharply from the European Union's Electronic Commerce Directive, which has implemented a takedown policy for material constituting ongoing torts.

To fall within the protection of CDA Section 230 immunity, a website must show: (1) it is an interactive service provider or user of such a service, (2) the cause of action considers the defendant as the publisher or speaker, and (3) the information at issue is provided by a third-party information content provider.

(D) DISTRIBUTOR LIABILITY

Courts have long distinguished between primary publishers—i.e. newspapers or book publishers— and secondary publishers or distributors—i.e. bookstores, libraries, or newsstands—in common law defamation lawsuits. A newspaper is a republisher with the same liability as the person who originally published a story or article if the newspaper has notice of any defamatory content. Republishers are classified as primary publishers and held to the same liability standard as the author of a defamatory work because of their active role in the publication.

Distributors traditionally are mere conduits, such as telegraph and telephone companies, who have no liability for content created by others unless they have specific knowledge of the defamatory message. Under Section 230, websites and other service liability are not liable for the defamatory postings of third parties absent proof that they qualify as creators of the objectionable materials. In the pre-Section 230 case of *Cubby v. CompuServe*, 776 F. Supp. 135 (S.D. NY. 1991), the court ruled that the service provider was not liable for third party content posted on its online bulletin board because the service provider was merely a distributor akin to a bookstore, library, or newsstand. When Congress enacted Section 230, its purpose was to adopt the *Cubby* court's view that websites are distributors, not publishers.

(1) Failure to Remove Content

U.S. courts have ruled consistently that service providers are not liable for ongoing torts (or crimes) committed by third parties on their services even after they have received notice. U.S. ISPs have no affirmative duty to either patrol or remove objectionable content constituting ongoing cybertorts. In *Zeran v. America Online*, 129 F.3d 327 (4th Cir. 1997), a malicious anonymous poster instructed members of the public to call Kenneth M. Zeran to order merchandise displaying tasteless slogans celebrating the 1995 bombing of the Alfred P. Murrah Federal Court Building in Oklahoma City. The incendiary messages by the hoaxer included Zeran's name and telephone number. An Oklahoma City radio broadcaster denounced Zeran on the air.

In the aftermath of the radio program, Zeran was deluged with threatening calls and even death threats but could not change his telephone number because it was also his business number. Zeran contended that AOL was negligent in failing to remove the incendiary posting from its service and for allowing the anonymous prankster to continue posting on AOL bulletin boards, even after the service provider was given notice of this continuing tort.

AOL defended on that grounds that it was Congress' intent to immunize service providers from tort liability in order to maintain robust Internet communications. The Fourth Circuit agreed, ruling that a service provider such as AOL was insulated from both publisher and distributor defamation lawsuits despite the fact that Section 230 only addresses publisher liability. The *Zeran* case established that intermediaries have no obligation to take down information posted by third parties, which is unlike their duty under copyright law under the takedown rules of the Digital Millennium Copyright Act covered in Chapter 10.

(2) ISP's Immunity for Online Gossip

In *Blumenthal v. America Online*, 992 F. Supp. 44 (D.D.C. 1998), commentator Matt Drudge posted a false report on AOL that Sidney Blumenthal, an aide to President Clinton, had a history of spousal abuse. Drudge later retracted the story and AOL published the retraction. Blumenthal contended that AOL should be liable for the defamatory communication, even though he conceded AOL was an interactive computer service. Blumenthal argued that because Drudge received a $3,000 monthly royalty payment from AOL for posting his column on its online service, his column was similar to writing for a newspaper or other mass media, making the ISP responsible as a publisher.

AOL was entitled under its contract with Drudge to edit the content of his online columns. Blumenthal contended AOL's editorial role made it a primary content provider rather than a mere conduit. The *Blumenthal* court concluded that AOL had no significant editorial role—even though it had the contractual right to edit, update, manage, or even remove objectionable content in its agreement to publish the Drudge Report, holding that AOL was immune for negligence claims as well as defamation under section 230. The Fourth Circuit's expansive interpretation of Section 230 conferred a tort shield on the service provider even though AOL manifested many attributes of a content creator.

(3) Islands of Section 230 Immunity

In *Mmubango v. Google, Inc.*, 2013 WL 664231 (E.D. Pa., Feb. 22, 2013), a federal court ruled Google was immunized by Section 230 for publishing (and refusing to remove) a link to a wikiscams.com website alleging defaming the plaintiff. The court ruled that Google was not an "information content provider" with respect to the allegedly defamatory material because Google did not create the content. A federal court in *Stevo Design Inc. v. SBR Marketing Ltd.*, 2013 WL 308996 (D. Nev. 2013) applied the Section 230 immunity to an offshore, sports-handicapping website's practice of awarding loyalty points to users who posted content on their website. The court noted that the test for liability "is whether the duty that the plaintiff alleges the defendant violated derives from the defendant's status or conduct as a publisher or speaker. If it does, 47 U.S.C. § 230(c)(1) precludes liability."

(4) Exceptions to Section 230 Immunity

A few courts have ruled that Section 230 immunity is not available if a website is too closely connected to the creation of content posted by third parties. In *Fair Housing Council of the San Fernando Valley* v. *Roommates.com*, 521 F.3d 1157 (9th Cir. 2008), the Ninth Circuit, sitting *en banc*, ruled that Section 230 did not immunize a roommate-matching website. The website required its users to answer potentially discriminatory questions about such things as age, race, and sexual orientation in order to complete a profile prior to getting suggested matches.

The site also encouraged subscribers to provide additional comments, which encouraged them to make discriminatory selections. The Ninth Circuit observed that a website is a content provider for content that it creates itself, whether in whole or in part. The court concluded a website might be immune from liability for some of the content it displays to the public but be subject to liability for content it had a significant role in creating.

§ 6-2. Intentional Cybertorts Against the Person

An intentional tort is committed where the defendant has acted with the desire to cause the consequence, or the desired consequence is substantially certain to occur. A virtual hate posting or online stalking is the gift that keeps on giving. Nevertheless, words alone do not make the actor liable for assault unless the plaintiff is placed in reasonable apprehension of an imminent harmful or offensive contact with his person. Battery, too, is virtually impossible because there can be neither a harmful or offensive contact nor an imminent apprehension of such a contact in cyberspace. See Restatement Third of Torts: Liability for Physical and Emotional Harm § 18, § 21 (2009).

(A) TORT OF OUTRAGE

To support the tort of outrage or what the intentional infliction of emotional distress, conduct must be so outrageous in character, and so extreme in degree, as to go beyond all possible bounds of decency. Restatement (3rd) Torts § 46. The tort of the intentional infliction of emotional distress ("IIED") or outrage is often pleaded in online stalking or anonymous bullying cases. The elements of IIED are that a defendant: (1) engages in extreme and outrageous conduct that (2) intentionally or recklessly (3) causes (4) severe emotional distress to another. States following Section 46 of the Restatement (Third) of Torts require only a showing of recklessness to prove IIED. Other states require the plaintiff to prove intent. The test for outrageous online conduct is conduct "so extreme as to exceed all bounds of that usually tolerated in a civilized community." The Restatement (Third) illustrates the tort of outrage by a stalking scenario adaptable to Internet stalking. See Restatement (Third) of Torts, § 46, illus. 1.

A Georgia girl filed an IIED and libel action against two classmates and their parents in a Facebook cyberbullying case. Her classmates created a fake Facebook page in her name, with photos and posts that were distorted to make her appear to be obese, racist, sexually active, and an illegal drug user. Even though the website that masqueraded as the plaintiff's was a cruel hoax, her IIED lawsuit is unlikely to succeed because of the difficulty of proving the conduct was so extreme to violate all bounds of decency or that it caused her such extreme distress that she needed to seek counseling.

The tort of outrage is not cognizable for "demeaning comments" that a company made on an ex-employee's Facebook page. *Murdock v. L.A. Fitness*, 2012 U.S. Dist. LEXIS 154478 (D. Minn. 2012). Specifically, Murdock based his IIED claim on L.A. Fitness employees "humiliating, bullying, making racially offensive statements . . . [and] posting demeaning comments on its Facebook [page]." The court stated that while these comments are insensitive, they do not amount to extreme or outrageous conduct. To qualify for IIED, conduct must be so atrocious that it passes the "boundaries of decency and is utterly intolerable to the civilized community." See Restatement (Second) Torts, § 46, cmt. 1. To be held liable for the tort of outrage, the Internet actor "must do more than intentionally or recklessly cause emotional harm. The actor must act in a ways that is extreme and outrageous." Restatement (Third) Torts, § 46, cmt. d.

(B) CYBERTORTS & THE FIRST AMENDMENT

The First Amendment of the U.S. Constitution trumps the tort of outrage when the statements are classified as protected speech. "Thus, a court may decide that although the First Amendment does not bar liability, the protection of speech is nonetheless a weighty enough concern in a given context that liability for intentionally inflicted emotional harm should not be imposed." Restatement (Third) Torts, § 46, cmt. b. A Texas court dismissed a Vice-Principal's claims for IIED against students who created a fake MySpace website masquerading as the school official's in *Draker v. Schreiber*, 2008 WL 3457023 (Tex. App. 2008). The website contained the Vice Principal's name, photo, and place of employment, and made explicit and graphic sexual references falsely depicting her to be a lesbian. The trial court entered summary judgment in the favor of the defendant on all claims, findings that were affirmed by the Texas Supreme Court.

The leading non-defamation case arose out of an IIED lawsuit that evangelist Jerry Falwell filed against Larry Flynt, publisher of Hustler Magazine. Falwell pleaded torts such as defamation, invasion of privacy and the intentional infliction of emotional distress for a tasteless parody that purported to describe Falwell's first sexual experience, with his mother in an outhouse. *Hustler Magazine, Inc. v. Falwell*, 485 U.S. 46 (S.Ct. 1988). The U.S. Supreme Court ruled that Falwell was a public figure and there could be no tort liability because his right of publicity was subject to the First Amendment.

(C) TRESPASS TO VIRTUAL CHATTELS

Trespass to chattel, sometimes called conversion's little brother, is a personal property tort that may be committed by intentionally: (A) dispossessing another of a chattel, or (B) using or intermeddling with a chattel in the possession of another. The standard remedy for trespass to chattels is the cost of repair or diminution in value of the property because of the intermeddling. Courts have stretched the ancient tort of trespass to include virtual property. The elements are: (1) there must be a disturbance of the plaintiff's possession and (2) the disturbance may be by an actual taking, a physical seizing and taking hold of the goods, removing them from their owner, or by exercising a control or authority over them inconsistent with the owner's possession.

(1) Spam E-Mail

The first court to apply trespass to chattels to spamming was *CompuServe v. Cyberpromotions, Inc.*, 962 F. Supp. 1015 (S.D. Ohio 1997). CompuServe filed for a preliminary injunction against Cyberpromotions, a bulk e-mailer. The *CompuServe* court ruled that there is no First Amendment constraint to enjoining spam. The spammer's use of CompuServe's computer system exceeded consent and constituted a trespass because the defendant deliberately bypassed CompuServe's spam blocking software.

The court also found Cyberpromotion's falsification of point of origin information was proof that it had misused the plaintiff's computer network. The "injury element" of trespass to chattels was the spammer's drain on the processing speed and disk space of the spammed computers.

The *CompuServe* court explained that a service provider could sustain an action for trespass to chattels but not conversion without a showing of substantial interference with its right to possession of its computer system. Under the logic of this modern case, physical contact can be satisfied by the mere reception of electrons.

(2) Bots as Trespassers

A web robot, or "bot," gathers and mines data from third party web sites. Most bot related litigation arises out of the misuse of bots that enable Internet users to submit auction bids. In *eBay Inc. v. Bidder's Edge Inc.*, 100 F.Supp.2d 1058 (N.D. Cal. 2000), the online mogul, eBay, filed suit against Bidder's Edge ("BE"), an aggregate auction website that enables consumers to do comparison-shopping.

BE's bots, or "spiders" searched and copied files on bidding activity from eBay and other online auction websites for use on its comparative, or aggregate, shopping auction site. Counsel for eBay sent BE a letter stating BE's spiders were unauthorized and contended that BE's activities constituted civil trespass to eBay's website. EBay sought a preliminary injunction against BE for trespassing on its website—trespass to chattels—as well as a variety of other business torts including trade libel and interference with prospective advantage. To obtain a preliminary injunction, eBay had the burden of proving: (1) a likelihood of success on the merits and the possibility of irreparable injury, or (2) that serious questions going to the merits were raised and the balance of hardships tips sharply in its favor. EBay offered to license BE's activities, but the parties ultimately could not agree on licensing terms.

EBay's software enabled it to monitor the extraordinary number of incoming requests from BE's IP address. EBay blocked 169 IP addresses it believed BE was using to query eBay's system. However, BE's bots continued crawling on eBay's site using proxy servers to evade eBay's filters, constituting trespass to chattels. BE argued its robot activity constituted no more than 1.1% of eBay's requests. The court found it unclear whether eBay's User Agreement included an anti-bot or spider term at the time BE was searching and copying listings from eBay's website but BE's web crawlers exceeded the scope of any such consent when they began acting like robots by making repeated queries. The court enjoined BE, finding eBay would suffer irreparable harm and be run out of business if BE was allowed to continue to crawl the eBay site. The court found that the balance of the equities favored enjoining BE.

(3) Intel v. Hamidi

Plaintiffs in Internet-related cases often have a difficult burden of proving concrete injuries amounting to damages. This issue arose in a trespass to chattels case in which the Intel Corporation filed suit against Ken Hamidi, an ex-employee. In *Intel Corp. v. Hamidi*, 30 Cal. 4th 1342, 71 P.3d 296, 1 Cal. Rptr. 3d 32 (Cal. Sup. Ct. 2003), the California Supreme Court held that Hamidi's e-mails to current Intel employees, despite requests by Intel to stop sending messages, did not constitute trespass of Intel's e-mail system. Ken Hamidi created an anti-Intel website, transmitting messages critical of Intel's employment practices to over 30,000 Intel employees on six separate occasions. Intel demanded Hamidi stop sending the messages, but he refused and bypassed Intel's firewall that employed routers to filter and transfer information between Intel's internal network and the Internet.

When Intel was unable to block or otherwise filter out the messages, it sent a letter demanding that Hamidi stop sending the mass e-mails to current employees. After Hamidi refused to heed this warning, Intel sought injunctive relief based upon the tort actions of nuisance and trespass to chattels. Intel ultimately dropped its nuisance theory and claim for damages, and only sought injunctive relief. The Superior Court issued a preliminary injunction, enjoining Hamidi from sending e-mail messages to Intel employees. The California Court of Appeals upheld the injunction, finding that Intel was likely to prevail on its claim that Hamidi trespassed onto Intel's computer system. Trespass to chattels based upon computer intrusions does not allow a nominal damages action; actual damages must be proven.

The California Supreme Court rejected Intel's trespass to chattels claim on the grounds it had proven no damages. The court found Hamidi's e-mails interfered with, but did not dispossess Intel of their computer system. Intel's computer system was not slowed down by Hamidi's e-mail messages nor did he damage the physical quality or value of

Intel's computer equipment. The court compared Hamidi's unwelcome e-mails to an unpleasant letter, which clearly does not cause injury to the recipient's mailbox.

Plaintiff attorneys have unsuccessfully attempted to overcome the "present injury" barrier by arguing that consumers are at risk of being victims of identity theft in the future. No plaintiff has been successful in receiving an award to compensate him or her for lost data where identity theft has not yet occurred. Courts ask plaintiffs to file their complaints once they have sustained damage from the hacked credit card numbers, which is similar to the ripeness doctrine.

(4) Spyware as Trespass to Chattels

In *Sotelo v. DirectRevenue*, 384 F. Supp. 2d 1219 (N.D Ill. 2000), the plaintiff sued the defendant for surreptitiously installing spyware on its computers. Direct Revenue's spyware delivered advertisements to consumers' computer screens through the Internet. To induce consumers to view the ads, the company offered them free software applications, such as screensavers, or games. When the consumer downloaded the free application, another piece of software known as an "advertising client" that generated the pop-up ads was also installed. The ads could be discarded by clicking on an "X" in the upper right hand corner of the display-box in which they appeared.

In *Sotelo*, the plaintiff claimed the spyware took up bandwidth, causing its computers to slow down and resulting in increased Internet charges. The *Sotelo* court found that the spam e-mailers caused an actionable injury to the provider's computer system. The court also refused to dismiss the plaintiff's Illinois Consumer Fraud Act and negligence claim that Direct Revenue breached its duty not to harm Sotelo's computers, as well as a computer-tampering claim.

(D) CONVERSION IN CYBERSPACE

Cyberconversion is the wrongful exercise of dominion over personal property on the Internet. This tort is committed by: (1) intentionally dispossessing another of a chattel, (2) intentionally destroying or altering a chattel in the actor's possession, (3) using a chattel in the actor's possession without authority, (4) receiving a chattel pursuant to sale, lease, pledge, gift or other transaction intending to acquire for himself or for another a proprietary interest in it, (5) disposing of a chattel by a sale, lease, pledge, gift or other transaction intending to transfer a proprietary interest in it, (6) misdelivering a chattel, or (7) refusing to surrender a chattel on demand. *Heidtman Steel Prods. v. Compuware Corp.*, 1999 U.S. Dist. LEXIS 21700 (N. Ohio 1999). No court has extended conversion to intellectual property misappropriation because federal or state statutes in most instances preempt this tort action.

(1) Cyberconversion of Domain Names

Conversion was originally a remedy for tangible goods appropriated by the defendant, not intangible assets such as a domain name. In *Kremen v. Cohen*, 337 F.3d 1024 (9th Cir. 2003), ex-convict Stephen Cohen forged a letter to a domain name registrar, Network Solutions. In the letter, Cohen masqueraded as the new contact person for Online Classifieds, Inc., the owner of the domain name, sex.com, requesting Network Solutions to deregister sex.com from Kremen and reregister it to him. Network Solutions, then the exclusive domain name registrar, transferred sex.com without making any effort to determine the authenticity of Cohen's letter. After Gary Kremen contacted Network Solutions some time later, protesting the transfer of the domain name to Cohen, a Network Solutions administrator informed him it was too late to undo the transfer. Cohen went on to transform sex.com into a multi-million dollar cyberporn empire.

Kremen sued Cohen in abstentia and was awarded $40 million in compensatory damages and another $25 million in punitive damages. The court ordered Cohen to disgorge profits gained by using the sex.com domain name and invoked a constructive trust over the ill-gotten gains. Cohen fled to Mexico, hiding the fruits of his fraud in offshore bank accounts. Kremen next filed suit against Network Solutions for the tort of conversion. The U.S. district court concluded that the letter to Network Solutions was a forgery but found that the registrar was not liable for conversion because domain names were intangibles, not personal property that could be converted. The Ninth Circuit reversed the lower court, ruling that Network Solutions converted Kremen's domain name.

This appellate case was the first time in Anglo-American legal history that a court stretched the tort of conversion to the misappropriation of a domain name. The court reasoned that corporations could be liable when they take away someone's shares of stock, which are pieces of paper symbolizing intangible assets. Since *Kremen*, other California courts have held that a domain name could be converted under California tort law despite it being an intangible. Few other U.S. jurisdictions have followed suit.

(2) Conversion of Websites

In *Budsgunshop.com ("BGS") v. Security Safe Outlet, Inc.*, 2012 U.S. Dist. LEXIS 72575 ("SSO") (E.D. Ky. 2012), a federal court ruled that the U.S. Copyright Act did not preempt a plaintiff's conversion claim arising out of the dispute over the ownership of a website. SSO and its officer expanded its online business selling firearms and its accessories through the www.budsgunshop.com website. SSO hired a consultant to oversee and improve its websites. The consultant and a co-defendant began to spin out the online business operations of SSO as a separate entity, which the plaintiff alleged was conversion, breach of fiduciary duty, and diversion of corporate assets. SSO responded with a counterclaim against BGS, asserting a conversion claim centering on three items of property:

(1) the www.budsgunshop.com website and all data pertaining to that website, including the e-mail database; (2) the . . . data stored on the SSO

server located in Paris, Kentucky, which also includes contact information for customers and other dealers; and (3) the www.Security SafeOutlet.com website and all data and electronic information stored within and pertaining to that website.

The federal court ruled that the U.S. Copyright Act did not preempt SSO's conversion claim, finding no authority that disputes over the ownership of websites were addressed by federal copyright law. The Kentucky ruling that the U.S. Copyright Act may not preempt conversion claims is a cautious first step to recognizing broader cyberconversion claims over websites and other virtual data. Battery, assault, false imprisonment and other intentional torts against the person have yet to evolve in cyberspace.

§ 6-3. Intentional Business Torts in Cyberspace

Business torts are often the last line of defense to protect intellectual property rights such as the right of publicity, trade secrets misappropriation, unfair competition and false advertising. Business torts include interference with contract, fraud, misrepresentation, trade libel, and the misappropriation of trade secrets. Misappropriation is defined as either acquisition of a trade secret by improper means or disclosure of a trade secret without permission. In addition to the tort of misappropriation for trade secrets covered in Chapter 12, there is also a tort action for breach of confidence, sometimes asserted in disputes over website development.

(A) INTERNET-RELATED BUSINESS TORTS

(1) Unfair Competition

The Restatement (Third) of Unfair Competition treats the appropriation of another company's intangible assets as unfair competition. Courts subdivide state unfair competition claims arising out of the defendant's misuse of trademarks into two general types: (1) consumer confusion as to the source of products, and (2) unfair trade practices, a residual category of unfair competition laws. Historically, trademark infringement was a tort; today it is governed by statute. Chapter 11 will cover trademark-related unfair competition causes of action in addition. Misstatements in advertisements and palming off are regarded as frauds against the consuming public. The FTC may prosecute unfair competition cases, a topic covered in Chapter 5 of this nutshell.

(2) Misappropriation of Intangible Data

In *International News v. Associated Press*, 248 U.S. 215 (S.Ct. 1918), a court recognized the misappropriation of intangible data for the first time in a case that arose out of the dispute between two news services. The plaintiff, Associated Press ("AP"), had a news wire and sold subscription services to individual newspapers on both coasts. The AP hired reporters in France to report on World War I battles. International News ("INS") would copy AP's "hot news" stories on battles in France when published in the East and sell them to West Coast customers unaltered or lightly edited. The U.S. Supreme Court recognized that this unauthorized copying of "hot news" constituted unfair competition. The Court upheld AP's misappropriation claim against INS stating, "You cannot reap where you have not sown."

In *NBA v. Motorola*, 105 F.3d 841 (2d Cir. 1997), the Second Circuit refined the "hot news" misappropriation tort further as having five factors: (1) a plaintiff generates or gathers information at a cost; (2) the information is time-sensitive; (3) a defendant's use of the information constitutes free riding on the plaintiff's efforts; (4) the defendant is in direct competition with a product or service offered by the plaintiffs; and (5) the ability of other parties to free-ride on the efforts of the plaintiff or others would so reduce the incentive to produce the product or service that its existence or quality would be substantially threatened. In that case, STATS, Inc. used Motorola's pagers to retransmit "real-time NBA game scores and statistics taken from broadcasts of games in progress to Internet sites. The court found that the NBA had not established misappropriation on these facts.

In *Barclays Capital Inc. v. Theflyonthewall.com*, 650 F.3d 876 (2d Cir. 2011), the Second Circuit found an Internet aggregator of financial data not to be liable for "hot news" misappropriation because the U.S. Copyright Act preempted the claim because it used its own resources to aggregate factual news information and was not diverting profits from Barclays and other companies.

(3) Interference with Business Contracts

The elements of a tortious interference with contractual relations claim are: (1) an advantageous (2) business relationship (3) under which plaintiff has legal rights, plus (4) an intentional and (5) unjustified (6) interference with that relationship (7) by the defendant which (8) causes (9) a breach of that business relationship and (10) consequential damages. In contrast, the interference with prospective contractual relations requires the plaintiff to prove: (1) the defendant intentionally interfered with the plaintiff's existing or potential economic relations (2) for an improper purpose or by improper means and (3) causes injury to the plaintiff. Plaintiffs deploy this tort in pop-up cases on the theory that these advertisements interfere with prospective economic relations. These business torts are often pleaded but seldom successful.

§ 6-4. Intentional Information-Based Torts

(A) CYBERFRAUD

The elements of a cyberfraud claim are the same as in the brick and mortar world: (1) a knowingly false representation by the defendant, (2) an intent to deceive or induce reliance, (3) justifiable reliance by the plaintiff, and (4) resulting damages. Fraud or misrepresentation includes willfully deceiving another with intent to induce a person to alter their position to their detriment. Despite the ubiquity of fraud on the Internet, relatively few plaintiffs have been successful in pursuing cyberfrauds. A common form of cyberfraud occurs when website owners pay people to click ads repeatedly in order to artificially increase advertising revenue.

In *Smallwood v. NCsoft Corp.*, 2001 U.S. Dist. LEXIS 82484 (D. Hawaii, 2010), an Internet user became physically and mentally ill after playing Linneage II, an online game, for 20,000 hours. The player filed suit after he was locked out of the game, contending that the game maker was liable for negligent misrepresentation by advertising that their virtual game was safe and fair. Elements of a negligent misrepresentation claim are that: (1) the defendant failed to exercise reasonable care in obtaining or communicating information, (2) caused pecuniary loss to the plaintiff, and (3) who justifiably relied on information supplied by the defendant. The court held that Smallwood repeatedly clicked agreement to the software maker's terms of service agreement that disclaimed warranties and limited remedies. The court dismissed all claims except the negligence claim but ruled that damages were limited by Linneage II's terms of service agreement.

(B) TRADE LIBEL IN CYBERSPACE

To prevail in a claim for trade libel, a plaintiff must demonstrate that the defendant: (1) made a statement that disparages the quality of the plaintiff's product; (2) that the offending statement was couched as fact, not opinion; (3) that the statement was false; (4) that the statement was made with malice; and (5) that the statement resulted in monetary loss. It is an essential element that a company must present evidence of special damages arising out of the online defamatory falsehood such as a Facebook posting. A court may presume as a matter of law that the defendant intended to make false statements (susceptible of only one meaning) that created public hatred, contempt or ridicule.

Private persons face the real risk of harm through the modern ease of defamatory publications now possible through use of the Internet. Presumed damages vindicate the dignitary and peace-of-mind interest in one's reputation that may be impaired through the misuse of the Internet. *Bierman v. Weier*, 826 N.W.2d 436 (Iowa 2013). Companies will have a cause of action for business disparagement (also known as trade libel) when defendants intentionally publish defamatory statements on their websites or in blast e-mails.

Online "publication" requires proof that the libelous statement reached even a single third person who understood both the defamatory meaning and its connection to the plaintiff. Trade libel requires proof of special damages, while libel *per se* does not have this requirement. "Special damages" are limited to actual pecuniary losses that must be specially pleaded and proved. Cyber-trade libel is the online publication of false and derogatory material regarding a website, calculated to discourage others from doing business with the defamed entity. An Internet company may not rely on a general decline in business arising from the falsehood but must instead identify particular commercial transactions or customers that it lost. Trade libel cases are often pleaded but difficult to prove because of the difficulties of establishing special damages and identifying the anonymous wrongdoer.

(C) INDIVIDUAL & MEDIA *PRIMA FACIE* CASE

Like trade libel, defamation of an individual consists of a false statement of fact rather than opinion. It is unclear how a defamation defendant would retract a libelous posting given the multiplicity of these sites. To date, there is no procedural mechanism for expunging ongoing Internet-related torts—let alone giving plaintiffs the right to remove postings that create ongoing injuries. Publication is an essential element of defamation and simply means a communication of statements to one or more third persons. If a statement is clear and unambiguous, the issue of whether the statement is libelous per se is for the court. Thus, the court may find a statement is libel per se if it unambiguously tends to provoke the plaintiff to wrath or expose him to public hatred, contempt, or ridicule.

To establish a *prima facie* defamation action against a media defendant, a private figure plaintiff must prove: (1) publication; (2) of a defamatory statement; (3) concerning the plaintiff; (4) in a negligent breach of the professional standard of care; and (5) that resulted in demonstrable injury. When deciding whether a statement is defamatory, a court must consider not only what the defendant explicitly stated but also the meaning that is insinuated or implied. In a virtual world, where user names are used as opposed to legal names, it may be difficult to establish that he or she was the target of a defamatory posting.

(1) Libel Per Quod

Libel *per quod* applies to a communication—which may not be defamatory on its face—that is defamatory when connected with other facts. To bring a libel *per quod* claim, a plaintiff must prove: (1) a false and defamatory statement concerning another, (2) an unprivileged publication to a third party, (3) fault amounting at least to negligence on the part of the publisher, and (4) either actionability of the statement irrespective of special harm or the existence of special harm caused by the publication. An online review is protected as long as it is opinion rather than fact-based. An online "opinion" may be actionable if it implies the allegation of undisclosed defamatory facts as the basis for the opinion. In *Hammer v. Amazon.com*, 392 F. Supp. 2d 423 (E.D. N.Y., 2005), a self-published author filed a defamation lawsuit against Amazon.com in relation to unfavorable reviews of his books on their website. The court dismissed the action because the reviews were pure opinion and therefore protected.

(2) Libel *Per Se*

Libel *per se* is available only when a private figure plaintiff sues a non-media defendant kinds of defamatory statements that do not concern a matter of public importance. In these cases, if the alleged defamatory statements have a natural tendency to provoke the plaintiff to wrath or expose him to public hatred, contempt, or ridicule, the plaintiff need not prove that the statement actually damaged her or him; damages are presumed. *Bierman v. Weier* (Iowa 2013). Under the common law, libel *per se* (for trade libel or ordinary defamation) requires proof that the plaintiff maliciously: (1) accused a person of commission of crime, (2) imputed unchastity to a woman, (3) stated that a person had a loathsome disease—e.g. AIDS, mental illness etc., or (4) made any statement that would damage a person in his business or standing in the community—e.g. crooked lawyer. A plaintiff need not prove actual damages with defamation *per se;* damages are presumed.

Courtney Love, widow of Nirvana's Kurt Cobain, posted a Tweet that alleged that Dave Grohl, former Nirvana drummer, tried to seduce her teenage daughter, Frances Bean Cobain. This statement would be a libel *per se*, assuming that it is a falsehood. Love settled this and another Twitter defamation case filed by a dress designer for $430,000. After several highly publicized libel claims against her, Ms. Love closed her Twitter account. Courts have yet to determine the meaning of the loss of online reputation in the relevant community of blogosphere or social network sites. If the defamation is not actionable *per se,* then, at common law, the plaintiff must plead and prove actual malice and special damages.

(3) Publishers & Conduits or Distributors

Defendants in defamation or trade libel cases may be classified as (1) primary publishers (such as a book publisher), (2) conduits (such as a telephone company), or (3) distributors (such as a bookstore). Distributors include conduits such as "telegraph and telephone companies, libraries and news vendors." DAN B. DOBBS, THE LAW OF TORTS § 402, at 1123 (2000). Distributors do not have liability for content created by others unless "the distributor knows or should know of the defamatory content in materials he distributes." *Id.* A bookstore owner, for example, would not be liable for defamatory statements made in books the store sold absent actual knowledge. A publisher, in contrast, is liable for defamatory statements in their works and the plaintiff need not prove the publisher had knowledge of the defamatory content. Distributors are subject to an intermediate standard between publishers and conduits.

Conduits are common carrier type defendants, who are generally not liable for defamatory content since they have no ability to screen or control defamatory material. Section 230 of the CDA treats websites as conduits so relatively few lawsuits for online defamation have been successful. The Internet has given estranged spouses, stalkers, and spurned lovers a worldwide forum for online defamation in the form of revenge porn. "The prototypical service qualifying for this statutory immunity is an online messaging board (or bulletin board) on which Internet subscribers post comments and respond to comments posted by others." *FTC v. Accusearch Inc.*, 570 F.3d 1187 (10th Cir. 2009).

(4) Single Publication Rule

Under U.S. law, the single publication rule limits tort liability arising out of mass communications to a single cause of action accruing when it is first published, thus preventing stale claims arising from a single publication. For purposes of the statute of limitations in defamation claims, a book, magazine, or newspaper has a single publication date, defined as when it was first posted or made generally available to the public. Copies of the original are still part of the single publication but republication in a new edition does create a new cause of action.

Courts have had no difficulty extending the single publication rule to an Internet posting. The Ninth Circuit in *Yeager v. Bowlin*, Nos. 10-15297 and 10-16503 (9th Cir. 2012), applied the single publication rule to an allegedly defamatory statement on a website that had not been modified since 2003. The court reasoned that the fact that other materials on the website had been modified did not restart the statute of limitations for the unaltered postings.

In *Alberghetti v. Corbis Corp.*, 476 Fed. Appx. 154 (9th Cir. 2012), the court ruled that a plaintiff's right of publicity claims were barred by California's two-year statute of limitations, because the single-publication rule applied to the images posted on defendant's website, and plaintiffs did not file suit until three years after the last image was posted. Chapter 3's discussion of Australian defamation law demonstrates that not every country follows this single publication rule.

(5) State Action

Generally, the First Amendment does not apply to speech on private property, such as a company's website because of the doctrine of state action. In *Noah v. AOL Time-Warner, Inc.*, 261 F. Supp.2d 532 (E.D. Va. 2003), the Virginia district court ruled that AOL's termination of an Internet service account because of pro-Islamic statements raised no First Amendment claim because the Constitution does not protect against actions taken by private entities. Public entities, in contrast, are subject to First Amendment actions because state action is satisfied.

(6) John Doe Subpoenas

John Doe subpoenas, also called *subpoena duces tecum*, are requested by prosecutors or private litigants to unveil anonymous bloggers, posters, and others potentially liable for trade libel or the infringement of intellectual property rights. The leading test was for granting these subpoenas was articulated in *Dendrite Int'l, Inc. v. Doe*, 775 A.2d 756 (N.J. Super. Ct., App. Div. 2001). The *Dendrite* court held that a plaintiff seeking to unveil an anonymous speaker must: (1) give notice, (2) identify the exact statements that constitute allegedly actionable speech, (3) establish a *prima facie* cause of action against the defendant based on the complaint and all information provided to the court, and (4) produce sufficient evidence supporting each element of its cause of action, on a *prima facie* basis, prior to a court ordering the disclosure of the identity of the unnamed defendant.

Assuming the plaintiff establishes a *prima facie* cause of action; the court must balance the defendant's First Amendment rights against the strength of the case presented, considering the importance disclosing the anonymous defendant's identity to allow the plaintiff to prove her case. Courts are disinclined to issue a John Doe subpoena unless the ISP gives notice to the anonymous speaker and an opportunity to be heard. A New Hampshire Jane Doe plaintiff filed suit against Friendfinder.com, an adult networking site, for defamatory third party postings under the screen name "petra03755."

The anonymous poster created a false defamatory profile of the Jane Doe plaintiff, which depicted her as a "swinger." The court granted Friendfinder.com's motion to dismiss the plaintiff's claims for invasion of privacy and defamation on grounds of the federal immunity under Section 230 of the Communications Decency Act. The federal court ruled that Friendfinder.com was not transformed into a content provider merely because it changed the wording about the age of Jane Doe's profile from age 40 or 41 into "early forties." However, a website operator making extensive editorial modifications risks losing its Section 230 immunity. See *Doe v. Friendfinder Network*, 2008 WL 2001745 (D. N.H. 2008).

Thomas M. Cooley Law School filed a complaint against John Doe 1 (Doe 1), alleging defamation arising from statements that Doe 1 made on a website. Under the pseudonym Rockstar, the blogger titled his website "THOMAS M. COOLEY

LAW SCHOOL SCAM." Cooley sought it unveil the anonymous blogger's identity to pursue a trade libel claim. Doe 1 moved the trial court to (1) quash a subpoena that Cooley obtained in California seeking his identity, and (2) issue a protective order. Doe 1 argued that the First Amendment's protections for anonymous free speech permitted him to shield his identity.

The court concluded that the trial court abused its discretion when it denied Doe 1's motion for a protective order after it adopted and applied foreign law. On remand, the trial court will determine whether it has the power to quash a California subpoena. If not, or if it declines to do so, the trial court is to determine whether Doe 1 is entitled to an order protecting his identity applying Michigan law. *Thomas M. Cooley Law School v. Doe 1*, 2013 WL 1363885 (Mich. Ct. of App. 2013).

In *Patrick Collins, Inc. v. Doe*, 2013 U.S. Dist. LEXIS 39187 (E.D. Pa. 2013), Collins filed "a copyright infringement action against 30 'John Doe' Defendants who allegedly used BitTorrent, a peer-to-peer file sharing protocol, to download a pornographic film." The plaintiff sought John Doe subpoenas because the defendants could only be located through their Internet Protocol ("IP") addresses. The third-party subpoenas served on Internet Service Providers ("ISPs"), sought "disclosure of each Defendant's name, address, telephone number, email address, and Media Access Control address." The court permitted Collins to serve the requested subpoenas, but required the ISPs to notify each affected subscriber of his or her right to challenge the subpoena before the court. The court quashed the subpoenas for all but one of the John Doe defendants. In *Barker v. Collins* No. 3:12-cv-372-S, *amended complaint filed* W.D. Ky. July 29, 2012), plaintiffs filed fraud and racketeering claims against Collins, claiming he was a "copyright troll" who allegedly misused John Doe subpoenas to extort settlements from Internet users that downloaded pornography from the Internet. Swarm joinder seeks John Doe Subpoenas in a single copyright infringement case against "unnamed defendants in order to avoid court filing fees, and then use subpoenas to ISPs to identify the IP account holders." The judicial concern is that "copyright tolls" are using "swarm litigation" to "pry a settlement out of [Internet users of pornography then, motivated in large part by an account holder's desire to avoid the embarrassment of being publicly labeled in a lawsuit as an Internet pornography voyeur." David McAuley, *Doe Defendants Take a Page From Plaintiffs Seek Judicial Remedies for Swarm Extortion,* BLOOMBERG BNA, ELECTRONIC COMMERCE & LAW REPORT (Aug. 28, 2012).

(D) DEFENSES IN DEFAMATION

(1) Public Official

If a plaintiff is a public official, he or she must demonstrate by clear and convincing evidence that a false and defamatory statement was made against him or her with actual malice. The statement must be false or made with reckless disregard as to the truth or falsity of the avowal. The rule requiring public officials to prove actual malice is based on First Amendment principles, reflecting the U.S. Supreme Court's consideration of the national commitment to robust and wide-open debate of public issues.

New York Times v. Sullivan, 376 U.S. 254 (S.Ct. 1964), was the most important defamation case in American history because of the Supreme Court's holding that Alabama's tort of defamation was subject to the constraints of the First Amendment. In *Sullivan*, the Montgomery, Alabama Police Commissioner filed a defamation suit against the New York Times after the newspaper published a full-page advertisement entitled: "Heed Their Rising Voices"—calling for support of Martin Luther King's peaceful protests. The Alabama trial court held that malice was presumed because the advertisement impugned the Police Chief's reputation by charging him with heavy-handed and illegal tactics. The Alabama jury awarded $500,000 to the plaintiff.

The significance of the *Sullivan* case is that it recognized for the first time that torts were subject to the First Amendment. The *Sullivan* Court noted that contentious public issues such as the extension of civil rights are protected as freedom of expression under the First Amendment. The Court's ruling that a public official cannot recover damages for defamation absent proof of actual malice has encouraged robust debate on public issues. The public official rules have been extended to cyberspace speech.

(2) Public vs. Private Figures

(a) General Purpose Public Figure

Public figures may be celebrities such as movie stars, athletes, or other well-known individuals. As with elected or appointed public officials, a celebrity must prove that a defamatory statement was made with malice. In 1967, the Court expanded *Sullivan's* constitutional limitations from public officials to public figures in *Curtis Publ'g Co. v. Butts*, 388 U.S. 130 (S.Ct. 1967). The Court in *Gertz v. Robert Welch, Inc.*, 418 U.S. 323 (S.Ct. 1974), distinguished between general-purpose public figures and limited public figures. General-purpose public figures are individuals who achieve pervasive fame or notoriety so that they qualify as public figures for all purposes and in all contexts.

To be liable for the defamation of a public figure, a distributor of allegedly defamatory material must act with actual malice—that is, with knowledge that the material was false or with reckless disregard of whether it was false or not. To prevail in a defamation action against a media defendant, a plaintiff must prove some sort of cognizable injury, such as injury to reputation. Hurt feelings alone cannot serve as the basis of a defamation action. When suing media defendants for defamation, plaintiffs no longer benefit from presumed fault or damages. Both public officials and private individuals must prove the falsity of the challenged statements.

(3) Limited Purpose Public Figure

"Limited purpose" public figures are only public figures on issues where they inject themselves into a public controversy. The U.S. Supreme Court created the "limited purpose" public figure classification to accommodate tort law to the First Amendment. It is unclear what level of Internet articulation turns a blogger or other Internet speaker into a limited purpose public figure. The Georgia Supreme Court in *Mathis v. Cannon*, 573 S.E.2d 376 (Ga. 2002) held that a poster to a Yahoo! message board qualified as a limited-purpose public figure in a controversy involving the county's recycling facility. Mathis posted several incendiary messages about Cannon on an Internet bulletin board as part of a local controversy about the unprofitable operation of a solid waste recovery facility. The Georgia Supreme Court reversed the lower court that conceptualized Matthias as a private person, concluding that he was a limited public figure. The court, however, dismissed the action because of the plaintiff's failure to demand a retraction, a requirement under Georgia's tort law.

(4) Standard for Private Persons

In online defamation cases against ordinary private individuals (not public figures or public officials), the plaintiff must prove: (1) a false and defamatory statement concerning another, (2) unprivileged publication to third party, (3) fault amounting to at least negligence on the publisher's part, and (4) either actionability of statement irrespective of special harm, or existence of special harm caused by publication.

(5) Truth as a Complete Defense

Under the law of defamation, truth is a complete defense. In U.S. defamation actions, the defense of truth is constitutionally required where the subject of the publication is a public official or public figure. The courts require only that the defendant establish that the gist of an Internet-related posting is true.

(6) Privileges and Qualified Privileges

A qualified privilege of common interest applies to communications made in good faith on any subject matter in which the party making the communication has an interest or in reference to which he has a duty, public or private, legal, either moral, or social, if made to a person having a corresponding interest or duty. An ex-employer giving an evaluation of an ex-employee will have a qualified privilege.

(7) Anti-SLAPP Suit Statutes

A number of states have enacted Strategic Lawsuits Against Public Participation Statutes ("Anti-SLAPP") that give a cause of action to a person who is sued while exercising their or free speech discussing public issue. Anti-SLAPP actions apply to either the First Amendment or an expression right recognized by a state constitution. California's Anti-SLAPP Statute, for example, was enacted in response to a "disturbing increase in lawsuits brought primarily to chill the valid exercise of the constitutional rights of freedom of speech." *Manufactured Home Communities Inc. v. County of San Diego*, 544 F.3d 959 (9th Cir. 2008).

In order to dismiss a cause of action under California's Anti-SLAPP Statute, the court must determine two things: (1) the court must decide whether the defendant has made a sufficient threshold showing that the challenged cause of action is subject to a special motion to strike and (2) the threshold showing has been made. The court must find that the plaintiff has demonstrated sufficient minimal merit to be allowed to proceed. A California appellate court ruled that websites were accessible to the public—thus being public forums for the purposes of California's Anti-SLAPP statute. *Kroneymer v. Internet Movie Database Inc.*, 150 Cal. App. 4th 941 (Cal. Ct. App. 2007). To date, many defendants who post derogatory statements on so-called "gripe websites" have successfully deployed anti-SLAPP suits.

(8) Retraction Statutes

Thirty-one U.S. states have enacted retraction statutes that require the plaintiff to demand a retraction before filing a libel lawsuit. In the physical world, retraction statutes are effective for many defamed individuals who are merely seeking to have their reputation repaired while avoiding costly and invasive litigation. In cyberspace, with its mirrored websites and Wayback machines, it is almost impossible to repair a reputation once lost. Retraction of defamatory statements is as futile as holding the ocean back with a broom.

(E) PRIVACY BASED CYBERTORTS

The right of privacy includes four causes of action: (1) the right to be free from invasion into one's solitude or intrusion upon seclusion, (2) the right to be free from public disclosure of private facts, (3) the right to be free from placement in a false light, and (4) the right not to have one's identity appropriated for commercial purposes. Not all jurisdictions recognize all four forms of this privacy-based tort and some have enacted statutes. Internet sites specialize in collecting "revenge porn," depicting former lovers in compromising sexual situations, are at the cutting edge of privacy tort lawsuits. In one case, an ex-boyfriend distributed nude pictures of a high school girl, which led to harassment by her classmates; later she committed suicide. To date, few plaintiffs have been successful in receiving civil recourse for violations of the right to privacy in large part because of the shield provided by Section 230.

(1) Intrusion Upon Seclusion

To establish liability for intrusion upon seclusion, a plaintiff must plead, and prove, that: (1) the defendant committed an unauthorized intrusion or prying into the plaintiff's seclusion, (2) the intrusion would be highly offensive or objectionable to a reasonable person, (3) the matter intruded upon was private, and (4) the intrusion caused the plaintiff anguish and suffering. A plaintiff must prove that they had an actual expectation of seclusion, or objectively reasonable solicitude. The rise of the Internet and of e-mail threatens privacy today just as the invention of the telephone or photography did in the early twentieth century. Eavesdropping, wiretapping, or intercepting e-mails could qualify as intrusions upon seclusion.

(2) Appropriation & Right of Publicity

The common law elements of the tort of the right of publicity are: (1) the defendant's use of the plaintiff's identity, (2) the appropriation of plaintiff's name or likeness to defendant's advantage, commercially or otherwise, and (3) the plaintiff has not given the defendant consent. The right of publicity applies to "[o]ne who appropriates the commercial value of a person's identity by using without consent the person's name, likeness, or other indicia of identity for purposes of trade is subject to liability." Restatement (Third) of Unfair Competition § 46 (2005). Appropriation is not actionable if the person's name or likeness is published for purposes other than taking advantage of the person's reputation, prestige, or other value associated with the person. The right of publicity or appropriation is the only property-based action of the four privacy-based torts.

The tort of commercial appropriation protects the "inherent right of every human being to control the commercial use of his or her identity." J. THOMAS MCCARTHY, THE RIGHTS OF PUBLICITY AND PRIVACY § 1.2, 1-8 (1992). In *C.B.C. Distribution and Mktg., Inc. v. Major League Baseball Advanced Media, L.P.*, 505 F.3d 818 (8th Cir. 2007), CBC marketed fantasy sports leagues on the Internet as well as by regular mail and telephone. Fantasy league participants form teams by drafting players from various Major League Baseball ("MLB") teams and use the cumulative statistics of the teams' players in actual games to determine the fantasy team's success.

The MLB players were unable to prove the fantasy league exploited their identity without their consent and for the purpose of commercial gain. The Eighth Circuit ruled that the MLB players' right of publicity does not encompass their personal statistics employed in fantasy sports leagues. The court decided the company's right to free speech outweighed the players' right to publicity.

The federal district court enjoined an adult entertainment website from distributing the video sex tape of Pamela Anderson Lee and musician Brett Michaels on its subscription website. The court found the site liable for copyright infringement, for infringing the celebrities' rights of privacy and publicity, and other intellectual property rights. *Michaels v. Internet Entertainment Group Inc.*, 5 F. Supp. 2d 823 (C.D. Cal. 1998). Nevertheless, the Ninth Circuit in *Perfect 10, Inc. v. CCBill*, 488 F.3d 1102 (9th Cir. 2007), stretched Section 230 of the Communications Decency Act to immunize websites for claims based upon the right of publicity. In *Perfect 10*, the plaintiff, a modeling agency, charged a website with violating its models' rights of publicity when it allowed third parties to post infringing copyrighted images on the site.

The defendant website responded with a claim that Section 230 of the CDA immunized them from the claim and the Ninth Circuit agreed. A growing number of states have enacted statutes addressing the right of publicity. Florida, for example, enacted a commercial misappropriation statute preventing the unauthorized use of the name, portrait, photography, or other likeness of any natural person without consent. Fla. Stat. § 540.08. This state statute requires the plaintiffs to allege that they are authorized in writing to use the names of natural persons. Fla. Stat. § 540.08(1)(b).

(3) Public Disclosure of Private Fact

In order to state a claim for public disclosure of private facts, the facts must not only be private but the matter revealed must be highly offensive to a reasonable person. To pursue a public disclosure of private facts action, the plaintiff must plead that: (1) publicity was given to the disclosure of private facts, (2) the facts were private, not public, (3) the matter made public was such as to be highly offensive to a reasonable person, and (4) the matter publicized was not one of legitimate public concern. "The tort of public disclosure of private facts is meant to protect against the disclosure of 'intimate . . . details the publicizing of which would be not merely embarrassing and painful but deeply shocking to the average person subjected to such exposure." *Chisholm v. Foothill Capital Corp.*, 3 F. Supp. 2d 925 (N.D. Ill. 1998).

The federal court in *In re Google Buzz Privacy Litigation*, 2011 WL 7460099 (N.D. Cal. 2011) approved an $8.5 million settlement in a class action suit brought by Gmail users who contended that Google exposed their personal information without authorization through "Google Buzz," a now-defunct social networking site. A California Appeals Court ruled that a preliminary injunction prohibiting an ex-wife from posting "false and defamatory statements and/or confidential personal information" on the Internet was an unconstitutional prior restraint. *Evans v. Evans*, 76 Cal. Rptr.3d 859 (Ct. App. 2008).

A Maine court considered a case in which a plaintiff filed a public disclosure of private facts case against a former classmate who published a book about their prolonged high school feud called, "Help Us Get Mia." The court rejected the plaintiff's claim for public disclosure for private facts since she had had posted many of the statements on her MySpace page. *Sandler v. Calcagni*, 565 F. Supp.2d 184 (D. Me. 2008).

In *Murdock v. L.A. Fitness*, 2012 WL 5331224 (D. Minn. 2012), an ex-employee of a health club asserted that a company manager invaded his privacy by the following posting to Facebook. "For those commenting and speculating about our group fitness coordinator/trainer who isn't there anymore—first, shame on you for gossiping about a man's career, and the decisions of his supervisors on an open forum . . . "The court found the complete posting not to be highly offensive to a reasonable person, an essential requirement of intrusion upon seclusion and the publication of private facts.

(4) False Light

One who gives publicity to a matter concerning another in a way that places the other before the public in a false light is subject to liability to the other for invasion of his privacy, if (1) the false light in which the other was placed would be highly offensive to a reasonable person; and (2) the actor had knowledge of or acted in reckless disregard as to the falsity of the publicized matter and the false light in which the other would be placed. False light is not a strict liability tort but requires proof of a defendant's negligence. The defendant must have knowledge of or have acted in reckless disregard as to the falsity of the published facts to be liable.

In 2007, a chiropractor's former patient posted negative reviews of his San Francisco chiropractic services on the website, Yelp.com. The defendant's postings suggested that the chiropractor was dishonest and engaged in insurance fraud through dishonest "time of service" billing practices. The plaintiff contended that the postings placed him in a false light in the public eye and that the publicity created by the Yelp.com posting was offensive and objectionable. False light, like the other privacy-based torts, is constrained by the First Amendment.

§ 6-5. Negligence Based Actions

(A) INTERNET RELATED NEGLIGENCE

To prove negligence based cybertorts, a plaintiff must prove, by a preponderance of the evidence, each element of negligence: duty, breach of duty, cause-in-fact, proximate cause, and damages. Duty is a legal obligation to conform to a reasonable person standard of care in order to protect others against unreasonable risks of harm. A breach of the duty of care is the failure of a defendant to conform to the standard of reasonable care. Courts construct tests for reasonable care such as whether the defendant has violated a statute, industry standard, or customary usage of trade.

Ninety percent of tort law is about negligence in the brick-and-mortar world but courts have been unwilling to recognize new duties of care for cyberspace activities, perhaps because of a fear of "opening the floodgates" to a tidal wave of litigation. None of the millions of consumers whose credit card numbers were stolen in the T.J. Maxx data heist will have a cause of action unless they can prove a concrete loss from the theft. The recognition of new tort duties is inevitably a policy-based determination.

The judiciary balances such factors as the foreseeability of the harm of computer viruses, or other breaches of security; the degree of certainty between software vulnerabilities and harm; the connection between lax Internet security practices and the injury suffered by a computer user; the policy of preventing future intrusions; the burden on the information industry, and the consequences to the community of imposing a duty to maintain adequate security; and the availability, costs, and prevalence of security solutions and insurance. In cybertort cases, as in the brick and mortar world, negligence is determined by a finding of excessive preventable danger. Companies that do not implement reasonable security measures to thwart hackers may be liable for negligent enablement of cybercrimes.

(B) NEGLIGENT ENABLEMENT OF CYBERCRIME

The negligent enablement of identity fraud or cybercrimes requires the plaintiffs to demonstrate a breach of the duty of care. Under this theory, a website would be liable for failing to implement reasonable security to thwart criminals using customer data to commit identity fraud. Most jurisdictions have declined to recognize the negligent enablement of cybercrime as a cause of action. Courts have been reluctant to construct a duty to maintain reasonable computer security.

The watchword of negligence liability is risk—the greater the risk, the greater the duty. The failure to implement reasonable cybersecurity poses great risks to our networked society. Increasingly, the world's infrastructure is software-driven and networked, which creates new vulnerabilities. LinkedIn.com, for example, used outdated methods to secure information of subscribers that enabled 6.5 million passwords to be purloined by some unknown cybercriminal. The biggest barrier to an enablement claim for stolen passwords is for plaintiffs to demonstrate a nexus between substandard security and a concrete injury even if they are able to prove duty and breach.

(C) NEGLIGENCE *PER SE*

The plaintiff must prove three things to establish negligence *per se*: (1) the injury must have been caused by the violation, (2) the injury must be the type intended to be prevented by the statute, and (3) the injured party must be one of the class intended to be protected by the statute. The negligence *per se* doctrine is based on the rule that a presumption of negligence arises from the violation of a statute that was enacted to protect a class of persons—of which the plaintiff is a member—against the type of harm the plaintiff suffered as a result of the violation.

Therefore, a party who seeks to prevail on a cause of action premised on the negligence *per se* doctrine must establish, among other elements, which the party is one of the class of persons who is protected by the statute, ordinance, or regulation. Defendants may use negligence *per se* to demonstrate a plaintiff's contributory negligence, if a user violates their statutory duty to secure their computer system or Internet passwords. President Barack Obama signed an Executive Order in 2013 mandating that the National Institute of Standards and Technology ("NIST") publish a draft cybersecurity framework for critical infrastructure owners and operators by February 2014.

The NIST standards may be the first step in developing statutory standards of care for Internet security, which can serve as surrogates for negligence. When federal cybersecurity standards are formulated, plaintiffs will be able to establish duty and breach in negligence *per se* actions.

Nevertheless, jurisdictions vary as to whether the violation of the statute is conclusive proof, presumptive proof, or just evidence of negligence.

(D) PREMISES LIABILITY IN CYBERSPACE

To prevail in a premises liability lawsuit, a plaintiff must establish that: (1) the defendant owed a duty to protect the injured crime victim, (2) the defendant breached that duty, and (3) the breach of the duty was a proximate cause of the criminal act and the victim's injuries. Section 314A of the Restatement (Second) of Torts lists a number of special relationships that create a duty to render aid; such as that of a common carrier (e.g. railroad, airlines) to its passengers, an innkeeper to their guest, or possessors of land. The analogy to premises liability is that the seller of inadequately configured software may expose its customers to cybercriminals—much like a shopping mall located in a high crime area that fails to implement reasonable security by hiring guards. The largest obstacle for Internet plaintiffs is to establish that websites owed them a duty or were not immunized by CDA Section 230.

Courts have been unreceptive to considering negligent Internet security claims. Plaintiffs are frequently left with no practical recourse but to file suit against a defendant website for failing to protect them from the direct criminal, who is unavailable or judgment-proof. Section 230 of the CDA blocks the development of premises liability arguments against websites that qualify as service providers. The most significant doctrinal obstacle to extending premises liability to the Internet is that this is a borderless instrumentality without a nexus to land or premises.

If courts were to recognized premises liability arguments, they would examine factors such as: (1) whether there have been prior similar cybercrimes, (2) the cost of increased Internet security measures, and (3) the degree to which intermediaries can reduce the radius of the cybercrime problem. In the absence of a history of similar intrusions and security breaches, foreseeability is based on all facts and circumstances.

The Fifth Circuit rejected a plaintiff's claim that the law of premises liability for owners of real property applied to a website. In *Doe v. MySpace, Inc.*, 528 F.3d 413 (5th Cir. 2008), the plaintiff contended that MySpace was liable under a premises liability theory for failing to prevent sexual predators from harming minors using its services. The plaintiff filed a complaint, alleging negligence, gross negligence, and strict products liability for failing to implement reasonable safety measures to protect minors.

A Texas federal court dismissed the claim against MySpace for enabling a sexual assault committed by a 19-year-old man on a 14-year-old girl he met online. The young girl misrepresented her age, claiming she was 18 years old when creating her My Space profile. The Fifth Circuit affirmed the federal district court's finding that Section 230 of the CDA immunized MySpace for liability. *Doe v. MySpace*, 528 F.3d 413 (5th Cir. 2008). The court found the law of premises liability was inapplicable to publishers and Internet service providers.

(E) COMPUTER PROFESSIONAL NEGLIGENCE

No U.S. court has recognized an action for computer or Internet security malpractice. New York, for example, does not recognize a cause of action for malpractice by computer professionals, *Nielsen Media Research Inc. v. Microsystems Software Inc.*, No. 99 Civ. 10876 (S.D. 2002). U.S. courts have held that computer consultants are not professionals for purposes of computer professional negligence. It is unclear whether cyber-malpractice applies where doctors give medical advice to online visitors. As Internet law matures, it is likely that software developers, website designers and Internet security specialists will begin to professionalize by developing industry standards of care. Courts are just beginning to construct new duties for Internet security so it is unlikely computer malpractice will be a cognizable action any time soon.

(F) NEGLIGENT DATA BROKERING

In Remsburg v. Docusearch, Inc., 816 A.2d 1001 (N.H. 2003), the New Hampshire Supreme Court held an online data broker owed a duty to a murder victim because it provided the killer with her personal contact information. On July 29, 1999, New Hampshire resident Liam Youens contacted Docusearch through its Internet website and requested the date of birth for Amy Lynn Boyer, a former high school classmate.

Youens provided Docusearch his name, New Hampshire address, and a contact telephone number along with a $20 fee. Youens e-mailed Docusearch inquiring whether it would be possible to get better results using Boyer's home address, which he provided, giving Docusearch a different contact phone number. Later that same day, Youens again contacted Docusearch and placed an order for Boyer's social security number (SSN), paying the $45 fee by credit card. On August 2, 1999, Docusearch obtained Boyer's social security number from a credit-reporting agency and provided it to Youens.

The next day, Youens placed an order with Docusearch for Boyer's employment information, paying the $109 fee by credit card, and giving Docusearch the same phone number he had provided originally. Shortly after obtaining information from Docusearch, Youens drove to Boyer's workplace and fatally shot her as she left work. Youens then shot and killed himself. The New Hampshire Supreme Court ruled that the data broker owed a duty to third persons whose information was disclosed if the company was subjecting them an unreasonable risk of harm.

(G) PRIVATE AND PUBLIC NUISANCE

No plaintiffs have successfully asserted either private or public nuisance causes of action against a website. Public nuisance theory, which has its origins in criminal law, does not mesh well with Internet websites. To date, no governmental unit has sought abatement of the nuisance of an annoying website. For a public nuisance to exist there must be proof that the activity substantially interferes with the common rights of the public at large. Generally, the plaintiff in a public nuisance action is a public official, such as a state attorney general, who is seeking a remedy for violation of a public right.

Private individuals may also sue for public nuisance, but only if they can demonstrate an injury separate and apart from the injury suffered by the public. A federal court found Craigslist to be immune from a public nuisance action in *Dart v. Craigslist, Inc.*, 665 F. Supp. 2d 961 (N.D. Ill. 2009). In *Dart*, a Cook County sheriff sought to hold Craigslist responsible for allegedly illegal content posted by users in Craigslist's erotic services section based upon public nuisance because it enabled prostitution. The federal court held that Craigslist was not susceptible to suit because of CDA Section 230(C) (1).

§ 6-6. Strict Liability in Cyberspace

(A) DEFECTIVE INFORMATION

Strict liability is the last frontier of tort law to accommodate to cyberspace. No court has applied the venerable doctrine of *Rylands v. Fletcher* [1868] UKHL 1) to software vendors that infect their user's computers with viruses. A few courts have recognized strict liability for defective information. The doctrine of *res ipsa loquitur* potentially applies to dangerously defective software. To date, no plaintiff has successfully deployed a strict liability-like standard such as *res ipsa* to failed computer vendors, programmers and others participating in the construction of software. Products liability for defective Internet information is undeveloped as a cause of action even though websites often enable downloads of software with viruses or other defective information products.

Courts have yet to apply strict liability to defective software or substandard website design. The term "products liability action" is broadly defined to include any action against a manufacturer or seller for recovery of damages, or other relief for harm allegedly caused by a defective product, whether the action is based on strict products liability, negligence, misrepresentation, breach of express or implied warranty, or any other theory or combination of theories, and whether the relief sought is recovery of damages or any other legal or equitable relief, including a suit for: (1) injury, damage to or loss of real or personal property, (2) personal injury, (3) wrongful death, (4) economic loss, or (5) declaratory, injunctive, or other equitable relief. Section 402A of the Restatement (Second) of Torts holds a manufacturer strictly liable for harm to person or property caused by "any product in a defective condition unreasonably dangerous to the user." Restatement (Second) Torts, § 402(A)(1).

The courts have recognized three paradigmatic types of defects in products litigation: (1) manufacturing defects, (2) design defects, and (3) the failure to warn or inadequate warnings. Courts have largely displaced the consumer expectation test with the risk utility test but California and a few other jurisdictions permit jury instructions on both tests. The Restatement (Third) of Torts: Products Liability requires the plaintiff to prove that there is a reasonable alternative design that would avert the risk of impugned design. Third, the product may lack adequate warnings or instructions. Products liability potentially applies to distributors of defective computer hardware and may even stretch to software. Software malfunctions of key infrastructure may have latent defects that prove deadly or economically disastrous.

The Sixth Circuit rejected a products liability claim arising out of a Kentucky school shooting. The plaintiffs contended the school shooter "regularly played video games, watched movies, and viewed Internet sites produced by the firms." *James v. Meow Media Inc.*, 300 F.3d 683 (6th Cir. 2002). The plaintiffs contended that the defendant's games "desensitized the shooter to violence" and caused the shooter to attack his classmates. Courts have generally been reluctant to classify Internet transmissions as "products" for purposes of products liability. The 24/7 virtual marketplace makes it even more likely that products liability cases will originate from a website sale.

The duty to warn licensees of known latent defects gives the customer the knowledge they need to protect themselves—much like the consumer of products. The Principles of the Law of Software Contracts discussed in Chapter 4 would also hold a computer vendor liable for statements made about software performance. In *Doe II v. MySpace Inc.*, 175 Cal. App. 4th 561, 96 Cal. Rptr. 3d 148 (Cal.

App. 2009), the parents of teenage girls filed strict products liability and negligence claims against MySpace, alleging that men they met through the site sexually assaulted them. The court sustained MySpace's demurrers without leave to amend and dismissed the complaints on the grounds of Section 230 immunity.

(B) ECONOMIC LOSS RULE

Under the economic loss rule ("ELR"), plaintiffs that incur only economic loss, as opposed to physical injury or collateral property damages, are limited to a contract remedy. In *East River Steamship Corp. v. Transamerica Deval Inc.*, 476 U.S. 858 (S.Ct. 1986), the U.S. Supreme Court held that a tort claimant could not recover for mere economic losses for product liability in admiralty. In *East River*, the problem was with the product itself, a massive turbine that continually malfunctioned. The Court recognized the availability of strict products liability in admiralty but established a boundary line between tort actions for physical harm and problems with the product itself. Tort damages are generally not recoverable in actions predicated upon bungled contract performance such as a defective computer system. The Court's distinction between injury to "the product itself" and "other property" is part of a continuing struggle to define the contours of the economic loss doctrine.

The ELR originated in the field of products liability but courts have stretched this doctrine beyond defective products cases to negligence, fraud, and virtually every other tort. The ELR shields design professionals from negligence claims for purely economic losses and privity is not an issue. In many Internet security cases, the loss is primarily the loss of data due to the failure of the firewall or other security precaution.

§ 6-7. Secondary Tort Liability

The common law doctrine of *respondeat superior* makes an employer liable for cybertorts, and even punitive damages, if the plaintiff shows the employee's action was committed within the scope of the employment. Vicarious liability or *respondeat superior* makes an employer liable for an employee's torts committed unless deemed a frolic outside the scope of duties. Secondary or indirect tort liability is not well developed in tort law beyond an employer's liability for an employee's torts committed within their scope of duties.

§ 6-8. Transborder Torts

Websites in the United Kingdom do not enjoy immunity for third party postings. In *Tamiz v. Google, Inc.*, No. 2013 EWCA Civ 68 (EWWA 2013), an English and Welsh court ruled that Google Inc. could be held liable as the publisher of an allegedly defamatory blog posting because of its failure to remove the post after receiving a complaint. Only a few tort cases have been filed against websites for third party postings in European courts. The strong administrative state in many civil code countries is an alternative to a strong cybertort regime. In Sweden, for example, claimants look to insurance first and to torts second. In Sweden, the tort system serves as a backup for those few individuals, such as foreigners, not covered by the nation's social security compensation agency, the *Forsakringskassan*.

In Europe, cybertorts are patrolled by consumer regulatory agencies, not private litigants. The United States is the only country connected to the Internet that depends so greatly upon the tort system to fulfill public law functions. The countries of the European Union, for example, arm consumer regulatory agencies with roving powers to protect privacy and other rights of persons.

CHAPTER 7

INTERNET-RELATED PRIVACY

In the late 1900s and early twentieth-century, privacy-based torts, along with remedies for misuse of novel technologies such as "instantaneous photographs," were being born. In the new millennium, American society is once again undergoing a technological revolution of great consequence. In the new millennium, America is evolving from a durable goods economy to one based on the licensing of information, software, and intellectual property.

Cyberspace privacy laws are in flux as legislatures attempt to accommodate to an ever-changing Internet. Apple was the target of a large number of class action lawsuits arising out of Apple-approved apps that collected personally identifiable information from iPhone, iPad, and iPod Touch users. The class action charged that Apple violated users' privacy by transmitting this information to third parties. *In re iPhone Application Litigation*, 2011 WL 4403963 (N.D. Cal. 2011).

In an era where cameras are standard features of mobile telephones, new websites such as People of Walmart.com have appeared. People of Wal-Mart has the feel of a Fellini-grotesque movie with its collection of grossly overweight, strangely dressed, or surrealistic shoppers at Wal-Mart. These online pictures, taken by fellow customers, are the modern equivalent of Tod Browning's 1932 movie, *Freaks*, featuring bearded women and conjoined twins.

Millions on social media sites such as Facebook and Twitter view People of Wal-Mart making it one of the largest successful degradation projects online. What rights do people have who are subject to ridicule on such websites?

Facebook has become an obsession, permitting narcissists to broadcast their most private thoughts twenty-four hours every day. Users are required to by the terms of service to indemnify Facebook and pay their own attorney's fees if a lawsuit is brought against the social media site for actions, content or information posted by these third parties. Are such terms of service agreements enforceable even though few consumers actually read them?

Companies have new legal obligations to protect data as transborder data flows go global on the Internet. In 2012, the FTC entered into a $22.5 million settlement with Google, requiring the social networking giant to implement comprehensive privacy programs. The settlement also prohibits social media sites from misrepresenting their compliance with the U.S.-E.U. Safe Harbor Principles that addresses cross-border transfers of personal data. Settlements of this type involve obvious jurisdictional and conflict of law dilemmas. The Internet is, by its very nature, a global phenomenon. Enormous conflict of law issues arise since the user crosses national borders seamlessly, without tollgates or even user awareness. This chapter examines the most significant online privacy issues including the problem of transborder data protection, where the legal norms are in flux.

§ 7-1. Online Privacy Issues

Two out of three Internet users utilize Google's search engine. Google collects information by planting cookies when users visit websites or interact with the service's ads and contents. Consumers' names, e-mail addresses, telephone numbers and credit card accounts, among other personal information, may be gathered. Google also harvests data through premium services such as its ad keywords, social media (Google+), e-mail, googlets, and search requests. If a consumer creates a Google profile, for example, the service will distribute a publicly visible Google Profile, which may include one's name and photo.

On March 1, 2012, Google revised its privacy policy, which now permits the company to collect device and mobile network information including the hardware model, operating system version, unique device identifiers, and the consumer's phone number. Each time a consumer accesses a location-enabled Google service; the service may collect and process information about her actual location. Google employs variegated technologies to determine location, such as sensor data to detect Wi-Fi access points and GPS signals sent by a mobile device. Google is a named in scores of class action lawsuits for unconsented tracking and collecting of users' personal information.

The Federation of German Consumer Organizations ("VZBV") filed an action against Facebook for violation of German consumer and privacy law in November 2010. A Regional Court of Berlin ruled that Facebook's "Friend Finder" and its terms of use agreement violated the Unfair Commercial Practices Directive as well as that country's data protection directive. Under the German court order, users must be clearly advised about how personal data is handled. Computer monitoring software permits workplace surveillance without the employees' knowledge. Current U.S. law imposes no duty on the part of employers to notify employees before implementing monitoring software. Many U.S. companies have installed GPS, web cams, and other software to track location or monitor their workers' e-mail and Internet usage. American employers monitor e-mail or Internet usage without notice to their employees with impunity, whereas European companies are liable for violations of human rights for the same policy according to rulings by the European Court of Human Rights.

U. S. companies employ electronic surveillance for diverse reasons including: (1) preventing the misuse of bandwidth as well as the loss of employee efficiency when employees surf the Internet, (2) ensuring that the company's networking policies are being implemented, (3) preventing lawsuits for discrimination, harassment or other online torts, (4) preventing the unauthorized transfer of intellectual property and avoiding liability due to employees making illegal copies of copyrighted materials, (5) safeguarding company records which must be kept to comply with federal statutes, (6) deterring the unlawful appropriation of personal information, and potential spam or viruses, and (7) protecting company assets including intellectual property and business plans.

The e-mail system is an efficient means of forwarding documents, including pornographic or obscene messages, and it is a common practice to forward off-color jokes or other objectionable materials to multiple recipients. The simple act of an employee forwarding tasteless jokes may unwittingly expose a company to a discrimination lawsuit under Title VII of the Civil Rights Act of 1964 and state discrimination laws as well as cybertort litigation. Employees not only e-mail or surf the web but also contribute to blogs or participate in social networks such as Facebook while at work. Employees in the private sector have no recourse if their employer terminates them for blogging about the company.

Private sector employees have no First Amendment right to criticize their company or employer as there is no state action. A state actor is someone acting on behalf of a governmental body and thus subject to the Bill of Rights, which includes the First Amendment. Under the doctrine of incorporation, the First Amendment as well as the Fourth and Fifth Amendment, also extends to state governmental actors. In contrast, public employees are protected by the First Amendment's qualified immunity if they are blogging about matters of "public concern."

U.S. employers frequently engage in social media "listening" to gather intelligence on applicants for employment and to manage the firm's reputation. E-mail monitoring software is so sophisticated that it can detect and correctly categorize employees' facial expressions. None of the EU countries would permit this form of intrusive monitoring because it would violate national privacy laws, the European-wide

Data Protection Directive, or fundamental human rights.

A growing number of U.S. employers are disciplining employees for anti-corporate or incendiary postings on social media sites. Employers are also monitoring social networking sites because of the risk that employees will misappropriate trade secrets. Prospective and current employers routinely patrol the Internet, studying Facebook profiles, Twitter postings, or other publicly available information to gain intelligence on job candidates, employees, and prospective customers.

Universities and colleges "cybervet" prospective students, faculty candidates, potential contributors, and others. Ratemyprofessor.com, for example, gives faculty recruitment committees publicly available, although certainly not statistically representative, information about a candidate's teaching evaluations. The most recent trend is for employers to ask job candidates for their Facebook or other social networking passwords, without giving them time to edit these pages, so that the company can view private profiles, timelines, and friends.

Facebook modified its terms of service in 2012, making all password sharing a breach. Maryland and Illinois have both enacted state statutes prohibiting companies from demanding that applicants give access to private social networking profiles. Facebook, Yelp, and Twitter, were among twelve other corporate defendants in a high profile privacy lawsuit alleging that their applications harvest consumer data without knowledge or consent. The class action, on behalf of mobile application users, seeks injunctive relief and damages to prohibit data collection without permission.

§ 7-2. Workplace Privacy Issues

(A) NATIONAL LABOR RELATIONS ACT

The National Labor Relations Act ("NLRA") considers it be an unfair labor practice to engage in surveillance of employees who are participating in "protected concerted activity" such as organizing their working conditions or attempting to increase their pay rates under section 7 of the NLRA, 29 U.S.C. § 1757. An employer monitoring e-mail or Internet communications for the purposes of constraining "concerted activity" will violate the NLRA. Congress needs to update this Depression era legislation to accommodate the Internet.

(B) CONCERTED ACTIVITIES

NLRA § 8 (A)(3) makes it unlawful for an employer to retaliate against employees participating in concerted activities. The National Labor Relations Board ("NLRB") has taken the position that employee posting and interaction on social media sites in an attempt to improve workplace conditions is classifiable as a "concerted activity." Employees who are fired after making derogatory comments about their employers have no remedy unless they can demonstrate that their social media postings constitute concerted activities. Four elements are required to prove concerted activity:

(1) online postings must relate to terms and conditions of employment, (2) there must be

evidence of concert—i.e. there must be discussions among employees of the posts or coworker responses to the posts, (3) there must be evidence the employee was seeking to induce or prepare for group concerns, and (4) the posts must reflect an outgrowth of employees' collective concerns.

(C) NLRA SECTION 8(A)(1)

Section 8(A)(1) of the NLRA makes it an unlawful or unfair labor practice for an employer to "interfere with, restrain, or coerce employees" with respect to their NLRA Section 7 organizational rights. An employer violates Section 8(A)(1) if the social media policy of the employer tends to chill their rights to organize. The NLRB applies a two-step test to determine if an employer's social media policy or other work rule violates Section 8(A)(1):

First, a rule is clearly unlawful if it explicitly restricts protected activities. If it will only violate Section 8(A)(1) upon a showing that: (1) employees would reasonably construe the language to prohibit Section 7 activity, (2) the rule was promulgated in response to union activity, or (3) the rule has been applied to restrict the exercise of Section 7 rights. NLRB, THE 2012 NLRB REPORT ON SOCIAL MEDIA (Jan. 24, 2012) at 4.

In one case described in the NLRB report, the Administrative Law Judge ("ALJ") examined a company's social networking policy and found it a violation of the NLRA to outright prohibit employees from commenting on work-related matters without the permission of a company's legal department. The NLRB upheld a second provision that prohibited employees from "posting any pictures or videos of employees in uniform or employees on a job site." The ALJ reasoned that a social media employment policy forbidding any comment on work-related legal matters is overly restrictive and thus violates employees' rights to concerted activity.

In 2012, the NLRB addressed the lawfulness of employer's rules prohibiting employees from "disparaging" the employer in any media. The NLRB concluded that the employer's rule prohibiting disparaging comments was unlawful and that the collection agency violated the NLRA when it terminated the charging party for her protected concerted Facebook postings.

An Administrative Law Judge found that a "nonprofit organization unlawfully discharged five employees after they posted comments on Facebook concerning working conditions, including work load and staffing issues." The ALJ ordered that the employers, Hispanics United, reinstate the five employees and awarded the employees back pay. In contrast, the NLRB has found individual gripes that do not encourage coworkers to engage in-group action to be unprotected and not concerted activity. The *2012 NLRB Report on Social Media* found the following emerging issues in social media-related cases:

(1) Collection agency's discharge of employee for Facebook comments and for violating non-disparagement rule was unlawful. Employee

used expletives in status update expressing frustration with her supervisor. Charging party had 10 coworker friends and therefore the gripes were an exercise of NLRA, Section 8(A)(1) rights. The NLRB ruled that the employer's social media policy violated Section 7 of the NLRA because it restricted protected activities.

(2) Home improvement stores that discharged employee for Facebook comments was lawful but social media policy and no-solicitation rules were overly broad.

(D) HARASSMENT BY CO-EMPLOYEES

Title VII of the Civil Rights Act of 1964 provides that it is unlawful to discriminate against an individual with respect to the terms of employment because of sex or race. Plaintiffs filing harassment claims may have tort actions as well. Courts have determined that employees may establish a "hostile workplace" claim if: (1) the conduct in question was unwelcome, (2) the harassment was sex or race-linked, (3) the sexual or racial harassment was severe, and (4) there was a causal connection to the employer.

Employee may base a hostile workplace claim upon an employer's failure to take prompt remedial responses to complaints about Internet harassment. For example, a federal court in California found Continental Express Airlines responsible for sexual harassment in a hostile workplace claim filed by a female pilot. In *Butler v. Krebs*, 100 F. Supp. 2d 1058 (N.D. Cal. 2000), co-employees depicted a female pilot in pornographic poses on the airline's intranet. Continental Airlines was found liable under theories of a hostile work environment and for ratification of sexual harassment.

In *Espinoza v. Orange County*, 2012 WL 420149 (Cal. Ct. App. 2012), a disabled employee of the Orange County probation department won a judgment for harassment based upon the California Fair Employment and Housing Act. The action arose from a co-employees' postings on a probation blog. Espinoza has no fingers on his right hand only two small stubs due to a birth defect and was self-conscious about people seeing it and often kept his hand in his pocket. An anonymous poster, who turned out to be a co-employee, wrote, "I will give anyone 100 bucks if you get a picture of the claw." The next day the same poster again referred to the offer of $100 for a picture of "the one handed bandit." Espinoza based his complaint against the probation department on disability, retaliation, failing to prevent harassment, wrongful termination, and the tort of the intentional infliction of emotional distress. The court granted a motion for nonsuit as to the wrongful termination and intentional infliction causes of action against defendant. The appellate court upheld a verdict against Orange County and awarded the plaintiff over $820,000 because of an abusive workplace.

(E) PUBLIC EMPLOYEE & FIRST AMENDMENT

In *Mattingly v. Milligan*, 2011 WL 5184283 (E.D. Ark. 2011), the government terminated an employee for incendiary comments she posted on a Facebook update. In this public employment case, the plaintiff had a First Amendment right to express opinions on

Facebook. In public employment cases, the court applies a two-step analysis. The first step is whether the speech is classifiable as a "matter of public concern." The second step is to balance the employee's First Amendment right against the employer's rights. In *Milligan*, the court found that the employee's postings on Facebook were protected and there was no evidence that the postings disrupted the county clerk's office.

§ 7-3. Fourth Amendment & Internet Technologies

The Fourth Amendment protects a person in the governmental workplace only if she has proved a subjective as well as an objective expectation of privacy in the place searched. In *Leventhal v. Knapek*, 266 F.3d 64 (2d Cir. 2001), a Department of Transportation investigation uncovered evidence of an employee's misuse of a computer. The Second Circuit recognized that the employee had a reasonable expectation of privacy, but concluded that the investigatory search for work-related misconduct did not violate his Fourth Amendment rights because the government's legitimate purpose outweighed the employee's privacy interest. The Fourth Amendment does not apply to a search unless the governmental intrusion infringes on the plaintiff's reasonable expectation of privacy, which is the legally protectable interest.

The *Knapek* court validated the investigatory search because it was reasonable in scope and advanced the employer's legitimate objective of searching for evidence of employee misfeasance. In the United States, courts balance privacy concerns against the employer's interest in the public sector, but they do not apply this balancing test to the private sector workplace. The Fourth Amendment only applies to governmental actions by law enforcement, other public law entities, or "state action." The Fourth Amendment does not apply to a search unless the governmental intrusion infringes the plaintiff's reasonable expectation of privacy.

Law enforcement officers must obtain a warrant before installing or executing electronic surveillance or seizing people's communications unless there is a showing of exigent circumstances. The U.S. Constitution logically does not constrain foreign law enforcement officers from monitoring Internet activities. The Fourth Amendment applies to governmental actions where the intrusion infringes on the plaintiff's reasonable expectation of privacy. Courts compel the plaintiff to prove that she had a subjective as well as an objective expectation of privacy in the place searched.

In *Katz v. United States*, 389 U.S. 347 (S.Ct. 2007), federal law enforcement officers attached an electronic eavesdropping device to a telephone booth in order to listen to conversations of a suspected illegal gambler. The Court ruled in any Fourth Amendment case, the issue would be whether the defendant had a reasonable expectation of privacy. The *Katz* Court held the Fourth Amendment protected people, not places, and that the defendant in *Katz* had a reasonable expectation of privacy when he shut the door on the telephone booth. The Court rejected the government's argument that it did not violate Katz's constitutional rights since it committed no trespass in its electronic surveillance.

Whether a defendant has a constitutionally protected reasonable expectation of privacy involves two questions: (1) whether a defendant is able to establish an actual, subjective expectation of privacy with respect to the place being searched or items being seized, and (2) whether that expectation of privacy is one which society recognizes as reasonable. At present, there is no freestanding privacy right for employees working in the private sector.

(A) INTERNET-RELATED SEARCH & SEIZURES

The Fourth Amendment's requirement of probable cause for the issuance of a search warrant "safeguards an individual's interest in the privacy of his home and possessions against the unjustified intrusion of the police." *Steagald v. United States*, 451 U.S. 204 (S.Ct. 1981). The Fifth Circuit upheld the denial of a motion to suppress evidence arising out of the search of a Texas fire marshal's office computer containing images of child pornography from a newsgroup titled "alt.erotica.xxx.preteen." *Slanina v. United States*, 283 F.3d 670 (5th Cir. 2002).

Investigators uncovered child pornography on each of the defendant's hard drives, and all together, these hard drives contained thousands of files with such images. "The zip disk from Slanina's office contained more than one hundred files of child pornography." The court found Slanina exhibited a subjective expectation of privacy in images of child pornography by storing them in containers away from plain view.

To limit access to his computer files, Slanina installed passwords, thereby making it more difficult for another person to access his computer.

The court found the supervisor's search of Slanina's computer was reasonable under the standard established in *O'Connor v. Ortega*, 480 U.S. 709 (S.Ct. 1987). The supervisor who conducted the search in *Slanina* had already learned about the accessing of child pornography newsgroups, which was evidence of the employee having downloaded child pornography onto his computer.

(1) Smyth v. Pillsbury

Smyth v. Pillsbury, 914 F. Supp. 97 (E.D. Pa. 1996) was the first reported case where a U.S. federal court upheld an employer's electronic monitoring and review of an employee's e-mails and Internet usage. In *Pillsbury*, a federal court held a company's interest in preventing inappropriate e-mail activity on its own system outweighed any employee privacy interest. The company had previously assured its employees that e-mail communications could not be intercepted. Smyth, a regional operations manager, sent a combustible e-mail attacking management to his supervisor that, threatened to "kill the backstabbing bastards."

Pillsbury terminated Smyth's employment for "inappropriate and unprofessional comments over defendant's e-mail system." The *Smyth* court ruled that the employee had no expectation of privacy in online messages and, in any case, the employer's reading of these messages was not a "substantial and highly offensive" invasion of his privacy. The court reasoned that Pillsbury's right to prevent unprofessional and illegal activity outweighed any privacy interest of its employee in e-mail comments. The court ruled Smyth's termination did not violate a public policy based upon right of privacy.

(2) Garrity v. John Hancock

John Hancock terminated two middle-aged female employees for forwarding sexually explicit e-mails from Internet joke websites and from other third parties in violation of the insurer's Internet usage policy. One of their co-employees complained to management after receiving a forwarded e-mail with off-color jokes from the plaintiffs. John Hancock promptly began an investigation of the plaintiffs' e-mail folders, as well as the folders of those to whom the plaintiffs e-mailed on a regular basis. The ex-employees disputed the insurer's characterization of the e-mails in question as sexually explicit or in any way in violation of the policy language. The *Garrity* court found the plaintiffs' off color e-mail violated the insurer's e-mail policy.

The Massachusetts federal court dismissed the plaintiffs' privacy-based actions since the Hancock employees had no reasonable expectation of privacy in e-mails transmitted on their employer's computer system. To determine whether a contract is unconscionable, a court will typically examine "the commercial setting of the transaction, the use of fine print in the contract, and the use of high-pressure contracting tactics." John Hancock's policy made it clear that all information stored on its e-mail system was property owned by the insurer.

Even in the absence of a company e-mail policy, employees do not have a reasonable expectation of privacy in their work e-mail. Further, the court said the interest of the employer to take affirmative steps against harassment outweighed the plaintiffs' privacy interest. *Garrity v. John Hancock Mut. Life Ins. Co.*, 2002 WL 974676 (D. Mass. 2005). U.S. courts' property-based approach to computer systems makes it difficult for plaintiffs to prevail even where employers' are engaging in secret e-mail surveillance.

(B) SEARCH AND SEIZURE OF TEXT MESSAGES[2]

(1) The Katz Balancing Test

The *sine qua non* of a Fourth Amendment inquiry is "whether the search or seizure was reasonable under the totality of the circumstances." *State v. Patino, State v. Patino*, 2012 R.I. Super. LEXIS 139 (R.I. Super. September 4, 2012) at *84. An expectation of privacy is determined by a two-fold test: (1) whether a person has a subjective expectation of privacy and (2) whether society recognizes that expectation as reasonable. When an individual has a legally recognized expectation of privacy, and was subject to a government search and/or seizure without a warrant or an exception to the warrant requirement, then the resulting evidence may be suppressed from trial under the exclusionary rule.

---

[2] This practice pointer was co-authored with Carl Alexander Chiulli, Suffolk University Law School, 2013.

(2) Fourth Amendment Stretched

In *City of Ontario v. Quon*, 130 S. Ct. 2619 (S.Ct. 2010), the United States Supreme Court recognized that in deciding questions of reasonableness, courts should consider "rapid changes in the dynamics of communication and information transmission. . . not just [in] the technology itself but in what society accepts as proper behavior." The issue before the Supreme Court in *Quon* was "whether text messages should be afforded Fourth Amendment privacy protection." In *State v. Smith*, 920 N.E.2d 949 (Ohio 2009), the Ohio Supreme Court found that the data contained within a cell phone, *i.e.* text messages, was protectable under the Fourth Amendment because a cell phone is not a container and therefore cannot be searched incident to arrest.

In *State v. Clampitt*, 364 S.W.3d 605 (Mo. App. Ct. 2012), a Missouri Appellate Court found that text messages stored on the defendant's phone, sent and received, were entitled to Fourth Amendment protection because text messages are a substitute for telephone calls and letters and worthy of the same protections. In *State v. Hinton*, 2012 WL 2401673 (Wash. App Div. 2012), a Washington Appellate Court found that the Fourth Amendment protects text messages but only in conjunction with cell phones. Similarly, in *United States v. Finley*, 477 F.3d 250 (5th Cir. 2007), the Fifth Circuit held that cell phones and text messages should be treated the same for purposes of analyzing standing and protection under the Fourth Amendment.

In reaching these holdings, the presiding courts were presented with a number of interconnected sub-issues. One of the foremost issues that courts have considered is whether text messages are a separate and distinct entity from a cellular phone. To make this decision courts must determine whether a cell phone is a container under its traditional legal definition. This determination is important because if a cell phone is a container, then its text messages are, logically, its contents. The Fourth Amendment law exclusionary rule exception for searching containers would then extend to cell phones.

A second issue that courts have weighed is the rigidity with which to apply the third-party doctrine. The third party doctrine states that an individual's expectation of privacy for information dissipates upon that information being voluntarily exposed or communicated to a third party. Courts taking a formalistic perspective on the third-party doctrine vitiate any expectation of privacy for text messages because electronic communications necessarily pass through a service provider's network during their transmission. Thus, the third-party doctrine is always activated for electronic communications if it is applied absolutely.

Another critical issue before courts is the proper use of analogies during the adjudication process. Courts must decide how similar older communication forms to new venues such as text messaging. Difficulties arise because analogies to letters, emails, and phone conversations are frequently imperfect due to the evolutionary nature of technology.

(3) State v. Patino

In *State v. Patino* 2012 R.I. Super. LEXIS 139 (R.I. Super. September 4, 2012) a Rhode Island trial court explored the search and seizure of text messages and its interconnected sub-issues in detail. The state indicted Michael Patino for the murder of his girlfriend's six-year-old son based upon a series of text messages that he exchanged with the mother of the child. Patino, in a motion to suppress, contended that the Cranston, Rhode Island police department violated his Fourth Amendment rights when they searched his girlfriend's cell phone and obtained his text messages without a warrant. Applying the *Katz* test, the court first determined that Patino had the necessary standing to challenge the constitutionality of the Cranston, Rhode Island Police Department's search and seizure of the defendant's text messages from his girlfriend's cellular phone.

To reach this holding, the court dealt with a number of factors including (1) whether cell phones are containers with text messages as their contents, (2) the appropriate application of the third-party doctrine to electronic communications, and (3) how text messages are analogous to traditional forms of communication. The court held that the Cranston Police Department's search of the girlfriend's cell phone violated the defendant's Fourth Amendment rights because it occurred without a warrant and outside of any established exception to the warrant requirement. Next, the court ruled that the text messages at issue, as well as a large amount of connected evidence, must be suppressed from Patino's murder trial as fruit of the poisonous tree.

(a) Cellular Phones as Containers

The *Patino* court classified the cell phone as an access point, rather than as a container, reasoning:

> A cell phone is the device by which text messages are sent, received, and stored. It is not, on accord of its physical dimensions or functionality, a closed container. In addition, text messages are not a tangible object that fit within a cell phone. They are, in fact, information born in non-tangible digital form. In this Court's view, therefore, a cell phone is better thought of not as a container but as an "access point" to potentially boundless amounts of digital information.

This is significant because containers, as defined by the law in *New York v. Belton*, 453 U.S. 454 (S.Ct. 1981), may be searched without a warrant pursuant to various well-established exceptions. In reaching this holding, the court indicated that the similarities between a cell phone and a "container" were too tenuous to apply the associated body of law. The court, in practical effect, precluded Rhode Island law enforcement from justifying the search and seizure of text message through the multiple warrantless exceptions recognized for physical containers.

(b) Third Parties' Text Messaging

The *Patino* court also weighed in on how the third-party doctrine applies to text messages. In the court's view, the third-party doctrine does not destroy an expectation of privacy in text messages because the doctrine is "ill-suited for contemporary forms of communication and thus should not wholly defeat an individual's expectation of privacy in the contents of his or her text messages." The court determined that "in an era before the advent of cell phones, that the exchange of content of the text messages ... would never have been public." The court held that this "theory of assumption of risk does not match today's realities of electronic communications."

(c) Imperfect Analogies for Text Messaging

The *Patino* court took great care to elaborate on the differences between text messages, oral communications, and letters. These are the forms of communications to which text messages have been most often compared. Text messages, the court held, "are not letters, email, or even an oral communication alone—they are a technological and functional hybrid." Therefore, "any consideration of people's subjective expectation of privacy in their text messages must reflect this reality."

§ 7-4. Federal Statutes Governing Internet Privacy

(A) PRIVACY ACT OF 1974

Congress enacted the U.S. Privacy Act of 1974 to prevent the federal government from collecting unnecessary private information about individuals. Enacted in the aftermath of the Watergate scandal, this statute was designed to curb U.S. governmental abuses as opposed to those of private companies. The federal statute specified the following fair information policies:

- There must be no personal data record-keeping systems whose very existence is secret;

- There must be a way for an individual to find out what information is in his or her file and how the information is being used;

- There must be a way for an individual to correct information in his or her records;

- Any organization creating, maintaining, using, or disseminating records of personally identifiable information must assure the reliability of the data for its intended use and must take precautions to prevent misuse; and

- There must be a way for an individual to prevent personal information obtained for one purpose from being used for another purpose without his or her consent.

CENTER FOR DEMOCRACY & TECHNOLOGY, UPDATING THE PRIVACY ACT OF 1974 (2009).

In *FAA v. Cooper*, 132 S. Ct. 1441 (S.Ct. 2012), the U.S. Supreme Court held that the Privacy Act does not authorize damages for mental or emotional distress, and therefore does not waive the government's sovereign immunity from liability for such harms. In *Cooper*, the Department of Transportation, and the SSA, in turn, provided the

DOT with a spreadsheet containing investigations of a pilot for not disclosing his HIV status to the FAA. The FAA revoked the pilot's certificate and the U.S. Department of Justice indicted him for making false statements to a government agency. Cooper pleaded guilty and was fined and sentenced to probation. He then filed suit, alleging that the FAA, DOT, and SSA violated the Privacy Act of 1974, which contains a detailed set of requirements for the management of federal records. The Court's holding that plaintiffs could not pursue non-pecuniary damages seemingly gives the U.S. Government a shield against most Internet-related claims, since the invasion of privacy action is seldom about money and largely about emotional injuries.

(B) HIPAA'S ONLINE PRIVACY RULES

Congress enacted The Health Insurance Portability & Accountability Act of 1996 ("HIPAA") to allay the increasing public concern about the threat to privacy posed by interconnected electronic information systems. HIPAA applies to information created or maintained by health care providers who engage in certain electronic transactions, health plans, and health care clearinghouses. HIPAA's goals include: (1) protecting and enhancing the rights of consumers by providing them access to their health information and controlling the inappropriate use of that information, (2) improving the quality of health care in the U.S. by restoring trust in the health care system among consumers, health care professionals, and the multitude of organizations and persons committed to the delivery of care, and (3) improving the efficiency and effectiveness of health care delivery by creating a national framework for health privacy protection building on efforts by states, health systems, and individual organization and persons. HIPPA prohibits a person from knowingly using your unique health identifier or wrongfully obtaining "individually identifiable health information relating to individual or disclosing individually identifiable health information to another person."

Online health providers will need to comply with information security requirements to comply with HIPAA. Section 501 of HIPAA requires each institution to protect the security and confidentiality of personal information. Fines for violating HIPAA range from $25,000 for multiple violations of the same standard in a calendar year up to $250,000. The criminal penalty for egregious violations of HIPPA is up to 10 years in prison.

(C) GRAMM-LEACH-BLILEY ACT

President Clinton signed the Gramm-Leach-Bliley Act ("GLBA") on November 12, 1999. Title V, Subtitle A of the GLBA on the "Disclosure of Nonpublic Personal Information" applies to many Internet transactions. Congress' intent in enacting the GLBA was to provide consumers with access and control over private financial information maintained by banks and other institutions along with the opportunity to correct any errors. The GLBA gives the Federal Trade Commission the power to enforce the financial privacy rules. This federal statute defines financial institutions as "any institution the business of which is engaging in financial activities as described in the Bank Holding Company Act of

1956." 12 U.S.C. § 1843(K). If a company is "significantly engaged" in providing financial products or services to consumers, it must comply with the privacy provisions of Title V, Subtitle A of the GLBA. 15 U.S.C. §§ 6801, 6809.

The GLBA requires financial institutions to inform their customers about the institution's privacy policies and practices with respect to information shared with both affiliated and non-affiliated third parties. The GLBA prohibits financial institutions from disclosing nonpublic personal information about customers to nonaffiliated third parties without first advising customers of the possibility of disclosure. Financial institutions must give customers an "opt out" procedure if they do not wish their financial information to be shared with third parties.

SEC's Regulation S-P ("S-P") implements the privacy rules of the GLBA. Section 504 requires the SEC and other federal agencies to adopt rules that implement notice requirements and restrictions on sharing a consumer's information. S-P requires brokers, dealers, investment companies, and investment advisers to provide notice of their privacy policy and to protect the privacy of customer information. Financial institutions must provide individuals with statutorily prescribed disclosures in initial as well as annual privacy notices. The GLBA regulation also specifies the affiliated and nonaffiliated third parties to which they may disclose personal information. Accordingly, financial institutions were required to post privacy notices and institute safeguards by July 1, 2001. S-P dictates that online companies provide customers with a clear and conspicuous notice of their privacy policies and practices. The online company needs to provide annual notices to its customers, post its privacy notice on its website, and offer its customers the option of opting out of disclosures.

§ 7-5. State Regulation of Online Privacy

"The digitization of personal information, along with increased internet usage, has dramatically increased the risks and frequency of identity theft." *Statement of the Federal Trade Commission on Identity Theft Before the Subcomm. on Tech., Terrorism and Gov't Infor.*, 106th Cong. (2000) (statement of Jodie Bernstein, Director of Consumer Protection, Federal Trade Commission).

California's 2004 online privacy statute applies to any operator of a website or online service collecting personally identifiable information about individual California residents, even if there has no physical presence in that state. An online company will be in violation of California law unless it "conspicuously posts its privacy policy on its website." Cal. Bus. & Prof. §§ 22575, 22579. Online companies have thirty days after being notified of noncompliance to post their online privacy policies.

California mandates every online company's policy must: (1) complete an audit of each category of personally identifiable information collected or shared with third parties or other entities on the Internet about website visitors, (2) give consumers notice if there is a process for reviewing and revising their personally identifiable information, and (3) describe the process by which the operator notifies consumers as to any material change in their privacy policy.

The California statute gives online companies alternative ways of complying with the statutory requirement that their online privacy policy must be conspicuously posted. The company may post its privacy policy on its homepage. Alternatively, a website may post an icon that hyperlinks to a web page displaying the actual privacy policy. This icon must be on the homepage or "the first significant page after entering the website, and if the icon contains the word privacy." A company must also use a color that contrasts with the background color of the web page or is otherwise distinguishable. Finally, a website operator may include a hyperlink to a web page on which the actual privacy policy is posted if the hyperlink is located on the website's homepage. The text link must include the word "privacy" and be written in capital letters equal to or greater in size than the surrounding text. The California online privacy statute determines conspicuousness by the standard of the reasonable person.

§ 7-6. Third Party Disclosure of Private Information

In *Bartnicki v. Vopper*, 532 U.S. 514 (S.Ct. 2001), the U.S. Supreme Court held that a journalist had an absolute First Amendment privilege to broadcast a private recording that was surreptitiously intercepted by an unknown person. Bartnicki was the teacher's union's chief negotiator in a contentious labor dispute with a high school. A third party intercepted his cell phone conversation with the union president in which the union president threatened to "blow off their front porches." A secretly taped copy of this cell phone statement was left in the journalist's mailbox by an unknown third party. The Court held the journalist was not liable for violation of the Electronic Communications Privacy Act ("ECPA") for broadcasting the illegally taped conversation. The Court commented, "The normal method of deterring unlawful conduct is to impose an appropriate punishment on the person who engages in it."

The *Bartnicki* Court noted it would be unusual to punish a law-abiding journalist for the criminal act of an anonymous third party interceptor. The U.S. Supreme Court in *Bartnicki* held the First Amendment prohibited imposition of civil liability for the journalist's disclosure of an illegally intercepted cell-phone call. This case "has significant implications for Internet law because of the vast opportunities for republication of information enabled by the Internet." MARK LEMLEY, ET. AL. SOFTWARE AND INTERNET LAW 955 (3rd ed. 2006). Notably, Chief Justice William Rehnquist commented, "We are placed in the uncomfortable position of not knowing who might have access to our personal and business e-mails, our medical and financial records, or our cordless and cellular telephone conversations."

§ 7-7. Consumer Privacy Bill of Rights

In February of 2012, the Obama Administration presented a Consumer Privacy Bill of Rights to extend consumer rights to commercial sectors that are not subject to other federal data privacy laws. The Consumer Bill of Rights incorporated privacy principles formulated by The Organization for

Economic Cooperation and Development ("OECD"), which were incorporated into the Directive on Data Protection that went into effect in October 1998 in the European Union. Online activities are increasingly likely to be subject to European privacy regulations in the interconnected world of the Internet. The proposed Consumer Privacy Bill of Rights, drawn in large part, from OECD principles, states:

Individual Control: Consumers have a right to exercise control over what personal data companies collect from them and how they use it.

Transparency: Consumers have a right to easily understandable and accessible information about privacy and security practices.

Respect for Context: Consumers have a right to expect that companies will collect, use, and disclose personal data in ways that are consistent with the context in which consumers provide the data.

Security: Consumers have a right to secure and responsible handling of personal data.

Access and Accuracy: Consumers have a right to access and correct personal data in usable formats, in a manner that is appropriate to the sensitivity of the data and the risk of adverse consequences to consumers if the data is inaccurate.

Focused Collection: Consumers have a right to reasonable limits on the personal data that companies collect and retain.

Accountability: Consumers have a right to have personal data handled by companies with appropriate measures in place to assure they adhere to the Consumer Privacy Bill of Rights.

THE WHITE HOUSE, CONSUMER DATA PRIVACY IN A NETWORKED WORLD (2012).

The Obama Administration seeks to improve global interoperability between the U.S. consumer data privacy framework and other countries' frameworks, through mutual recognition, the development of codes of conduct through multi-stakeholder processes, and enforcement cooperation. If Congress enacts this proposed statute, it will help to harmonize U.S. privacy law with the Eurozone's Data Protection Directive.

§ 7-8. State Security Breach Notification

Forty-six states, the District of Columbia, Guam, Puerto Rico and the Virgin Islands have enacted legislation requiring notification of security breaches involving personal information. Data breach notification statutes require entities that maintain personally identifiable information to give notice if there is a breach in the security of the information. In 2013, California's state senate approved a proposal to extend their data protection statute to address "email addresses, passwords, user names, and security questions and answers for online accounts." Data Breaches: California Data Breach Notice Law Would Apply to User Names, Passwords, BLOOMBERG BNA, ELECTRONIC COMMERCE & LAW REPORT (May 22, 2013).

Massachusetts, for example, defines breach of security" as "the unauthorized acquisition or unauthorized use of unencrypted data or, encrypted electronic data and the confidential process or key that is capable of compromising the security, confidentiality, or integrity of personal information, maintained by a person or agency that creates a substantial risk of identity theft or fraud against a resident of the commonwealth." Mass. Gen. Laws § 93H-1 et seq. Many states limit the data breach notification requirement to unencrypted data. Massachusetts, like other states, imposes civil penalties for failing to give consumers notice of security breaches. Data breaches for e-commerce companies, for example, will rarely affect citizens in a single state. Counsel must ensure that their client complies with the data breach statutes for all states.

§ 7-9. Global Privacy Issues

Cross-border flows of personal data are necessary for the expansion of E-Commerce but new dangers arise when personal data is transferred. Counsel for 24/7 companies must oversee what personally identifiable information is collected and how long such data is kept. If a website business processes information, the European Union Directive on Data Protection, which became effective on October 25, 1998, will classify it as a service provider.

(A) DATA PROTECTION DIRECTIVE

The Council of Europe adopted the European Convention on Human Rights ("ECHR") in 1950. Article 8 of the ECHR treats the right to respect for an individual's private and family life, home, and correspondence as a basic right. The Data Protection Directive of October 1995 commands any EU company to comply with specific rules for processing and transferring European consumer data. Each EU Member State has enacted legislation fulfilling the legal grounds defined in the Directive: consent, contract, legal obligation, vital interest of the data subject, and the balance between the legitimate interests of the people controlling the data versus the people on whom data is held (i.e., data subjects). Article 8 requires providers to implement reasonable security.

The Data Protection Directive gives data subjects control over the collection, transmission, and use of personal information. The Directive gives data subjects the right to be notified of all uses and disclosures about how their personal data is collected and processed. Directive 95/46/EC. An Internet business must procure explicit consent for the collection of personal data concerning race, ethnicity, or political opinions. Data handlers are required to protect personal information with adequate security. Data subjects have the right to get copies of information collected as well as the right to correct or delete personal data. Article 7 requires the provider to obtain consent from the data subject before entering in to the contract. Data handlers may not transfer data to other countries without "adequate level of protection" under Article 25.

(B) U.S. SAFE HARBOR

The European Community achieved greater harmonization of data protection when the EC approved the Data Protection Directive, which expects each of the twenty-seven Member States to enact national legislation protecting "the fundamental rights and freedoms of natural persons, and in particular their right to privacy with respect to the processing of personal data." The EC negotiated a safe harbor with the United States' Department of Commerce that obliges companies to certify their compliance with the Data Protection Directive. Companies may join a self-regulatory privacy program by developing their own self-regulatory privacy policies.

(C) GENERAL DATA PROTECTION REGULATION

On January 1, 2012, the EC proposed the *Regulation on the Protection of Individuals with Regard to the Processing of Personal Data and on the Free Movement of Such Data* ("General Data Protection Regulation"). The General Proposed Data Protection Regulation will displace the Data Protection Directives. (Directive 95/46/EC). The proposed Regulation offers the EU countries greater harmonization than directives that require national legislation to implement them.

(1) Central Provisions

The Data Protection Regulation, which will be directly applicable to all of the Member States, was proposed to reduce legal fragmentation by developing a common core of rules protecting privacy. Article 1 of the proposed regulation sets out the same objectives as Directive 95/46/EC. The key provisions of the General Data Protection Regulation are: (1) an expanded jurisdictional reach applied to non-European companies that process the data of European consumers, (2) the duty to notify consumers of a data breach within 24 hours, (3) require companies to obtain a "specific, informed and explicit" consent before collecting personal data (opt-in provision), and (4) a company's duty to erase personal data upon demand (right to be forgotten). Jeffrey M. Goetz, *A New World of EU Protection*, MARTINDALE.COM (Feb. 2012).

Under the EU data protection proposal, consumers have a right of access, right to be forgotten and erasure, right to object to inaccurate information, and fortified rights of notice. "The legal regime applicable to profiling is tightened, and stricter rules will apply. Profiling will be allowed only in limited situations, in particular: (i) with the individuals' consent (which has to be freely given, specific, informed, and explicit); (ii) when profiling is explicitly permitted by legislation; or (iii) when profiling is "necessary" for entering into or the performance of a contract, subject to certain restrictions." Cédric Burton, et. al. *The Proposed EU Data Protection Regulation One Year Later: The Albrecht Report,* ELECTRONIC COMMERCE & LAW REPORT (Jan. 18, 2013). The chief provisions of the General Data Protection are:

- A single set of rules on data protection, valid across the EU. Unnecessary administrative requirements, such as notification requirements for companies, will be removed. This will save businesses around €2.3 billion a year.

- Instead of the current obligation of all companies to notify all data protection activities to data protection supervisors—a requirement that has led to unnecessary paperwork and costs businesses €130 million per year, the Regulation provides for increased responsibility and accountability for those processing personal data.

- For example, companies and organizations must notify the national supervisory authority of serious data breaches as soon as possible (if feasible within 24 hours).

- Organizations will only have to deal with a single national data protection authority in the EU country where they have their main establishment. Likewise, people can refer to the data protection authority in their country, even when a company based outside the EU processes their data. Wherever consent is required for data to be processed, it is clarified that it has to be given explicitly, rather than assumed.

- People will have easier access to their own data and be able to transfer personal data from one service provider to another more easily (right to data portability). This will improve competition among services.

- A "right to be forgotten" will help people better manage data protection risks online: people will be able to delete their data if there are no legitimate grounds for retaining it.

- EU rules must apply if personal data is handled abroad by companies that are active in the EU market and offer their services to EU citizens.

- Independent national data protection authorities will be strengthened so they can better enforce the EU rules at home. They will be empowered to fine companies that violate EU data protection rules. This can lead to penalties of up to €1 million or up to 2% of the global annual turnover of a company.

- A new Directive will apply general data protection principles and rules for police and judicial cooperation in criminal matters. The rules will apply to both domestic and cross-border transfers of data.

The proposed General Data Protection Regulation imports principles for processing personal data drawn from its predecessor, the Data Protection Directive, but also strengthens protections. Article 3 defines key concepts such as data subject, personal data, processing, controller, processor, and sets forth the following principles for processing personal data:

(1) This Regulation applies to the processing of personal data in the context of the activities of an establishment of a controller or a processor in the Union.

(2) This Regulation applies to the processing of personal data of data subjects residing in the

Union by a controller not established in the Union, where the processing activities are related to:

(A) the offering of goods or services to such data subjects in the Union; or

(B) the monitoring of their behavior.

(3) This Regulation applies to the processing of personal data by a controller not established in the Union, but in a place where the national law of a Member State applies by virtue of public international law. EU Parliament and Council, *Proposed General Data Protection Directive* (2012).

(2) Opt-in Rules for Cookies

Article 3(2) asserts that non-Eurozone Internet sellers must comply with the Regulation if they target consumers within the EU or monitor their behavior. This provision would make Internet sellers liable for dropping cookies without the consent of EU consumers. Article 5 sets out the principles relating to personal data processing. Personal data must be:

(A) processed lawfully, fairly and in a transparent manner in relation to the data subject;

(B) collected for specified, explicit and legitimate purposes and not further processed in a way incompatible with those purposes;

(C) adequate, relevant, and limited to the minimum necessary in relation to the purposes for which they are processed; they shall only be processed if, and as long as, the purposes could not be fulfilled by processing information that does not involve personal data;

(D) accurate and kept up to date; every reasonable step must be taken to ensure that personal data that are inaccurate, having regard to the purposes for which they are processed, are erased or rectified without delay;

(E) kept in a form which permits identification of data subjects for no longer than is necessary for the purposes for which the personal data are processed; personal data may be stored for longer periods insofar as the data will be processed solely for historical, statistical or scientific research purposes in accordance with the rules and conditions of Article 83 and if a periodic review is carried out to assess the necessity to continue the storage;

(F) processed under the responsibility and liability of the controller, who shall ensure and demonstrate for each processing operation the compliance with the provisions of this Regulation.

(3) Data Minimization

The Regulation adopts a new transparency principle as well as a principle of data minimization. Comprehensive responsibility and liability of the controller was also established. Article 6 sets out the basic principle that consent is the *sine qua non* of fair data collection. Data processing is limited to specified purposes. Article 7 of the Regulation sets out the importance of valid consent as a legal predicate ground for lawful processing of subject data. Subjects have the right to withdraw consent at any time.

Article 8 is a special provision for the processing of personal data of children in relation to services offered directly to them. Article 9 prohibits the processing or revealing of data on "race or ethnic origin, political opinions, religion or beliefs, trade-union membership, and the processing of genetic data or data concerning health or sex life or criminal convictions or related security measures." The Regulation recognizes exceptions including the consent of the subject and processing to protect the interests of the subject.

(4) Duties of Controllers

Article 4(5) defines controllers as those natural persons or others who control the processing of data. The new Regulation requires controllers to have transparent, and easy to understand policies as well as mechanisms for data subjects to exercise their rights, which are spelled out in Articles 11 and 12. Article 11 introduces the obligation on controllers to provide transparent and easily accessible and understandable information. Article 12 requires the controller to provide procedures and mechanisms for exercising the data subject's rights including means for electronic requests, respond to the data subject's request within a defined deadline, and provide explanations for any refusal to act on a data subject's request. Article 15 provides the data subject with the right of access to their personal data and the right to be informed of their right to rectification and to erasure, with a mechanism for complaint.

(5) The Right to Be Forgotten

Under the proposed Data Protection Regulation, European citizens will have the right to expunge or erase personal data and "abstention from further dissemination" under Article 17. It further elaborates and specifies the "right of erasure ... including the obligation of the controller which has made the personal data public to inform third parties on the data subject's request to erase any links to, or copy or replication of that personal data." EU Commission, Detailed Explanation of the Data Protection] Proposal (2012) The right to be forgotten "should also be extended in such a way that a controller who has made the personal data public should be obliged to inform third parties which are processing such data that a data subject requests them to erase any links to, or copies or replications of that personal data." EU Commission, Explanatory Memorandum at 54.

The Data Protection Regulation establishes a general standard of reasonableness for controllers to employ technical measures, in relation to data for the publication of which the controller is responsible. The regulation requires controllers to give notice to third parties that a data subject has revoked consent for data that the subject demands be forgotten. Subjects should have the fundamental right that their personal data be erased and no longer processed. The right to be forgotten is "relevant, when the data subject has given their consent as a child, when not being fully aware of the risks involved by the processing, and later wants to remove such personal data especially on the Internet." Article 17(1) of the EC's new privacy regulation states:

> The data subject shall have the right to obtain from the controller the erasure of personal data relating to them and the abstention from further dissemination of such data, especially in relation to personal data, which are made available by the data subject while he or she was a child, where one of the following grounds applies:
>
> (A) the data are no longer necessary in relation to the purposes for which they were collected or otherwise processed;
>
> (B) the data subject withdraws consent on which the processing is based according to point (A) of Article 6(1), or when the storage period consented to has expired, and where there is no other legal ground for the processing of the data;
>
> (C) the data subject objects to the processing of personal data pursuant to Article 19;
>
> (D) the processing of the data does not comply with this Regulation for other reasons.

In addition, the controller has a duty to inform third parties processing data that it is subject to erasure. The proposed directive requires the controller to:

> take all reasonable steps, including technical measures, in relation to data for the publication of which the controller is responsible, to inform third parties which are processing such data, that a data subject requests them to erase any

links to, or copy or replication of that personal data. Where the controller has authorized a third party publication of personal data, the controller shall be considered responsible for that publication.

The right to be forgotten, as conceptualized by the EC, applies to "every photo, status update, and tweet," which "could precipitate a dramatic clash between European and American conceptions of the proper balance between privacy and free speech." Jeffrey Rosen, *Right to Be Forgotten*, 64 STAN. L. REV. ONLINE 88 (2012). Data providers face ruinous monetary sanctions for any data controller that does not comply with the right to be forgotten or to erasure'—a fine up to 1,000,000 Euros or up to two percent of Facebook's annual worldwide income. This "right to be forgotten" provision will be difficult to implement because of Internet archiving that captures a past Internet site. The beta version of the Wayback Machine enables browsing through over 150 billion web pages archived from 1996 to within a few months of 2012. Social media such as Facebook or Twitter and search engines such as Google "need to demonstrate that they are taking reasonable steps to delete data permanently from the internet in accordance with the 'right to be forgotten.'" Ali Qassim, *Businesses Must Show 'Reasonable Steps,' to Delete Data*, ELECTRONIC COMMERCE & LAW REPORT (Sept. 18, 2012).

(6) Profiling & Aggregating Data

Article 19 provides for the data subject's rights to object to the use of their data for direct marketing purposes. Article 20 concerns the data subject's right not to be subject to a measure based on profiling. Articles 31 and 32 introduce an obligation to notify the data subject of personal data breaches, building on the personal data breach notification in article 4(3) of the E-Privacy Directive 2002/58/EC. Article 33 introduces the obligation of controllers and processors to carry out a data protection assessment prior to risky processing operations. This establishes a negligence-like standard in determining the radius of the risk. The EC's reform of the 1995 EU data protection is designed to update and modernize the law to reflect the impact of the Internet.

(D) PRIVACY AND ELECTRONIC COMMUNICATIONS

Europe follows an "opt-in" approach to cookies, versus the U.S. approach, which is "opt-out." The Privacy and Electronic Communications Regulation (2011) implements a new provision that requires users to give consent before dropping a cookie. Osborne Clark, *New ePrivacy Regulations in Force* (June 17, 2011). "Under Regulation 6 of the 2003 Regulations, users of cookies were allowed to deploy them provided that those whose devices they were being dropped on were given clear and comprehensive information about the cookies and were given the opportunity to refuse their having access to the device or store information on it." Stephen Groom, *New E-Privacy Rules in Force* (Sept. 2012).

In the twenty-seven countries of the European Union, cookies cannot be used without a user's permission except for the current session (session cookies.) For persistent cookies (beyond the current session), companies must seek explicit permission (opt-in.) EU COMMISSION, COOKIES, INTERNET PROVIDERS GUIDE, THE EU INTERNET HANDBOOK (2012). The E-Privacy Directive, effective May 26, 2012, requires websites disclose that they use cookies to track users and requires user's consent before dropping them. A U.S. company targeting European consumers need to comply with the EU Directive by May 26, 2012, which is the end of the one-year grace period.

(E) NATIONAL DIFFERENCES

In the U.S., Section 230 immunizes websites for postings by third parties even if they invade the privacy of users. In the U.S., no court has ordered a website to remove third party content that invades privacy or is otherwise tortious. In contrast, in *Lefebure v. Lacambre,* Ref. 55181/98, No. 1/JP (Tribunal de Grande Instance de Paris, 1998), a French court found an ISP liable for publishing erotic images of the plaintiff on its Web site. "Under French law, an Internet Service Provider is responsible for the morality of the content distributed via the client-operated Web sites it hosts, and may be liable for violations of privacy." The French plaintiff contended that the ISP violated her privacy and damaged her professional reputation by allowing a subscriber to publish nude photographs of her on a website. The French court ordered the offending website be shut down under the threat of a fine of 100,000 francs per day.

CHAPTER 8
INTERNET-RELATED CRIMES

§ 8-1. Overview of Cybercrimes

A time-traveler could be an eyewitness to the early 1990s, when Internet-related crimes were first conceived. In 1991, a federal court mentioned the term "Internet" for the first time in a decision upholding the conviction of the creator of an Internet worm that caused interconnected university computers to crash. *U.S. v. Morris*, 928 F.2d 504 (2d Cir. 1991). The first criminal conviction under the federal Electronic Communications Privacy Act did not occur until 1990 (*U.S. v. Riggs*, 739 F. Supp. 414 (N.D. Ill. 1990)).

In the new millennium, cybercrime encompasses violations of criminal law perpetrated online or using the Internet as an instrumentality. Internet crime respects no national borders and is often difficult to detect because although online criminals sometimes leave digital footprints, there is no traditional crime scene. Internet crimes, unlike traditional crimes, do not involve face-to-face criminality, although traditional crimes may be enabled by careless behavior in cyberspace. The Internet has lowered the barrier of perpetuating bricks and mortar crimes because victim's personal information is posted on websites. For example, the BBC reported that an Australian teenager posted a picture of a massive cache of cash that she was helping to count. Within hours, masked men appeared at the door and demanded the money at gunpoint.

The Internet has also created new categories of crime such as virtual trespass, identity theft, online stalking, hacking into websites, and the misappropriation of intangible data. Cybercriminals, for example, maintain websites where one can buy names, addresses, and Social Security or credit card numbers to be used in financial crimes. Cybercrimes often occur across borders creating difficult problems of detection. For causes of action based upon privacy violations or espionage, there may be little by way of provable damages.

This chapter investigates the evolving law of cybercrimes, including computer hacking, viruses, economic espionage, trade secret misappropriation, intellectual property theft, and cyber terrorism. An examination of the leading U.S. federal computer statutes will reveal the shortcomings of the criminal law in constraining cybercriminals. The second part of this chapter examines the rapidly evolving duty to implement reasonable security against cybercriminals.

(A) OVERVIEW OF COMPUTER CRIMES

(1) What Computer Crime Includes

The first computer crime statutes were enacted in the 1980s at both the U.S. state and federal level. Orin Kerr divides computer crime into two categories: computer misuse crimes and traditional crimes. ORIN S. KERR, COMPUTER CRIME LAW 1 (2d. ed. 2009). Computer misuse is a relatively new category of computer crime, involving deliberate interference with the functioning of the computer. Traditional computer crimes, which use the computer to facilitate long-established crimes such as child pornography, trade secret misappropriation, and stalking, take on new forms in the Internet age. For example, online stalking does not fit neatly into the traditional tort of assault because it lacks the element of imminence except perhaps in the case of a live chat. Orin Kerr identifies three major legal controversies in computer crime: (1) Fourth Amendment search and seizure (procedural computer crime law), (2) Statutory Privacy Law, which includes the Electronic Communications Privacy Act ("ECPA" or federal wiretap act) and the Stored Communications Act ("SCA"), and (3) Disputes where the victim and the defendant are in different jurisdictions. Questions regarding cross border enforcement of state criminal statutes often arise in the field of cybercrime.

(2) The Nature of Computer Crime

Computer crimes are often more difficult to detect and resolve than crime in the streets. Most cybercriminals are not physically present at the crime scene. The Internet enables anonymous communication, which are difficult to trace because of false e-mail headers and anonymous re-mailers. Relational crimes are easier to prosecute in the physical world because police can focus on multiple physical clues and eliminate suspects who were not in the area when the crime was committed. Internet crimes may involve creating small economic losses for many consumers, making it unlikely that any one victim will report it or file a claim. Victims may be unaware that their information or identity has been stolen until long after the crime has been completed.

§ 8-2. Computer Fraud and Abuse Act

(A) CRIMINAL LAW PROVISIONS

The Computer Fraud and Abuse Act ("CFAA") is a criminal anti-hacking statute designed to prohibit unauthorized access to electronic data. The CFAA prohibits unauthorized access to a computer and thus is applicable in most computer hacking scenarios. The CFAA makes it a crime to intentionally obtain information from computers without authorization. The CFAA also makes it a crime to damage a "protected computer." In addition to its criminal provisions, the CFAA enables the victims of authorized computer intrusions to file civil actions in federal court and recover damages as well as attorney's fees. The CFAA is a leading cause of action in computer-based trade secret misappropriation, a topic discussed in Chapter 12.

The enactment of CFAA illustrates the problem of legal lag as technology outpaces the criminal law. Prior to the CFAA, there was no statute addressing unauthorized computer access. The CFAA has "been invoked involving a variety of Web-based activities that the drafter did not contemplate at all." JULIE E. COHEN, CONFIGURING THE NETWORKED SELF: LAW,

CODE, AND THE PLAY OF EVERYDAY PRACTICE 159 (2012). The CFAA, for example, could not have foreseen the use of bots or automated software to extract information from websites or other online misconduct.

The CFAA creates liability for a person who: (1) intentionally accesses a computer without authorization or exceeds authorized access, and thereby obtains information from any protected computer, in violation of § 1030(A)(2)(C), (2) knowingly and with intent to defraud, accesses a protected computer without authorization, or exceeds authorized access, and by means of such conduct furthers the intended fraud and obtains anything of value, in violation of § 1030(A)(4), or (3) intentionally accesses a protected computer without authorization, and as a result of such conduct, recklessly causes damage, or causes damage and loss, in violation of § 1030(A)(5)(B)–(C).

The CFAA prohibits anyone from intentionally accessing a computer used in interstate or foreign commerce without authorization (or by exceeding authorized access) and thereby obtains access to information. 18 U.S.C. § 1030(A)(2)(C). Exceeding authorized access is defined as accessing a computer with authorization but then using such access to obtain or alter information that the computer user is not entitled to acquire or change. 18 U.S.C. § 1040(E)(6).

The CFAA refers to "exceed[ing] authorized access" and accessing a computer "without authorization" but there is some question as to whether these terms are interchangeable or have different meanings. 18 § 1030(A)(1); § 1030(A)(5)(A)(I). Prosecutors in Internet crime cases use the CFAA to punish the release of viruses, worms or malware to penetrate a computer's firewall in order to steal or destroy data. Section 1030(A) (5) criminalizes those who deliberately attack computers or infect data with harmful code. Originally, only a criminal statute, the CFAA now enables the victims of computer crimes to file civil actions against cybercriminals, provided the access is either "without authorization" or "exceeds authorized access." 18 U.S.C. § 1030(G). The civil action provision is covered later in this chapter.

Summary of Computer Fraud & Abuse Act

Type of Offense	Section in the CFAA	Initial Prison Sentence
Obtaining National Security Information	18 U.S.C. § 1030(A)(1)	10 years (rarely used)
Accessing a Computer and Obtaining Information	18 U.S.C. § 1030(A)(2)	1 or 5 years
Trespassing in a Government Computer and	18 U.S.C. § 1030(A)(3)	1 year

Obtaining Information		
Accessing a Computer and Obtaining Information (Without Authorization)	18 U.S.C. § 1030(A)(2)	1 or 5 years
Accessing a Computer to Defraud & Obtain Value	18 U.S.C. § 1030(A)(4)	5 years
Intentionally Damaging by Knowing Transmission	18 U.S.C. § 1030(A)(5)	10 years
Recklessly Damaging by Intentional Access	18 U.S.C. § 1030(A)(5)(B)	1 or 5 years
Negligently Causing Damage & Loss by Intentional Access	18 U.S.C. § 1030(A)(5)(C)	1 year
Trafficking in	18 U.S.C.	1 year

Passwords	§ 1030(A)(6)	
Extortion with Computers	18 U.S.C. § 1030(A)(7)	5 years

(1) Obtaining National Security Information

The elements of an (A)(1) criminal offense require that a defendant: (1) knowingly accessed computer without or in excess of authorization, (2) obtained national security information, (3) had reason to believe the information could injure the U.S. or benefit a foreign nation, and (4) made a willful communication, delivery, transmission (or attempt) or willfully retained the information. National security cybercrimes are rarely prosecuted; most computer crime enforcement is directed at domestic cybercriminals.

(2) Accessing Computer Without Authorization

The CFAA prohibits exceeding authorized access to a computer and obtaining information. 18 U.S.C. § 1030(A)(2) but *United States v. Drew*, 259 F.R.D. 499 (C.D. Cal. 2009) rejected the theory that "the latter two elements of the § 1030(A)(2)(C) crime [obtaining information from a protected computer] will always be met when an individual using a computer contacts or communicates with an Internet website." The CFAA prohibits exceeding authorized access to a computer and obtaining information. 18 U.S.C. § 1030(A)(2).

The Fourth Circuit in *WEC Carolina Energy Solutions LLC v. Miller*, 2012 U.S. App. LEXIS

15441 (4th Cir. 2012) held that an ex-employee who downloaded trade secrets during the course of his employment and used that information for a presentation to his new employer did not access his employer's computer without authorization. While still employed by WEC the energy company provided "him with a laptop computer and cell phone, and authorized his access to the company's intranet and computer servers." Miller had access to numerous confidential and trade secret documents stored on the company's computer servers. WEC instituted a policy to protect its trade secrets that prohibited using the information without authorization or downloading it to a personal computer. These policies did not restrict Miller's authorization to access the information.

The court ruled that the CFAA does not impose liability for a mere violation of a terms of use policy. Under the WEC court's narrow reading of the CFAA, the terms "without authorization" and "exceeds authorized access" only apply when an individual accesses a computer without permission, or obtains or alters information on a computer beyond that which he is authorized to access. The path of CFAA law suggests that employers will find it difficult to pursue civil actions against ex-employees.

In *State Analysis, Inc. v. American Financial Services Assoc.*, 621 F. Supp. 2d 309 (E.D. Va. 2009), the court considered a case where one defendant has a password to a website and shares it with a third party who did not have the password. The court found that the password sharer did not act "without authorization" even though the terms of service agreement prohibited sharing passwords. The *State Analysis* court acknowledged, however, that the third person would be without authorization if they used the shared password to access the website.

(3) Trespassing in a Government Computer

Trespassing in a government computer and obtaining information is covered by 18 U.S.C. § 1030(A)(3). Under (A)(3), the government must prove that the defendant: (1) intentionally accessed, (2) without authorization, (3) a nonpublic computer that was exclusively for the use of the U.S. Government, or was used by or affected by the use of a U.S. Government computer.

(4) Accessing to Defraud

The CFAA provides that whoever "knowingly and with intent to defraud, accesses" a computer covered by the Act "without authorization, or exceeds authorized access, and by means of such conduct furthers the intended fraud and obtains anything of value" shall be punished as provided in the Act. In an "unauthorized use" case, the CFAA requires a defendant to: (1) knowingly and (2) with intent to defraud (3) access a protected computer (4) without authorization or exceeding authorized access (5) in order to further the intended fraud and (6) the defendant obtained something of value, including use of the computer or data that exceeded $5,000 over a one-year period. 18 U.S.C. § 1030(A)(4). In *Shurgard Storage Centers, Inc. v. Safeguard Self Storage, Inc.*, 119 F. Supp. 2d 1121 (W.D. Wash.

2000), the court determined that a plaintiff need not prove common law fraud in order to have a CFFA action under 1030(A)(4). In denying the defendant's motion to dismiss *in* this civil CFAA action, the court held that the word "fraud" as used in section 1030(A)(4) simply means "wrongdoing."

(5) Damaging Computers or Data

Damaging a computer or its information is addressed by 18 U.S.C. § 1030(A)(5), which criminalizes multiple offenses. Section 1030(A)(5)(A) makes it a crime to knowingly cause transmission of a program, information, code, or command such as a computer virus that intentionally causes damage. Similarly, Section 1030(A)(5)(B) criminalizes the intentional access of a computer without authorization resulting in damage. Finally, Section 1030(A)(5)(C) makes it a crime to intentionally access a protected computer without authorization causing damage or loss.

Section 1030(A)(5)'s offenses will constitute felonies if they result in damage or loss of $5,000 during the year, or, modify medical care of a person, cause physical injury, threaten public health or safety, or damage computer systems used for justice, national defense, national security, or civil liability. Finally, it is a felony to affect ten or more protected computers during a year regardless of damages or loss. U.S. DEP'T OF JUSTICE, PROSECUTING COMPUTER CRIMES 35 (2012).

(6) Trafficking in Passwords

Section 1030(A)(6) prohibits a person from knowingly trafficking in computer passwords and similar information with intent to defraud, when the trafficking affects interstate or foreign commerce, or when the password may be used to access a computer used by or for the U.S. Government without authorization. The elements of the CFAA for trafficking in passwords include: (1) trafficking, (2) in computer password or similar information, (3) knowingly and with intent to defraud, and (4) trafficking affects interstate or foreign commerce or a computer used by or for the U.S. Government. The term "trafficking" in section 1030(A)(6) is defined by reference to the definition of the same term in 18 U.S.C. § 1029, and means "transfer, or otherwise dispose of, to another, or obtain control of with intent to transfer or dispose."

(7) Threatening to Harm a Computer

Section 1030(A)(7) addresses extortion, which prohibits threats to harm a computer or data. Prosecutors must prove that the defendant has: (1) intent to extort money or any other thing of value, (2) transmitted the threat in interstate or foreign commerce, and (3) made a threat to damage a protected computer, reveal confidential information, or demand money in connection with the extortion. Attempts and conspiracy to commit computer crimes are crimes addressed in amendments to the CFAA. Inchoate offenses such as attempt, conspiracy, and aiding and abetting are commonly covered in federal computer statutes. However, to date, federal prosecutors are unable to prosecute inchoate or attempted cybercrime.

(8) CFAA Criminal Law Featured Cases

In *United States v. Morris*, 928 F.2d 504 (2d Cir. 1991), a graduate student was convicted of accessing a federal interest computer without authorization since his worm broke into computers and exploited a "hole" or "bug" (an error) in both "SEND MAIL" an e-mail program and a "finger demon" program, a program providing information about the users of another computer.

Morris' computer replicated and reinfected Internet-linked computers exponentially, causing computers around the country to either crash or freeze in a catatonic-like state. The Second Circuit Court of Appeals upheld the CFAA conviction, finding Morris to be without authority to transmit his worm to protected computers. In *United States v. Ivanov*, 175 F. Supp. 2d 367 (D. Conn. 2001), a federal court addressed the issue of whether a defendant in a foreign country could be prosecuted for violating the CFAA.

Aleksey Vladimirovich Ivanov of Chelyabinsk, Russia, was indicted for CFAA offenses including conspiracy, extortion, and possessing illegal access devices. The indictment alleged that these crimes had been committed against the Online Information Bureau ("OIB"), whose business and infrastructure were based in Vernon, Connecticut. Ivanov filed a motion to dismiss since these computer crimes were committed in Russia.

The district court refused to dismiss the action, ruling that the detrimental effects were felt by OIB in Connecticut. Ivanov was caught in a sting when he was invited to interview for a position in a fake computer company set up by FBI agents in Seattle. He was arrested during the "job interview." The Russian hacker was convicted upon proof that he knowingly obtained, altered, or caused the transmission of information with the intent to defraud. Ivanov pleaded guilty to accessing a company's computers without authorization and was sentenced to serve 48 months and following his release, an additional period of supervised probation. In 2001, Congress amended the CFAA to encompass computers located outside the United States when it enacted the Patriot Act.

In *United States v. Drew, 259 F.R.D. 449* (C.D. Cal. 2009), a federal prosecutor charged Lauri Drew, a homemaker, with violating the CFAA by masquerading as a teenage boy, stalking a 13-year-old girl, and inducing her to commit suicide. Drew's fictitious profile violated MySpace's terms of service agreement, which prohibited users from creating fictitious accounts. Prosecutors charged Drew and unnamed co-conspirators with intentionally accessing a computer used in interstate and foreign commerce without authorization or in excess of authorized access to further the intentional infliction of emotional distress. The issue in *U.S. v. Drew* was whether Drew's intentional breach of MySpace's Terms of Service, the only basis for finding her guilty of violating the CFAA, constituted a misdemeanor crime for purposes of 18 U.S.C. § 1030(A)(2)(C).

The court held that treating a violation of a website's terms of use agreement as a statutory offense violated the U.S. constitutional doctrine of void for vagueness. Massachusetts proposed that it be a crime "to knowingly impersonate someone on a web page or blog without authorization, punishable by up to 30 days' jail time or a $500 fine for first offense; 6 months or a $1,000 fine for subsequent offenses." Mass H.B. 230. This bill was set aside for further study in April 2010, largely because of the problem of overcoming the vagueness hurdle.

In 2011, open Internet activist Aaron Swartz was charged with violating the CFAA and the ECPA, when he downloaded scores of academic journals, violating terms of service. In January of 2013, Swartz committed suicide and many argue that his death was causally connected to an overzealous prosecution. Members of Congress have cosponsored legislation called "Aaron's Law" to amend the CFAA so that terms of service breaches are excluded from the sphere of the statute.

(B) CFAA'S CIVIL LIABILITY

The CFAA extends a private cause of action to a victim who suffers "loss" because of a violation of the Act's prohibitions. The CFAA allows for private right of action if the violation caused:

(I) loss to one or more persons during any [one]-year period (and, for purposes of an investigation, prosecution, or other proceeding brought by the

United States only, loss resulting from conduct affecting one or more other protected computers) aggregating at least $5,000 in value;

(II) the modification or impairment, or potential modification or impairment, of the medical examination, diagnosis, treatment, or care of [one] or more individuals;

(III) physical injury to any person;

(IV) a threat to public health or safety; [or]

(V) damage affecting a computer used by or for an entity of the United States Government in furtherance of the administration of justice, national defense, or national security . . . 18 U.S.C. § 1030(G).

The CFAA requires the plaintiff to prove "that [the defendant] accessed a protected computer without authorization and, as a result caused an annual loss of at least $5,000." The CFAA defines the term "loss" as the reasonable cost to any victim, including the cost of responding to an offense, conducting a damage assessment, and restoring the data, system, or information to its condition prior, as well as "any revenue lost, cost incurred, or other consequential damages." 18 U.S.C. § 1030(E)(11).

(1) Int'l Airport Centers v. Citrin

Many CFAA cases center on the meaning of using a protected computer "without authorization" or in a manner that "exceeds authorized access." In *Int'l Airport Centers v. Citrin*, 440 F.3d 418 (7th Cir. 2006), Citrin was employed by International Airport

Centers ("IAC"), a real estate business. IAC issued Citrin a computer so that he could compile data on properties. When Citrin left the company, he deleted data from his corporate-issued computer before returning it, and erased the backup files. IAC filed a CFAA lawsuit against Citrin that did not even allege that he accessed a computer; much less, that he had exceeded authorization.

Judge Richard Posner, writing for the Seventh Circuit panel, nevertheless found that Citrin violated the CFAA because, by writing over backup files, he exceeded authorized access. Citrin is cited for the proposition that a breach of loyalty alone is enough to render an employee to be "without authorization." U.S. DEPT. OF JUSTICE, MANUAL ON PROSECUTING COMPUTER CRIMES 7 (2012).

(2) LVRC Holdings v. Brekka

In *LVRC Holdings LLC v. Brekka*, 581 F.3d 1127 (9th Cir. 2011), the Ninth Circuit determined that an employee does not exceed authorized access to a computer by accessing information unless the employee has no authority to access the information under any circumstances. Brekka was an employee at an addiction treatment center who was negotiating with his employer, LVRC Holdings, for an ownership stake in the business. During negotiations, Brekka e-mailed several business documents to himself and to his wife's personal e-mail accounts. The negotiations broke down and Brekka left his employment with LVRC. LVRC later discovered the e-mails Brekka had sent to himself and sued him under § 1030(G), which provides for a private right of action under the CFAA.

The Ninth Circuit held in *Brekka* that the employer's policies determine whether an employee acts without authorization or not and not just the language of the statute. The court reasoned that there would have been no dispute if Brekka had accessed LVRC's information on their website after he left the company in September 2003.

(3) United States v. Nosal

The Ninth Circuit, in an *en banc* opinion, rejected the *Brekka* court's expansive interpretation of the CFAA in its decision in *United States v. Nosal*, 676 F.3d 854 (9th Cir. 2012). In *Nosal*, a former employee of Korn-Ferry no longer had access to the search firm's computer system. Nosal convinced current employees to use their legitimate credentials to access Korn-Ferry's computer system and download data from the firm's computer system, which he would use to form a competing executive recruiting firm. The court reasoned that the plain language of the CFFA addresses unauthorized access rather than misuse of computer data.

The court rejected the government's argument that the CFAA could apply to someone who has unrestricted physical access to a protected computer, but is limited in the uses to which he can make of the information. A court applying *Nosal* will not find a CFAA violation if an employee or ex-employee simply exceeds authorization. In contrast, a court applying Brekka will stretch the CFAA to treat violations of use restrictions as a federal criminal offense. Recently, more courts are following Nosal's conservative reading of CFAA that exceeding authorized access is not a CFAA offense. See *Serbite Agency Inc. v. Platt*, No. 11–3526 (D. Minn. 2012).

(4) Weingand v. Harland Financial Solutions

In *Weingand v. Harland Financial Solutions*, 2012 WL 2327660 (N.D. Cal. 2012), Michael Weingand filed suit against his ex-employer, contending that Harland Financial wrongfully terminated him. Harland Financial counterclaimed that Weingand violated the CFAA, accessing business files without permission by misrepresenting that he was only retrieving his personal files. The court held that the ex-employee violated the CFAA when he exceeded the scope of authorized access, even though he had legitimate access to the company's network for his own records. The court also ruled that a number of business torts claimed by the company survived summary judgment.

(5) Harris v. Comscore. Inc.

An Illinois federal court certified a class action against marketer comScore Inc. for its non-consensual online harvesting and transferring a large amount of users' personal data. The e-mail marketer bundled tracking software with its free screensaver. The defendant marketer was accused of collecting social security and credit card numbers and information on what websites users visited. The court found that the plaintiff's complaint alleged a basis for the Computer Fraud and Abuse Act and the Electronic Communications Privacy Act.

§ 8-3. Electronic Communications Privacy Act

(A) OVERVIEW OF THE ECPA

Congress enacted the Electronic Communications Privacy Act ("ECPA") in 1986 to "clarify federal privacy protections and standards in light of dramatic changes in new computer and telecommunication technologies." 132 Cong. Rec. S. 14441 (1986). Many states have enacted functionally equivalent little ECPA statutes, which are often referred to as "wiretap statutes." The ECPA prohibits the interception of any wire, oral, or electronic communication in the absence of a defense such as consent, business necessity, or a warrant. Title I of the ECPA amended the federal wiretap statute to update the meaning of interception of electronic communications to accommodate new technologies. The term "electronic communication" now applies broadly to e-mail or other Internet-related communications.

Title I of the ECPA criminalizes three types of activities: (1) intercepting or endeavoring to intercept electronic communications, (2) disclosing or endeavoring to disclose unlawfully intercepted information, and (3) using the content of unlawfully intercepted information. The ECPA recognizes a civil act for private plaintiffs who have been victimized by the unauthorized or unconsented interception or access of electronic communications. The ECPA requires proof that the defendant knew or had reason to know the electronic communication had been illegally intercepted. Electronic communication is broadly defined to include "any transfer of signs, signals, writing, images, sounds, data, or intelligence of any nature transmitted in whole or in part by a wire, radio, electromagnetic, photoelectric, or photo-optical system that affects interstate or foreign commerce, with certain exceptions." 18 U.S.C. § 2510(12).

Under the ECPA, federal courts may order Internet service providers to disclose stored communications and transaction records. The ECPA requires prosecutors to prove facts, capable of articulation, illustrating reasonable grounds relevant to a criminal investigation to support orders for service providers to turn over confidential customer information. The subscriber whose information is turned over to the government has no reasonable expectation of privacy and is thus not protected under the Fourth Amendment.

The prohibitions enumerated in the ECPA are subject to certain specific exceptions. Providers of wire or electronic communications services may monitor their services to ensure adequacy. The "ordinary course of business" exception allows employers to access stored or electronic communications, which enables them to monitor their employees' e-mail. To meet the "ordinary course of business" exception, the employer has to show: (1) the device used to intercept the electronic communication, and (2) the device is used by the employer within the ordinary course of the business. The employer is only allowed to intercept electronic communications long enough to determine the topic being discussed. If the communication is personal, the employer must stop intercepting the communications further.

ECPA Key Provisions

Intercepting a Communication	18 U.S.C. § 2511(1)(A)
Disclosing an Intercepted Communications	18 U.S.C. § 2511(1)(C)
Using an Intercepted Communications	18 U.S.C. § 2511(1)(D)

Within the ECPA, Congress also created a private action that authorizes plaintiffs to seek monetary damages against a person who "intentionally intercepts, endeavors to intercept, or procures any other person to intercept or endeavor to intercept, any wire, oral, or electronic communication." 18 U.S.C. § 2511(A)(4). To establish a *prima facie* case for a civil violation of § 2511(1)(A), a plaintiff must prove five elements: that a defendant (1) intentionally (2) intercepted, endeavored to intercept or procured another person to intercept or endeavor to intercept (3) the contents of (4) an electronic communication (5) using a device.

(B) ECPA DEFENSES

As noted above, the ECPA includes two statutory exceptions: the "ordinary course of business" exception and for activities incidental to rendering services. The business exception to ECPA provides that a provider may intercept electronic communications within its network for incidental activities. The ECPA allows service providers or anyone else to intercept and disclose an electronic communication where either the sender or recipient of the message has effectively consented to disclosure, explicitly or implicitly. Section 2511(2)(D) of the ECPA prohibits employers from intercepting e-mail messages, but the ECPA does not apply if an employee consents to e-mail monitoring. Consent, as defined by the ECPA, also encompasses implied consent, which in the context of e-mail monitoring, is an employer's prior notice that it will monitor Internet usage and e-mail.

The USA Patriot Act amended the ECPA to list crimes for which investigators may get a wiretap order for wire communications. The Act permits federal government agents to intercept e-mail and monitor other Internet activities in order to battle terrorism. The FBI can seek National Security Letters ("NSL") that enable it to gain access to subscriber information in order to investigate terrorism. A NSL is defined as an administrative subpoena that allows the FBI to gain access to, among other things, subscriber information, or electronic communication transactional records held by Internet service providers when this information is relevant to international terrorism or clandestine intelligence activities.

§ 8-4. Stored Communications Act

(A) SCA *PRIMA FACIE* CASE

Congress enacted the Stored Communications Act ("SCA"), 18 U.S.C. § 2701–2711 in 1986 as Title II of the ECPA, governs the privacy of stored Internet communications. An SCA violation requires that a person: (1) intentionally access without authorization a facility through which an electronic communication service is provided or intentionally exceed authorization to access that facility, and (2) thereby obtain, alter, or prevent authorized access to an electronic communication while it is in electronic storage. Section 2701(C)(1) exempts from subsection (A) "conduct authorized by the person or entity providing a wire or electronic communications service." 18 U.S.C. § 2701(C)(1).

The SCA creates rights held by "customers" and "subscribers" of network service providers in both content and non-content information held by two particular types of providers. The SCA bars electronic communications service providers from divulging to any person or entity the contents of a communication while held in their electronic storage. The SCA created a service provider exception for the provider of that service. Service providers are within the definition of "electronic communication service" or "remote computing service."

Title II of the ECPA or the SCA addresses access to stored wire and electronic communications and transactional records. Generally, the SCA prevents providers of communication services from divulging private communications to certain entities and/or individuals. The SCA defines an electronic communication service ("ECS") as "any service which provides to users thereof the ability to send or receive wire or electronic communications." 18 U.S.C. § 2510(5). The SCA creates a civil right of action to protect against persons who gain unauthorized access to an electronic communication storage facility. A person violates § 2701 if he or she "intentionally accesses without authorization a facility through which an electronic communication service is provided; or intentionally exceeds an authorization to access that facility; and thereby obtains, alters, or prevents authorized access to a wire or electronic communication while it is in electronic storage in such system." 18 U.S.C. § 2701.

An Internet actor such as employer will violate the SCA by intentionally accessing an e-mail server through which they provide an electronic communication service. Service providers are prohibited from disclosing stored communications absent the consent of the sender or other exceptions. The SCA requires the government to obtain a search warrant for electronic communications in storage for 180 days or less. For information stored greater than 180 days, the government can obtain a search warrant and rely upon either a subpoena or a court order so long as the owner of the information has prior notice.

(B) SCA DEFENSES

The SCA posits a statutory exception for conduct that is authorized by the person or entity providing the electronic communications service. This means a company providing e-mail service to its employees may access the service without violating the SCA. Non-providers do not violate the SCA by accessing computer communications in electronic storage if it acts with the knowledge and consent of the person or entity that provides the electronic communication service. The SCA explicitly provides that good faith reliance on a warrant is a complete defense to a civil action. Defendants in ECPA cases will have a functionally equivalent defense for good faith reliance on a warrant. Many states have enacted "little SCA" that are state law equivalents.

§ 8-5. Computer Crime Case Law

(A) FEATURED CASES

(1) *U.S. v. Councilman*

The First Circuit in *United States v. Councilman*, 418 F.3d 67 (1st Cir. 2005), held e-mail messages no longer in electronic storage could not be intercepted under the ECPA. In *Councilman*, the defendant, both a book dealer and an e-mail service provider, created software that redirected incoming e-mails from Amazon.com to customers of the defendant's company. Federal prosecutors charged the defendant with conspiring to intercept electronic communications. The First Circuit dismissed the indictment against Councilman, reasoning that he copied incoming e-mails from Amazon already in storage. By definition, a message in storage cannot be intercepted. E-mails already in storage (opened or unopened) could not be intercepted but were subject to the SCA.

(2) U.S. v. Riggs

In *United States v. Riggs*, 739 F. Supp. 414 (N.D. Ill. 1990), the court held that defendants were in violation of the ECPA when they gained unauthorized access to Bell South computers. The violation arose when hackers, known as "Prophet" and "Knight Lightning," gained unauthorized access to Bell South's 911 computer files and published them in a hacker's newsletter. The defendants also sent communications to each other via electronic mail and published an issue of PHRACK, which contained a series of tutorials about breaking into computer systems. Similarly, many of the U.S. Justice Department's prosecutions under the Economic Espionage Act also bring charges arising from the ECPA as well as the CFAA. One of the greatest dangers for companies is that malicious hackers, disaffected employees, or unknown third parties will maliciously divulge trade secrets online.

(3) Konop v. Hawaiian Airlines

In *Konop v. Hawaiian Airlines, Inc.*, 302 F.3d 868 (9th Cir. 2002), a Hawaiian Airlines pilot sued his employer for violation of the SCA; claiming the airline had viewed his secure website without his consent. Konop controlled access to his website by requiring visitors to log in with a user name and password. At the request of a Hawaiian Airlines vice president, one of the authorized users allowed management to access Konop's website. The pilot who revealed the password had permission to access Konop's site, but had never used it.

The SCA exempts conduct authorized by a user of an electronic communication service from liability. Later that day, the pilot received word that the Hawaiian Airlines VP was upset by the contents of Konop's website, leading the authorized users to suspect that management was secretly monitoring their website. The Ninth Circuit affirmed the lower court's ruling that the airline did not violate Title I of the ECPA because the pilot's website was not intercepted during transmission, but rather while in electronic storage. The *Konop* court's *en banc* opinion reasoned that they were following precedent in construing the definition of intercept narrowly when it comes to electronic communications. The seizure of unread e-mail residing on a host computer does not match up well with the narrow meaning of "intercept" as required by Title I of the Wiretap Act, which contemplates "intercept" as occurring during or contemporaneously with transmission. Since the *Konop* case, Congress has amended the ECPA to eliminate storage from the definition of wire communication.

(4) Bohach v. City of Reno

The court rejected an ECPA claim by two police officers in *Bohach v. City of Reno*, 932 F. Supp. 1232 (D. Nev. 1996). While under internal investigation, the police officers sought an injunction pursuant to the ECPA, to prevent disclosure of the contents of electronic messages sent between them. The issue in *Bohach* was whether a government employee has a reasonable expectation of privacy in messages sent through government-issued communications equipment when his employer has notified him that his use of the equipment is subject to monitoring without notice. The court held that the police officers had no right to restrain disclosure of electronic messages and that the police department had a right to retrieve pager text messages saved on the department's computer system under Title II of the ECPA.

The *Bohach* court reasoned that the department was a provider of electronic communications services and that stored transmissions of a paging system are in storage, irrespective of whether the storage of paging messages was classifiable as temporary, intermediate, or incidental electronic transmission. The court found that the employee had no expectation of privacy in police pagers because users knew that the department stored all messages by logging them into a system. The court held that the retrieval of alphanumeric pager messages stored in computer files did not constitute an interception for purposes of the ECPA.

(5) In re Pharmatrak, Inc.

In re Pharmatrak, Inc., 329 F.3d 9 (1st Cir. 2003), the First Circuit reversed a lower court ruling that Pharmatrak violated the ECPA with website monitoring software that captured personally identifiable information including name, address, telephone number, and e-mail address-entered by users visiting the software maker's customers' web pages. Pharmatrak assured their pharmaceutical company customers that their software product did not compile or store information about individual website visitors. In fact, the software routinely recorded the full URLs of the web pages accessed by a user before and after visiting a client pharmaceutical company's website and on occasion recorded personal information appended to the next URL.

The court found the defendant's monitoring software to qualify as a "device" under ECPA that captured consumer personally identifiable information and thus was classifiable as an "interception." The software's capture of personally identifiable information was not by design and only captured data from a very small number of users. The affected plaintiffs filed a class action against Pharmatrak and the pharmaceutical companies, asserting an ECPA complaint.

The First Circuit held that the lower court incorrectly interpreted the "consent" exception to the ECPA and remanded the case for further proceedings. The court ruled Pharmatrak had the burden to prove it had the consent of the few users on whom it collected data. The court concluded that it did not need to address the "real-time requirement" of the ECPA since Pharmatrak acquired the information contemporaneously with transmission by the Internet users. The court held that Pharmatrak intercepted electronic communications without their consent. The court observed, "Traveling the Internet, electronic communications are often—perhaps constantly—both "in transit" and "in storage" simultaneously, a linguistic but not a technological paradox."

(B) SOCIAL MEDIA & THE ECPA

An ex-boyfriend opened a fake Twitter account, masquerading as his former girlfriend, in *Doe v. Hofstetter*, No. 11-CV02209-DME-MJW (D. Colo. June 13, 2012). The defendant published a blog containing intimate and private photographs of the plaintiff. The defendant published false statements about the plaintiff's marriage and his relationship with her. The court concluded that the defendant did not violate the Stored Communications Act when he violated Twitter's terms of service by creating an account in his ex-girlfriend's name. The court observed that the defendant did not hack into the plaintiff's account to obtain stored communications. The court declined to find a violation of the ECPA or the CFAA, but did recognize a cause of action for the intentional infliction of emotional distress.

A U.S. Judicial Panel on Multidistrict Litigation ordered consolidation of scores of complaints against Facebook for improperly tracking users' Internet activities after they had logged out of their Facebook accounts. Many of these claims are asserted under the CFAA and the SCA. *In re Facebook Privacy Litigation*, 791 F. Supp. 2d 705 (N.D. Cal. 2011), Facebook users filed a class action, contending that the social media site divulged private information about users to advertisers without users' consent and were thus liable under SCA. The plaintiffs alleged that their privacy was invaded when they clicked on an advertisement banner displayed on the site, which sent personally identifiable information to the advertiser.

The court found that, as a matter of law, the Facebook users had no ECPA or SCA causes of action. The federal court found that the Facebook users did not allege that the communications at issue were sent to Facebook or to its advertisers and thus could not state a claim under the SCA. The court denied Facebook's motion to dismiss on the ground that the plaintiffs lacked standing under Article III of the Wiretap Act, but granted defendant's motion to dismiss on all other counts.

In *Low v. LinkedIn Corp.*, No. 11–1468 (N.D. Cal. 2011), the district court dismissed a class action suit against LinkedIn under the SCA. The class action complaint alleged the social networking site dropped cookies that tracked class members' browsing history in violation of the SCA. The court reasoned that the plaintiffs did not demonstrate proof of how they were injured and that the bare assertion of embarrassment and humiliation was not enough. The court reasoned that emotional or economic harm from online disclosure of personal information or browsing histories must be concrete and particularized to individual plaintiffs to permit recovery under the SCA.

The class representative in LinkedIn contended that the personal information of the class members, including personally identifiable browsing histories, was disclosed to third party advertisers and marketers using cookies. The plaintiff's class action included a count that charged LinkedIn with violating the SCA and several California consumer laws. The court granted LinkedIn's motion to dismiss with leave to amend.

(C) CHILD PORNOGRAPHY & SEXTING

In the United States, it is a criminal offense in every state to create, use, or distribute child pornography. The relevant elements prohibit the transmission of child pornography as stated in section 2252(A) and include: (1) an active intention to give or transfer a specific depiction [of a minor] to another person and (2) active participation in the actual delivery. Overzealous prosecutors have charged underage girls with "sexting;" in this case, the sending nude pictures of themselves to peers.

A federal court ruled in *Backpage.com v. McKenna*, 2012 U.S. Dist. LEXIS 105189 (W.D. Wash. 2012) that Section 230 of the CDA likely preempts a Washington state statute, which criminalizes commercial advertisements that sexually exploit minors. Philip Alpert faced criminal charges for violating child pornography laws for the unauthorized e-mailing of his ex-girlfriend's nude picture. The constitutionality of the Washington statute was challenged by Backpage.com, a service that obtains revenue from commercial sex advertising.

The court reasoned that online service providers such as Backpage.com were neither publishers nor speakers of information because third party advertisers provided the information, thus expanding CDA Section 230 to include crimes. The federal court therefore granted the plaintiffs' motion for a preliminary injunction, barring enforcement of the law. The unintended consequence of immunizing all ISPs from liability is that this confers an absolute immunity on feral ISPs.

§ 8-6. Other Internet-Related Criminal Statutes

(A) IDENTITY THEFT

The Identity Theft Penalty Enhancement Act ("ITPEA"), which took effect July 15, 2004, established a new offense of aggravated identity theft. 18 U.S.C. § 1028(A). Section 1028A applies when a defendant "knowingly transfers, possesses, or uses, without lawful authority, a means of identification of another person" during and in relation to any felony violation of certain enumerated federal offenses. This statute can be deployed against hackers that steal credit card information or "phishers," who misappropriate trade secrets or other information through fraudulent e-mails. In general, those who violate section 1028A are subject to a mandatory two-year term of imprisonment. In cases of terrorism related aggravated identity theft, including that related to section 1030(A)(1), Section 1028A imposes an additional five-year term of imprisonment.

(B) ACCESS DEVICE FRAUD

Access device fraud is a relatively new cybercrime to address theft using payment devices. 18 U.S.C. § 1029. Congress defined access broadly to avoid the problem of legal lag as new technologies evolve. "Unauthorized" access devices include lost, stolen, or revoked devices, whereas "counterfeit" ones include fictitious, altered, or forged devices. 18 U.S.C. § 1029(E)(2) & (3). Conviction for access device fraud may result in a 10-year prison sentence. 18 U.S.C. § 1029(A)(E) & (C)(1)(A)(I).

(C) ANTI-STALKING

Scores of states have enacted anti-stalking criminal law statutes. Nevertheless, litigants have been more likely to use the federal anti-stalking statute. To prove stalking, the government must establish that defendants: (1) employed a facility of interstate commerce, (2) to engage in a course of conduct with the intent to place a person in reasonable fear of death or serious bodily injury either to that person or to a partner or immediate family member, and (3) the course of conduct actually put that person in reasonable fear of death or serious bodily injury to himself or his partner or immediate family member. Anti-stalking statutes are notoriously difficult to draft.

To prove a conspiracy to commit interstate stalking, the government must also prove that the charged defendants agreed to participate in this conspiracy. Finally, with regard to aiding and abetting, a defendant is punishable as the principal if the government establishes, beyond a reasonable doubt, that the defendant committed the stalking or aided, abetted, counseled, commanded, induced or procured the substantive act of stalking by another person. 18 U.S.C. § 2.

§ 8-7. International Cybercrime Enforcement

At present, there is no Internet wide treaty addressing cybercrimes or even the procedural aspects of policing cybercrime. Not all countries connected to the Internet regard computer attacks as crimes. Many countries connected to the global Internet do not embrace U.S. style free expression and have no equivalent to U.S. constitutionally based legal norms and values. The Convention on Cybercrime, sponsored by the Council of Europe ("COE"), is the first international treaty addressing computer crime and Internet-related crime. The Cybercrime Convention, concluded in Budapest in 2001, is an international treaty to improve cooperation between nation states in the fight against cybercrime, harmonize the law, and improve investigative techniques. The United States became a signatory country in 2006.

Articles 2–4 compel signatory states to enact national legislation addressing computer crimes such as illegal access, illegal interception, and data interference. Article 5 criminalizes the creation or transmission of computer viruses or malware and expects states to enact legislation adopting the doctrine of corporate liability for cybercrimes. Articles 7 and 8 of the Convention criminalize computer related forgery and fraud. Article 9 constitutes an agreement to criminalize the production and distribution of child pornography. In Articles 10 and 11, the signatories agreed to criminalize copyright infringement, as well as aiding and abetting computer crimes. Article 17 of the Cybercrime Convention also treats computer crime as an extraditable offense and calls for mutual assistance in the investigation and prosecution of computer crimes. Article 24 provides mechanisms for obtaining an "expeditious preservation of data" on a computer system or server in another territory.

CHAPTER 9

CONTENT REGULATION ON THE INTERNET

§ 9-1. Overview of Internet Regulations

Billions of Internet users around the world, who come from radically different legal cultures, interact in cyberspace. Thailand, for example, demanded that Google remove 149 YouTube videos for allegedly insulting the monarchy. Google blocked access to a 14-minute trailer entitled "Innocence of Muslims" in a few Islamic nations. Nevertheless, the U.S. government refused to cede to demands by seventeen countries to remove the controversial video. In the widely circulated film trailer, Mohammed, the founder of Islam, is depicted as a child molester, sexual deviant, and as an uncouth barbarian. Fundamentalist clerics called for a fatwā, advocating that Muslims kill the film's director, actors, actresses and others who helped to make this controversial film.

Immediately after the translation of the film trailer into Arabic and its posting on YouTube, it incited violence in many countries including Afghanistan, Somalia, Syria, Turkey and the United Kingdom. The cascading after effects of posting this amateurish, low budget film trailer on YouTube illustrates how the Internet can be used to incite violence on a scale far greater than with the use of traditional media.

The U.S. government is no longer in a position to control Internet governance. U.S. companies, for example, must comply with the EU's regulations for data protection, distance sales, jurisdiction, choice of law, and mandatory consumer rules. E-Businesses must continually respond and adapt to diverse legal systems. Google, for example, received over 1,000 requests to remove content in the second half of 2011. Google's *2012 Transparency Report* acknowledges that foreign governments make routine demands for them to censor or remove content they find objectionable.

A large number of countries connected to the Internet do not have a strong tradition of the right of expression. A traditional Islamic jurist would likely find an unveiled female face on a social media site to be shameful. Not just Islamic republics have blasphemy laws. The Republic of Ireland outlaws cyberspace incitement including "blasphemous Internet statements in defiance of the law." DAVID NASH, BLASPHEMY IN THE CHRISTIAN WORLD (2012) at Preface. Lawyers of the twenty-first century need to be less U.S. centric because cyberspace is a cross-border legal environment. This chapter examines problems of regulating content communities that originate on the World Wide Web. Internet businesses targeting China's 1.4 billion consumers will need to comply with that country's Internet regulations. Carnegie-Mellon researchers found widespread evidence that the Chinese government was deleting messages containing politically sensitive terms from popular micro blogs.

The researchers "conducted a statistical analysis of 56 million messages (212,583 of which have been deleted out of 1.3 million checked, more than 16 percent) from the domestic Chinese micro blog site, Sine Web, and 11 million Chinese–language messages from Twitter." David Bamman, Brendan O'Connor, & Noah A. Smith, *Censorship and Deletion Practices in Chinese Social Media*, 17 FIRST MONDAY 3 (Mar. 5, 2012). This chapter examines the controversial issue of Internet content regulation and discusses leading developments around the world. Today the leading questions are: Who should regulate the Internet? How extensive should content regulations be and by what authority?

§ 9-2. Indecent Speech & Censorship

(A) COMMUNICATIONS DECENCY ACT

In 1996, Congress enacted the Communications Decency Act ("CDA") through Title V of the Telecommunications Act. The CDA criminalized the transmission of materials deemed to be either "obscene or indecent" for Internet users under the age of eighteen. Shortly after Congress enacted the CDA, plaintiffs filed a declaratory judgment, asking a U.S. district court to declare the statute unconstitutional. A three-judge panel of the federal appeals court enjoined enforcement of the CDA's framework for controlling obscenity on the Internet. In *Reno v. ACLU*, 521 U.S. 844 (S.Ct. 1997), the U.S. Supreme Court upheld a lower court's judgment that the CDA violated the First Amendment because it was overly vague.

In particular, the Court found the CDA's "contemporaneous community standard" for obscene materials to be overly broad. The local community test is inappropriate for a cross-border Internet, with radically different communities and groups likely to be offended by a given message. Section 230, which as noted in Chapter 6, immunizes providers for third parties' postings, is all that survives from the original legislation.

The CDA states in relevant part that service providers are not liable for "Good Samaritan" block and screening of offensive material. Section 223(a) of the CDA criminalizes the transmission via a telecommunications device of a "suggestion, proposal, image, or other communication which is obscene, lewd, lascivious, filthy, or indecent, with intent to annoy, abuse, threaten, or harass another person." 47 U.S.C. § 223(A).

(B) CHILD ONLINE PROTECTION ACT

After the U.S. Supreme Court struck down the CDA in *Reno* v. *American Civil Liberties Union,* Congress enacted the Child Online Protection Act ("COPA"). 47 U.S.C. § 231. COPA prohibits any person from knowingly and with knowledge of the character of the material, in interstate or foreign commerce by means of the World Wide Web, making any communication for commercial purposes harmful to minors. COPA imposes criminal penalties of six months in prison and a $50,000 fine.

COPA's scope was restricted to obscene materials on the World Wide Web, whereas the earlier statute applied to all electronically disseminated information.

Under COPA, whether material published on the World Wide Web is "harmful to minors" is governed by a three-part test: (1) Would the average person, applying contemporary community standards, find after taking the material as a whole and with respect to minors, to pander to the prurient interest?, (2) Does the material depict, describe, or represent, in a manner patently offensive with respect to minors, an actual or simulated sexual act or sexual contact, an actual or simulated normal or perverted sexual act, or a lewd exhibition of the genitals or post-pubescent female breast?, and (3) Taken as a whole, does the material lack serious literary, artistic, political, or scientific value for minors? The dictionary definition of prurient interest is that it is evidenced by or arousing an immoderate or unwholesome interest or sexual desire. COPA sought to use digital certificates to verify users were old enough to view online pornography. Websites could assert, as a complete defense, that they restrict access to minors by requiring a credit card, debit card, or access cards.

After a decade of litigation and a remand from the U.S. Supreme Court, COPA was struck down after a complicated series of opinions. In *ACLU v. Reno*, 31 F. Supp.2d 473 (E.D. Pa. 2009), the federal court granted a preliminary injunction enjoining enforcement of COPA. The United States Supreme Court vacated and remanded for consideration, on the narrow question of whether COPA's use of "community standards" to identify material that was harmful to minors violated the First Amendment.

The U.S. Supreme Court vacated the Third Circuit's judgment in *Ashcroft v. ACLU*, 535 U.S. 564 (S.Ct. 2002). The *Ashcroft* Court found that COPA's reliance on "community standards" to identify what material is harmful to minors did not by itself make COPA substantially overbroad. The Court did not decide whether COPA was unconstitutionally vague or could withstand strict scrutiny.

In *ACLU v. Mukasey*, 534 F.3d 181 (3rd Cir. 2008), the Third Circuit considered these issues on remand and again struck down COPA on grounds of vagueness and overbreadth, finding the statute violated the First Amendment in failing to tailor its restrictions to survive strict scrutiny. The Third Circuit held that the government failed to demonstrate that COPA was a more effective and less restrictive alternative to the use of filters.

(C) CHILDREN'S INTERNET PROTECTION ACT

In 2000, Congress enacted the Children's Internet Protection Act ("CIPA"), which requires public libraries and schools to install software filters to block obscene or pornographic images. Schools and libraries subject to CIPA are required to adopt and implement an Internet safety policy addressing: (1) access by minors to inappropriate matter on the Internet, (2) the safety and security of minors when using electronic mail, chat rooms and other forms of direct electronic communications, (3) unauthorized access, including so-called "hacking," and other unlawful activities by minors online, (4) unauthorized disclosure, use, and dissemination of personal information regarding minors, and (5) measures restricting minors' access to materials harmful to them.

In *United States v. American Library Ass'n*, 539 U.S. 194 (S.Ct. 2003), the Court upheld CIPA, reasoning that the statute did not violate the First Amendment because the purpose of the software was to block obscene or pornographic images and to prevent minors from obtaining access to harmful material. The plurality opinion stated that the federal assistance programs for helping libraries secure Internet access was a valid statutory purpose. "Under the Spending Clause of the Constitution, Congress has "wide latitude" to appropriate public funds, and to place conditions on the appropriation of public funds, in furtherance of the general welfare." Const. Art. I, § 8, cl. 1.

Justice Rehnquist's plurality opinion found that Internet access in public libraries is neither a "traditional" nor a "designated" public forum. The plurality stated that any concerns over filtering software's alleged tendency to erroneously "overblock" access to constitutionally protected speech was dispelled by the ease with which library patrons could have the filtering software disabled. The Court also observed that because public libraries had traditionally excluded pornographic material from their collections, they could impose a parallel limitation on its Internet assistance programs. In *PFLAG v. Camdenton R–III School Dist.*, 2012 WL 510877 (3rd Cir. 2011), a court entered an injunction against a school district's use of filters to block websites directed at lesbian, gay, bisexual, and transgendered ("LGBT") youth.

(D) THE CHILD PORNOGRAPHY PREVENTION ACT

The Child Pornography Prevention Act of 1996 ("CPPA") made it a crime to create sexually explicit images that appear to depict minors but were produced without using any real children. The statute prohibits, in specific circumstances, possessing or distributing these computer images, which may be created by using adults who appear under the age of consent.

In *Ashcroft v. Free Speech Coalition*, 535 U.S. 234 (S.Ct. 2002), the U.S. Supreme Court held that the ban on virtual child pornography was unconstitutionally overbroad since it proscribed speech that was neither child pornography nor obscene and thus abridged the freedom to engage in a substantial amount of lawful speech. The Court also held that the government was not permitted to bar protected virtual child pornography as a means of enforcing its proper ban of actual child pornography.

(E) THE PROTECT ACT OF 2003

After the Court's decision in *Free Speech Coalition*, Congress enacted the Prosecutorial

Remedies and Other Tools to end the Exploitation of Children Today ("Protect Act of 2003"). The Protect Act criminally sanctions the advertising, promotion, presentation, distribution, and solicitation of child pornography. This federal criminal statute also penalizes speech accompanying, or seeking the transfer of, child pornography via reproduction or physical delivery, from one person to another. 18 U.S.C. § 2252A (A)(3)(B). The Protect Act classifies primary producers as including anyone who creates a visual representation of actual sexually explicit conduct, through videotaping, photographing, or computer manipulation. Secondary producers upload such images to a website or otherwise manage the content of the website. The producer must inspect the depicted individual's government issued picture identification and determine her or his name and date of birth. 18 U.S.C. § 2257(B) (1).

In *United States v. Williams*, 128 S. Ct. 1830 (S.Ct. 2008), the U.S. Supreme Court upheld the pandering provision of the Protect Act of 2003 that makes it illegal to send material, or purported material, in a way that "reflects the belief, or is intended to cause another to believe," that the material contains illegal child pornography. 18 U.S.C. § 2252A(A)(3)(B). In *Williams*, the defendant used a sexually explicit screen name, signed in to a public Internet chat room and conversed with a Secret Service agent masquerading as a mother of a young child.

The defendant offered to trade the agent sexually explicit pictures of his four-year-old daughter in exchange for similar photos. His chat room message said "Dad of toddler has "good" pics of her an [sic] me for swap of your toddler pics, or live cam." The defendant was charged with one count of promoting, or "pandering," material intended to cause another to believe the material contained illegal child pornography and carried a sixty-month mandatory minimum sentence.

The defendant challenged the constitutionality of the Protect Act's pandering provision and the Eleventh Circuit found this part of the statute both substantially overbroad and vague, and therefore facially unconstitutional. In a 7-2 opinion, the U.S. Supreme Court reversed the Eleventh Circuit. Justice Scalia's majority opinion concluded that the federal anti-child pornography statute did not, on its face, violate the First Amendment's right to free speech. The *Williams* Court found offers to provide or obtain child pornography to be categorically excluded from the First Amendment.

(F) SCHOOL CENSORSHIP OF INTERNET CONTENT

School districts around the United States face difficult policy decisions about social media postings that "threaten academic environments when they are used to bully, defame or engage in hate speech against students, administrators, and faculty." Karen M. Bradshaw & Souvik Saha, *Academic Administrators and the Challenge of Social Networking Sites* in SAUL LEVMORE & MARTHA NUSSBAUM, THE OFFENSIVE INTERNET: PRIVACY, SPEECH, AND REPUTATION (2010).

In *Layshock v. Hermitage Sch. Dist.*, the school district suspended Justin Layshock for ten days and demoted him to an academically inferior educational program because of his Internet posting that mocked his high school principal. The issue in *Layshock* was whether the school district violated a student's First Amendment free-speech rights. The federal court granted the student summary judgment as to his expression claim, but ruled in favor of the district as to the due process claim. The Third Circuit in *Layshock v. Hermitage Sch. Dist.*, 593 F.3d 249 (3rd Cir. 2005) affirmed the lower court decision. An *en banc* opinion of the Third Circuit vacated this district court decision.

The unsettled issue is whether the school district has any authority to punish students for postings that defame administrators, teachers, or fellow students. In *J.S. v. Blue Mt. Sch. Dist.*, 650 F.3d 915 (3rd Cir. 2011), the Third Circuit held that a student's sexually explicit internet "profile" of her principal caused no substantial disruption in school, as it was not taken seriously, access was limited to her friends, and it did not identify him. The court held that her suspension due to the website profile violated the First Amendment. The principal basis for this finding was that the school's policy purported to control a student's home use of their computer.

§ 9-3. Applying the First Amendment in Cyberspace

The Federal Communications Commission controls decency in broadcast media but has no jurisdiction to control decency on the Internet. In *Sable Communications Inc. v. FCC*, 492 U.S. 115 (S.Ct. 1989), the U.S. Supreme Court struck down a Communications Act provision that would have prohibited all indecent "dial-a-porn" telephone messages. The Court's reasoning was that the First Amendment protects sexual expression that is indecent but not obscene. The *Sable* Court required the prosecution to demonstrate that it was promoting a compelling interest and it choose the least restrictive means to further that interest. As a content based restriction on expression, the statute will be subject to strict scrutiny. A court will strike down government regulations unless the legislature has narrowly tailored it to serve a compelling government interest.

(A) DORMANT OR NEGATIVE COMMERCE CLAUSE

A "dormant" or "negative" aspect of this grant of power is that a state's authority to impinge on interstate commerce may be limited in some situations. In *Am. Library Ass'n v. Pataki*, 969 F. Supp. 160 (S.D.N.Y. 1997), libraries challenged the constitutionality of a New York state statute that attempted to keep people from transmitting material harmful to minors via the Internet. The plaintiffs filed a lawsuit seeking declaratory and injunctive relief, contending that the state statute violated the First Amendment and burdened interstate commerce in violation of the Commerce Clause.

The court granted the preliminary injunction, holding that the plaintiffs showed a likelihood of success on the merits. The *Pataki* court analogized the Internet to highways and railroads in reaching its decision. In this case, the burden on interstate commerce exceeded the benefits of preventing indecent materials from being available to minors.

In this case, the burden on interstate commerce exceeded the benefits of preventing indecent materials from being available to minors.

(B) CONTENT-SPECIFIC REGULATIONS

An injunction enjoining Internet speech is a prior restraint, which will be upheld only in the most exceptional circumstances. Geoffrey R. Stone, *Content Regulation and the First Amendment,* 25 WM. & MARY L. REV. 189 (1983). In *Federal Communications Commission v. Pacifica Foundation*, 438 U.S. 726 (S.Ct. 1978), the U.S. Supreme Court upheld the Federal Communications Commission's ability to restrict the use of "indecent" material in broadcasting.

(C) CONTENT-NEUTRAL REGULATIONS

In the context of the First Amendment, "a content neutral regulation with an incidental effect on speech component must serve a substantial governmental interest, the interest must be unrelated to the suppression of free expression, and the incidental restriction on speech must not burden substantially more speech than is necessary to further that interest." Geoffrey R. Stone, *Content Regulation and the First Amendment,* 25 WM. & MARY L. REV. 189 (1983). A content neutral regulation need not employ the least restrictive means but it must avoid burdening "substantially more speech than is necessary to further the government's legitimate interests." Courts uphold content neutral restrictions on the time, place, or manner of protected speech so long as the government narrowly tailors the regulation to serve a significant governmental interest. *City of Renton v. Playtime Theatre,* 475 U.S. 41 (S.Ct. 1986).

(D) FACIAL ATTACKS ON INTERNET SPEECH

A court considering a facial challenge on either overbreadth or vagueness must first determine whether and to what extent the statute reaches protected conduct or speech.

(1) Vagueness

Void for vagueness occurs when a regulation is so ambiguous a person cannot know with certainty what acts are proscribed. Plaintiffs may challenge content-based restrictions of speech on vagueness grounds. The vagueness doctrine is an outgrowth of the Due Process Clause of the Fifth Amendment. In *Reno v. American Civil Liberties Union,* 521 U.S. 844 (S.Ct.1997), the Court struck down a part of the Communications Decency Act ("CDA") on grounds of vagueness and over breadth. The Court reasoned the CDA's use of the undefined terms "indecent" and "patently offensive" would have a chilling effect on speakers and therefore, raised special First Amendment concerns. The CDA's vagueness undermined the likelihood it had been carefully tailored to the congressional goal of protecting minors from potentially harmful materials.

(2) Overbreadth

Overbreadth is the constitutional infirmity where a regulation prohibits more conduct or protected speech than is necessary. The First Amendment's "overbreadth doctrine" is a tool for striking down Internet-related content regulations as facially invalid if they prohibit a substantial amount of protected speech. The breadth of this content-based restriction of speech imposes an especially heavy burden on the Government to explain why a less restrictive provision would not be as effective. *Reno v. ACLU*, 521 U.S. 844, 879 (1997). The Court in *Reno* found the CDA's expansive coverage of content unprecedented, and acknowledged that the breadth of the content-based restriction placed a heavy burden on the government to explain why they could not enact a less restrictive provision.

(E) CATEGORIES OF UNPROTECTED SPEECH

The Virginia Supreme Court struck down a notorious spammer's criminal conviction on First Amendment overbreadth grounds. In *Jaynes v. Commonwealth of Virginia*, 666 S.E.2d 303 (Va. 2008), the court upheld the conviction of a defendant who violated Virginia's Computer Crime Act by sending over 10,000 commercial e-mails within a 24-hour period to subscribers of America Online, Inc. ("AOL") on each of three separate occasions. The spammer used routing and transmission information, bypassing AOL's security controls, which trespassed on AOL's proprietary network.

Jaynes intentionally falsified the header information and sender domain names before transmitting the e-mails to the recipients. The *Jaynes* court found Virginia's statute criminalizing the falsification of IP addresses as overly broad and unacceptably burdening the right to engage in anonymous speech. The court applied the strict scrutiny standard, requiring the state computer crime statute to be narrowly tailored. The *Jaynes* court found the computer crime statute was overbroad in prohibiting communications that contained political, religious, or other speech.

In *United States v. Kilbride*, 584 F.3d 1240 (9th Cir. 2009), an e-mail spammer was indicted under an eight-count complaint, including the CAN-SPAM Act, for distributing pornographic e-mail spam messages. The spammers were convicted of transmitting e-mails with materially false header information because they used fictitious e-mail addresses and registered domain names using a false contact name and phone number. The court also found that Kilbride materially falsified information within the meaning of Section 1037, when he had a third party alter headings. The federal appeals court affirmed the defendants' convictions and sentences for CAN-SPAM, fraud and conspiracy to commit fraud in connection with electronic mail, interstate transportation and interstate transportation for sale of obscene materials, and conspiracy to commit money laundering.

§ 9-4. Cyberbullying

(A) FEDERAL LEGISLATIVE PROPOSALS

In 2008, the U.S. House of Representatives introduced the Cyberbullying Prevention Act in response to a middle-aged woman whose cyberbullying caused a thirteen-year-old girl to commit suicide. This federal statute states: "Whoever transmits in interstate or foreign commerce any communication, with intent to coerce, intimidate, harass, or cause substantial emotional distress to a person, using electronic means to support severe, repeated, and hostile behavior, shall be fined under this title or imprisoned." Cyberbully Prevention Act, H.R. 6123, 110th Congress (2d sess. 2008). The proposed statute would make cyberbullying a federal crime, but it will not survive constitutional scrutiny, as it is likely to be overly broad or too vague.

(B) STATE ANTI-BULLYING LEGISLATION

New Jersey enacted the Anti-Bullying Bill of Rights after Tyler Clemente, a Rutgers undergraduate, committed suicide because a roommate used a webcam to record him kissing a male. The roommate streamed the secret video on the Internet and tweeted about it. The Berkman Center found that forty-eight states have enacted statutes addressing school bullying.

§ 9-5. Adult Entertainment & Pornography

Many federal courts apply the standard of *Miller v. California*, 413 U.S. 15 (S.Ct. 1973) in determining whether an Internet-related work is subject to regulation as obscenity. The *Miller* test has three prongs: (1) whether the average person, applying contemporary community standards would find that the work, taken as a whole, appeals to the prurient interest, (2) whether the work depicts or describes, in a patently offensive way, sexual conduct specifically defined and (3) whether the work, taken as a whole, lacks serious literary, artistic, political, or scientific value. Federal criminal statutes also address Internet pornography. Section 2252(A)(A)(2) prohibits any person from knowingly receiving or distributing child pornography that has traveled in interstate or foreign commerce. The statute requires proof that the defendants knowingly possessed and distributed photographs of minors. Section 2257 requires publishers of pornographic material to verify the age of models and this provision applies equally well to cyberspace.

In *Breitfeller v. Playboy*, No. 8:05CV405 T30TGW, 2007 WL 294233 (M.D. Fla. 2007), the 17-year-old girls filed suit against several defendants for distributing a video of them that was taken when the girls were participating in a wet t-shirt contest. The court ruled that Playboy knew or should have known that there was a risk the images contained minors, and that its decision to remain ignorant as to the plaintiffs' ages therefore satisfied the statute's *knowingly* requirement.

Underage minors have been charged with violating 18 U.S.C. § 2252(A), by taking sexually explicit photos of themselves and sending them to friends. In *Clark v. Roccanova*, 2011 WL 665621

(E.D. Ky. 2011), the court ruled that sexting by a 14 year old girl to other minors could constitute a violation by the girl of child pornography laws. Criminal prosecutions for online pornography often turn on whether a community standard has been violated. Courts differ as to whether there should be a national versus a local community standard in Internet-related obscenity cases.

CHAPTER 10

COPYRIGHTS IN CYBERSPACE

This chapter will focus on the unique copyright issues posed by Internet-related transmission and distribution. The law governing copyright protection was once a sleepy backwater but today Internet copyright disputes are the subject of weekly front-page stories in the *Wall Street Journal* and *The Economist*. Courts have stretched copyright law through cases and statutes that preserve the idea of property interests in cyberspace. Peer-to-peer file sharing, the licensing of content, the Digital Millennium Copyright Act, and social media content have required a vast reworking of the concept. It is now difficult to imagine the contours of copyright law without bandwidth, browsers, and digital data.

§ 10-1. Overview of Copyright Law

Copyright is a form of protection provided by federal law to the authors of works including software programs, digital content, and materials on websites. The U.S. Supreme Court takes a utilitarian approach ("the greatest good for the greatest number"), stating "[t]he sole interest of the United States and primary object in conferring the monopoly [of copyright protection] lie in the general benefits derived by the public from the labors of authors." *Sony Corp. v. Universal City Studios, Inc.*, 464 U.S. 417 (S.Ct. 1984). The federal law of copyright recognizes property interests in products of the human intellect that are expressive.

(A) WHAT IS PROTECTABLE UNDER COPYRIGHT LAW

Courts have had little difficulty extending copyright protection to software, websites, and other Internet-related intellectual property. Copyright is secured automatically when the work is created, and a work is "created" when it is fixed in a copy or phonorecord for the first time. Section 102 of the Copyright Act extends copyright protection to original works of authorship fixed in any tangible medium of expression. This includes: (1) literary works, (2) musical works, including any accompanying words, (3) dramatic works, including any accompanying music, (4) pantomimes and choreographic works, (5) pictorial, graphic, and sculptural works, (6) motion pictures and other audiovisual works, (7) sound recordings, and (8) architectural works. 17 U.S.C. § 102(A). A "derivative work" is a work based upon one or more preexisting works.

Section 103 of the Copyright Act provides that compilations and derivative works fall within the subject matter of copyright. 17 U.S.C. § 103. Software programs may qualify as derivative works if they recast, transform, or adapt extant software. Websites, too, may be protectable. The requirements of originality and fixation for copyright protection are the same for Internet-relate works of authorship. G. Peter Albert, Jr. & Rita Abbati, *Using and Protecting Copyrighted Works on the Internet*, Chapter 4 in G. Peter Albert Jr. and AIPLA (2011) at 127.

(B) EXCLUSIVE RIGHTS OF COPYRIGHT OWNERS

Authors receive a bundle of rights under Section 106 that include the right: (1) to reproduce the copyrighted work in copies or phonorecords, (2) to prepare derivative works based upon the copyrighted work, (3) to distribute copies or phonorecords of the copyrighted work to the public by sale or other transfer or ownership, or by rental, lease, or lending, (4) in the case of literary, musical, dramatic, and choreographic works, pantomimes, motion pictures, and other audiovisual works, to perform the copyrighted work publicly, (5) in the case of literary, musical, dramatic, and choreographic works, pantomimes and pictorial, graphic, or sculptural works—including the individual images of a motion picture or other audiovisual work—to display the copyrighted work publicly, and (6) in the case of sound recordings, to perform the copyrighted work publicly by means of a digital audio transmission. 17 U.S.C. § 116.

(C) THE PATH OF COPYRIGHT LAW

The protection of literary works by copyright coincided with the invention of the printing press. ROBERT P. MERGES & JANE C. GINSBURG, FOUNDATIONS OF INTELLECTUAL PROPERTY 271 (2006). Copyright law was prefigured in England when Queen Mary chartered the stationers—the book publishers and sellers—by letters patent on May 4, 1557. The earliest copyright statute to grant rights to authors, as opposed to stationers was the Statute of Anne, enacted on April 10, 1710, which set the term of copyrights for authors at twenty-one years. The sole rights of copyright owners were to print and reprint works.

(D) COPYRIGHT TERM EXTENSION

The Copyright Act of 1976 extended the term for the life of the author plus 50 years, or 75 years for a work made for hire. The Copyright Term Extension Act ("CTEA") of 1998 extended U.S. copyright terms by an additional 20 years, to life of the author plus 70 years and for works of corporate authorship to 120 years after creation or 95 years after publication, whichever endpoint is earlier. A joint work is prepared by two or more authors with the intention that their contributions be merged into inseparable or interdependent parts of a unitary whole.

For joint authors, the copyright term is the life of the last surviving author plus 70 years. The constitutionality of the latest copyright term extension was upheld in *Eldred v. Ashcroft*, 537 U.S. 186 (S.Ct. 2003). The Court held that Congress had the discretion to extend the copyright term and did not violate the "limited terms" provision of Article I, § 8, Cl. 8 or the First Amendment.

§ 10-2. Elements of Copyright Law

Copyright protection, whether on a website, social media, or any other Internet-related medium, applies only if a work satisfies two criteria: originality, and fixation. Section 102(A) of the Copyright Act describes copyright subject matter: "Copyright protection subsists in original works of authorship fixed in any tangible medium of expression, now known or later developed, from which they can be perceived, reproduced, or otherwise communicated, either directly or with the aid of a machine or a device." 17 U.S.C. § 102. A website that consists of predominately-historical facts receives "thin" protection versus the "thick" protection provided to a digital work of authorship that is purely expressive. The copyright owner is generally the author, but a major U.S. exception to this rule is the Copyright Act's conclusive presumption that works created by employees in the scope of employment vest with the employer, a legal policy that is sharply at odds with European practices.

(A) ORIGINALITY

"Original," as the term is used in copyright, means the work originated with the author and had some minimum degree of creativity. In *Feist Publications, Inc. v. Rural Telephone Service Co.*, 499 U.S. 340 (S.Ct. 1989), the U.S. Supreme Court held the plaintiff's database composed of "white pages" telephone number listings was not entitled to copyright protection because it did not fulfill the minimum threshold of originality required under the U.S. Copyright Act. The *Feist* Court conceded that a compilation of facts could possess the requisite originality if the author made choices as to what facts to include, their ordering, and arrangement. However, even under these circumstances copyright protection extends only to those components of the work that are original to the author—not to the telephone numbers. This fact/expression dichotomy severely limits the scope of protection in fact-based works such as databases. The *Feist* Court rejected a "sweat of the brow" theory adopted by the European Union, which extends a compilation's copyright protection beyond selection and arrangement to the facts themselves.

(B) FIXATION

An author must fix a work of authorship in a tangible medium of expression to satisfy the fixation requirement. A work is "fixed" in a tangible medium of expression when it is "sufficiently permanent or stable to permit it to be perceived, reproduced, or otherwise communicated for a period of more than transitory duration." 17 U.S.C. § 101. The creator may communicate the fixation with the help of a machine or device.

The acts of transmitting an e-mail or viewing a web page—both of which store copies in the user's computer RAM—qualify as copies for purposes of the Copyright Act. However, it is unclear whether something in dynamic RAM is fixed for establishing a copyright. The Ninth Circuit, in *MAI Systems Corp. v. Peak Computer*, 991 F.2d 511 (9th Cir. 2003), held that simply loading a computer operating system into RAM, which is accomplished by turning the computer on, created a fixed copy for purposes of the Copyright Act. Internet copying, such as caching temporary copies of websites, would qualify as a fixed copy under the reasoning of the *MAI* court. Generally, a "cache" is "a computer memory with very short access time used for storage of frequently or recently used instructions or data." *United States v. Ziegler*, 474 F.3d 1184, 1186 (9th Cir. 2007). Title III of the Digital Millennium Copyright Act modifies *MAI v. Peak* by amending the U.S. Copyright Act (Section 117) to permit limited copies to be made in the course of computer repair.

(C) WHAT IS NOT PROTECTABLE

(1) Idea/Expression

Copyright protects expression, not ideas. The U.S. Supreme Court in *Baker v. Selden*, 101 U.S. 199 (S.Ct. 1880) first conceptualized the "idea/expression" dichotomy. Selden copyrighted a book in which he described a method of bookkeeping and sued Baker when the latter published a book on bookkeeping with functionally equivalent methods, but with different columns and headings. The Court ruled that Selden could not copyright his method of accounting because it was an idea, but could copyright the forms used to implement his system of bookkeeping, which was expression. In practice, it is difficult to separate functionality from expression. Courts, for example, hold that mannequins and Halloween costumes are entitled to copyright protection, even though the aesthetic aspects of those works are inseparable from their functionality.

(2) Governmental Works

Works of the U.S. government, or its employees acting within the scope of their professional duties, are not protectable by copyright.

(3) Functionality or Utility

The functionality or utility of any work of authorship is not protectable. Thus, a website, protocol, or programming language's utility does not qualify for copyright protection but still may be covered by patent law.

(4) Public Domain Information

Copyright law does not encompass information in the public domain. For example, a code writing organization could not enjoin a website operator from posting the text of a city's model building code because the code was in the public domain and not protected by copyright, notwithstanding software licensing agreement and a copyright notice prohibiting copying and distribution.

(5) Fair Use

"Fair use" is a statutory exception to the copyright owner's exclusive right "to reproduce the copyrighted work in copies." 17 U.S.C. § 106(1). A defendant has the burden of proof and production in demonstrating its copying is shielded by copyright law's doctrine of fair use. The fair use doctrine evolved from a common law doctrine and is now codified as Section 107 of the Copyright Act. The Copyright Act's four statutory factors that determine whether a given copyrighted work constitutes fair use are:

> (1) The purpose and character of the use including whether such use is of a commercial nature or is for nonprofit educational purposes,

(2) the nature of the copyrighted work, (3) the amount and substantiality of the portion used in relation to the copyrighted work as a whole, and (4) the effect of the use upon the potential market for or value of the copyrighted work. 17 U.S.C. § 107.

The first factor in a fair use inquiry is determining the "purpose and character of the use." Courts determine whether the new work "supersedes" the original work, or is transformative in the sense that it "adds something new, with a *further purpose* or different character." *Harper & Row v. Nation Publishers*, 471 U.S. 539 (S.Ct. 1985). Transformative use is a fundamental change in a plaintiff's copyrighted work, or use of the copyrighted work in a radically different context, through which the plaintiff's copyrighted work is "transformed" into a new creation. *Campbell v. Acuff-Rose,* 510 U.S. 569 (U.S. 1994). In *Campbell v. Acuff-Rose Music, Inc.*, Acuff Rose filed suit against members of the rap music group 2 Live Crew and their record company, claiming that 2 Live Crew's song, "Pretty Woman," infringed Acuff Rose's copyright in Roy Orbison's rock ballad, "Oh Pretty Woman." The Court reasoned that a parody might not violate copyright protection, even if the transformed version is highly profitable. The greater the transformative nature of the new work, the less important the other factors, including commercialism, become. Parody, like other comment and criticism, may claim fair use. Under the first of the four §107 factors, "the purpose and character of the use, including whether such use is of a commercial nature . . . ," the Court focuses on whether the new work merely supersedes the objects of the original creation, or whether and to what extent it is "transformative," altering the original with new expression, meaning, or message. The more transformative the new work, the less will be the significance of other factors, like commercialism, that may weigh against a finding of fair use.

To date, no court has addressed how fair use applies to Twitter and hundreds of other social networking sites. "If Pinterest users post or pin another's work without permission, have they violated copyright law? Does it matter if the work posted or pinned by a user was originally posted to Pinterest by the author or creator of the work? If users impermissibly post or pin a copyrighted work, are they then contributing to infringement when another user in turn re-posts it or pins it on their own page? There is a surplus of questions but is a shortage of answers." Mary Ann L. Wymore, *Social Media and Fair Use: Pinterest as a Case Study*, Bloomberglaw.com (2013).

(D) DERIVATIVE WORKS

A "derivative work" is a work based upon one or more preexisting works such as "a translation, musical arrangement, dramatization, fictionalization, motion picture version, sound recording, art reproduction, abridgment, condensation, or any other form in which a work may be recast, transformed, or adapted." 17 U.S.C. § 101. Films based upon books are classifiable as derivative works. Editorial revisions, annotations, elaborations, or other modifications such as an altered or updated website, may qualify as a derivative work.

(E) COPYRIGHT CREATION

Copyright arises automatically during creation of a work of authorship—even if the author does not include a copyright notice or fails to register the work with the U.S. Copyright Office. It is advisable, however, to include a copyright notice—i.e. the letter c in a circle: ©, or the word "Copyright" and the first year of a publication of a work (e.g. Copyright 2013, Michael L. Rustad)—because registration and notice confer benefits to the copyright owner. A copyright registration certificate is evidence of the validity of the copyright so the holder of the registration certificate need not produce additional evidence of ownership or originality of the copyrighted work. A defendant in a copyright infringement suit cannot use an "innocent infringer" defense to mitigate actual or statutory damages if there is a proper copyright notice affixed to a work, 17 U.S.C. § 401(D).

(F) WORK MADE FOR HIRE

In general, the creator of a copyrightable work is the rights holder. The "work for hire" doctrine is an exception to this general rule; it applies where a person creates, but is not the owner of a copyrightable work. The "Work for Hire" doctrine makes an employer the copyright owner for works prepared by their employee within the scope of employment—even if the employer does nothing more than hire the employee who creates the work.

§ 10-3. Overview of Copyright Infringement

In the past two decades, courts have generated a distinct body of copyright law to accommodate cyberspace. The discussion of direct and secondary infringement cases demonstrates how the Internet shapes and will continue to shape copyright law for the foreseeable future. To establish infringement, a copyright owner must demonstrate that: (1) the defendant has actually copied the plaintiff's work and (2) the copying is illegal because a substantial similarity exists between the defendant's work and the protectable elements of the plaintiff's creation. Federal copyright law recognizes four kinds of copyright infringement: (1) direct copyright infringement, (2) contributory copyright infringement, (3) vicarious copyright infringement and (4) inducement to commit infringement.

The early Internet-related copyright cases were against computer bulletin boards. In 1993, a Florida federal court became the first to find a computer bulletin board liable for copyright and trademark infringement when it displayed unauthorized copies of Playboy's copyrighted photographs. *Playboy Enterprises, Inc. v. Frena*, 839 F. Supp. 1552 (M.D. Fla. 1993).

In the past ten years, the cutting edge of online copyright law is peer-to-peer ("P2P") software litigation. The ten-year war against P2P file sharing networks has resulted in a number of high profile victories for copyright owners, but has done little to stem the tide of P2P sharing, particularly among younger web users. REBECCA GIBLIN, CODE WARS: 10 YEARS OF P2P SOFTWARE LITIGATION vi (2011) (foreword by Jane Ginsburg). Social-media related-copyright cases have dominated the legal landscape in recent years.

(A) DIRECT INFRINGEMENT

To prove a claim of direct copyright infringement, a plaintiff must prove that the defendant violated one or more of the plaintiff's exclusive rights under the U.S. Copyright Act. Copyright owners must therefore satisfy two requirements to prove a *prima facie* case for direct copyright infringement: (1) ownership of the allegedly infringed material, and (2) the copying of original works violated at least one exclusive right granted to copyright holders. Liability for direct copyright infringement arises from the violation of any one of the exclusive rights of a copyright owner, including the exclusive right to authorize others to reproduce, distribute, perform, display, and prepare derivative works from the copyrighted work. Sharing music or video files on BitTorrent, for example, is an infringement of the copyright owner's distribution right if unauthorized. In the past decade, the U.S. music industry has begun to file and win direct infringement lawsuits against the individuals who share copyrighted files on P2P services.

(B) SECONDARY COPYRIGHT INFRINGEMENT

Secondary Copyright Liability

Contributory	Vicarious	Inducement
One who, with knowledge of the infringing activity, induces, causes, or materially contributes to the infringing conduct of another	One who has the right and ability to supervise the infringing activity and also has a direct financial interest	One who distributes a device with the object of promoting its use to infringe copyright, as shown by clear expression or other affirmative steps taken to foster infringement

All three indirect infringement theories depend on a showing of underlying direct infringement. Secondary copyright infringement is analogous to aiding and abetting on the criminal side of the law. Evidence of active steps to induce direct copyright infringement includes activities such as advertising an infringing use or instructing users how to access infringing content. Until the last few years, nearly all P2P copyright infringement enforcement actions targeted the secondary infringers rather than the primary users.

ReDigi, a web-based storage locker, was found liable for infringing copyright owners' exclusive rights because it allowed users to resell their users tracks that had been legally purchased on iTunes. Once a user chose to sell the file, his access to it was immediately terminated. The file was then transferred to the purchaser, who in turn may stream, download, or sell the song.

The court found that ReDigi infringed two of the exclusive rights of record companies, the reproduction and distribution rights. Neither the fair use defense nor the first sale doctrine excused that infringement. ReDigi satisfied the volitional conduct requirement to render the company liable for direct infringement. ReDigi was also liable for secondary infringement: liability for contributory infringement because they knew or should have known that the service would encourage infringement and they materially contributed to their users' infringement. *Capitol Records, LLC v. ReDigi, Inc.*, 2013 WL 1286134 (S.D. N.Y. 2013).

(1) Contributory Infringement

Contributory infringement is a doctrine drawn in large part from tort law. To prevail in a contributory copyright infringement lawsuit, the plaintiff must prove: (1) direct copyright infringement by a third party, (2) knowledge by the defendant the third party was directly infringing, and (3) defendant's material contribution to the infringement. In an Internet case, plaintiffs will have a claim for contributory copyright infringement if a third-party website hosts and distributes infringing content while contributing to this infringing conduct. In P2P copyright infringement cases, the meaning of the secondary infringer's "knowledge" and the definition of materially contribute is unsettled doctrine.

(2) Vicarious Infringement

A defendant is liable for vicarious copyright infringement if the defendant "profit[s] from direct infringement while declining to exercise a right to stop or limit it." *Metro-Goldwyn Mayer Studios v. Grokster*, 545 U.S. 913 (S.Ct. 2005). To state a claim for vicarious copyright infringement, a plaintiff must allege the defendant has: (1) the right and ability to supervise the infringing conduct and (2) a direct financial interest in the infringing activity. In *Perfect 10,* the plaintiff, a publisher of an adult magazine and the operator of that magazine's subscription website—both of which featured copyrighted images of models owned by the plaintiff—asserted that the defendants were contributorily and vicariously liable because they processed credit card payments to allegedly infringing websites. The appellate court held the defendants were not vicariously liable because they had no right or ability to control the infringing activity. The infringement stemmed from the failure to get a license to distribute the copyrighted images, not from processing payments.

(3) Inducement or Encouraging Infringement

In *MGM Studios, Inc. v. Grokster Ltd.*, 545 U.S. 913 (S.Ct. 2005), the U.S. Supreme Court imported the secondary infringement theory of inducement from patent law. To establish a claim for inducement, a plaintiff must show that the defendant intentionally engaged in purposeful conduct that encouraged copyright infringement. A defendant's intent to foster infringement is established by evidence of the defendant's clear expression of such intent, or affirmative steps taken by the defendant to foster infringement.

An advertisement or solicitation that broadcasts a message designed to stimulate others to commit violations is direct evidence of inducement. Such evidence, however, is not the exclusive way of proving inducement liability. The *Grokster* Court explained that, "[o]ne infringes contributorily by intentionally inducing or encouraging direct infringement." The Court made it clear that "mere knowledge of infringing potential or actual infringing uses would not be enough here to subject [a defendant] to liability." In the wake of *Grokster*, it remains unclear whether inducement is a separate secondary copyright cause of action or merely a type of contributory copyright infringement.

In *Viacom Int'l, Inc. v. YouTube, Inc.*, 676 F.3d 19 (2d Cir. 2012), the Second Circuit affirmed in part, vacated in part, reverse in part and remanded the case back to the lower court affirming the lower court's holding that the § 512(C) safe harbor requires knowledge or awareness of specific infringing activity. The appeals court stated that the "first and most important question on appeal is whether the DMCA safe harbor at issue requires "actual knowledge" or "aware[ness]" of facts or circumstances indicating "specific and identifiable infringements." The Second Circuit instructed the lower court to consider first the scope of the statutory provision and then its application to the record in this case.

Nevertheless, the court vacated the lower court's entry of summary judgment ruling, "[a] reasonable jury could find that YouTube had actual knowledge or awareness of specific infringing activity on its website." The lower court erred by interpreting the "right and ability to control" infringing activity to require "item-specific" knowledge. Finally, the court affirmed the district court's holding that three of the challenged YouTube software functions fell within the safe harbor for infringement that occurs "by reason of" storage at the direction of the user, and remanded for further fact-finding with respect to a fourth software function.

§ 10-4. The Path of Peer-to-Peer File Sharing

Peer-to-peer ("P2P") sharing of video and music files is an Internet-related development that has shaped the law of secondary copyright infringement.

(A) NAPSTER

Napster.com ("Napster") was the pioneering P2P sharing service, permitting the exchange of MP3 music files stored on individual computer hard drives with other Napster users. Many record companies and music publishers filed copyright infringement lawsuits against Napster for facilitating P2P transmissions of copyrighted content. Napster defended its actions by asserting fair use. *A & M Records v. Napster, Inc.*, 239 F.3d 1004 (9th Cir. 2001). The court found Napster had diminished the copyright owners' commercial sales because users were downloading content without paying royalties or fees. The court rejected Napster's fair use argument, finding that commercial use of the copyrighted material occurred through Napster's users' "repeated and exploitative unauthorized copies of copyrighted works...made to save the expense [of] purchasing authorized copies."

The federal appeals court rejected Napster's argument that it was not liable for direct or contributory copyright infringement, ruling that DMCA § 512(A) did not protect Napster's referencing and indexing activities. In addition, the court held Napster liable for contributory infringement because Napster not only had knowledge of the infringing activity, it also contributed to the infringing conduct. Napster was also found to be vicariously liable because it had a direct financial interest in the visitors' infringing activities.

(B) GROKSTER

In *Metro-Goldwin-Mayer Studios, Inc. v. Grokster, Ltd.*, 545 U.S. 913 (S.Ct. 2005) the Supreme Court unanimously held that "one who distributes a device with the object of promoting its use to infringe copyright, as shown by clear expression or other affirmative steps taken to foster infringement is liable for the resulting acts of infringement by third parties." The *Grokster* Court decided the case on an "intentional inducement" theory, declining to rule on the continuing vitality of the *Sony* test for contributory infringement. The *Sony* test determines "whether a company's product is capable of substantial or commercially significant noninfringing uses." (citing *Sony Corp. of Am. v. Universal City Studios, Inc.*, 464 U.S. 417 (S.Ct. 1984).

The *Grokster* Court found that "[o]ne infringes contributorily by intentionally inducing or encouraging direct infringement." The *Grokster* Court based its inducement theory upon evidence that P2P networks intended and encouraged the use of their products for file sharing. The Court unanimously held that because the P2P defendants intentionally distributed their software, they knowingly promoted copyright infringement. Grokster induced direct infringement in its advertising and business model. "The probable scope of copyright infringement," just with respect to the two networks at issue, was "staggering" because Grokster targeted millions of consumers. "The probable scope of copyright infringement," just with respect to the two networks at issue, was "staggering." The Court demonstrates in *Grokster* that it is receptive to imposing secondary liability on third parties that facilitate IP crimes or widespread infringement.

(C) CYBERLOCKER SERVICES

"Cyberlockers" are third party file sharing services that provide password-protected hard drive space online. A user has the option of sharing the cyberlocker password information with friends, who can then privately download any content a user has placed online. This easily leads to the unauthorized sharing of copyrighted works. In *Perfect 10, Inc. v. Megaupload Ltd.*, 2011 No. 11CV0191–IEG (S.D. Cal. 2011), Perfect 10 contended that Megaupload, an online storage company, stored billions of dollars of pirated media on their servers, uploaded by users, including its copyrighted images and videos. When a visitor to Megaupload's website attempted to download this content, they were "offered the opportunity to purchase a membership" to Perfect 10's subscription-only website. The court dismissed the vicarious liability claim but denied Megaupload's motion to dismiss the claim of contributory infringement.

The FBI seized Megaupload's servers and arrested Kim Dotcom, also known as Dr. Evil, Megaupload's founder, director, and sole shareholder of Vestor Ltd. The FBI and Justice Department charged Megaupload with generating $175 million in illicit copyright proceeds. The Motion Picture Association of America ("MPAA") filed suit against Hotfile.com, another cyberlocker. Many cyberlocker services are shutting down in the wake of the FBI takeover of Megaupload. Copyright owners have won nearly every P2P case, but these victories have done little to deter widespread file sharing.

§ 10–5. Links, Framing, Bookmarks, and Thumbnails

(A) HYPERLINKS

Typically, there is no copyright infringement when merely linking to a third party's website that contains infringing materials. In *Bernstein v. J.C. Penney*, 1998 WL 906644 (C.D. Cal. 1998), a federal court in California dismissed a copyright infringement claim against J.C. Penney for linking to a Swedish website with infringing content. In that case, the site with the infringing material was several links distant from J.C. Penney's website. "Deep linking" occurs when a defendant's link bypasses the principal web page containing the trademark owner's logo and third party advertising. The Canadian Supreme Court in *Crookes v. Newton*, 2011 SCC 47 (SCC 2011) held that a mere hyperlink could not be considered a publication.

(B) FRAMING

"Framing" is displaying content from another website while still maintaining advertisements from the original site. Framing allows the user to visit one website while remaining in a prior one. This method of online advertising causes a second website to appear on a part of another site. Eugene R. Quinn Jr., *Web Surfing 101: The Evolving Law of Hyperlinking*, 2 BARRY L. REV. 37, 46, 59 (2001).

To date, no appellate court has weighed in on framing. In *Washington Post v. Total News, Inc.*, No. 97 Civ. 1190 (S.D. N.Y. 2011), the Washington Post along with other publishers charged that Total News infringed its copyrights and trademarks, and misappropriated their news material but the case settled before an appellate opinion.

(C) BOOKMARKS

The Seventh Circuit in *Flava Works v. Gunter, 2012* U.S. App. LEXIS 15977 (7th Cir. 2012), determined that myVidster was not a contributory infringer merely because a website visitor bookmarks a video and later clicks on the bookmark and views the video. The federal district court issued a preliminary injunction against the social media site, which was vacated by the U.S. Court of Appeals. Flava Works produced and distributed videos "of black men engaged in homosexual acts." The court acknowledged that myVidster "may have done a bad thing by bypassing "Flava's pay wall" by enabling viewing the uploaded copy, but it does not constitute copyright infringement." The direct infringers are Flava's customers who copied his copyrighted videos and posted them to the Internet. The court stated that myVidster could be liable for contributory infringement under an inducement theory but there was no evidence in the record supporting that claim.

(D) THUMBNAILS OF IMAGES

In *Kelly v. Arriba Soft Corp.*, 77 F. Supp.2d 1116 (C.D. Cal. 1999), ditto.com, a search engine, retrieved images by matching the keyword searched with the description of image files sorted in Ditto's database. Leslie Kelly, a Western art photographer filed suit against ditto.com for reproducing and displaying his copyrighted art on its search engine in miniature. Ditto would index the images and "display them in 'thumbnail' form on the search results page." The Ninth Circuit found Arriba Soft's use of thumbnails was transformative because the greatly reduced copies of copyrighted images used in the thumbnails were for a different purpose.

In 2002, the Ninth Circuit affirmed the district court's holding that thumbnails infringed Kelly's copyrighted photographs, but fair use permitted the use of the thumbnails in Ditto.com's image index. In a 2003, decision, the Ninth Circuit upheld the panel's ruling that search engines could use thumbnails of images, but withdrew the portion of the opinion dealing with inline linking or framing.

In *Perfect 10, Inc. v. Google, Inc.*, 508 F.3d 1146 (9th Cir. 2007), the plaintiff created photographs of nude models for commercial distribution. After publishing its magazine, Perfect 10, began offering access to these pictures on its password protected paid subscription website. Google's search engine used a web crawler to copy thumbnail images of Perfect 10's copyrighted photographs for use in its search engine. In *Perfect 10*, the Ninth Circuit held Google's thumbnail sized reproduction of entire copyrighted images in its search engine results page to be "highly transformative."

Google's use of the copyrighted images was to find content, which was a radically different purpose than the original copyright owner's use. The Ninth Circuit held that Perfect 10 was not likely to prevail it its copyright infringement arising out of Google's "in-line links" that allowed Internet users to view infringing copyrighted images on third party's websites. In addition, the court found no vicarious or contributory infringement in its use of thumbnails or in-line links.

§ 10-6. Database Protection

As noted earlier in this chapter, in 1991, the U.S. Supreme Court held in *Feist Publications, Inc., v. Rural Telephone Service Co.* (S.Ct. 1989) that compiling information alone without a minimum of original creativity does not satisfy the originality element of the U.S. Copyright Act. The Court rejected Rural's "sweat of the brow" argument, finding that there was no infringement since Rural had no copyright in the telephone white databases. The U.S. rejection of sweat of the brow diverges sharply with the EU's approach. The European Union enacted the Database Directive in 1996, granting legal protection of databases in any form.

Article 6 of the Directive provides for copyright protection for databases, while Article 9 provides for a *sui generis* right of protection. Article 7 notes that the object of "protection" is to protect database developers who have made "qualitatively and/or quantitatively a substantial investment in either the obtaining, verification or presentation of the contents to prevent extraction." Under EU's dual system for protecting databases, copyright law protects compilations meeting the requirements of fixation, and origination, for a 70-year term.

Prior to the Database Directive, EU countries differed in their approaches to database protection. The United Kingdom, for example, endorsed the "sweat of the brow" approach and granted protection to database works considering "skill, labour and judgment," even though the databases might not be either creative or original. JOHN CROSS ET. AL, GLOBAL ISSUES IN INTELLECTUAL PROPERTY LAW 108 (2010).

Article 10(1) provides that the EU's *sui generis* term of protection for databases (not satisfying the originality requirement for copyright protection) is "fifteen years from the first of January of the year following the date of completion. Article 9 of the Database Directive recognizes an exception to the *sui generis* protection for data used in either teaching, or scientific research. *Sui generis* database protection was prefigured by the Nordic countries' "catalogue rule," providing "short-term protection for catalogues, tables and similar fact-based compilations." The U.S. publishing industry has lobbied Congress to adopt similar *sui generis* legislation to protect U.S.-based databases. In an attempt to circumvent the *Feist* opinion on sweat of the brow, U.S. database developers lobbied for similar legislation.

§ 10-7. Limitations on Exclusive Rights

Under the "first sale" doctrine, a topic covered in Chapter 4, once the copyright holder sells a copy of the copyrighted work, the owner of the copy can "sell or otherwise dispose of the possession of that copy" without the copyright holder's consent. Because of the first sale doctrine, the owners of software license rather than sell copies of software. In *UMG Recordings, Inc. v. Augusto*, 558 F.Supp.2d 1055 (C.D. Cal. 2009), the federal court held that the boilerplate language used on a promotional CD did not create a license, and therefore the resale of these already-distributed copies was protected by the first sale doctrine.

Courts determine whether there has been a sale or licensing using an economic realities test, as opposed to the labels parties to the sale use. Calling an agreement a license does not make it so. Courts determine whether there has been a sale or licensing using an economic realities test, as opposed to the labels used by the parties to the sale. Calling an agreement a license does not make it so. Courts look at economic realities such as whether the software publisher has placed limits on the use of copyrighted content or other attributes of a license versus a sale. Courts will unveil a sale masquerading in the clothing of a license.

§ 10-8. Digital Millennium Copyright Act

(A) OVERVIEW OF THE DMCA

Congress enacted the Digital Millennium Copyright Act ("DMCA"), 17 U.S.C. § 1201 et seq. to fulfill its obligations under the 1996 World Intellectual Property Organization ("WIPO") Copyright treaties. The DMCA created both civil remedies, *see* 17 U.S.C. § 1203 and criminal sanctions against circumventing copyright protection or marketing anti-circumvention devices.

See 17 U.S.C. § 1204. The DMCA specifically authorizes a court to grant temporary and permanent injunctions on such terms, as it deems reasonable to prevent or restrain a violation. *See* 17 U.S.C. § 1203(b)(1). The Digital Millennium Copyright Act ("DMCA") was the first time that Congress revised copyright law to accommodate Internet technologies.

The DMCA was enacted in 1998 to implement two World Intellectual Property Organization treaties: the WIPO Copyright Treaty ("WCT"), and the WIPO Performances and Phonograms Treaty ("WPPT"). The DMCA also addresses other significant copyright-related issues and is part of the frequently amended U.S. Copyright Act. Title I, the "WIPO Copyright and Performances and Phonograms Treaties Implementation Act of 1998," implements the WIPO Copyright and Performances and Phonographs Treaty Implementation Act by criminalizing the circumvention or removal of Digital Rights Management ("DRM")—digital locks on copyrighted materials—and by prohibiting trafficking in tools that are primarily designed, valued or marketed for such circumvention.

Title II, the "Online Copyright Infringement Liability Limitation Act" ("OCILLA") creates four "safe harbors" that enable qualifying service providers to limit their liability for claims of copyright infringement when engaging in certain types of activities. Titles III, IV, and V contain miscellaneous provisions addressing other copyright issues.

(B) TITLE I'S PROVISIONS

Title I of the DMCA added Chapter 12, entitled "Copyright Protection and Management Systems," to the U.S. Copyright Act. The DMCA distinguishes between circumvention and trafficking. Trafficking in qualified technology that circumvents technological measures that controls either access to a copyrighted work, or protects the author's rights, are both prohibited, while the actual act of circumvention is only prohibited when it circumvents a technological measure that controls access, not protecting the author's rights. The DMCA provides legal protection for anti-copying technology as well as anti-access technology.

The WCT requires signatory powers to provide remedies against defendants circumventing digital rights management tools or tampering with copyright management information. DRM tools restrict the use and copying of digital information such as music or movies. Congress had the statutory purpose of facilitating "the robust development and world-wide expansion of electronic commerce, communications, research, development, and education in the digital age." S. Rep. No. 105-190 (1998) at 1-2.

(1) Anti-Circumvention Provisions

Section 1201 prohibits the circumvention of anti-access technology as well as the making and selling of anti-circumvention devices. To "circumvent a technological measure" means that the defendant has descrambled a scrambled work, decrypted an encrypted work, or bypassed a technological measure protecting a copyrighted work. 17 U.S.C. § 1201(A)(3)(A). The DMCA makes it a crime to "circumvent a technological protection measure that effectively controls access" to copyrighted works. 17 U.S.C. § 1201(A)(1)(A). "A technological measure "effectively controls access to a work" if the measure, in the ordinary course of its operation, requires the application of information, or a process, or a treatment, with the authority of the copyright owner, to gain access to the work." 17 U.S.C. § 1201(A)(3)(B). The DMCA proscribes circumventing anti-access measures, but does not prohibit circumventing anti-copying measures. Apple's FairPlay and Microsoft Windows Digital Rights Managers, for example, provide controls on the viewing or playing of copyright materials, which is accessing a service.

Software "that circumvents "digital walls" in violation of the DMCA . . . is like a skeleton key that can open a locked door, a combination that can open a safe, or a device that can neutralize the security device attached to a store's products" or "a digital crowbar." *Universal City Studios v. Corley*, 273 F.3d 429 (2d Cir. 2001). The DMCA's anti-circumvention prohibitions essentially criminalize picking digital locks guarding access to copyrighted materials. It does not, however, prohibit circumvention of technological measures that protect the exclusive rights of an author under § 106 of the Copyright Act, such as copying or distribution, as such infringement may be protected by "fair use." This bifurcation between access and copying differs from the anti-trafficking provisions, which proscribes both. In *Lexmark Int. v. Static Control Components*, 387 F.3d 522 (6th Cir. 2004), the Sixth Circuit held that software on a printer cartridge did not qualify as a protected access control device. The court reasoned that computer code did not control access, but was to prevent copying of the program.

(2) Anti-Trafficking Provisions

The DMCA's anti-trafficking provisions cover those who traffic in, or manufacture, import, offer to the public, or provide, any technology, product, service, device, component, or part thereof, that can circumvent "a technological measure" controlling *access* to a copyrighted work. 17 U.S.C. § 1201(A)(2). The DMCA protects the rights of an author—such as copying, distribution, or any of the other exclusive rights embodied in Section 106 of the Copyright Act. A "Prohibited Device" is one that (1) is primarily designed for circumvention, (2) has limited uses for legitimate commercial purposes (other than circumvention), or (3) is marketed for use in circumventing copyright protection. The penalty is up to five years imprisonment for a defendant's first offense in manufacturing, importing, offering to the public, or trafficking in such a device, technology, product, or service.

(C) TITLE II'S SAFE HARBORS

Title II of the DMCA, OCILLA, protects online service providers ("OSPs") who meet certain safe harbor requirements from liability for all monetary relief for direct, vicarious, and contributory infringement. To qualify for protection under any of the DMCA § 512 safe harbors, a party must meet a set of threshold criteria. First, the party must in fact be a service provider, defined, in part, as an OSP, network access administrator, or the operator of facilities. A party that qualifies as an OSP must also satisfy certain conditions of eligibility, including adopting, reasonably implementing, and informing subscribers of a policy that provides for the termination of accounts of recidivist copyright infringers. They must also accommodate, and not interfere with, standard technical measures that are used by copyright owners to identify or protect copyrighted works, or they are divested of the safe harbors of § 512(A)–(D).

Under the DMCA, ISPs are immunized from secondary copyright infringement claims for four activities: (1) transitory communications; (2) caching; (3) content of websites hosted by the ISP; and (4) information location tools. Section 512(a) of the DMCA limits the liability of a service provider where the ISP merely transmits digital information that may include infringing material. The next section is a guide to the four OSP safe harbors, which vary significantly in their preconditions.

(1)   Transitory   Digital   Network Communications

The DMCA immunizes OSPs for all copyright infringement "by reason of the provider's transmitting, routing, or providing connections for, material through a system or network controlled or operated by or for the service provider, or by reason of the intermediate and transient storage of that material." 17 U.S.C. § 512(A). The definition of an OSP is narrower for transitory digital network communications than the other safe harbors in § 512(B)–(D). This safe harbor applies only to OSPs qualifying under OCILLA's narrow definition, which means those "entities that transmit, route, or provide connections for digital online communications, between or among points specified by user." To qualify for the transitory digital network communications safe harbor, OSPs may not modify content transmitted, routed, or connected. Someone other than the OSP must initiate the transmission of the material.

(2) System Caching

The DMCA immunizes service providers for caching so long as they provide online services or network access. 17 U.S.C. § 512(k)(1)(B). OSPs claiming the caching safe harbor must expeditiously respond to takedown notices and remove, or disable, objectionable content. Assuming these preconditions are satisfied, Section 512(B) shields service providers from injunctive or monetary remedies for caching copyrighted materials.

(3) Storage Exemption

The storage exemption safe harbor provision of DMCA limits the liability of online service providers for copyright infringement that occurs, "by reason of the storage at the direction of a user of material" residing on a system or network, controlled, or operated by or for the service provider. 17 U.S.C.

§ 512(C)(1). To qualify for this safe harbor, OSPs cannot have actual knowledge the material or activity is infringing or be aware infringing activities are apparent.

In addition, they must: (1) perform a qualified storage or search function for Internet users, (2) lack actual or imputed knowledge of the infringing activity, (3) receive no financial benefit directly from such activity in a case where the provider has the right and ability to control it, (4) act promptly to remove or disable access to the material when the designated agent is notified that it is infringing, (5) adopt, reasonably implement, and publicize a policy of terminating repeat infringers, and (6) accommodate and not interfere with standard technical measures used by copyright owners to identify or protect copyrighted works.

(a) OSP's Registered Agent for Responding to Complaints

To qualify for the storage exemption safe harbor for information residing on systems or networks, the OSP must designate an agent to receive notice from copyright owners when there is a complaint of infringement. The OSP must also post the agent's name on its website and register the agent with the Library of Congress' Copyright Office and provide required information such as contact telephone numbers and working e-mail addresses.

OSPs are required to maintain a DMCA agent to receive takedown notices and respond expeditiously to takedown notices. Suffolk University Law School, for example, must appoint an agent designated to receive notification of a claimed copyright infringement under the DMCA. If a website did not maintain an agent, or fulfill the other requirements of § 512, they would be subject to secondary copyright liability arising out of third party postings, even when they are not the content creator. A service provider must act "expeditiously to remove, or disable access to, the material" when it (1) has actual knowledge, (2) is aware of facts or circumstances from which infringing activity is apparent, or (3) has received notification of claimed infringement meeting the requirements of § 512(C)(3).

(b) Takedown & Put-Back Rules

In order to meet the requirements of § 512(a)'s safe harbor, the ISP must meet stringent criteria. Section 512(c) of the DMCA immunizes service providers from copyright infringement claims so long as they do not have actual knowledge of the infringing activity and promptly block allegedly infringing sales once notified. To qualify for such protection, an ISP must meet three requirements: (i) the service provider must either lack both actual knowledge of the infringing activity and awareness of facts or circumstances from which infringing activity should be apparent, or it must promptly, upon gaining such knowledge move to prevent the use of its service to further such infringing activity; (ii) the service provider must not receive a financial benefit directly attributable to infringing activity it has the ability to control; and (iii) the service provider must expeditiously remove material from its service on receipt of an appropriate written notice in order to qualify for safe harbor protection under the DMCA.

The DMCA's complex notice, takedown, and put-back procedures are triggered when a copyright owner, or an assignee, gives written notice to the designated agent of the service provider under § 512(C)(3)(A). The copyright owner is able to find the contact information for the service provider's agent because, as mentioned above, that information is posted on the website of the U.S. Copyright Office. The copyright owner must give the provider's designated agent a written takedown notice which includes: (1) a physical or electronic signature of a person authorized to act on behalf of the copyright owner of the right allegedly infringed, (2) identification of the copyrighted works allegedly infringing, (3) identification of the parts of the copyrighted work that are infringing and thus should be removed, (4) sufficient information to contact copyright owner or complaining party, (5) a statement by the complainant in the good faith belief that the material is infringing, and (6) a statement that the information in the notice is accurate.

Congress' "red flag" test strips service providers of their immunity if they fail to take action with regard to infringing material if they gain awareness of facts or circumstances where infringement is apparent (red flags). Section 512(F)(1)–(2) of the DMCA provides remedies if a person "knowingly materially misrepresents" information "(1) that

material or activity is infringing, or (2) that
material or activity was removed or disabled by
mistake or misidentification." 17 U.S.C.
§ 512(F)(1)(2). Those persons who knowingly
misrepresent the facts in take-down notices:

> shall be liable for any damages, including costs
> and attorneys' fees, incurred by the alleged
> infringer, by any copyright owner or copyright
> owner's authorized licensee or by a service
> provider, who is injured by such
> misrepresentation, as the result of the service
> provider relying upon such misrepresentation *in
> rem*oving or disabling access to the material or
> activity claimed to be infringing, or in replacing
> the removed material or ceasing to disable
> access to it. 17 U.S.C. § 512(F)(2).

Once the OSP's designated agent receives a notice
that substantially complies with the DMCA's
requirements, it must expeditiously remove the
identified material. The DMCA provides that a user
whose material has been removed or disabled may
have a right to a put back of the disputed content.
After the user who posted the objectionable material
receives notice, he or she, has a statutory right to
send a written counter-notification to the OSP's
designated agent. The counter notice must
minimally contain the subscriber's signature—
physical or digital—identify the material removed,
and give a statement that the user has a good-faith
belief that the material was mistakenly removed or
disabled. 17 U.S.C. § 512(G)(3)(C).

After receiving a counter-notification, the agent then must promptly (1) provide the person who filed the original takedown notice with a copy of the counter notification, and (2) advise that it will replace the removed material or cease disabling access to it in ten business days. 17 U.S.C. § 512(G)(2)(B). Unless the person who provided the takedown notice—the copyright owner or their assignee—gives notice that he or she has filed a copyright infringement lawsuit or other judicial action, the OSP must replace or reactivate the removed material no sooner than 10, and no later than 14 business days. 17 U.S.C. § 512(G)(2)(C). The takedown procedures of the DMCA only apply to copyright materials because a website has no duty to takedown material that constitutes trademark infringement, torts, crimes, or other ongoing wrongdoing.

(4) Information Location Tools

Section 512(D) is the OSP safe harbor used by search engines such as Google, or Yahoo! The OSP safe harbor limits an Internet Service Provider's liability for monetary relief, as well as injunctive relief, for secondary copyright infringement for activities such as "linking users to an online location containing infringing material or infringing activity, by using information location tools" such as "a directory, index, reference, pointer, or hypertext link." 17 U.S.C. § 512(D).

(D) EXEMPTIONS & THE FIRST AMENDMENT

The DMCA exempts nonprofit libraries, archives, and educational institutions so long as these organizations make a good faith determination when acquiring a copy of a protected work. Academic commentators view these anti-circumvention measures as an inappropriate extension of copyright impediments to fair use. Courts are still determining the proper balance between the DMCA's copyright protection measures and the doctrine of fair use. In *Universal City Studios, Inc. v. Reimerdes*, 111 F. Supp. 2d 294 (S.D.N.Y. 2000), several motion picture studios brought action under the DMCA to enjoin Internet website owners from posting, or downloading, computer software decrypting digitally encrypted movies on digital versatile disks ("DVDs"), and from including hyperlinks to other websites making decryption software available. The federal court ruled the Internet posting of decryption software violated DMCA provisions prohibiting trafficking in technology circumventing measures controlling access to copyrighted works. The *Reimerdes* court also ruled that posting hyperlinks to other websites offering decryption software violated DMCA. The court rejected the defendant's First Amendment challenge finding the DMCA's anti-trafficking provision to be content-neutral as applied to a decryption computer program. The court ruled that the DMCA's anti-trafficking provision was not overly broad, and that the plaintiffs were entitled to an injunction enjoining the defendants from posting decryption software, or hyperlinking to other websites making such software available.

The Second Circuit upheld the *Reimerdes* decision in *Universal City Studios, Inc. v. Corley* (2d Cir. 2001). The Second Circuit held the decryption software qualified as "speech" for First Amendment purposes because the computer code combined non-speech and speech elements. The *Corley* court found the DMCA anti-circumvention regulation to have an incidental effect on a speech component and found the government's interest in preventing unauthorized access to encrypted copyrighted material to be substantial as the governmental interest was unrelated to the suppression of free expression. The federal appeals court upheld the injunction finding it to be a content neutral restriction on owners' speech. The court also found the injunction did not burden substantially more speech than necessary to further the government's interest. Finally, the injunction did not eliminate owners' "fair use" of copyrighted materials and was therefore constitutional.

(E) TAKEDOWN AND PUTBACK CASES

In *Lenz v. Universal Music Corp.*, 2008 WL 3884333 (N.D. Cal. 2008), a California district court ruled that a copyright owner had to consider the fair use doctrine in formulating good faith belief in connection with takedown notice under the DMCA. A California court held Universal acted in bad faith by issuing a takedown notice for a 29-second video of her 18-month-old child dancing to Prince's song, Let's Go Crazy that had been uploaded to YouTube.

YouTube removed the video and Lenz sent a counter notification pursuant to 17 U.S.C. § 512(G), asserting that her family video constituted fair use of the song and thus did not infringe Universal's copyrights. Universal sent her a removal notice asserting Prince's wishes not to have his songs posted on YouTube.

The court found Universal's failure to consider fair use as sufficient to state a misrepresentation claim pursuant to the DMCA. The *Lenz* court also ruled the plaintiff alleged a cognizable injury in responding to a bad faith takedown notice. The court sent a deterrent message to copyright owners that mechanically file DMCA takedown notices without considering fair use. In the post-*Lenz* period, copyright owners risk being penalized for filing takedown notices for material protected by fair use.

§ 10-9. Copyright Issues in the Cloud

Cloud computing raises new concerns for copyright owners seeking to protect content from being illegally shared by mobile users. Cloud computing enables copyrighted works to be illegally transmitted and distributed as never before. Myxer.com, for example, is a cloud service that allows users to upload sound files and create ringtones, which they can then download and send to their phones. In *Capitol Records Inc. v. MP3tunes LLC*, No. 1:07–CV–09931–WHP-FM (S.D. N.Y. 2011), a cloud music provider, ran a music locker service where users could upload their music library onto MP3tunes servers and access their music over the Internet. The *MP3tunes* court ruled that the music locker business did not infringe on copyright by observing that the cloud provider stored only one copy of a particular song, no matter how many users added it to their music library. The court held that the DMCA does not require vigilant copyright monitoring by a company having users that upload infringing content. A DMCA takedown notice for a song in the locker of one user does not require removal of that song from all users' accounts.

§ 10-10. International Issues

(A) EXTRATERRITORIALITY

Takedown disputes will increasingly involve parties in different countries, which raise extraterritoriality issues. In general, intellectual property rights are left to each nation to enforce. A copyright infringement claim may not be brought in U.S. courts for conduct committed entirely outside the territorial boundaries of the United States.

(B) SOPA

In the fall of 2011, Congress considered several controversial bills that would allow blocking orders against infringing ISPs and the removal of pirate websites. The Stop Online Piracy Act ("SOPA") was a proposed U.S. House of Representatives statute to expand the ability of U.S. law enforcement to fight online trafficking in copyrighted works. The companion statute in the U.S. Senate was the Protect IP ACT ("PIPA"). Reddit, TwitPic, and 7,000 other websites went "black" to express their opposition to SOPA and PIPA. The worldwide backlash against overly expansive online copyright forced governments to withdraw their support.

(C) ACTA

The Anti-Counterfeiting Trade Agreement ("ACTA") was a proposed multinational treaty to establish uniform standards for enforcing intellectual property rights. ACTA fortified the enforcement provisions of the TRIPS agreement by targeting counterfeit goods, infringing generic goods, and widespread copyright infringement. In March of 2012, the European Parliament voted to refer ACTA to the European Court of Justice, which stalled ratification for Eurozone countries.

(D) MORAL RIGHTS

Victor Hugo's descendants filed an action based on moral rights against a French journalist who wrote and published a sequel to Hugo's *Les Miserables*. Likewise, the great-grandson of Victor Hugo argued that Disney's cartoon film *The Hunchback of Notre Dame* violated the integrity of the author's work; a moral right not followed in U.S. copyright law, but recognized in the Berne Convention for the Protection of Literary and Artistic Works protecting the moral rights of authors (*droit moral*).

Article 6(B) of the Berne Convention provides that "the means of redress for safeguarding the [right of integrity] shall be governed by the legislation of the country where protection is

claimed." PATRICK W. BERGOS, THE BERNE
CONVENTION (1997). The right of integrity, for
example, is "inalienable and perpetual" thereby
protecting the artist against "any distortion or
alteration of his or her creation once the completed
work has been transferred or made the subject of
publication performance." Moral rights include the
right of attribution, integrity, spirit, and
personality.

The United States enacted the Visual Artists
Rights Act of 1990 ("VARA") to implement the
Berne Convention. Regardless of assignment or
ownership of rights, VARA protects the expectation
that a visual work will not be revised, altered, or
distorted. VARA has little application to the
Internet since it only protects works of visual art
that have attained the status of "recognized
stature." "The Internet raises the potential for
infringement of an author's *moral rights*. Issues
raised specifically by the Internet include the
circumstances"—where their creations are
presented when a website links to another site.
MAREE SANSBURY, MORAL RIGHTS AND THEIR
APPLICATION IN AUSTRALIA 147 (2003).

While moral rights have been applied primarily to
works of art created in a tangible medium, they can
apply to online modifications as well. "Two moral
rights are of primary importance in respect of works
placed on the Internet: the right of attribution and
the right of integrity." PETER GRABOSKY & RUSSELL
G. SMITH, CRIME IN THE DIGITAL AGE: CONTROLLING
TELECOMMUNICATIONS AND CYBERSPACE 116 (1998).
The right to false attribution could be extended to

computer programs or website creations. Similarly, manipulating an electronic or digitalized photograph could violate the right not to have an artist's work distorted, mutilated, or modified.

Any "assignment of economic rights is not accompanied by assignment of moral rights. . . French rights, may provide a remedy where infringement relating to a digital work is disseminated over the Internet." CATHERINE COLSTON & JONATHAN GALLOWAY, MODERN INTELLECTUAL PROPERTY 450 (2010). In *Gilliam v. American Broadcasting Co.*, 538 F.2d 14 (2d Cir. 1976), the British creators of the television series, *Monty Python's Flying Circus*, argued that the rebroadcasted series that shortened the programs and edited them greatly violated their moral rights. The *Gilliam* court held that the Lanham Act protected the creators from the excessive mutilation or altered versions of their comedic television series. The court defined the concept of *droit moral*, or moral right, as, "including the right of the artist to have his work attributed to him in the form in which he created it." The Second Circuit stated that: "American Copyright Law, as presently written does not recognize moral rights or provide a cause of action for their violation, since the law seeks to vindicate the economic rather than the personal rights of authors."

(E) EXTRATERRITORIAL REACH

The Copyright Act has only limited extraterritorial reach. *Litecubes LLC v. Northern Light Products, Inc.*, 523 F.3d 1353 (Fed. Cir. 2008).

The Copyright Act provides that "[i]mportation into the United States, without the authority of the owner of copyright under this title, of copies . . . of a work that have been acquired outside the United States is an infringement of the exclusive right to distribute copies . . . under section 106, 17 U.S.C. § 106. It is well established that the Copyright Act does not "reach acts of infringement that take place entirely abroad." *Subafilms Ltd. v. MGM-Pathe Commn'ns Co.*, 24 F.3d 1088 (9th Cir. 1994).

(F) EUROPEAN ISPS & NO DUTY TO MONITOR

The issue of whether Internet service providers should monitor illegal content remains a contentious issue. The European Court of Justice ("ECJ") in *Belgische Vereniging van Auteurs, Componisten en Uitgevers CVBA (Sabam v. Netlog NV,* 2012) ruled that an Internet Service Provider had no obligation to monitor illegal content. The court reasoned that imposing an injunction would be the functional equivalent of requiring ISPs to monitor content, contrary to European Directives.

CHAPTER 11

TRADEMARKS ON THE GLOBAL INTERNET

A trademark is a word, phrase, symbol or design, or a combination thereof, that identifies and distinguishes the source of the goods of one party from those of others. Trademarks not only identify the origin of goods and services, which is the traditional function of trademarks, they also fulfill a consumer protection role in being a mark of quality. New goods and services are promoted online at "Internet speed," creating strains in trademark law. The Internet's disregard of geographic borders creates conflicts between concurrent users, which would never have arisen between distant companies in the purely brick-and-mortar world. Courts have come to recognize an "Internet trio" of confusion factors: (1) similarity of the marks, (2) relatedness of the goods and services, and (3) simultaneous use of the Internet for marketing. While trademark law traditionally works well in product counterfeiting cases, it is increasingly ill fitted to the Internet.

An emergent Internet-related issue is to the intersection between trademark law and torts—such as trade secret misappropriation, defamation, privacy/publicity and e-personation. New trademark issues such as using a competitor's name in metatags and/or domain names are also evolving at a rapid pace. The latest trademark-related abuse is "username squatting," where entrepreneurs register usernames containing another's mark with the intent to sell the username to the mark holder for a profit. For example, Coca-Cola and Nike were allegedly "victims of squatters of their Twitter identities." Lisa P. Ramsay, *Brandjacking on Social Networks: Trademark Infringement for Impersonation of Markholders*, 58 BUFF. L. REV. 851, 852 (2010). Social media such as Facebook and Twitter have created new venues for trademark infringement. Trademark owners, like copyright owner, monitor social media for trademark misuse. In contrast to copyright law, Congress has yet to enact revisions to the trademark law covering notice-and-takedown procedures as they did with the DMCA. Websites such as eBay monitor their sites and takedown auctions involving infringing content.

§ 11-1. Overview of Internet-Related Trademark Law

The federal trademark statute establishes a system for the registration and protection of trademarks used in commerce. U.S. trademark law is found in the common law, state statutes and the federal Lanham Act of 1946 ("Lanham Act"), which provides a civil action against any person who shall, without consent of the registrant, use in commerce any reproduction, counterfeit copy, or colorable imitation of a registered mark in connection with the sale, offering for sale, distribution, or advertising of any goods with which such use is likely to cause confusion, or to cause mistake, or to deceive." 15 U.S.C. § 1114(A). The Lanham Act describes a trademark as being a limited property right in a particular word, phrase, or symbol, and federal trademark protection is only available for marks "used in commerce." 15 U.S.C. § 1127. In the twenty first century, trademark law has evolved to address websites and domain names. Mobile application names and icons, for example, constitute a new frontier for trademark protection.

(A) THE DISTENSION OF TRADEMARKS

Traditional or conventional trademarks are unique identifiers that employ words, logos, pictures, symbols, or combinations of these elements. The nonconventional use of trademark has expanded to include single color trademarks, sound trademarks, three dimensional trademarks, shape trademarks and even scent trademarks. In the last decades of the twentieth century, courts expanded what could be trademarked. Coca-Cola®'s bottle was registered as a three dimensional mark in 1977. In 1987, Owens-Corning was granted a trademark for the color pink in insulation. Clarke's Osewez® was granted a trademark on a fragrance for use on their sewing thread and embroidery yarn in 1991.

(B) FEDERAL TRADEMARK REGISTRATION

The Trademark Act of 1946, as amended, 15 U.S.C. § 1051, governs the federal registration of trademarks. Trademark applicants need to consider (1) the mark they want to register, (2) the goods and/or services in connection with which you wish to register the mark, and (3) whether they will be filing the application based on actual existing use of the mark or a *bona fide* intention to use the mark in

the future. A trademark application "must specify
the proper "basis" for filing, whether current use of
the mark in commerce or on an intent to use the
mark in commerce in the future." The U.S.
Trademark Office publishes approved trademarks
on the Principal Register of the United States
Patent and Trademark Office ("USPTO"). A
trademark must be distinctive and thus functions as
a source identifier. America Express, for example,
trademarked the phrase, "Don't Leave Home
Without it." Microsoft's Window's icon is an example
of a picture or symbol. IBM is an example of using
letters. Beginning in the late twentieth century, the
Trademark Office recognizes more nonconventional
trademarks as represented in the chart below.

Type	Company	Trademark
Color Marks	Owens-Corning	Pink Color for Insulation
Trade Dress	Coca Cola	Shape of the Coke Bottle
Sound Marks	MGM	MGM's lion's roar
Motion Marks	Sony Ericsson	Flipbook of twenty images
Lacquered Sole on Shoes	Christian Louboutin	Lacquered red sole on

		footwear.
Fragrance Marks	Kalin Manchev	Rose oil scent

A company will claim rights in its trademarks or service marks by labeling its product with the "™," "ˢᴹ," and "®" symbols. A *service mark* is the same as a trademark, except that it identifies and distinguishes the source of a service rather than a product and is defined by the USPTO as a, "word, phrase, symbol or design, or a combination thereof, that identifies and distinguishes the source of a service rather than goods." The USPTO refers to the term, "trademark" to include both trademarks and service marks. The USPTO has registered Internet Domain Names as trademarks since 1997.

The term of a federal trademark registration is 10 years and can be renewed indefinitely for 10-year periods. Trademark owners must file an affidavit, or a declaration of continued use, with the USPTO to keep the registration alive between the fifth and sixth year after the date of initial registration. Failure of the registrant to provide the affidavit results in cancellation of the trademark registration. Trademarks may be established by using a mark in commerce, without a federal registration. However, the USPTO explains the advantages of owning a federal trademark registration on the Principal Register:

- Public notice of your claim of ownership of the mark;

- A legal presumption of your ownership of the mark and your exclusive right to use the mark nationwide on or in connection with the goods/services listed in the registration;

- The ability to bring an action concerning the mark in federal court;

- The use of the U.S. registration as a basis to obtain registration in foreign countries;

- The ability to record the U.S. registration with the U.S. Customs and Border Protection (CBP) Service to prevent importation of infringing foreign goods;

- The right to use the federal registration symbol ® and

- Listing in the United States Patent and Trademark Office's online databases. USPTO, Trademark FAQs, *What Are the Benefits of Trademark Registration?* (2012).

Famous trademarks like Coca-Cola will have trademark protection in perpetuity; so long as they continue to renew their registration with the USPTO. The two principal rights in a trademark are a federal trademark registration and the right to use the mark. In general, the first party who either uses a mark in commerce or files an application in the trademark office has the ultimate right to register that mark. The date of first use anywhere is the date when the goods were first sold or transported, or, the services were first rendered under the mark, if such use is *bona fide* and in the ordinary course of trade. 15 U.S.C. § 1127.

Under U.S. trademark law, it is the first person to use a mark in interstate commerce rather than the first to register it who has priority. Factors determining first use include which party first affixed the mark to a product, or whose party's name appeared with the trademark. Other factors considered are which party maintained the quality and uniformity of the product, or created the good will associated with a product. Registration with the Trademark Office gives the owner exclusive rights only in the United States. However, marks may be registered in different countries; a practice that is recommended for companies selling goods and rendering services on the Internet to foreign countries.

The registration of trademarks signals constructive notice of mark ownership, and creates a legal presumption in favor of ownership. Trademark registrants have the right to bring infringement or dilution actions in federal court. Finally, registration is a predicate to the U.S. Customs Department preventing the importation of infringing goods.

(C) STATE TRADEMARK LAW

Trademark registration procedures vary widely from state to state. Under the California state trademark law, online companies need to register their trademarks to receive protection. However, under the Massachusetts commonwealth trademark law, online companies need not register with the

Commonwealth to receive protection, but they may if they want to. In 2006, Massachusetts adopted the International Trademark Association's Revised Model State Trademark Bill ("INTA-MSTB"); an online company, or an individual, may register a trademark or service with the Corporation Division, so long as the mark is used in the Commonwealth. The use must be *bona fide*, and not to reserve a right in the mark.

A trademark is considered in use when it is affixed on the goods or containers, and on the tags, labels, displays or documents associated with the goods, and those goods are sold or transported within the Commonwealth. Similarly, service marks are used or displayed in the sale or advertising of services. The Internet has marginalized the value of state trademark registration because by definition, cyberspace disputes are rarely between citizens of the same state.

(D) TRADEMARK APPLICATIONS

(1) Elements of an Application

Trademark applications, filed in the USPTO, must include: (1) the name of the applicant, (2) a name and address for correspondence, (3) a clear drawing of the mark, (4) a listing of the goods or services, and (5) the filing fee for at least one class of goods or services. The Madrid system for the international registration of trademarks is administered by the International Bureau of WIPO located in Geneva, Switzerland. One of the advantages of the Madrid system is that a trademark owner may obtain protection in several countries by filing a single application within their own national or regional trademark office provided they are members of the Madrid Union.

(2) Actual & Intent to Use Applications

The Lanham Act allows two types of use applications: (1) actual use, and (2) intent to use ("ITU"). ITU applications require intent to use the trademark in commerce in the future. The Lanham Act requires proof of "use in commerce" meaning there is a *bona fide* use of a mark in the ordinary course of trade—the mark cannot only be used to reserve a right to a particular mark. In the brick-and-mortar world, the term "use in commerce" originated when trademarks where affixed on goods or containers.

In website sales, in general, the first party who either uses a mark in commerce or files an application in the U.S. Trademark Office holds the first right to register that mark. The Trademark Office may accept evidence an applicant has used a mark "in commerce" for five years as *prima facie* evidence of distinctiveness. 15 U.S.C. § 1054. An owner will typically use trademarks on its product and packaging, while service marks advertise services.

(E) THE SPECTRUM OF DISTINCTIVENESS

Courts considering whether a mark is sufficiently distinctive to warrant trademark protection evaluate the mark based on a hierarchy of classifications. Marks are classified on a continuum of increasing distinctiveness: (1) generic, (2) descriptive, (3) suggestive, (4) arbitrary, or (5) fanciful. Fanciful or "coined" marks are the strongest marks, followed by arbitrary, suggestive, and descriptive marks. "Context is critical to a distinctiveness analysis, and the level of distinctiveness of a mark can be determined only by reference to the goods or services that the mark identifies." *Advertise.com, Inc. v. AOL Adver., Inc.*, 616 F.3d 974 (9th Cir. 2010). For example, the mark 'Super-encrypted software' connotes computer security. Notably, a weak descriptive mark may gain secondary meaning through online advertising or publishing. "Courts classify the distinctiveness or conceptual strength of a mark as either (1) generic, like 'Diet Chocolate Fudge Soda'; (2) descriptive, like 'Security Center', (3) suggestive, like 'Coppertone', or (4) arbitrary or fanciful, like 'Kodak.' " *Sabinsa Corp. v. Creative Compounds, Inc.*, 609 F.3d 175 (3rd Cir. 2010).

(1) Arbitrary Trademarks

Arbitrary marks do not suggest or describe but are arbitrarily assigned to the goods or services. Arbitrary marks, which are also inherently distinctive, typically involve common words that have no connection with the actual product. Apple Computer Corp. is an arbitrary mark for computers. Lotus software is also arbitrary, as is SUN for computers.

(2) Fanciful Trademarks

Fanciful marks are not words in the dictionary, and there is no logical connection to the goods or services. Fanciful marks are coined, or made up, by the trademark owner and therefore not found in the dictionary. "Fanciful marks, which are inherently distinctive, typically involve made-up words. Clorox®, Kodak®, Polaroid®, and Exxon® are examples of fanciful marks.

(3) Suggestive Trademarks

Suggestive trademarks "suggest, but do not describe, the nature or characteristics of the product." Stephen M. McJohn, INTELLECTUAL PROPERTY: EXAMPLES AND EXPLANATIONS, 384 (2012). "Suggestive marks require consumer "imagination, thought, or perception" to determine what the product is," whereas descriptive marks conveys "an immediate idea of the ingredients, qualities or characteristics of the goods" and include "JAGUAR for fast, luxurious cars and EXPLORER for an Internet search engine." American Bar Association, What is a Trademark? (2009). "Microsoft" is a trademark that is suggestive as is "Netscape" when referencing the Internet landscape. Other examples of suggestive marks are Coppertone®, Orange Crush®, and Playboy®."

"The primary criteria for distinguishing between a suggestive mark and a descriptive mark are the imaginativeness involved in the suggestion, that is, how immediate and direct is the thought process from the mark to the particular product." *City of*

Carlsbad v. Shah, 850 F. Supp.2d 1087 (S.D. Cal. 2012).

(4) Descriptive Trademarks

Descriptive marks "define a particular characteristic of the product in a way that does not require any exercise of the imagination." "Examples of descriptive marks include 'After Tan post-tanning lotion' and '5 Minute Glue.'" *George & Co. v. Imagination Entm't Ltd.*, 575 F.3d 383 (4th Cir. 2009). "Descriptive" marks are not inherently distinctive, but "may acquire the distinctiveness which will allow them to be protected. This acquired distinctiveness is generally called "secondary meaning." "Secondary meaning" identifies the source of the product, not the product itself.

(5) Generic Trademarks

Generic marks are marks that lack the distinctive qualities to be protectable. "Generic terms are those that refer to the genus of which a particular product or service is a species, i.e., the name of the product or service itself." MCCARTHY ON TRADEMARKS AND UNFAIR COMPETITION, § 12.23 (4th ed. 2012). To determine whether a term is generic, the court looks at whether consumers understand the word as one that only refers to a particular producer's goods, or whether the consumer understands the word to refer specifically to the goods themselves. A company may not register generic marks such as "website," "e-mail", "spam" or "social media site."

(F) TRADE NAME

Apple is a "trade name," meaning that it is a name used by a person to identify his or her business or vocation. 15 U.S.C. § 1127. Amazon.com, eBay, YouTube, and Facebook, are examples of Internet-related trade names. Trade names, like trademarks, must be distinctive to be protectable. A domain name may qualify as a trade name if the domain name is used to distinguish the company, for instance to give information on that company and its activities. GRAHAM J.H. SMITH, INTERNET LAW AND REGULATION 209 (2007). Domain names may also be perceived as a trademark when the website itself is a product or a service such as Amazon.com or eBay.

(G) SERVICE MARKS

A service mark, as its name suggests, identifies the source of services as opposed to a source of goods. E*Trade, for example, is a service mark for online investing. The U.S. Patent and Trademark Office uses the terms "trademark," and "mark" to refer to both trademarks and service marks whether they are word marks or other types of marks. Those claiming rights in a mark will label their products with the symbols "TM," "SM," or "7". The Trademark Office allows a company to use the "TM" (trademark) or "SM" (service mark) designation, which signals rights even if the mark has not been registered. However, a company may not use the federal registration symbol "7" until the USPTO actually registers a mark—not while an examination is still pending.

(H) FUNCTIONAL LIMITS OF TRADEMARKS

Congress adopted the functionality doctrine by explicitly prohibiting trademark registration or protection under the Lanham Act for a functional product. Section 1052(E) (5) prohibits the registration of a mark, which comprises any matter that, as a whole, is functional, which means it is essential to the use or purpose of the article or if it affects the cost or quality of the article. This doctrine developed as a common law rule prohibiting trade dress or trademark rights in the functional features of a product or its packaging in order to ensure that the proper boundaries are kept between patent law and trademark law. In *Rosetta Stone Ltd. v. Google, Inc.*, 2012 U.S. App. LEXIS 7082 (4th Cir. 2012), the Fourth Circuit found that the functionality doctrine was inapplicable to the keywords, reversing the district court's conclusion that Rosetta Stone's trademarked keywords marks were functional product features "or that Rosetta Stone's *own use* of this phrase was somehow functional when it entered into Google's AdWord program." While the keywords have an indexing function, they served a classic trademark purpose identifying goods or services.

(I) WHAT A DOMAIN NAME IS

The Internet Corporation for Assigned Names and Numbers is seeking ways to minimize deceptive and fraudulent practices as well as other abuses of domain name registrations. Besides cybersquatting, forms of abuse include:

Gripe/Complaint Sites a.k.a. "Sucks Sites": Websites that complain about a company's or entity's products or services and uses a company's trademark in the domain name (e.g. companysucks.com).

Pornographic/Offensive Sites: Websites that contain adult or pornographic content and uses a brand holder's trademark in the domain name (e.g. brandporn.com).

Offensive strings: Registration of stand-alone dirty words within a domain name (with or without brand names).

Registration of deceptive domain names: Registration of domain names that direct unsuspecting consumers to obscenity or direct minors to harmful content—sometimes referred to as a form of "mousetrapping."

INTERNET CORPORATION FOR ASSIGNED NAMES & NUMBERS (ICANN), REGISTRATION ABUSE POLICIES WORKING GROUP FINAL REPORT (submitted 29 May 2010) at 36.

§ 11-2. Website Trade Dress

It is an unsettled issue whether trade dress can be protected for websites. The design or packaging of a product may acquire distinctiveness, serving to identify the product with its manufacturer or source. The Bubble Calculator, for example, employs bubbly trade dress to call Internet consumer's attention to the name of trademarked product, "Bubble Calculator." A design or package, which acquires this secondary meaning, assuming other requisites are met, is a "trade dress" which may not be used in a manner likely to cause confusion as to the origin, sponsorship, or approval of the goods. In these respects, protection for trade dress exists to promote competition. Trade dress generally refers to characteristics of the visual appearance of a product or its packaging that signify the source of the product to consumers. 1 MCCARTHY ON TRADEMARKS AND UNFAIR COMPETITION § 8:1 (4th ed. 2012). In *Two Pesos, Inc. v. Taco Cabana, Inc.*, 505 U.S. 763 (S.Ct. 1992), the U.S. Supreme Court decided that the term "trademark" extends to "trade dress," which means a product's "total image and overall appearance" if it is a source identifier. The Court also found trade dress to be protectable under Section 43(A) of the Lanham Act prohibiting the use of false designations of origin, false descriptions, and false representations in the advertising and sale of goods and services.

Section 43(A) of the Lanham Act recognizes two distinct protectable interests: (1) protection against unfair competition in the form of an action for false advertising, and (2) protection against false association in the form of a lawsuit for false endorsement. The Court explained that trade dress, which is inherently distinctive, is protectable under Section 43(A) even if the plaintiff cannot demonstrate secondary meaning since the trade dress itself identified products or services as coming from a specific source. The Court noted the shape and general appearance of the restaurant as well as "the identifying sign, the interior kitchen floor plan, the decor, the menu, the equipment used to serve food, the servers' uniforms, and other features [all reflected] on the total image of the restaurant." Trade dress is entitled to protection under the Lanham Act if: (1) it is inherently distinctive or has acquired distinctiveness through secondary meaning, (2) it is primarily nonfunctional, and (3) its imitation would result in a likelihood of confusion in consumers' minds as to the source of the product. *Faegre & Benson v. Purdy*, 367 F. Supp. 2d 1238 (D. Minn. 2005).

§ 11-3. Road Map of Internet-Related Trademark Claims

Tens of thousands of domain name/trademark disputes have been decided over the past decade. In a domain name infringement action, a trademark owner will typically have causes of action such as: (1) trademark infringement, (2) state and federal dilution, (3) false designation of origin, (4) false advertising and (5) Anticybersquatting Act remedies.

Internet Trademark Cases

Cause of Action	Type of Claim	Liability Standard
Trademark Infringement Act, 15 U.S.C. § 1114(1)	Trademark Infringement by incorporating owner's trademark in	Likelihood of Confusion Test: with the sale of a good constitutes infringement if

	defendant's mark.	it is likely to cause consumer confusion as to the source of those goods or as to the sponsorship or approval of such goods.
Trademark Dilution Revision Act of 2006 ("TDRA"): 15 U.S.C. § 1125(C)	Dilution of Famous Trademarks by incorporating mark in domain name.	Impairs the mark's distinctiveness, whether or not the mark is used on a competing product or in a way that is likely to cause customer confusion. Must be a famous mark, meeting statutory standards.
False designation of origin and unfair competition:	False designation of origin by incorporating an owner's	False designation origin, use in commerce, causes

15 U.S.C. § 1125(A)(1)(A)	trademark in domain name.	confusion, mistake, or deception.
False or misleading description or representation: § 43(A)(1)(B) of the Lanham Act, 15 U.S.C. § 1125(A)(1)(B)	False or misleading description of fact, or false *or* misleading statements.	False or misleading representations in commercial advertising.
ACPA: 15 U.S.C. § 1125(D)	Domain names registered in bad faith identical or confusingly similar to a trademark.	Bad faith intent to profit from the mark and registers, traffics in, or uses a domain name that is (A) identical or confusingly similar to a distinctive mark, or dilutes a famous mark.

§ 11-4. Internet-Related Trademark Infringement

(A) DIRECT INFRINGEMENT

Section 32 of the Lanham Act provides liability for trademark infringement if, without the consent of the registrant, a defendant uses "in commerce any reproduction, counterfeit, copy, or colorable imitation of a registered mark: which is likely to cause confusion, or to cause mistake, or to deceive." 15 U.S.C. § 1114. To establish trademark infringement under the Lanham Act, a plaintiff must prove: (1) that it owns a valid mark; (2) that the defendant used the mark in commerce and without plaintiff's authorization; (3) that the defendant used the mark (or an imitation of it) in connection with the sale, offering for sale, distribution, or advertising of goods or services; and (4) that the defendant's use of the mark is likely to confuse consumers. 15 U.S.C. § 1114(A).

Similar elements are required in claims under 15 U.S.C. § 1125(a) for false designation of origin. To state a claim for false designation of origin and false advertising under the Lanham Act, plaintiff must allege that the defendant in connection with goods or services used in commerce the plaintiff's mark in a manner likely to confuse consumers about the source or sponsorship of the goods or services. Lanham Act, § 43(a), 15 U.S.C. § 1125(a).Whether the court calls the violation infringement, unfair competition or false designation of origin, the test is identical: is there a likelihood of confusion? In general, the more unique or arbitrary a mark, the more protection a court will afford it.

There are two requirements a plaintiff must allege to survive a Fed. R. Civ. P. 12(B)(1) motion to dismiss for lack of subject matter jurisdiction: (1) the trademark violation was in connection with any goods or services, and (2) the defendant used the trademark in commerce. To prevail in a trademark infringement case, plaintiffs must meet a three-prong test: (1) Did the plaintiff own a valid and enforceable mark? (2) Did the defendant cause confusion? (3) Did the plaintiff use the mark in commerce? Stephen W. Feingold & Howard S. Hogan, *Unique Online Trademark Issues*, Chapter 7 in G. PETER ALBERT, JR. AN AIPLA, INTELLECTUAL PROPERTY IN CYBERSPACE (2d ed. 2011) at 308.

Under Section 32 of the Lanham Act, the owner of a mark registered with the Patent and Trademark Office can bring a civil action against a person alleged to have used the mark without the owner's consent. 15 U.S.C. § 1114. The Lanham Act specifically prohibits person from reproducing, counterfeiting, copying, or colorably indicating a registered mark, which is likely to cause confusion. A plaintiff claiming infringement of an incontestable mark must show likelihood of consumer confusion as part of the *prima facie* case. 15 U.S.C. § 1115(B).

Courts consider the following factors in determining whether there is a likelihood of confusion or unfair competition: (1) strength or weakness of plaintiff's mark, (2) the degree of similarity with defendant's mark, (3) class of goods,

(4) marketing channels used, (5) evidence of actual confusion, and (6) intent of the defendant. No one factor is determinative as the likelihood of confusion test considers the totality of facts under the circumstances. Under Section 35 of the Lanham Act, a plaintiff seeking damages for counterfeiting and infringement has the option of seeking either actual or statutory damages—but not both. Feingold & Hogan, Issues *Unique Online Trademark Issues*, *Id.* at 308–309.

For example, Louis Vuitton, a French high-end retailer and subsidiary of the Louis Vuitton Moet-Hennessey holding company ("LVMH"), will have an action against an Internet website that advertises colorable imitations or counterfeits of its handbags, wallets, luggage, shoes, belts, scarves, sunglasses, charms, watches, and jewelry and other branded merchandise. The French luxury goods manufacturer will contend that consumers will be misled, confused, and disappointed by the quality of these imposter products, and that the brand will suffer loss of sales for their genuine products.

A high-end designer, retailer, and brand holder, like Louis Vuitton, may recover actual damages equal to (1) defendant's profits, (2) any damages sustained by the plaintiff, and (3) the costs of the action. 15 U.S.C. § 1117(A). The brand holder may elect instead to recover statutory damages for the use of a counterfeit mark that is computed per counterfeit mark per type of goods or services sold, offered for sale, or distributed. 15 U.S.C. § 1117(C). In 2006, statutory awards for trademark infringement ranged from not less than $500 to

$100,000 per counterfeit mark per type of goods sold if the use of the mark was not willful, or up to $1,000,000 per mark if the use was willful. These amounts were doubled beginning in October 13, 2008.

Trademark owners can seek remedies for infringement including: (1) injunctive relief, (2) accounting for profits made while misusing the owner's trademarks, (3) damages including treble damages for willful infringement, (4) attorney's fees in the "exceptional case," and (5) costs. The usual test used to measure a likelihood of confusion is whether the similarity of the marks is "likely to confuse consumers about the source of the products." *North Am. Med. Corp. v. Axiom Worldwide, Inc.*, 522 F.3d 1211 (11th Cir. 2008).

Likelihood of confusion case law instructs courts to examine nine factors: (1) the strength or distinctiveness of the plaintiff's mark as actually used in the marketplace, (2) the similarity of the two marks to consumers, (3) the similarity of the goods or services that the marks identify, (4) the similarity of the facilities used by the mark holders, (5) the similarity of advertising used by the mark holders, (6) the defendant's intent, (7) actual confusion, (8) the quality of the defendant's product, and (9) the sophistication of the consuming public. *George & Co. v. Imagination Entm't Ltd.*, 575 F.3d 383 (4th Cir. 2009). No single factor is determinative, as the likelihood of the confusion test considers the totality of facts under the circumstances. The three most important factors in conflicts between domain names and trademarks are: (1) the similarity of the marks, (2) relatedness of the goods and services offered, and (3) simultaneous use of the Internet as a marketing channel. In trademark infringement cases based upon initial interest confusion, the owner of the mark must demonstrate the likelihood of confusion, not just diversion of Internet traffic.

In cybersquatting cases, a trademark owner may claim actual damages that include the profits the domain name registrant made from his use of the mark, as well as losses sustained by the mark holder as a result of the domain name registrant's actions, such as lost sales or harm to the mark's reputation. Under the Anticybersquatting Consumer Protection Act of 1999, the trademark owner has the option of pursuing either actual damages or statutory damages, which range between $1,000 and $100,000 per domain. 15 U.S.C. § 1117(D). The court exercises its discretion to fix the actual amount awarded. In "exceptional cases," a trademark owner can recover attorney's fees against the domain name registrant found to have registered the infringing domain name in bad faith.

(B) CONTRIBUTORY TRADEMARK INFRINGEMENT

To be liable for contributory trademark infringement, a defendant must have: (1) intentionally induced the primary infringer to infringe, or (2) continued to supply an infringing product to an infringer with knowledge that the infringer is mislabeling the particular product supplied. To support a contributory trademark dilution claim, plaintiff must show that defendants either encouraged others to dilute plaintiff's trademark, or continued to supply their product to one whom it knows or has reason to know is engaging in trademark infringement. Lanham Act, § 43(c), 15 U.S.C. § 1125(c).

When the primary infringer supplies a service rather than a product, a court must consider the extent of control exercised by the defendant over the third party's means of infringement. The knowledge requirement is objective and is satisfied where the defendant knows or has reason to know of the infringing activity.

Any liability for contributory infringement will depend upon whether or not the contributing party intended to participate in the infringement, or actually knew about the infringing activities. Secondary liability for infringement arises when "a manufacturer or distributor intentionally induces another to infringe a trademark, or . . . continues to supply its product to one whom it knows or has reason to know is engaging in trademark infringement." *Inwood Labs Inc. v. Ives Labs, Inc.*, 456 U.S. 844 (S.Ct. 1982).

When the alleged direct infringer supplies a service rather than a product, under the second prong of this test, the court must consider the extent of control exercised by the defendant over the third party's means of infringement. For liability to attach there must be direct control and monitoring of the instrumentality used by a third party to infringe the plaintiff's mark. In *Sony Corps. v.*

Universal City Studios (S.Ct. 1984), the U.S.
Supreme Court determined the manufacturers of
Betamax video tape recorders were not secondarily
liable because these machines had a substantial
legitimate use.

The first Internet-related case to address
contributory trademark infringement was *Lockheed
Martin Corp. v. Network Solutions, Inc.*, 194 F.3d
980 (9th Cir. 1999), where the Ninth Circuit held
that Network Solutions was not contributorily liable
for the trademark infringement of a domain name.
In *Gucci America, Inc. v. Hall & Assocs.*, 135
F.Supp.2d 409 (S.D.N.Y. 2001), the court refused to
dismiss Gucci's claim against an ISP for
contributory trademark infringement predicated
upon the claim it hosted a direct trademark
infringer. Mere knowledge of third party
infringement is an insufficient basis for contributory
trademark infringement.

(C) SECONDARY TRADEMARK INFRINGEMENT

(1) Vicarious Liability

Vicarious liability for trademark infringement
requires a finding that the defendant and the
infringer have an apparent or actual partnership,
have authority to bind one another in transactions
with third parties or exercise joint ownership or
control over the infringing product." *Perfect 10, Inc.
v. Visa Int'l Serv. Ass'n*, 494 F.3d 788, 807 (9th Cir.
2007). One of the greatest hurdles is to find an
apparent or actual partnership. *Hard Rock Café
Licensing Corp. v. Concession Servs. Inc.*, 955 F.2d

1143 (7th Cir. 1992). Courts apply a four-part test to determine partnership: (1) parties' sharing of profits and losses, (2) parties' joint control and management of business, (3) contribution by each party of property, financial resources, effort, skill, or knowledge to business, and (4) parties' intention to be partners.

In *Perfect 10 v. Visa International*, 494 F.3d 788 (9th Cir. 2007), the Ninth Circuit refused to find Visa vicariously liable for its role in enabling payment for website access to content violating the copyrights and trademarks of a third party magazine publisher. The appeals court uncovered no affirmative acts by the defendants suggesting to third parties that they should infringe the publisher's trademarks. The Ninth Circuit said even if defendants allowed the infringing merchants to use their logos, trade name, or trademarks, they would not be liable for false advertising because they had no duty to investigate the truth of the statements made by others. Moreover, the court found that Visa did not encourage the improper conduct at issue; they merely processed credit card payments.

(2) Contributory Infringement

To be liable for contributory trademark infringement, a defendant must have (1) 'intentionally induced' the primary infringer to infringe, or (2) continued to supply an infringing product to an infringer with knowledge that the infringer is mislabeling the particular product supplied." *Id.* (quoting *Inwood Labs., Inc. v. Ives*

Labs., Inc., 456 U.S. 844, 855 (1982). The tests for secondary trademark infringement are even more difficult to satisfy than those required to find secondary copyright infringement." *Perfect 10, Inc. v. Visa Int'l Serv. Ass'n,* 494 F.3d 788, 806 (9th Cir.2007)

§ 11-5. Trademark Dilution Revision Act of 2006

Federal dilution claims only extend to famous marks, those marks with such powerful consumer associations that even non-competing uses can impinge on their value. Under the statute, "a mark is famous if it is widely recognized by the general consuming public of the United States as a designation of source of the goods or services of the mark's owner." 15 U.S.C. §1125(c)(2)(A). Federal dilution claims require the plaintiff to show that its mark is famous and distinctive, that the defendant began using its mark in commerce after the plaintiff's mark became famous and distinctive, and that the defendant's mark is likely to dilute the plaintiff's mark. Congress enacted the Trademark Dilution Revision Act of 2006 that displaced the FTDA of 1996. For § 1125(c)(1) to apply, the defendant must have "commence[d]" a diluting use of the plaintiff's mark *after* the point at which the mark became famous.

The TDRA amended the Lanham Act to render one liable to the owner of a trademark who, with "a bad faith intent to profit from that mark," "registers, traffics in or uses a domain name" that is either identical or confusingly similar to a "distinctive" mark or is identical, confusingly similar or dilutive of a "famous mark." 15 U.S.C. § 1125(C). The Federal Trademark Dilution Act (FTDA) recognized new remedies for the dilution of famous trademarks. The FTDA factors include the duration and extent of use of the mark, the nature of the advertising, and the acquired distinctiveness of the mark. 15 U.S.C. § 1125(c)(1).

To state a *prima facie* dilution claim under the TDRA, the plaintiff must show the following:

(1) that the plaintiff owns a famous mark that is distinctive;

(2) that the defendant has commenced using a mark in commerce that allegedly is diluting the famous mark;

(3) that a similarity between the defendant's mark and the famous mark gives rise to an association between the marks; and

(4) that the association is likely to impair the distinctiveness of the famous mark or likely to harm the reputation of the famous mark. 15 U.S.C. § 1125(C).

(A) BASICS OF FEDERAL DILUTION CLAIMS

(1) Dilution by Blurring

The TDRA defines "dilution by blurring" as the "association arising from the similarity between a mark or trade name and a famous mark that impairs the distinctiveness of the famous mark." 15 U.S.C. § 1125(c)(2)(B). Blurring under the federal statute involves the classic "whittling away" of the selling power and strength of the famous mark.

A plaintiff seeking relief under the blurring prong of the TDRA must show that its mark is famous and distinctive, that defendant began using its mark in commerce after plaintiff's mark became famous and distinctive, and that defendant's mark is likely to dilute plaintiff's mark. In determining whether a mark or trade name is likely to cause dilution violative of the Lanham Act by blurring, the court may consider all relevant factors, including (i) the degree of similarity between the mark or trade name and the famous mark, (ii) the degree of inherent or acquired distinctiveness of the famous mark, (iii) the extent to which the owner of the famous mark is engaging in substantially exclusive use of the mark, (iv) the degree of recognition of the famous mark, (v) whether the user of the mark or trade name intended to create an association with the famous mark, and (vi) any actual association between the mark or trade name and the famous mark. Lanham Act, § 43(c), 15 U.S.C.A. § 1125(c). To prove dilution by blurring, the plaintiff must show that the association between the plaintiff's mark and the defendant's mark weakens the mark's ability to evoke the first product in the minds of consumers. (*Jada Toys Inc. v. Mattel, Inc.*, 518 F.3d 628 (9th Cir. 2008). The TDRA, 15 U.S.C. § 1125(c), grants "[t]he owner of a famous mark" the right to seek "an injunction against another person's commercial use in commerce of a mark or trade name, if such use begins after the mark has become famous and causes dilution of the distinctive quality of the mark."

(2) Dilution by Tarnishment

"[D]ilution by tarnishment" is defined as the "association arising from the similarity between a mark or trade name and a famous mark that harms the reputation of the famous mark." 15 U.S.C. § 1125(c)(2)(C). Dilution by tarnishment occurs where the plaintiff's mark is linked with something unsavory or degrading. This category includes things like X-rated movies, hard-core pornography, revenge porn websites, crude humor, and pirated goods. The TDRA applies when a website blurs a famous trademark by incorporating the mark in a domain name. 15 U.S.C. § 1125(c). A domain name can tarnish a famous trademark, as in *Mattel, Inc. v. Jcom, Inc.*, 48 U.S. P.Q.2d (BNA) 1467 (S.D.N.Y. 1996), where the court held that the use of the Barbie trademark by an adult entertainment web site, combined with particular fonts and color schemes, tarnished the mark.

The TDRA amended the Trademark Act of 1946 to describe the factors determining whether a mark is "distinctive and famous," 15 U.S.C. § 1125(c)(1), and defines "dilution" as "the lessening of the capacity of a famous mark to identify and distinguish goods or services," 15 U.S.C. § 1127. The TDRA amended Section 43(C) of the Lanham Act to enable trademark owners of famous trademarks to file a federal anti-dilution action. This 2006 amendment to the Lanham Act overrules the Supreme Court's ruling in *Moseley v. Victoria Secret*

Catalogue, Inc., 537 U.S. 418 (S.Ct. 2003), which interpreted the prior federal Anti-Dilution Act to require prevailing plaintiffs to prove actual dilution. In *Moseley,* the Court settled a circuit court split as to whether plaintiffs had to prove actual dilution in a federal dilution action. The TDRA overturned *Moseley* when it provided relief for "likely," as opposed to actual, dilution. 15 U.S.C. § 1125(c)(1).

Dilution, under the TDRA, is defined as lessening the capacity of a famous mark to identify and distinguish goods or services regardless of the presence or absence of: (1) competition between the owner of the famous mark and other parties, or (2) likelihood of confusion, mistake, or deception. 15 U.S.C. § 1127. In order to establish its trademark dilution claim, a plaintiff must show that: (1) its marks are famous; (2) the defendant adopted its mark after its marks became famous; (3) the defendant's mark is likely to cause dilution of the trademark; and (4) the defendant is using its mark in commerce for commercial purposes. Under the TDRA, there is still a cause of action "regardless of the presence or absence of actual or likely confusion, of competition, or of actual economic injury." 15 U.S.C. § 1125(C)(1).

To obtain relief under the TDRA, a trademark owner must first show that their mark is both famous and distinct. The TDRA extends to those marks that are inherently distinctive, and to those deriving distinctiveness from secondary meaning. Second, the owner must show one of two forms of dilution: blurring and tarnishment as first developed under the common law. Under the TDRA, there are two types of dilution, but one, dilution by blurring, occurs when a mark previously associated with one product also becomes associated with a second. 15 U.S.C. § 1125(c)(2)(B).

Blurring weakens the mark's ability to evoke the first product in the minds of consumers. Many courts describe blurring as a whittling away of a mark's distinctiveness. The TDRA states: (1), "dilution by blurring" is association arising from the similarity between a mark or trade name and a famous mark that impairs the distinctiveness of the famous mark. In determining whether a mark or trade name is likely to cause dilution by blurring, the court may consider all relevant factors, including the following:

(i) The degree of similarity between the mark or trade name and the famous mark.

(ii) The degree of inherent or acquired distinctiveness of the famous mark.

(iii) The extent to which the owner of the famous mark is engaging in substantially exclusive use of the mark.

(iv) The degree of recognition of the famous mark.

(v) Whether the user of the mark or trade name intended to create an association with the famous mark.

(vi) Any actual association between the mark or trade name and the famous mark.

15 U.S.C. § 1125(c)(2)(B).

Congress has enumerated factors courts may use to analyze the likelihood of dilution, including the similarity between the two marks and the distinctiveness and recognition of the plaintiff's mark. 15 U.S.C. § 1125(c)(2)(B)(i). "Dilution by tarnishing occurs when a junior mark's similarity to a famous mark causes consumers mistakenly to associate the famous mark with the defendant's inferior or offensive product." *Hasbro, Inc. v. Internet Entm't Group, Ltd.*, 1996 U.S. Dist. LEXIS 11626 (W.D. Wash. 1996).

The Ninth Circuit explains the essence of blurring as the weakening of the ability of a trademark "to evoke the first product in the minds of consumers. "For example, Tylenol snowboards, Netscape sex shops, and Harry Potter dry cleaners would all weaken the 'commercial magnetism' of these marks and diminish their ability to evoke their original associations." *Levi Strauss & Co. v. Abercrombie & Fitch Trading Co.*, 633 F.3d 1158 (9th Cir. 2011).

Under the FTDA, "a mark is famous if it is widely recognized by the general consuming public of the United States as a designation of source of the goods or services." 15 U.S.C. § 1125(C)(2)(A). The statute establishes that the junior user, to be liable for dilution, must use "a mark or trade name . . . after *the* mark has become famous." 15 U.S.C. § 1125(c)(1).

In *Avery Dennison Corp. v. Sumpton*, 189 F.3d 868 (9th Cir. 1999), the trademark owner of the "AVERY" and "DENNISON" brands of office products filed suit against Jerry Sumpton, an entrepreneur who sold vanity domain names and registered domain names with these trademarks. The Ninth Circuit held that Avery Dennison did not establish the "famousness" element and therefore had no TDRA cause of action. The court also found that the plaintiff failed to demonstrate commercial use by the defendant as Mr. Sumpton was selling the domain names for use for surname domain names—not for commercial use.

The court did not find the words "AVERY" and "DENNISON" to constitute famous marks although they had been used for over seventy years and had generated sales of $3 billion. The lesson from this case is that the FTDA's delimiters of famousness and commercial use prevent many trademark owners from pursuing a federal dilution claim.

In *Visa Int'l Service Ass'n v. JSL Corp.*, 610 F.3d 1088 Supp.2d 1089 (9th Cir. 2010), the Ninth Circuit affirmed a lower court opinion that held that use of "evisa.com" by a business to promote its language service diluted the Visa International trademark. The court stated that the defendant's use of the trademark "evisa.com" created "actual dilution" because it was substantially similar to the plaintiff's famous "Visa" mark.

Moreover, the court explained that businesses commonly place an "e" before their trademark to denote the online version of their business. Specifically, the *Visa* court held that dilution occurred because of Visa being unable to use "evisa.com" to market its product. More significantly, the court did not rely on direct evidence of actual dilution or that consumers actually associated defendant's evisa.com mark with the plaintiff. The court found the TDTA of 2006 only required the holder of a famous mark to show a likelihood of dilution arising out of defendant's use of a mark. The court found it likely that consumers would "form new and different associations" with Visa's mark.

Notably, the district court was obligated to interpret the FTDA as directed by the U.S. Supreme Court in *Moseley*, because the case was filed before the 2006 amendment of the FTDA. Accordingly, the Visa court held that the plaintiff did not need to prove actual confusion given the near identity of the parties' respective marks. The district court further found the FTDA protected Visa because the "evisa" mark weakened the ability of the Visa to identify its respective goods and services. The "evisa" mark diverted Internet searchers because consumers were not brought to Visa's website when entering "evisa.com."

Because the Visa mark was famous, the court granted Visa International's motion for summary judgment, finding that JSL Corp. violated the FTDA. After the 2006 amendments, a federal antidilution cause of action requires proof that (1) the mark is famous and distinctive; (2) the defendant is making use of the mark in commerce; (3) the defendant's use began after the mark became famous; and (4) the defendant's use of the mark is likely to cause dilution. *Jada Toys, Inc. v. Mattel, Inc.* (9th Cir. 2008).

(B) TDRA REMEDIES

The remedy under the TDRA is limited to an injunction, ". . . unless the person against whom the injunction is sought willfully intended to trade on the owner's reputation or to cause dilution of the famous mark." 15 U.S.C. § 1125(c)(2). Under the FTDA, the owner of a famous mark may obtain injunctive relief against any "person who, *at any time after* the owner's mark has become famous, *commences use* of a mark . . . in commerce that is likely to cause dilution." 15 U.S.C. § 1125(c)(1).

(C) DEFENSES TO THE TDRA

In response to First Amendment, or associational policy concerns, the TDRA exempts certain uses of a famous mark. TDRA defenses include the following: (1) the mark is not famous, (2) the use is classified as a parody, (3) noncommercial use of the mark, (4) fair use of a famous mark is permitted in comparative advertisements and (5) dilution is not likely. The TDRA expressly excludes from its reach "[a]ny fair use, including a nominative or descriptive fair use, or facilitation of such fair use, of a famous mark by another person other than as a designation of source for the person's own goods or services." 15 U.S.C. § 1125(c)(3)(A). The federal antidilution statute specifically provides comparative advertising and parody as examples of non-dilutive fair uses. See 15 U.S.C. § 1125(c)(3)(A)(i) & (ii). Just as with any trademark action, a defendant may assert a right to use a trademark in a news commentary, a comparative advertisement. Fair use is a statutory defense under the FTDA.

§ 11-6. False Designation of Origin

To prevail in a false designation of origin, or in an infringement case, the plaintiff needs proof that defendant's use of the trademark in cyberspace would likely cause an appreciable number of Internet users to be misled or confused as to the source, sponsorship, or affiliation of defendant's goods or services. The unfair competition or, "consumer confusion" provision, of Section 43 of the Lanham Act, is intended to prevent confusion, mistake, or deception regarding the source of goods or services and applies equally well to cyberspace

The core element of any trademark infringement cause of action, or false designation of origin, is whether there is a likelihood of confusion. Under trademark infringement, unfair competition, or false designation of origin claim, a plaintiff is required to show that its marks are valid and that a defendant's use of those marks is likely to cause consumer confusion.

In *Ron Paul 2012 Presidential Campaign Comm., Inc. v. Does*, 2012 U.S. Dist. Lexis. 30911 (N.D. Cal. Mar. 8, 2012), the defendants owned a YouTube and Twitter account named "NHLiberty4Paul." Under this pseudonymous website, the defendants uploaded a video on YouTube entitled "Jon Huntsman's Values" that attacked the former Republican primary nominee before concluding with the text: "American Values and Liberty—Vote Ron Paul." Shortly after the video's release, the Ron Paul Campaign filed a complaint asserting a claim for: (1) false designation of origin in violation of the

Lanham Act, (2) false description and representation in violation of the Lanham Act, and (3) common law libel and defamation. The federal court denied the Paul Campaign's request for expedited discovery stating it had grave doubts about whether the commercial use requirement for false designation was met.

§ 11-7. False Endorsement

To state a false endorsement claim, the plaintiff must allege facts that, if true, would establish that his or her name was: (1) used in commerce, (2) is distinctive and (3) a likelihood of confusion exists. The elements of a false endorsement claim are akin to the tort of the right of publicity. Section 43(A) covers a false or misleading misrepresentation of fact, which ". . . is likely to cause confusion, or to cause mistake, or to deceive as to the affiliation, connection, or association of such person with another person, or as to the origin, sponsorship, or approval of his or her goods, services, or commercial activities by another person." 15 U.S.C. § 1125(A)(1)(A). A false endorsement claim requires allegations of an unauthorized use of a celebrity's identity and this includes their visual characteristics, voice, or other distinctive qualities.

§ 11-8. Anticybersquatting Act of 1999

The Anticybersquatting Consumer Protection Act ("ACPA") is the principal tool used by trademark owners to reclaim domain names containing their trademarks and trade names from cybersquatters. Cybersquatting is defined as the: "Offer to transfer, sell, or otherwise assign the domain name to the mark owner or any third party for financial gain without having used, or having an intent to use, the domain name in the bona fide offering of any goods or services, or the person's prior conduct indicating a pattern of such conduct." *See Corsair Memory, Inc. v. Corsair7.com,* 2008 U.S. Dist. LEXIS 110067 at *20 (N.D.Cal. Nov. 3, 2008) (quoting The ACPA protects the owner of a distinctive or famous trademark from another's bad faith intent to profit from the trademark owner's mark by registering or using a domain name which is identical or confusingly similar to, or dilutive of, the trademark owner's mark without regard to the goods or services of the parties. 15 U.S.C. § 1125(d).

The ACPA, which amended the Lanham Act, addresses the: (1) registration, use, or trafficking in, a domain name, (2) that is identical or confusingly similar to a distinctive or famous trademark, (3) with a bad-faith intent to profit from the mark. Under the ACPA, 15 U.S.C. § 1125(d), a person commits cybersquatting, if, without regard to the goods or services of the parties, that person (i) has a bad faith intent to profit from that mark, including a personal name which is protected as a mark under this section; and (ii) registers, traffics in, or uses a domain name that—(I) in the case of a mark that is distinctive at the time of registration of the domain name, is identical or confusingly similar to that mark; (II) in the case of a famous mark that is famous at the time of registration of the domain name, is identical or confusingly similar to or dilutive of that mark; or (III) is a protected trademark, word, or name. 15 U.S.C. § 1125(d).

(A) ELEMENTS OF ACPA CLAIMS

To prevail under the ACPA, a plaintiff must prove: "(1) its mark is distinctive or famous and entitled to protection; (2) the defendant's domain name is identical or confusingly similar to the plaintiff's mark; and (3) the defendant registered or used the domain name with a bad faith intent to profit." *Bavaro Palace, S.A. v. Vacation Tours, Inc.*, 203 F. App'x 252, 256 (11th Cir. 2006) (citing *Shields v. Zuccarini*, 254 F.3d 476, 482 (3d Cir. 2001)). The inquiry under the ACPA is "narrower than the traditional multifactor likelihood of confusion test for trademark infringement." *Newport News Holdings Corp. v. Virtual City Vision*, 650 F.3d 423, 437 (4th Cir. 2011) (citing *Coca-Cola Co. v. Purdy*, 382 F.3d 774, 783 (8th Cir. 2004)).

The ACPA provides that a court may order the cancellation of the domain name or its transfer to the owner of the mark as remedy to the owner. *Id.* at § 1125(d)(1)(C).The core element in a cybersquatting case is proof of a bad faith intent to profit from a distinctive or famous mark. A trademark is famous only if the owner can prove that the mark "is widely recognized by the general consuming public of the United States as a designation of source of the goods or services of the mark's owner." 15 U.S.C. § 1125(C)(2)(A).

The ACPA's statutory purpose is to protect trademark holders from misuse of domain names intending to "divert consumers from the mark owner's online location to a site accessible under the domain name that could harm the goodwill represented by the mark, either for commercial gain or with the intent to tarnish or disparage the mark, by creating a likelihood of confusion." *See* 15 U.S.C. § 1125(d)(1)(B). The ACPA lists factors to assist courts in determining whether there has been a registration of a domain name in bad faith.

(B) ACPA SAFE HARBOR

The ACPA recognizes a safe harbor provision for a defendant who acted in good faith. If "the court determines that the person believed and had reasonable grounds to believe that the use of the domain name was a fair use or otherwise lawful," then the defendant will not be held liable under the ACPA. 15 U.S.C. § 1125(D)(1)(B)(ii). In *Panavision Int'l, L.P. v. Toeppen*, 141 F.3d 1316 (9th Cir. 1998), Dennis Toeppen registered scores of domain names containing the trademarks of famous companies, and then sought to sell them to the owners of the marks for a profit. Toeppen posted an aerial vision of Pana, Illinois on the website Panavision.com as a pre-textual gesture to try to prove legitimate use.

The federal court rejected this ploy finding Toeppen liable for misappropriating the trademark of Panavision through his practice of registering trademarks as domain names and then selling them to the trademark owners. The court found that Dennis Toeppen registered the domain name "panavision.com" in order to extort a ransom from Panavision.

Toeppen was using the domain panavision.com to display photographs of Pana, Illinois and, when asked to cease using the domain name, he offered to sell it for $13,000. After Panavision refused to buy the domain name from Toeppen, he registered their other trademark, Panaflex, as a domain name. Because Toeppen registered the "PANAVISION" mark as a domain name to palm off on the recognition of the "PANAVISION" name and mark, the Ninth Circuit determined that this misuse or exploitation of the value of the mark rose to the level of commercial use under the Lanham Act, even though Toeppen never used it to sell goods or services.

(C) *IN REM* JURISDICTION

The ACPA allows a trademark owner to file an *in rem* civil action against a domain name and provides instructions on how to provide sufficient notice of such an action. Specifically, the ACPA provides that service of process in an *in rem* action may be accomplished by sending notice of the alleged violation and intent to proceed under the ACPA to the registrant of the domain name at the postal and e-mail addresses provided by the registrant to the registrar, and by publishing notice of the action as the court may direct promptly after filing the action. 15 U.S.C. § 1125(d)(2)(A) and (B). Trademark owners may assert *in rem* jurisdiction only if the domain name is confusingly similar or identical to its mark and the abusive registrant is not locatable. A trademark owner may proceed *in personam* against an infringer or, in certain circumstances, *in rem* against the domain name only if they have exhausted reasonable efforts to locate the bad faith registrant. Trademark owners may seek an *in rem* remedy if the abusive domain name registrant is not locatable despite a diligent effort to find him or her. An illustrative case occurred in July of 2012 when a Virginia federal court ordered VeriSign, an accredited domain name registrar, to transfer 265 "infringing domain names" from VeriSign to Go Daddy. The disputed domain names were registered in the name of Richemont International, Ltd, but in fact, the registrants were based in China. The domain names were being used to sell fake Mont Blanc pens, violating the pen company's famous trademarks. The court ordered that the domain names used in selling knockoffs all be transferred to Mont Blanc.

The ACPA gives trademark owners the right to file an *in rem* action against the domain name in the judicial district where the domain name registrar, domain name registry, or other domain name authority registered or assigned the domain name is located. See e.g., *Cable News Network L.P., L.L.L.P. v. cnnews.com*, 162 F. Supp. 2d 484 (E.D. Va. 2001) (holding that plaintiff properly perfected service under ACPA's *in rem* service procedure in domain name litigation).

(D) ACPA REMEDIES

Under the ACPA, plaintiff may elect as its measure of damages statutory damages in the amount of not less than $1,000 and not more than

$100,000 per domain name, as the court considers just. 15 U.S.C. § 1117(d).

§ 11-9. Keyword Trademark Litigation

In keyword advertising cases such as *Hearts on Fire Co. v. Blue Nile, Inc.*, 603 F. Supp. 274 (D. Mass. 2009), the "likelihood of confusion is determined by what the consumer saw on the screen and reasonably believed, given the context." In *Hearts on Fire*, a diamond wholesaler alleged that an Internet diamond retailer infringed its trademark when it used the wholesaler's trademark as a keyword to trigger search engine advertisements known as "sponsored links."

The Massachusetts federal court determined that dismissal of the trademark owner's lawsuit was not warranted and found the purchase of trademarks to trigger pop-up or banner advertisements to be use in commerce. The purchase of the trademarked keyword to trigger sponsored links constituted a "use" within the meaning of the Lanham Act because, on the facts of the case, a computer user's search for the trademarked phrase necessarily involved a display of that trademark as part of the search-results list.

The court found the diamond wholesaler to have stated a claim for trademark infringement, even where the Internet retailer's sponsored links did not display the protected mark. The court reasoned that the (1) initial interest confusion could support a claim under the Lanham Act where the wholesaler plausibly alleged that consumers were confused, and not simply diverted, and (2) the wholesaler offered sufficient allegations to support its claim that consumers were likely confused, and potentially misled, by the retailer's use of the trademark as a trigger for its sponsored links.

(A) THE MEANING OF USE IN COMMERCE

Many Internet-related cases turn on the element of "use in commerce," which is essential in a trademark infringement claim. In *Intermatic Inc. v. Toeppen*, 947 F. Supp. 1227 (N.D. Ill. 2006), the federal court held that the defendant's use of the Internet satisfied the "in commerce" requirement when the defendant registered a domain name identical to the plaintiff's trademark name and used it on the Internet. In more recent cases, the issue of commercial use often turns on whether "use" of a trademark under the Lanham Act requires that the trademark is displayed or visible to consumers. Commercial use, the third requirement of any trademark infringement lawsuit, is a major obstacle especially where the use of the plaintiff's trademark is invisible.

Many of the Internet-related commercial use issues involve the question of whether covert use of trademarks by advertisers constitutes "use in commerce under the Lanham Act." In many of the "covert use" cases, plaintiffs are unable to clear the use in commerce hurdle.

(B) KEYWORDS AND COMMERCIAL USE

Keywords "keyed" to famous trademarks that trigger pop-ups is an example of the covert use of trademarks by online advertisers. The problem is that keywords use a competitor's trademark to tout the products and services of the competitor rather than the keyworded trademark owner. "Adware" is software that generates advertisements while a consumer browses the Internet. Trademark owners argue that this covert use of a competitor's trademarks in adware essentially misappropriates their goodwill by, diverting sales and thus constituting infringement.

Google has created the AdWords program, which, in effect, is a full-employment act for trademark litigators. AdWords allows an advertiser to bid on keywords or terms that an Internet user might enter into a Google search thereby triggering the display of a sponsor's advertisement. When a user enters a keyword, Google displays the links generated by its own algorithm in the main part of the page, along with the advertisements in a separate "sponsored links" section next to or above the objective results. Trademark owners have filed multiple trademark infringement lawsuits against Google and its customers arising out of the use of the AdWords context-advertising program.

A leading trademark scholar, views the issue as whether keyword placement is unfairly "drawing [the] power and goodwill of these famous marks. The question is whether this activity is fair competition or whether it is a form of unfair free

riding on the fame of well-known marks." 4
MCCARTHY ON TRADEMARKS AND UNFAIR
COMPETITION § 25-171 (4th ed. 2012).

(1) 1–800 Contacts, Inc. v. WhenU.Com, Inc.

In *1–800 Contacts, Inc. v. WhenU.com, Inc.*, 414
F.3d 400 (2d Cir. 2005), the Second Circuit reversed
the district court's issuance of a preliminary
injunction that enjoined WhenU.com from causing
"pop up" advertisements to appear on Internet
user's computer screens when they went to the 1–
800 Contacts website or each time a trademark is
entered into a search engine. The federal appeals
court reasoned that WhenU.com's use of 1–800
Contacts' trademarks did not constitute "use in
commerce," a predicate for a finding of trademark
infringement under the Lanham Act. However, the
plaintiff's trademark claim failed because
WhenU.com's pop-up ads did not actually display
the 1–800 Contacts' trademark. The court found the
defendant's use of the plaintiffs' trademarks as
"analogous to an individual's private thoughts about
a trademark. Such conduct simply does not violate
the Lanham Act." The *1–800 Contacts* case ended
when the U.S. Supreme Court refused to accept the
contact maker's writ of certiorari. Some courts have
held that the use of keywords satisfies the
commercial use requirement of the Lanham Act.

(2) Rescuecom Corp. v. Google

In *Rescuecom Corp. v. Google*, 456 F. Supp. 2d 393
(2d Cir. 2009), the Second Circuit held that Google
used Rescuecom's trademark in commerce when

Google sold keywords containing Rescuecom's mark. Google used the trademark in its Keyword Suggestion Tool, where it was suggested to potential advertisers that the keyword was available for a fee. Thus, whenever an Internet user typed "Rescuecom" as a search term, the competitor's hyperlink appeared linked to the competitors' websites among the search results.

The court found Google's use of Rescuecom's trademark in a keyword did not satisfy the "trademark use" requirement as it applies to 15 U.S.C. § 1051, whereby it is necessary for establishing infringement and false origin actions. Rescuecom was unable to establish "trademark use" because they could not prove that: (1) any of the search results, except the links belonging to plaintiff, displayed plaintiff's trademark, that (2) defendant's activities affected the appearance or functionality of plaintiff's website, or that (3) defendant placed plaintiff's trademark on any goods, containers, displays, or advertisements.

(3) Google Keyword Cases

In *Google, Inc. v. American Blind & Wallpaper Factory, Inc.*, 2007 WL 1848665 (N.D. Cal. 2007), the court found Google's sale of trademarked terms in its advertising program did constitute "use in commerce" for purposes of the Lanham Act, and denied summary judgment to Google. In *Rosetta Stone Ltd. v. Google, Inc.*, 2012 U.S. App. LEXIS 7082 (4th Cir. 2012), the Fourth Circuit affirmed the district court's order with respect to the vicarious infringement and unjust enrichment claims, but vacated the court's order with respect to the direct infringement, contributory infringement and dilution claims and remanded these claims for further proceeding.

In *Network Automation, Inc. v. Advanced Systems Concepts, Inc.*, 638 F.3d 1137 (9th Cir. 2011), the Ninth Circuit ruled that Network Automation Incorporated's ("Network") use of keywords incorporating Advanced System Concepts ("Systems") trademarks did not violate the Lanham Act. Network and Systems were competitors, both selling job scheduling and management software. Network purchased the keyword "ActiveBatch" from Google—ActiveBatch being the name of the product produced by Systems. When Internet users typed "ActiveBatch" into various search engines, a results page was produced showing Network's website as a sponsored link. The Ninth Circuit court determined that the federal trial court was correct in finding Network's use of keywords to constitute the prerequisite "use in commerce."

Commercial use was found in Network's use of System's mark to purchase keywords to advertise its products for sale on the Internet. Nevertheless, the Ninth Circuit reversed the district court ruling that System was not entitled to an injunction. The appellate court held that the district court did not apply the *Sleekcraft* factors correctly and further that the lower court did not determine whether there was a likelihood of confusion.

§ 11-10. Sponsored Banner Advertisements

Trademark infringement claims may be predicated upon the defendant's use of unidentified banner ads on the Internet user's search page. Playboy, for example, objected to a competitor's ad appearing as a pop-up banner ad along the margin of the search result when the searcher entered "Playboy" and/or "Playmate"—both trademarked terms owned by Playboy. *Playboy Enterprises v. Netscape Communications Corp.*, 354 F.3d 1020 (9th Cir. 2004). The search engine incorporated calibration keywords in its software application. The *Playboy* court found the banner advertisements objectionable because they did not clearly identify the sponsor of the ad, thereby creating a likelihood of confusion.

§ 11-11. Metatags

(A) INVISIBLE TRADEMARK VIOLATIONS

Some search engines index each discernible word on every web page, while others index by metatags. A "metatag" is an invisible code in Hypertext Markup Language ("HTML") that describes the contents of a Web page. Trademark owners file suit against individuals or companies that incorporated the metatags of popular companies in their website to jump-start their page rank. The recent trend is for courts to find that merely incorporating the plaintiff's trademark in invisible code does not demonstrate use in commerce. Nevertheless, if a website uses metatags deceptively to misrepresent its sites, courts will find liability for trademark infringement. A few courts continue to find that use of a plaintiff's trademark in metatags constitutes infringement.

(B) INITIAL INTEREST CONFUSION

Initial Interest Confusion ("IIC") occurs on the Internet when a company creates confusion "from the unauthorized use of trademarks to divert Internet traffic, thereby capitalizing on a trademark holder's goodwill." Aust. Gold Inc. v. Hatfield, 436 F.3d 1228 10th Cir. 2006). IIC ". . . occurs when a customer is lured to a product by the similarity of the mark, even if the customer realizes the true source of the goods before the sale is consummated." Initial interest confusion is, in effect, a misappropriation of good will. What is important is not the duration of the confusion; it is the misappropriation of goodwill. A growing number of courts are skeptical about the continuing vitality of IIC.

Terri Welles graced the cover of Playboy in 1981 as the Playboy Playmate of the Year. Playboy Enterprises International ("PEI") challenged her use of the title "Playboy Playmate of the Year 1981," and her use of other trademarked terms on her website. PEI contended that Welles infringed the following trademarked terms on her website: (1) the terms "Playboy" and "Playmate" in the metatags of the website, (2) the phrase "Playmate of the Year 1981" on the masthead of the website, (3) the phrases "Playboy Playmate of the Year 1981" and "Playmate of the Year 1981" on various banner ads, and (4) her repeated use of the abbreviation "PMOY '81" as the watermark on the pages of the website.

In *Playboy Enterprises, Inc. v. Welles*, 279 F.3d 796 (9th Cir. (2002), the Ninth Circuit reversed a federal district court's grant of a preliminary injunction that restrained Welles from using the registered trademarks "Playboy" and "Playmate" as metatags in her websites. Playboy sued Welles on various theories, including a federal trademark dilution claim under the prior statute. The appeals court determined that most of Welles's use of "Playmate of the Year" were nominative uses and, therefore, excepted from coverage. To use a mark as a trademark, the defendant must attempt to identify the source of the mark with the defendant itself. Trademark mention is any other use of a mark, such as to refer to a particular product for purposes of comparison, criticism, or point of reference. The court found Welles's use of the abbreviation "PMOY" on the wallpaper of her site was not nominative, and, therefore was "not excepted from the anti-dilution provisions." In finding nominative use, the court ruled that Welles was not trying to divert traffic from *Playboy*. A party raising the statutory affirmative defense of nominative use to a claim of trademark infringement must prove she is using the term fairly and in good faith and for description.

§ 11-12. Trademark Law Defenses

(A) NOMINATIVE FAIR USE

In order to assert a successful fair use defense to a trademark infringement claim, the defendant must prove three elements: that the use was made (1) other than as a mark, (2) in a descriptive sense, and (3) in good faith. 15 U.S.C. § 1115(b)(4). To qualify under nominative fair use, there are three requirements. First, the product or service in question must not be readily identifiable without use of the trademark. Second, the defendant may only use as much of the mark as is reasonably necessary to identify the product or service. Third, the defendant must not do anything in conjunction with the mark that would suggest sponsorship or endorsement by the trademark holder. The nominative fair use analysis allows a defendant to use the plaintiff's mark to describe the plaintiff's product, so long as the goal is for the defendant to describe her own product. A computer repair shop, for example, can advertise that it fixes Dell laptops even though "Dell" is a registered trademark. In *New Kids On The Block v. News America Publishing, Inc.*, 971 F.2d 302 (9th Cir. 1992), the Ninth Circuit adopted a nominative fair use test in which the defendant must prove that:

> first, the product or service in question must be one not readily identifiable without use of the trademark, second, only so much of the mark or marks may be used as is reasonably necessary to identify the product or service, and third, the user must do nothing that would, in conjunction

with the mark, suggest sponsorship or endorsement by the trademark holder.

Fair use also enables comparative advertising and the use of another's trademark in a manner such as the Pepsi Challenge that featured taste tests between Coca-Cola and Pepsi in malls around the country in the 1980s.

(B) FIRST AMENDMENT IN CYBERSPACE

(1) Gripe Sites

Fan Sites, rogue sites, or grip sites that mention trademarks in the course of criticizing companies are generally protected by the First Amendment unless a court finds that those sites are deceptive, and create consumer confusion. Gripe sites must make it clear that they are not affiliated with trademarks. In *Bihari v. Gross* (S.D.N.Y. 2000), the court found that a "Gripe Site" that was critical of the plaintiff's interior design work did not violate Marianne Bihari's trademark because no reasonable consumer would believe that the plaintiff or her company, Bihari Interiors, sponsored the site. The court also found that the "Gripe Site" was not diverting users from the Bihari Interior site. Companies will find it difficult to enjoin websites critical of their goods and services, which have become ubiquitous on the Internet. In the early years of the Internet, trademark owners often won lawsuits against domain name registrants who incorporated their trade names or marks.

An early example of such a complaint occurs in, *Bally Total Fitness Holding Corp. v. Faber*, 29 F. Supp. 2d 1161 (C.D. Cal. 1998), where a critic of the chain of health clubs set up an anti-Bally website entitled, "Bally's sucks" filed suit for trademark dilution because the defendant was using its trademarks in an unauthorized manner. The federal court in California granted summary judgment in favor of Faber, reasoning, "no reasonable person would think Bally's is affiliated with or endorses [the anti-Bally site]." The court also found "fair use" in the website's use of Bally's intellectual property.

In a UDRP proceeding, the domain name, AirFranceSucks.com, was transferred to Air France but "the airline's victory at arbitration was not without controversy: panelists disagreed about what the word 'sucks' really means to Internet users." *Société Air France v. Virtual Dates, Inc.*, Case No. D2005–0168 UDRP 2005).

(2) Lamparello v. Falwell

The Fourth Circuit found the FTDA applies only to a commercial use in commerce of a mark, leaving no doubt, "that it did not intend for trademark laws to impinge the First Amendment rights of critics and commentators." Lamparello v. Falwell, 420 F.3d 309 (4th Cir. 2005).   In *Lamparello*, the Fourth Circuit determined that Christopher Lamparello's domain name, www.fallwell.com, a website critical of Reverend Jerry Falwell and his views on homosexuality, did not constitute cybersquatting. The appellate court reasoned that Reverend Falwell was unable to show that Lamparello had a bad faith

intent to profit from his use of the fallwell.com
domain name. Lamparello had not engaged in the
type of conduct described in the statutory factors as
typifying the bad faith intent to profit essential to a
successful cybersquatting claim.

(3) People for the Ethical Treatment of Animals v. Doughney

In *People for the Ethical Treatment of Animals v.
Doughney*, 263 F.3d 359 (4th Cir. 2001), the
organization People for the Ethical Treatment of
Animals ("PETA") brought action against Michael
Doughney, citing trademark infringement, dilution,
and cybersquatting for Doughney's use of the
domain name, peta.org. Doughney argued that his
website, People Eating Tasty Animals, was a parody
of People for the Ethical Treatment of Animals, and
thus protected by the First Amendment. A Virginia
district court granted summary judgment to PETA.

The court, using the *Bantam* test, held that
Doughney's site did not constitute a parody because
there was no "simultaneous conveyance," that the
site was at once a PETA site and a parody.
Similarly, for the infringement and unfair
competition claims, the court found that Doughney
used PETA's trademark "in commerce" based on a
two-part rationale. First, because his website
offered links to other websites offering "goods and
services" thereby providing the needed "connection
with goods and services" required by the Lanham
Act, and second, because Doughney recommended
that PETA "settle" or "make him an offer" in order

to purchase the domain name from him thereby making Doughney a cybersquatter.

(C) TRADEMARK PARODIES

A parody is a "simple form of entertainment conveyed by juxtaposing the irreverent representation of the trademark with the idealized image created by the mark's owners." *L.L. Bean, Inc. v. Drake Publishers, Inc.*, 811 F.2d 26 (1st Cir. 1987) . In *Lyons Partnership v. Giannoulas*, 179 F.3d 384 (5th Cir. 1999), the Fifth Circuit ruled that the Ted Giannoulas creation of the sports mascot The Famous Chicken stepping on a Barney lookalike constituted a parody protectable by the First Amendment of the U.S. Constitution. A parody makes a trademark the brunt of its joke, or satirical message, and therefore does not infringe upon the trademark.

In *Louis Vuitton Mallettier S.A. v. Haute Diggity Dog,* the Fourth Circuit ruled that a "Chewy Vuiton" dog chew toy was a successful parody of the French manufacturer's luxury handbags and the "LOUIS VUITTON" marks and trade dress used in marketing those handbags. To state a claim for trade dress infringement, plaintiffs must show (1) their trade dress is primarily non-functional; (2) the alleged infringement creates a likelihood of confusion; and (3) the trade dress either is inherently distinctive or has acquired secondary meaning. Lanham Act, § 43(a), 15 U.S.C. § 1125(a).

The *Louis Vuitton* court reasoned the "Chewy Vuiton" toy was obviously an irreverent and intentional representation of the famous designer's handbag. *Louis Vuitton Malletier, M.A. v. Haute Diggity Dog,* 507 F.3d 252 (4th Cir. 2007) . The *Louis Vuitton* court found that the dog toy was not an "idealized image" of a mark created by the manufacturer. Moreover, the toy's name immediately conveyed a joking and amusing parody by using something a dog would chew on to poke fun at the elegance and exorbitance of the famous French designer's rather pricey handbags. The parody doctrine is not well developed outside the United States.

(D) TRADEMARK LACHES

Laches is an equitable defense consisting of three elements (1) delay in asserting one's trademark rights, (2) lack of excuse for the delay, and (3) undue prejudice to the alleged infringer caused by the delay. To avoid the equitable defense of laches, or "sleeping on your rights," trademark owners should conduct public searches of social media and other websites. Non-generic, non-misleading, genuine and continuous use of trademarks is necessary for continuous protection. In cybersquatting cases, the trademark owner should not wait too many years to file a complaint either in federal court or in a UDRP dispute-resolution proceeding.

§ 11-13. False Advertising

To prevail in a Lanham Act false advertising case, the plaintiff must prove: (1) the online advertisements of the defendant were false or misleading, (2) the online ads deceived, or had the capacity to deceive website visitors, (3) the deception had a material effect on purchasing decisions, (4) the misrepresented product or service affects interstate commerce, and (5) the plaintiff has been, or is likely to be, injured as a result of the false advertising.

§ 11-14. Typosquatting

"Typosquatting" is the practice of registering a domain name to benefit from users who mistype a domain name. A classic example is the "typosquatter" who registered domain names that employed misspellings of popular child oriented websites. The typosquatter took advantage of children's foreseeable misspellings to receive a fee for each child's clickstream. Typosquatters rely upon adult Internet users mistyping domain names as well. Dotster, a domain name registrar, registered the domain name "wwwVulcanGolf.com," which is a period away from the domain name www.VulcanGolf.com. *Vulcan Golf LLC v. Google, Inc.*, 552 F. Supp. 2d 752, 760 (N.D. Ill. 2008).

Vulcan filed suit against Dotster claiming the defendant "intentionally registered this domain name without the period after the 'www,' expecting that a certain number of Internet users will mistype the name and will land on the webpage." Dotster was liable because it benefited from their blatantly deceptive domain. Each time a user clicks on links or other online ads, Google, the parking companies and domain name owners receive advertising revenue. This is the business model for many commercial websites

§ 11-15. Domain Name Hijacking & Reverse Hijacking

Trademark hijacking is when a cybersquatter registers a domain name that is identical or confusingly similar to a plaintiff's trade name or trademark. In contrast, a "reverse domain name hijacking" occurs when a cybersquatter or person with no legitimate interest in a mark files a complaint against the domain name registrant who does have a legitimate interest in the mark. Reverse cybersquatting lawsuits are filed in order to extract a nuisance settlement. Under the Lanham Act, "a domain name registrant who is aggrieved by an overreaching trademark owner may commence an action to declare that the domain name registration or use by the registrant is not unlawful under the Lanham Act." 15 U.S.C. § 1114(2)(D)(v).

In *Telemedia Network Inc. v. Sunshine Films, Inc.*, 2002 WL 31518870 (Cal. Ct. App. 2d Dist. 2002), an adult entertainment company modified a domain name to redirect traffic of a rival to its own website, a practice known as "domain name hijacking." The diversion of traffic occurred when customers who were trying to access Sexnet found a website operated by Sunshine with no content. Sunshine's purpose was to raise revenue through deceptive means.

§ 11-16. Uniform Domain Name Resolution Policy

(A) OVERVIEW OF UDRP PROCEEDINGS

The World Intellectual Property Organization ("WIPO") developed the Uniform Domain Name Resolution Policy ("UDRP") for the arbitration of domain name disputes. WIPO is an agency of the United Nations that administers many international treaties. WIPO, for example, entered into a cooperative agreement with the World Trade Organization ("WTO") in 1996. WIPO's UDRP policy and rules play a role in harmonizing IP law by providing uniform remedies for trademark owners against cybersquatters and other abusive domain name practices. In 2012 alone, trademark holders filed 2,884 cybersquatting cases covering 5,084 Internet domain names under procedures based on the Uniform Domain Name Dispute Resolution Policy ("UDRP"). WIPO, *WIPO Arbitration and Mediation Center-2012 Review* (2012). UDRP arbitral panels have the power to cancel or transfer domain name registration. ICANN can also order such relief upon receipt of an order from a court or arbitral tribunal. Nevertheless, UDRP panels have no arbitral authority to award monetary damages, statutory damages, or any other remedies typically other than the power to cancel or transfer domain names.

(B) UDRP PROVIDERS

Under the UDRP, most types of trademark-based domain-name disputes are resolvable by agreement, court action, or arbitration before a registrar will cancel, suspend, or transfer a domain name. The UDRP arbitration panel decides cases arising out of abusive registrations of domain names such as cybersquatting. Under the UDRP's expedited proceedings, the owner of trademark rights files a complaint with an approved dispute-resolution service provider.

UDRP panels are limited in what remedies they may impose. Panels may order that a registrar cancel, transfer, or change a domain name registration but have no authority to award monetary damages or attorney's fees. The UDRP rules have been adopted by ICANN and are incorporated by reference in every new domain name registration. Jurisdiction is not an issue because the domain name registrant has agreed in advance to submit to UDRP should a trademark dispute arise.

(C) HOW THE UDRP WORKS

(1) Domain Name Registration

The year 1999 marked the release of the WIPO's Uniform Dispute Resolution Policy ("UDRP"). All ICANN-accredited registrars have adopted the UDRP. Certain managers of country-code top-level domains (e.g., .nu, .tv, .ws) have also adopted it. The UDRP policy provides trademark owners with an expedited administrative procedure to resolve disputes over abusive practices such as "cybersquatting," "reverse cybersquatting", and other abusive domain name registration abuses.

A federal court described the three principal UDRP institutions key to understanding the management of domain names:

> First, companies called "registries" operate a database (or "registry") for all domain names within the scope of their authority. Second, companies called "registrars" register domain names with registries on behalf of those who own the names. Registrars maintain an ownership record for each domain name they have registered with a registry. Action by a registrar is needed to transfer ownership of a domain name from one registrant to another. Third, individuals and companies called "registrants" own the domain names. Registrants interact with the registrars, who in turn interact with the registries. *Office Depot Inc. v. Zuccarini*, 2010 U.S. App. LEXIS 4052 (9th Cir. 2010).

Under the DNS, the registrant is the company or individual to whom the domain name actually belongs. A website operator must signify an administrative contact at the point of registration, who is a person authorized by the registrant to make changes in the domain name. For example, the administrative contact may transfer, cancel, or assign rights to the domain name.

Registrars are companies that register domain names and accredited by ICANN. During the accreditation process, registrars agree to adhere to the Uniform Domain Name Dispute Resolution Policy. ICANN posts a list of Approved Dispute-

Resolution Service Providers. In addition, to this Policy, there are Rules for Uniform Domain Name Dispute Resolution Policy. Dispute-Resolution service providers do the administrative work of processing complaints, vetting arbitrators, and overseeing cases. . Charges for domain name registration are competitive, as little as $10.

Domain name registrants agree in advance to settle disputes with trademark owners under the UDRP policy. "The Uniform Domain-Name Dispute Resolution Policy ("UDRP") has been adopted by ICANN-accredited registrars in all gTLDs (.aero, .asia, .biz, .cat, .com, .coop, .info, .jobs, .mobi, .museum, .name, .net, .org, .pro, .tel and .travel)." ICANN, UDRP Dispute Resolution Policy (2012). Domain name registrants agree to UDRP proceedings arising from alleged abusive registrations of domain names—for example, cybersquatting—may be initiated by a holder of trademark rights. In 2013, the ICANN will significantly expand domain name space with internationalized domain names (IDNs) and non-Latin characters such as Chinese, Cyrillic, and Arabic characters. BLOOMBERG BNA, ELECTRONIC COMMERCE & LAW REPORT *Keeping Up With the Domain Name Explosion,* (Dec. 28, 2012).

Trademark owners will generally prevail under the UDRP if they can prove a domain name is either identical or confusingly similar to their trademark or service mark. Bad faith registrations may have their registration cancelled or transferred to the true owner. The emblem of bad faith is when a registrant obtains a domain name for the sole purpose of selling, renting, or transferring the registration to the true owner for a profit, which is the classic test for cybersquatting. Another test for bad faith is whether the registrant registers the domain name to prevent the true owners from using it.

(2) Liability of the Domain Name Registrars

A federal court in 1999 became the first to rule that a domain name registrar was not liable for direct infringement or liable for dilution if it had not made commercial use of the mark in its capacity as the sole and exclusive domain name registrar. Domain name registrars have no liability for direct, contributory, or vicarious trademark infringement for accepting the registration of an Internet domain name that is confusingly similar to a plaintiff's service mark or trademark. Domain name registries may not face liability for intellectual property infringement, but may be liable for negligence, conversion, or other torts, where they do not act reasonably.

In *Solid Host, NL v. Namecheap, Inc.*, 652 F. Supp.2d 1091 (C.D. Cal. 2009), a California court held that a domain name registrar is immune from trademark infringement claims for failing to prevent the registration of domain names infringing a trademark owner's registered marks. In *Kremen v. Cohen* (9th Cir. 2003), the Ninth Circuit reversed a lower court ruling and held that Network Solutions converted a registrant's domain name when it transferred it to an ex-convict based on a forged letter.

In *Baidu Inc. v. Beijing Baidu Netcom Science & Technology Co.*, 2010 WL 2900313 (S.D. N.Y. 2010) 2010 WL 2900313 (S.D. N.Y. 2010), a domain name registrar was liable under a theory of negligent enablement. Baidu filed a lawsuit for trademark infringement, breach of contract, and gross negligence against Register.com, a domain name registry, for negligent security in enabling a cyberattack on its website. "Baidu, Inc. provides Chinese and Japanese language Internet search services," that enables Internet users to locate online information such as, "Web pages, news, images, multimedia files, and blogs through the links provided on its websites." Bloomberg Business Week, Baidu (Jan., 14, 2010). On January 11, 2010, a hacker who gained "unauthorized access to Baidu's account at Register," hijacked Baidu's website.

The cybercriminal, masquerading as Baidu's agent, requested a change of its e-mail address in an online chat with Register.com's service representative. The Baidu service representative asked the intruder to provide security information and the intruder gave the incorrect answer. Nevertheless, the Register.com representative gave the intruder information that enabled him to gain unauthorized access to Baidu's account. The hacker rerouted Internet traffic intended for Baidu to a web page displaying an Iranian flag and a broken Star of David proclaiming: "This site has been hacked by the Iranian Cyber Army." The hijacking of the Baidu website diverted Internet traffic for approximately five hours.

Baidu filed suit in a New York federal court, bringing claims for breach of the terms of service agreement, gross negligence, and secondary trademark infringement. Register.com's terms of service agreement limits its liability for interrupted service and other errors or omissions. The federal court held that Baidu's complaint for negligence could go forward because Register.com's gross negligence was outside the sphere of the terms of service. The court ruled that Register.com was not entitled to immunity because it was acting as a registrar. The *Baidu* court found that Register.com was neither registering a domain name nor maintaining it when it gave the intruder unauthorized information that enabled it to control Baidu's website. Nevertheless, the court held that Register.com was not secondarily liable for trademark infringement.

The *Baidu* court applied the contributory trademark infringement test articulated in its 2010 decision in *Tiffany (NJ) Inc. v. eBay, Inc.*, 600 F.3d 93 (2d Cir. 2010) Tiffany, Inc. ("Tiffany") a renowned jewelry seller, instituted a trademark lawsuit against eBay, asserting diverse causes of action including trademark infringement, trademark dilution and false advertising, arising from eBay's advertising and listing practices. Tiffany alleges that eBay directly infringed its trademark in violation of Section 32 of the Lanham Act. Under the *Tiffany* test, a provider like Register.com must have knowledge of infringement in order to have secondary liability. The court found that Register.com did not induce infringement given that the intruder had tricked the registrar and that it had no knowledge of direct infringement. Trademark owners sometimes assert the right to a DMCA takedown, but the takedown procedures do not cover trademark infringement on a website.

§ 11-17. Types of UDRP Cases

The first WIPO UDRP proceeding was initiated in 2000 when the World Wrestling Federation (WWF) submitted an electronic complaint to the World Intellectual Property Organization's Arbitration and Mediation Center in order to gain control over the domain name www.worldwrestlingfederation.com. The WIPO Panel ruled that the registrant of this domain name acted in bad faith when it offered to sell the domain name to third parties for a significant profit. The Panel decided the contested domain name was identical or confusingly similar to the trademark and service mark in which the WWF had rights. The WIPO panel transferred the disputed domain name to WWF, ruling that the respondent had no legitimate rights in the domain name. Since this first case, UDRP panels have decided tens of thousands of disputes between domain name registrants and trademark owners.

Five paradigmatic categories of cases are typically decided by WIPO arbitral panels in deciding whether a given domain name is "confusingly similar" to a trademark: (1) cases where the domain name and trademark are wholly identical, or, in cases where the trademark owner has a registered domain name, the generic Top-Level Domain ("gTLD") might be different, (2) cases where a registrant's domain name incorporates the surname of a celebrity, (3) cases where a generic or descriptive word has been added to the trademark (such as "my," "direct," or "e-"), (4) cases where anti-corporate websites append the word "sucks" at the end of trade names, and (5) typosquatting cases where the domain name registrant relies on Internet users mistyping famous trademark names.

(A) INCORPORATING ANOTHER'S TRADEMARK

The classic illustration of incorporating another's trademark in a domain name was *Playboy Enterprises International, Inc. v. Good Samaritan Program*, D2001-0241 (WIPO, 2001). In this WIPO case, *Playboy* magazine founder and complainant in the case, Hugh M. Hefner, objected to Good Samaritan's registration of the domain name "hughhefner.com" with BulkRegister, a domain name registry. Playboy Enterprises, which holds the trademark "Hugh M. Hefner," met the three elements of UDRP Policy 4(A) because: (1) Good Samaritan's domain name was identical to Playboy's trademarks, (2) Good Samaritan had no rights or legitimate interests in the domain name, and (3) Good Samaritan's domain name was registered and was used in bad faith.

The UDRP panel decided the case on the complaint given compelling evidence Good Samaritan was a cybersquatter. The panel found it appears from Good Samaritan's own statements that it sought substantial consideration in the form of celebrity endorsement or linkage to successful commercial websites in return for its services. The UDRP panel concluded, "Good Samaritan registered 'hughhefner.com' for the purpose of transferring it to Playboy in return for valuable consideration in excess of its costs directly related to the domain name."

(B) COMMON LAW TM RIGHTS OF CELEBRITIES

The USPTO maintains a database of trademarks. The complainant must prove common law rights if the trademark or service mark is not registered. A celebrity's name alone is not protected under the UDRP or the common law. The *sine qua non* of common law rights is that the personal name is a source of goods or services. The purpose of trademark law is to protect consumers by providing accurate product identification. Kevin Spacey, for example, has common law rights in his name because he uses his name as a trademark as a way of identifying his performances. A single cybersquatter took advantage of the goodwill in the names of well-known personalities by registering domain names that contained the names of celebrities.

UDRP panels ruled against the cybersquatter who registered Kevin Spacey's name, as well as domain names containing the names of other well-known celebrities including Larry King, Pierce Brosnan, Celine Dion, Pamela Anderson, Carmen Electra, Michael Crichton, and Julie Brown. UDRP panels typically refuse to transfer or cancel domain name registrations of surnames unless the plaintiff proves he or she has common law rights or that their name has a secondary meaning in the marketplace.

(C) APPENDING DESCRIPTIVE OR GENERIC WORDS

Cybersquatting registrants with no rights to famous trademarks palm off on their goodwill by simply adding one or more generic or descriptive words to the celebrity or company's name. A UDRP panel is likely to find a domain name confusingly similar when it is used in the same industry as a well-known trademark, as with "statefarm-claimshelp.com." However, in *Safeguard Operations LLC v. Safeguard Storage*, NAF Case No. FA0604000672431 (NAF 2006), the NAF panel ruled the respondent had a legitimate interest in the domain name "safeguard-storage.com" because of the preparations it undertook to operate a self-storage business under the name "Safeguard Storage" before receiving notice of the instant domain name dispute. As a result, the UDRP panel refused to direct the respondent to transfer the disputed domain to Complainant Safeguard Operations LLC, owner of several federally registered trademarks containing the word "Safeguard," which marks its uses in connection with its operation of self-storage facilities.

(D) ANTI-CORPORATE WEBSITES

Companies seeking to shut down gripe sites are far more likely to find success through the UDRP panels than in the U.S. federal courts, which often refuse to enjoin gripe sites because of the First Amendment. The fourth category of UDRP cases deal with complaint sites, a.k.a. "sucks" domain names (i.e., names with the complainant's trademark and a negative term such as "sucks"). Most panels facing the issue have found such domain names are confusingly similar to the complainants' marks.

A UDRP panel found that that the domain name Radioshacksucks.com was pointing to a website with various pay-per-click links that were mainly aimed at directing visitors to competing third party commercial websites. The Panel ruled in favor of Radio Shack and transferred the name. In one case, the "sucks" site was found to be confusingly similar to the complainant's mark because a search engine would bring up the "sucks" site when the mark itself was entered as a search term.

UDRP panels distinguish between complaint websites expressing feelings about products and services, and those constructed for the sole purpose of extorting money from the trademark owners. Rather than asking whether the domain name causes confusion as to source, the panel should compare the domain name and the mark for similarity. Other panels have noted that many Internet users do not speak English or do not know the word "sucks." Ultimately, these panels have held domain names adding the word "sucks" to a trademark of another company was confusingly similar to the mark incorporated. A minority of panels have ruled "sucks" sites are not confusingly similar.

(E) UDRP TYPOSQUATTING

The fifth paradigmatic UDRP case is the "typosquatting" case, i.e., where one letter in a well-known brand is replaced with another letter in order to direct traffic to the typosquatter's website. UDRP panels generally disfavor such strategies, especially when evidenced by bad faith. In *Toronto-Dominion Bank v. Karpachev*, WIPO Case No. D2000–1571 (WIPO 2001), the WIPO panel concluded the domain name "tdwatergouse.com" was confusingly similar to the TD WATERHOUSE mark.

John Zuccarini, a recidivist typosquatter, was the respondent in *Six Continents Hotels, Inc. v. John Zuccarini*, Case D2003-D5009 (WIPO 2003). The WIPO panel found that Zuccarini acted in bad faith, and transferred the domain name "hoildayinn.com" to the owner of the Holiday Inn hotel chain.

(F) UDRP PANELS V. DOMAIN NAME LITIGATION

U.S. trademark owners have a choice as to whether to file federal trademark lawsuits under the ACPA or pursue UDRP remedies. The advantage of the UDRP is speed and low expense. Trademark litigation may cost hundreds of thousands of dollars and take years to complete the appellate process. UDRP panels, in contrast, make decisions in a few weeks and there is no appeals process. However, UDRP panels have no power to award damages, attorneys' fees, or costs.

Another advantage of the UDRP is that every domain name registrant is subject to its jurisdiction, whereas a plaintiff will need to demonstrate minimum contacts to hale a defendant into federal court. In many instances, a trademark owner is only seeking transfer or termination of the domain name, which can be accomplished more efficiently under the UDRP.

§ 11-18. Global Trademark Issues

(A) GLOBAL E-BUSINESS CONCERNS

It is now difficult to imagine the contours of trademark infringement without considering new methods of infringement enabled by bandwidth, browsers, and digital data. Beginning in the mid-1990s, entrepreneurs registered thousands of domain names containing the trademarks of famous companies in the hopes of selling them back for a ransom price. In the past two decades, global trademark law has been reworked to address challenges posed by domain names and cybersquatting. The UDRP rules for deciding domain name disputes are drafted to bridge disparate legal cultures and thus help resolve disputes that cross national borders. Without Internet websites, no court would need to decide issues such as whether a pop-up ad infringed a company's trademark or constituted an unfair business practice in cyberspace.

Lawyers representing information-based companies must make difficult decisions to determine where to seek protection. Trademarks, by their very nature, are symbols and often language-based signifiers. Lawyers seeking trademark protection in foreign countries must consider translation challenges "particularly where multiple language may be spoken within a particular nation." JOHN CROSS, ET. AL, GLOBAL ISSUES IN INTELLECTUAL

PROPERTY LAW 162 (2010). Trademark law has been harmonized but there are still differences in how a company obtains trademark rights. U.S. trademark protection tends to be broader than in Europe giving protection to "nontraditional marks such as colors, smells, sounds, and taste."

(B) EUROPEAN COMMUNITY TRADEMARKS

The Community Trademark ("CTM") is a trademark valid across the countries in the European Union registered in OHIM in Alicante, Spain, in accordance with CTM Regulations, which is Council Regulation (EC) No 40/94 of 20 December 1993 on the Community trademark) ("CTMR"). The EU trademark regulation has been amended and the European Commission has adopted implementing rules for the CTMR, the fees payable to OHIM ("Office of Harmonization for the Internal Market"), and the rules of procedure of the Boards of Appeal of OHIM. A CTM is a trademark valid across the European Union ("EU") assuming it is registered with OHIM in accordance with the provisions of the CTM Regulations.

(C) MADRID PROTOCOL

The Madrid System for the International Registration of Marks ("the Madrid system") was established in 1891 and now functions as the Madrid Protocol (1989), which is administered by the International Bureau of WIPO. International registration is governed by the Madrid Protocol system, which allows one-stop registration in multiple countries. Under the Madrid Agreement, an international application must be based on a mark that has already been registered ("basic registration") in the Office of origin. An international mark so registered is equivalent to an application or a registration of the same mark effected directly in each of the countries designated by the applicant.

The Madrid Protocol has been in operation since April 1996 and has been ratified by many countries around the world, including most European countries individually, as well as the US, Japan, Australia, China, Russia, and, in October 2004, by the European Community. A registered Community Trademark is valid for ten years from the date of filing of the application. It can be renewed indefinitely for further periods of ten years.

CHAPTER 12

TRADE SECRETS IN CYBERSPACE

One of the greatest dangers facing companies is the possibility that spiteful hackers, disaffected employees, or unknown third parties will maliciously divulge trade secrets online. Ex-employees can destroy the trade secret status of new product blueprints, customer lists, or other proprietary information with the push of a button. Once a trade secret is revealed to millions on the Internet, it is reasonably certain that it can no longer be classified as a trade secret. This chapter examines Internet-related trade secret issues. Trade secret protection is perilous in a networked world where intangible assets may be lost at the click of a mouse. Calling something a trade secret is not enough in a world of mobile technology, mobile phones, and instant messaging. Theft of trade secrets is now occurring on portable devices, such as mobile phones.

§ 12-1. What Trade Secrets Are

The common law of trade secrets was first conceptualized as a business tort in the nineteenth century. Today trade secrets are classified as the fourth branch of intellectual property ("IP") law, whether based upon on a contract or torts theory and covered by state rather than federal law. Trade secrets are neither patentable nor subject to copyright because these forms of intellectual property mandate disclosure. Disclosure is the death knell for a trade secret, destroying its emblematic feature of secrecy.

Coca Cola company officials have kept the recipe for Coca Cola syrup locked in a vault for more than a century, in order to prevent rivals from producing an identical copy of the company's best-known product that could be sold at a lower price. Unlike patents, copyrights, or trademarks, state tort law is the only protection for trade secrets.

§ 12-2. Trade Secrets Governed by State Law

Trade secrets were originally a tort of misappropriation governed by the Restatement (First) of Torts, § 757. The elements of the misappropriation tort are that (1) the plaintiff must have invested time, money, or effort to extract the information, (2) the defendant must have appropriated the information without a similar investment, and (3) the plaintiff must have suffered a competitive injury because of the taking. Today, the Uniform Trade Secrets Act ("UTSA") provides that a trade secret includes "a formula, pattern, compilation, program, device, method, technique, or process, that: (1) Derives independent economic value, actual or potential, from not being generally known to the public or to other persons who can obtain economic value from its disclosure or use, and (2) Is the subject of efforts that are reasonable under the circumstances to maintain its secrecy."

UTSA is a Model Statute drafted by the National Conference of Commissioners on Uniform State Law ("NCCUSL") to update and harmonize the law concerning the misappropriation of trade secrets. As of May 1, 2012, only Massachusetts, New Jersey, New York, Pennsylvania, Tennessee, Texas, and Wyoming have not enacted UTSA's broad definition of a trade secret. The few states that have yet to adopt UTSA follow the Restatement (First) or the Restatement of the Law (Third) of Unfair Competition and treat trade secret misappropriation as a business tort.

(A) UTSA'S DEFINITION OF SECRECY

Secrecy is the principal issue in most trade secret litigation. Courts consider six factors in determining whether confidential information constitutes a trade secret: (1) the extent to which the information is known outside the business, (2) the extent to which it is known to those inside the business, i.e., by the employees, (3) the precautions taken by the holder of the trade secret to guard the secrecy of the information, (4) the savings effected and the value to the holder in having the information as against competitors, (5) the amount of effort or money expended in obtaining and developing the information, and (6) the amount of time and expense it would take for others to acquire and duplicate the information.

(B) UTSA MISAPPROPRIATION ACTION

Misappropriation means acquiring a trade secret by "improper means" or from someone who has acquired it through "improper means." To state a claim for misappropriation of trade secrets under the Uniform Trade Secrets Act, a plaintiff must allege that: (1) the plaintiff owned a trade secret, (2) the defendant misappropriated the trade secret, and (3) the defendant's actions damaged the plaintiff. *Nexsales Corp. v. Salebuild, Inc.*, 11–CV–3195, 2012 WL 216260 (N.D. Cal. 2012).

(C) REASONABLE MEANS TO PROTECT SECRETS

Trade secret laws require companies to take reasonable steps to prevent the public disclosure of source. Accidental or other public disclosure of a trade secret destroys its status as a trade secret. Trade secrets in software derive their economic values from their secrecy. For example, trade secret protection lasts indefinitely so long as the software vendor is able to keep its source code secret. At a minimum, an Internet company must label source code, plans, and other documents with a legend that proclaims these materials are confidential and proprietary.

(1) Nondisclosure Agreements

Licensors will typically enter into nondisclosure agreements ("NDAs") with their employees, consultants, and joint ventures as a reasonable means of protecting software code. An NDA is a contractual arrangement that requires a recipient of confidential information to keep that information secret. Counsel will typically draft NDAs that bind its employees, consultants, customers, and other third parties when the software maker is developing customized software or building a specialized company website.

In April of 2009, a Rhode Island jury ruled that Microsoft should pay Uniloc USA and Singapore $388 million in damages for patent infringement arising out of a breach of a NDA. This case arose out of Microsoft's study of Uniloc's product activation software to address its piracy problem. Uniloc had a § 216 patent for a registration system that required the user to enter an identification code on the client that matched the server side for the software to be activated. The court ruled that Microsoft breached the NDA and violated Uniloc's patent in producing software relying upon the patent. This case illustrates the multiple functions of NDAs, which can be drafted to protect patents.

Typically, the nondisclosure agreement will stipulate that the customers, without the developer's prior written consent, are not permitted to disclose trade secrets. Therefore, software developers and their customers will enter into mutual nondisclosure agreements because the developer will typically have access to its customer's intellectual property when configuring or customizing software. Courts will typically determine the enforceability of nondisclosure agreements by asking a series of questions:

(1) Is the restraint, from the standpoint of the employer, reasonable in the sense that it is no greater than is necessary to protect the employer in some legitimate business interest? (2) From the standpoint of the employee, is the restraint reasonable in the sense that it is not unduly harsh and oppressive in curtailing his legitimate efforts to earn a livelihood? (3) Is the restraint

reasonable from the standpoint of a sound public policy? *Decision Insights, Inc. v. Sentia Group, Inc.*, 2009 U.S. App. LEXIS 2654 (4th Cir. 2009).

In the late 1980s, Par Microsystems, Inc. developed a computer software accounting program with the help of Robert S. Johnson, a computer designer employee. Johnson accepted employment with Pinnacle Development Corporation and shortly after, Pinnacle began the marketing and sale of a similar computer software accounting program. Upon Par's discovery of this program, they took legal action against Johnson and Pinnacle for copyright infringement, and the jury awarded them $100,000. *PAR Microsystems Inc. v. Pinnacle Development Corp.*, Case No. 93–2114–D (D. Tex. 1997). The remedies for the misappropriation of trade secrets include damages (UTSA, § 3), injunctive relief (UTSA, § 2), and attorneys' fees (UTSA, § 4) if the plaintiff proves bad faith.

In determining whether to grant a preliminary injunction in trade secret litigation, courts weigh four factors: (1) the probability that the movant will succeed on the merits, (2) the threat of irreparable harm to the movant, (3) the balance between the harm to the movant and any harm that granting the injunction will cause to other parties to the litigation, and (4) the public interest. UTSA permits the owner of a trade secret to recover damages (actual), profits, and punitive damages up to two times the actual amount of damages if the misappropriation is willful and malicious.

(2) Idea Submission Policies

Florida joins the growing number of states that recognize a common law action for idea misappropriation, but it requires a showing of confidentiality and novelty. Information-based businesses will often adopt idea submission policies to avoid conflicts concerning ownership or interests in intellectual property rights. Idea submission policies are terms of service when customers, employees, or third parties submit ideas to the company. One of the chief purposes of an idea submission policy is to avoid disputes over whether the company misappropriated or disclosed a trade secret.

(D) UNIFORM TRADE SECRET ACT REMEDIES

The UTSA provides a broad range of remedies, including: preliminary injunctive relief, monetary damages, lost profits, consequential damages, lost royalties, attorney's fees, and punitive damages. A plaintiff will often seek injunctive relief if they suspect that former employees are violating or about to violate NDAs. Courts may enjoin actual or threatened misappropriation of trade secrets. Trade secret owners may claim a reasonable royalty for the loss of revenue attributable to the misappropriation of a trade secret.

UTSA, § 4 states that attorney's fees may be recoverable where a claim of misappropriation is made in bad faith, a motion to terminate an injunction is made or resisted in bad faith, or willful and malicious misappropriation exists. Section 3 of UTSA also gives the court the power to award "exemplary damages in an amount not exceeding twice any award," upon a finding of "willful and malicious misappropriation." Section 6 of the UTSA statute of limitations states that aggrieved parties may seek relief within three years after the owner discovers the misappropriation or should have discovered it.

(E) DEFENSES IN UTSA LITIGATION

(1) Reverse Engineering

In the anti-reverse engineering clause, a customer will be in breach of the license agreement if it discloses, decompiles, disassembles, or reverse engineers licensed software. In *Mid-Michigan Computer Sys. v. Marc Glassman Inc.*, 416 F.2d 505 (6th Cir. 2005), the Sixth Circuit upheld a $2 million compensatory damages award and a $5 million punitive damages award against a licensee that secretly copied source code from its licensor. The licensor entered into a license agreement with the defendant to maintain prescription and billing records for customers. The parties also entered into a Source Code Agreement, which provided that defendant would access the escrowed source code only in certain specified emergencies. The evidence at trial showed that defendant secretly copied software that was then used to reconstruct the plaintiff's source code. Such activity helped save research and manufacturing resources in developing the software that would ultimately replace the plaintiff's pharmacy software. Thus, while reverse engineering is proper, the acquisition of the known product must, of course, also be by fair and honest means to be lawful. UTSA § 1, cmt. 2.

The Reporters for the ALI's Principles of the Law of Software Contracts, discussed in Chapter 4, acknowledge that anti-reverse engineering clauses are "troublesome terms." European courts would not likely enforce clauses that prohibited reverse engineering to achieve interoperability because of the Software Directive. In Europe, all users of software have a right to reverse engineer code to achieve interoperability of computer programs under the Software Directive adopted in 1991.

(2) First Amendment Defenses

In recent years, U.S. courts have ruled that the tort of misappropriation must give way to the First Amendment. The First Amendment of the U.S. Constitution protected a website operator's posting of DeCSS, which enabled users to evade the "content scramble system" that both encrypts DVDs and is designed to prevent their unauthorized use and duplication. The California appellate court ruled that since the DeCSS that the website operator posted was already public knowledge, the defendant could not be liable for misappropriation since there was no trade secret. In *Ford Motor Co. v. Lane*, 67 F. Supp. 2d 745 (E.D. Mich. 1999), the federal court denied a motion for a preliminary injunction to prevent Lane from disclosing alleged trade secrets on the Internet because the proposed injunction would "constitute an invalid prior restraint of free speech in violation of the First Amendment."

§ 12-3. Restatement (Second) of Torts

The First Restatement of Torts defines a trade secret as "any formula, pattern, device, or compilation of information which is used in one's business, and which gives him an opportunity to get an advantage over competitors who do not know or use it." Restatement (Second) of Torts, § 757. Massachusetts, New York, Texas, and the District of Columbia continue to follow the Restatement of Torts' approach to trade secrets and have yet to adopt UTSA. Trade secret misappropriation evolved as a tort and the Restatement (First) of Torts, 757–758 (1939) was followed by most states until the UTSA swept the country.

The definition of a trade secret under Section 757 is based in part "upon the ease or difficult with which the information could be properly acquired or duplicated by others." Restatement (Second) of Torts, § 757, cmt. b. The Restatement of Torts, Section 757 requires trade secrets to contain "a substantial element of secrecy so that, except by the use of improper means, there would be difficulty in acquiring the information." A key factor of secrecy is the ease or difficulty with which others can acquire information properly.

§ 12-4. Internet-Related Trade Secret Misappropriation

To prevail on a trade secret claim, a plaintiff must show that (1) the misappropriated information constitutes a trade secret, (2) the defendant "used" the trade secret, and (3) the plaintiff was actually damaged by the misappropriation or the defendant was unjustly enriched by such misappropriation and use. The secrecy need not be absolute; the owner of a trade secret may, without losing protection, disclose to a licensee, if the disclosure is made in confidence, express or implied. The UTSA provides that misappropriation may be demonstrated by alleging the "[a]cquisition of a trade secret of another by a person who knows or has reason to know that the trade secret was acquired by improper means." *Dealertrack, Inc. v. Huber*, 460 F. Supp. 2d 1177 (C.D. Cal. 2006).

To prove misappropriation of a trade secret, the plaintiff must show: (1) it possessed a valid trade secret, (2) the defendant acquired its trade secret, and (3) the defendant knew or should have known the trade secret was acquired by improper means or by breaching an agreement, confidence, or fiduciary duty. A fact finder will calculate damages in a misappropriation case by several methods. First, damages may be computed by the plaintiff's losses including the cost of developing the trade secret. A second approach is to determine damages based upon a plaintiff's lost profits. If the first two methods do not adequately compensate the plaintiff, a court may award reasonable royalties. *In re Cross Media Mktg. Corp. v. Nixon*, 2006 WL 2337177 (S.D. N.Y. 2006). The first online trade secrets cases arose out Church of Scientology's lawsuit to enjoin further electronic distribution of secret church doctrine. A California federal court said, "posting works to the Internet makes them 'generally known,' at least to the relevant people interested in the news group."

Religious Technology Center v. Netcom, 907 F. Supp. 1361 (N.D. Cal. 1995).

In the Internet economy, employees are highly mobile. Courts often balance the employees' right to work against the employer's right to protect trade secrets. In *DoubleClick, Inc. v. Henderson*, No. 116914/97, 1997 WL 731413 (N.Y. Sup. Ct. 2007), several employees planned to leave the Internet advertising mogul in order to start a dot-com startup. DoubleClick confiscated one of the employee's laptops and found information on the hard drive, including e-mails and future business plans that suggested he was engaged in economic espionage. DoubleClick summarily fired the employees and sought an injunction to enjoin them from sharing trade secrets with competitors. The ex-employees argued that much of the information DoubleClick classified as trade secrets was already made public because it was displayed on the online company's website.

The court found there was evidence the ex-employees intended to use trade secrets to advise Alta Vista, DoubleClick's largest client. The court, however, refused to enjoin the ex-employees for the one-year period sought by DoubleClick, noting it was too long given the ever-evolving Internet advertising industry. The court limited the injunction to six months.

In *PhoneDog v. Kravitz*, 2011 WL 5415612 (N.D. Cal. 2001), the court refused to dismiss a claim that an ex-employee misappropriated the password/login information for a Twitter account. Kravitz,

PhoneDog's ex-employee, continued to access a Twitter account used to publicize PhoneDog's website after his employment had ended. Kravitz argued that passwords to Twitter accounts do not derive any actual or potential independent economic value under the UTSA because they do not provide any substantial business advantage. He also contended that PhoneDog did not make any reasonable efforts to maintain the secrecy of the Twitter password.

The court ruled that PhoneDog had sufficiently pleaded a misappropriation claim. The company requested that its ex-employee relinquish use of the account but he merely changed the Twitter handle on the account, while continuing to misappropriate confidential information. The extent of Internet security measures taken by the owner of the trade secret need not be absolute but must be reasonable under the circumstances. Trade secret owners must protect the confidentiality of software and documentation.

§ 12-5. Trade Secrets in a Global Internet

Congress enacted the Economic Espionage Act ("EEA") in 1996 to criminalize the misappropriation of trade secrets. An empirical study of all EEA prosecutions from the federal criminal statute's enactment in 1996 to August 1, 2005 uncovered fewer than fifty economic or espionage prosecutions filed in federal courts. Michael L. Rustad, *The Negligent Enablement of Trade Secrets*, 22 SANTA CLARA COMPUTER & HIGH TECH J. 455 (2006). In the first decade of EEA prosecutions, the Department of

Justice did not file a single case against a hacker stealing trade secrets by "exploiting known software defects" during an **Internet** transmission. The causes of action for EEA causes of action are highlighted in the table below.

Economic Espionage Act

Section 1831(A)(3)	The defendant intended or knew his actions would benefit a foreign government, foreign instrumentality, or foreign agent.	The defendant knowingly received, bought, or possessed a trade secret, knowing the same to have been stolen or appropriated, obtained, or converted without authorization.
Section 1832(A)(3)	The defendant intended to convert a trade secret to the economic benefit of anyone other than the owner.	The defendant knowingly received, bought, or possessed a trade secret, knowing the same to have

		been stolen or appropriated, obtained, or converted without authorization; must satisfy interstate commerce.

The EEA criminalizes two types of offenses: (1) economic espionage that benefits foreign governments or entities (§ 1831); and (2) the theft of trade secrets to benefit any person but the true owner (§ 1832). Both Sections 1831 and 1832 require proof of a trade secret. A defendant violates federal law when he "steals" or "without authorization . . . photographs" a trade secret, "intending or knowing that the offense will . . . injure any owner of that trade secret." See § 1832(A) The government may not charge a defendant with violating the EEA unless "the owner thereof has taken reasonable measures to keep such information secret." Section 1831 of the EEA addresses the problem of misappropriation by foreign governments or their agents and criminalizes data theft with fines of up to $500,000 and imprisonment of up to fifteen years. Offending organizations may be subject to fines of up to $10,000,000. In contrast, § 1832 applies to domestic trade secrets theft. It is a broader provision, applying "to anyone who knowingly engages in the theft of trade secrets, or an attempt or conspiracy to do so." Under § 1832, individuals are subject to fines and up to ten years of imprisonment, while organizations are subject to fines of up to $5,000,000.

Section 1839(3)(B) of the EEA requires that information must derive "independent economic value, actual or potential, from not being generally known to, and not being readily ascertainable through proper means by the public." 18 U.S.C. § 1839(3)(B). Although the EEA provides criminal sanctions and civil damages for the misappropriation of trade secrets, it does not permit civil actions to be filed by private attorneys general. Most recent EEA cases have been against Chinese employees of U.S. companies who stole trade secrets and transmitted them to Chinese companies, the government, or universities. For example, in April 2011, Yu Xiang Dong was sentenced to 70 months in federal prison for violating the Economic Espionage Act. Yu was an employee of Ford Motor Company employee who resigned to work at Beijing Automotive Company taking with him 4,000 confidential Ford documents copied on his hard drive.

All but a few of the EEA prosecutions have been under Section 1832, not 1831. The U.S. Justice Department has been reticent to initiate prosecutions against foreign governments and foreign agents. In 2012, the Justice Department launched a high profile EEA prosecution to include a Chinese company that was, in fact, an operation of the Chinese Government.

§ 12-6. International Trade Secret Protection

Trade secrets in the United States are generally protected by the common law, rather than statute. Foreign countries that recognize trade secrets may have limitations on the duration of protection. U.S. E-Businesses can restrain the importation of products into the United States using a misappropriated trade secret complaint. World Trade Organization member states are required to provide adequate protection for undisclosed information. Article 39(2) of the Agreement on Trade Related Aspects of Intellectual Property Rights ("TRIPS") also establishes an obligation to protect trade secrets. In February 2013, the Obama Administration released a report on trade secret theft that there were "indications that U.S. companies, law firms, academia, and financial institutions are experiencing cyber intrusion activity against electronic repositories containing trade secret information." President Barack Obama, Administration Strategy on Mitigating the Theft of U.S. Trade Secrets (Feb. 20, 2013) at 1. "Trade secret theft threatens American businesses, undermines national security, and places the security of the U.S. economy in jeopardy."

CHAPTER 13

PATENT LAW AND THE INTERNET

§ 13.1 Overview of Internet-Related Patents

(A) WHY INTERNET PATENTS

The goal of this chapter is to present the basic concepts and methods of Internet-related patent law. The Internet-related foundations of patent protection, patentability, and the patenting process will be discussed. A patent grants the patent holder the right to exclude others from making, using, or commercially exploiting an invention. Patent law is increasingly harmonized for countries connected to the Internet, but there remain variations in practices from country to country. The importance of patent law for today's Internet is reflected in skyrocketing patent awards. Patent litigation is costly; the median cost of a patent lawsuit is $1 million to $3 million. Apple's patent lawsuit alleging that Samsung copied software in its smartphones gained momentum in June of 2012 when a federal judge enjoined sales of Samsung's Galaxy Tab 10.1 tablet computer. Ashby Jones & Jessica E. Vascellaro, *In Silicon Valley, Patents Go on Trial: Tech Giants Near A Landmark Jury Trial Over Performance of an iPhone; Is it Innovation or Litigation?*, WALL ST. J (July 24, 2012) at B1.

Apple contends that Samsung infringed its "rubber banding," the term used to describe the way smartphone images pull away from the edge and bounce back when a user overscrolls with a finger. A

California federal jury held that Samsung violated several of Apple's patents, awarding a billion dollar verdict for willful infringement. Shortly after this verdict was announced, a Seoul court ruled that Apple infringed two of Samsung's patents, while Samsung violated one of Apple's design patents. The South Korean court awarded nominal damages to both companies.

America's information-based economy is increasingly built on a foundation of patents defined as limited duration property rights. An estimated 11,000 patents cover Internet-related business methods. JAMES BESSEN & MICHAEL J. MEURER, PATENT FAILURE 8-9 (2005). *Internet patents* deploy software and other computer-related technologies to perform various business procedures. Critics of Internet-related method patents contend that these innovations would develop more efficiently without patent protection. Internet related business methods give the holder the right to control the use of the technology. The level and extent of the control depends upon the business method. All patents balance antitrust concerns against market dominance. Patent holders who obtain a patent to discourage competitors will have a chilling impact on e-commerce.

The United States Patent and Trademark Office ("USPTO") is the federal agency responsible for examining U.S. patent applications and issuing patents. The USPTO determines whether a patent should be granted in a particular case. The *quid pro quo* for these rights is to disclose the invention to enhance the public knowledge, or the state of the art. Inventors must reveal the best mode for their invention and enable one skilled in the art to practice to it. *Internet patents* deploy software and other computer-related technologies to perform various business methods.

(B) CONSTITUTIONAL AND STATUTORY BASIS

Article I, Section 8 of the U.S. Constitution gave Congress the power to "promote the Progress of Science and [the] useful Arts, by securing for limited Times to Authors and inventors the exclusive Right to their respective Writings and Discoveries." Patent law, like copyright law, arises out of federal statutes. Congress enacted the first Patent Act in 1790 and soon after legislated the Patent Act of 1793, which today is embodied in the Patent Act of 1952. The primary source for U.S. patent law is Title 35 of the United States Code, referred to as the Patent Act.

(C) AMERICAN INVENTS ACT

(1) First Inventor to File ("FITF")

On September 16, 2011, President Obama signed into law the Leahy-Smith America Invents Act ("AIA"), which represents a sea change in U.S. patent law. The United States now aligns its law with the rest of the world in adopting the first-to-file ("FITF") system, which jettisons the older U.S. rule of awarding patents to the first-to-invent ("FI") system. Under the FI system, applicants got a patent "after disclosing the invention as long as a patent is filed within one year of the disclosure."

MARK V. CAMPAGNA, UNDERSTANDING PATENT REFORMS IN THE CONTEXT OF LITIGATION 9 (2009). The newly aligned FITF system is equivalent to U.C.C. Article 9's chief rule that the first to file or perfect obtains protection under the law. The FITF is determined by the race to the registry, in this case to the USPTO.

(2) Expedited Procedures

The U.S. adopted a registration system for patents where examiners determine whether a given claim is patentable and whether an applicant has the rights to a patented invention. The process of obtaining a patent is called patent prosecution. Patent examiners in the USPTO determine whether the boundaries of the claim sought by the applicant qualify for patent protection. Under the AIA reforms, the USPTO now offers applicants an opportunity to have patent applications reviewed on an expedited basis. Small entity and independent inventors receive a 50 percent discount on the $4800 fee to use this new fast track option. This reform was made in response to criticism of the long and drawn-out patent evaluation process.

(3) Other Patent Reforms

The AIA initiated new methods for challenging patents, developed several new third-party challenges, including post grant review, *inter partes* review and devised a transitional program for covered business method patents. An *inter partes* review may be instituted upon a showing that there is a reasonable likelihood that the petitioner would prevail with respect to at least one claim challenged. *Inter partes* review is a new trial proceeding conducted at the Board to review the patentability of one or more claims in a patent.

The grounds for review are limited to those issues that could be raised under Sections 102 or 103, and only because of prior art consisting of patents or printed publications. Prior art consists of all pre-existing patents and published patent applications, printed publications and other non-patent literature anywhere in the world. After the AIA, prior art is assessed after the effective filing date, not as of the date of invention. The *inter partes* review process can only be initiated by a third party or someone who does not own the patent. The petition is filed after the later of either: (1) 9 months after the grant of the patent or issuance of a reissue patent, or (2) if a post grant review is instituted, the termination of the post grant review. The patent owner may file a preliminary response to the petition. The AIA eliminated the possibility of false patent marking complaints by *qui tam* plaintiffs.

The AIA replaces the former interference procedures with post-grant procedures in the form of a new trial proceeding at the Patent Trial and Appeal Board. Under this procedure, a patent may be challenged on any grounds available under 35 U.S.C. § 282 (b)(2) or (3). The AIA no longer permits a patent to be invalidated because the applicant did not satisfy the "best mode" requirement.

(D) TYPES OF PATENTS

A patent lasts for a specific period, usually twenty years, and represents a bargain made between the government and the inventor. Patent protection is available for the invention of "any new and useful process, machine, manufacture, or composition of matter, or any new and useful improvement thereof." 35 U.S.C. § 101. Federal patent law recognizes three ideal types of patent protection: (1) utility patents, (2) design patents, and (3) plant patents. Utility patents, as their name connotes, are any new or useful process. Design patents protect the ornament design of products. Plant patents cover the invention and discovery of new plants. 35 U.S.C. § 161.

(1) Utility Patents

Greater than ninety percent of all patents are utility patents, issued for four general types of inventions/discoveries: machines, human made products, compositions of matter, and processes. 35 U.S.C. § 101. Utility patents protect the way an article is used and works (35 U.S.C. § 101), while a "design patent" protects the way an article looks or its appearance. (35 U.S.C. § 171). Internet-related patents are typically utility patents, subcategorized as process patents if they qualify as new and useful.

Articles of manufacture may possess both functional and ornamental characteristics. . "Both design and utility patents may be obtained on an article if invention resides both in its utility and ornamental appearance. While utility and design patents afford legally separate protection, the utility and ornamentally of an article are not easily separable." USPTO, A GUIDE TO FILING DESIGN PATENTS, DEFINITION OF DESIGN 1 (2013). Crocs, a popular form of footwear, for example, have both a utility patent and a design patent.

(2) Design Patents

Whoever invents any new, original, and ornamental design for an article of manufacture may obtain a patent. 35 U.S.C. § 171. An Apple computer, an iPad, or smart phone are all-protectable by design patents or the visual ornamental characteristics of an article of manufacture. Design patents, with a term of 14 years, protect the ornamental exterior appearance of an object and that appearance must be non-functional. The ornamental design of a Coca Cola bottle or a Budweiser bottle may be protectable by design patents as are cell phones, Sketcher shoes, or Coach Purses. "Design patents may relate to the configuration or shape of an article, to the surface ornamentation applied to an article, or to the combination of configuration and surface ornamentation. A design for surface ornamentation is inseparable from the article to which it is applied and cannot exist alone." USPTO, A GUIDE TO FILING DESIGN PATENTS, DEFINITION OF DESIGN 1 (2013). A design patent is a "definite pattern of surface ornamentation, applied to an article of manufacture." A design patent application may only have a single claim (37 CFR § 1.153).

"Designs that are independent and distinct must be filed in separate applications since they cannot be supported by a single claim." Design patents are relevant to Internet inventions because the USPTO considers computer-generated icons, including full screen images and type fonts, to constitute surface ornamentation. Design patents must be original and cannot be considered offensive to any race, religion, sex, ethnic group, or nationality. 35 U.S.C. 171 and 37 CFR § 1.3.

(3) Plant Patents

Plant patents are granted to those who invent or discover, and asexually reproduce any distinct and new variety of plant. Plant patents apply to new varieties of plants, other than a tuber-propagated plant or a plant found in an uncultivated state. The grant, which lasts for 20 years from the date of filing the application, protects the inventor's right to exclude others from asexually reproducing, selling, or using the plant so reproduced. Plant patent have no obvious connection to Internet law as the U.S. Department of Agriculture administers the statute.

(E) PATENT LAW TERMS

Generally, the term of a new utility patent, which accounts for most Internet-related patents, is 20 years from the date on which the patent was issued. Plant patents also have a 20-year term, while design patents only have a term of 14 years from the issue date. Utility or plant patents issued on applications filed before June 8, 1995 have a term of

17 years from the issuance of the patent or 20 years from the filing, whichever is greater.

(F) SECTION 101 PATENTABLE SUBJECT MATTER

Section 101 of the Patent Act states that "any new and useful process, machine, manufacture, or composition of matter, or any new and useful improvement thereof" is patent-eligible, "subject to the conditions and requirements of this title." Congress used "expansive terms" in defining the four categories of inventions eligible for patent protection under § 101: processes, machines, manufactures, and compositions of matter. Courts set forth three judicial limits on patentability: (1) laws of nature (2) natural phenomena and (3) abstract ideas. Algorithms and formulas are not patentable because they do not fit within any of the aforementioned four categories. "Laws of nature, natural phenomena, and abstract ideas (e.g., in the guise of mathematical algorithms) are not eligible under Section 101." 35 U.S.C. § 101.

Abstract ideas are not patentable because they serve as the tools for scientific inquiry and technology. Physics formula such Newton's second law of motion or other laws of nature are not patentable, but the expression of an idea is within the scope of patentable subject matter. The tipping point between an abstract idea and a commercially viable invention is often murky. Patent examiners must reject a claim if it drawn from an ineligible abstract idea.

The USPTO cites the following examples of patentable concepts: (1) Basic economic practices or theories (e.g., hedging, insurance, financial transactions, marketing); (2) Basic legal theories (e.g., contracts, dispute resolution, rules of law); (3) Mathematical concepts (e.g., algorithms, spatial relationships, geometry); (4) Mental activity (e.g., forming a judgment, observation, evaluation, or opinion); (5) Interpersonal interactions or relationships (e.g., conversing, dating); (6)Teaching concepts (e.g., memorization, repetition); (7) Human behavior (e.g., exercising, wearing clothing, following rules or instructions); and (8) Instructing "how business should be conducted." USPTO, PATENT SUBJECT MATTER ELIGIBILITY (2012). Patents are not granted for all new and useful inventions and discoveries.

In *Diamond v. Chakrabary*, 447 U.S. 303 (Sup. Ct. 1980), the U.S. Supreme Court interpreted the subject matter of patents "to include anything under the sun that is made by man." Can microorganisms qualify as patentable subject matter absent Congress' statutory authorization?

The Court answered that question affirmatively, holding that a live, human-made microorganism that is useful in breaking up crude oil is patentable subject matter under 35 U.S.C. § 101. Justice Burger, writing for the Court, found that Chakrabary's microorganism constitutes a "manufacture" or "composition of matter" within the meaning of the patent statute. The idea/expression dichotomy is found in copyright law as well as patent law. A treatise applying Newton's second law of motion would be copyrightable but Newton's insight about motion would not be afforded protection.

(G) THE ESSENTIALS OF PATENTABILITY

The four statutory categories in Section 101 are (1) processes, (2) machines, (3) manufactures, and compositions of matter. The four categories fill out the meaning of "useful arts" in the constitutional reference to patents. ROGER E. SCHECHTER & JOHN B. THOMAS, INTELLECTUAL PROPERTY: THE LAW OF COPYRIGHTS, PATENTS, AND TRADEMARKS 291 (2003). The federal patent statute requires a claim to have some utility (§ 101), be novel (not anticipated prior to the invention) (§ 102), and be nonobvious (§ 103).

Patentability Demystified

Issues Defined	Section in Patent Act
Novelty, Utility Statutory Bar	Section 101
Novelty, Anticipation	Section 102
Nonobviousness	Section 103

(H) PATENTABILITY: NOVELTY

A patent provides legal protection for an invention only as it is defined in a patent application by what are known as "claims." A "claimed invention" is the invention as it is defined in the application for legal protection. Claims must demonstrate novelty as well as utility. What destroys novelty? Section 102(a)(1) states there is no novelty "if before filing date the patented or claimed invention as patented, was described in a printed publication, in public use, or on sale, or otherwise available to the public. Section 102(a)(2) also vitiates novelty when there is an issued patent or published application filed before the application. Novelty means that a patent claim was not anticipated by technology disclosed in the prior art. 35 U.S.C. § 102.

(1) Anticipation

An examiner rejects a claim as anticipated under 35 U.S.C. 102 when a single prior art reference discloses every element of the claim. "If an invention was anticipated by prior art, it is not patentable. A person shall be entitled to a patent "unless –(a) the invention was known or used by others in this country, or patented or described in a printed publication in this or a foreign country, before the invention thereof by the applicant for a patent." 35 U.S.C. § 102(A). Anticipation includes evidence that the patent application was filed one year before any of the following events: (1) invention known by others in the U.S., (2) invention used by others in the U.S., (3) invention patented in the U.S. or abroad, and (4) invention described in a printed publication in the U.S. or abroad. 35 U.S.C. § 102(A).

(2) Statutory Bar

Section 102(b) is the statutory bar if "the invention was patented or described in a printed publication in this or a foreign country or in public use or on sale in this country, more than one year prior to the date of application for patent in the United States" 35 U.S.C. § 102(B).

(I) PATENTABILITY: NONOBVIOUSNESS

The obviousness requirement is the most difficult obstacle to overcome. Section 103 requires that the claim to be nonobvious when measured against prior art. The test is whether the subject matter as a whole would have been obvious at the time the invention was made to a person having ordinary skill in the art. An invention must also not be the functional equivalent of an invention covered by a previously issued patent. An invention is not patentable if the claimed subject matter was disclosed before the date of filing or before the date of priority, if a priority is claimed, of the patent application. An invention is not patentable if it would have been obvious to one of ordinary skill in the art.

Each element or limitation of the claimed invention does not need to be contained in a single reference or event unlike novelty. Under the obviousness doctrine, a patent should not be granted if the invention could readily be deduced from the prior art. In *Graham v. John Deere Co.*, 383 U.S. 1 (S.Ct. 1966), the Court set forth criteria to determine whether an invention is nonobvious. A court must (1) determine the scope and content of the prior art, (2) determine the scope and content of the prior art, (3) ascertain the differences between the claimed invention and the prior art, and (4) resolve the level of ordinary skill in the pertinent art.

In *KSR International Co. v. Teleflex Inc.*, 550 U.S. 398 (S.Ct.2007), the Court reaffirmed the basic tests outlined in the John Deere case. "In Graham, the Court set out a framework for applying the statutory language of § 103 ... [T]he factors continue to define the inquiry that controls. If a court, or patent examiner, conducts this analysis and concludes the claimed subject matter was obvious, the claim is invalid under § 103." In *KSR*, Teleflex filed a patent infringement suit claiming that a KSR product infringed its patent on connecting an adjustable vehicle control pedal to an electronic throttle control. KSR defended against this lawsuit by contending that Teleflex's patent was obvious and therefore the claim was not patentable.

The U.S. Supreme Court agreed with KSR that Telefex's claim was obvious reversing the Federal Circuit Court. The Court noted that it was following the *John Deere* test for obviousness. The Court stated that the Federal Circuit Court's teaching-suggestion-motivation (TSM) test is just one of a number of valid rationales that may be employed when determining obviousness under 35 U.S.C. § 103. In *KSR*, the Supreme Court emphasized "the need for caution in granting a patent based on the combination of elements found in the prior art." Under the *KSR* test, if the subject matter was obvious, the claim is invalid under § 103.

(J) PATENTABILITY: UTILITY

Utility is the requirement that a patentable invention be useful. To satisfy the utility requirement, the invention must be operable or capable of being used as either a product or process. Section 101 of Title 35 requires that inventions have novelty and utility. The utility requirement is seldom a significant barrier against patent seekers. The examiner must reject a patent if it does not achieve a useful result. "Cold fusion is not patentable because of the lack of enablement under 112 and as inoperative and lacking utility under § 101." McCarthy's Desk Encyclopedia of Intellectual Property 3rd ed. 2004 at 651.

(K) THE ANATOMY OF PATENT APPLICATIONS

Issued patents are public documents and contribute to the storehouse of practical knowledge. An applicant must disclose information in the application. 35 U.S.C. § 112. The written description in an application must explain what precisely is being claimed. Utility patent applications in the U.S. consist of a brief abstract of the invention, background about the invention, descriptions of drawings, a detailed explanation of how to make/use the invention, and one or more claims. This section should include a statement of the field of endeavor to which the invention pertains. 35 U.S.C. § 111. Patents can be conceptualized as having two parts:

the specification and the claims. A specification is simply a written description of the claim. The specification "must enable a person of ordinary skill in the art to make and use the invention without further experimentation." Specifications include a "best mode" which requires the inventor to disclose the best way of making or using the invention. Claims come after the invention description "and are intended to define the invention by setting forth the boundaries of the patentee's rights." The specification shall conclude with one or more claims particularly pointing out and distinctly claiming the subject matter, which the applicant regards as his invention. 35 U.S.C. § 112.

(1) Anatomy of Patent Applications

The USPTO recognizes two kinds of patent applications, provisional and regular. Provisional applications are never examined and serve as placeholders. An applicant who decides to file a provisional application must file a corresponding nonprovisional application during the 12-month pendency period of the provisional application in order to benefit from the earlier provisional application filing. 35 U.S.C. § 111(B). Regular or nonprovisional applications are examined by a patent examiner, and may be issued as a patent if all the requirements for patentability are met. USPTO, NONPROVISIONAL (UTILITY) PATENT APPLICATION FILING GUIDE (2012). Each year the USPTO receives approximately 500,000 regular patent applications.

Most of the applications filed with the USPTO are nonprovisional applications for utility patents. The elements of a nonprovisional utility application are: (1) Utility Patent Application Transmittal Form or Transmittal Letter, (2) Appropriate Fees, (3) Application Data Sheet (see 37 CFR § 1.76), (4) Specification (with at least one claim), (5) Drawings (when necessary), (6) Executed Oath or Declaration, (7) Nucleotide and/or Amino Acid Sequence Listing (when necessary), and (8) Large Tables or Computer Listings (when necessary). A nonprovisional patent application will typically include (1) a specification, (2) a drawing, and (3) an oath by the applicant. 35 U.S.C. § 111. Every patent begins with a short title of the invention.

The specifications are "a written description of the invention, and of the manner and process of making it and using it, in such full, clear, concise, and exact terms ... to make and use the same." 35 U.S.C. § 112. Section 112(a) requires that the written description be in such "full, clear concise and exact terms as to enable any person skilled in the art" to make and use the invention. 35 U.S.C. § 112.

The specification concludes with one or more claims, particularly pointing out and distinctly claiming the subject matter, which the applicant regards as his invention. Claims define the contours of the property rights conferred by a patent. Patent examiners "identify the boundaries of the protection sought by the applicant and to understand how the claims relate to and define what the applicant has indicated is the invention." MPEP, 2106,

PATENT SUBJECT MATTER ELIGIBILITY [R-6]-2100
PATENTABILITY (2012).

Claims may be drafted as independent claims,
dependent claims and multiple dependent claims.
With a dependent form, reference is made to a claim
previously described. "A claim in dependent form
shall be construed to incorporate by reference all the
limitations of the claim to which it refers." 35 U.S.C.
§ 111. Multiple dependent claims are construed to
incorporate by reference all limitations of a
particular claim in relation to the one being
considered. An applicant for a patent may include a
drawing "where necessary for the understanding of
the subject matter sought to be patented." 35 U.S.C.
§ 113. The USPTO Commissioner may require a
patent applicant to furnish a model of convenient
size to exhibit advantageously the several parts of
his invention. 35 U.S.C. § 114. In general, pending
applications are confidential until a patent grant.

(2) Examination of Patent

The USPTO patent examiners are "persons of
legal knowledge and scientific ability" who
determine the patentability of inventions. 35 U.S.C.
§ 7. Examiners investigate whether the "five
primary requirements of patentability are satisfied:
(1) Patentable subject matter, (2) novelty, (3) utility,
(4) nonobviousness, and (5) enablement." ROBERT
MERGES, ET. AL. INTELLECTUAL PROPERTY IN THE
NEW TECHNOLOGICAL AGE 133 (5th ed. 2012). Every
case involving a § 101 issue must begin with this
question: "What, if anything, did the applicant
invent or discover?" *In re Alappat*, 33 F.3d 1526

(Fed. Cir. 1994). Stated generally, examiners determine whether the applicant adequately describes how to make and use the invention.

Specifically, patent examiners determine if the applicant claims are novel, useful, and nonobvious at creation. An examiner must also evaluate whether the combination of claimed elements exists in prior art. "A claim in a patent provides the metes and bounds of the right, which the patent confers on the patentee to exclude others from making, using or selling the protected invention." *Burke, Inc. v. Bruno Indep. Living Aids, Inc.*, 183 F.3d 1334 (Fed.Cir. 1999). An applicant may amend claims during prosecution as long as the amendment is supported by the specification as originally filed.

(3) Specifications

The specifications will generally summarize or describe the invention as a whole. The specification shall conclude with one or more claims particularly pointing out and distinctly claiming the subject matter, which the applicant regards as his invention. 35 U.S.C. § 112. The patent applicant must describe the features of the present invention, limiting its scope. A specification is broadly defined as a written description of the invention and of the manner and process of making and using it. To be complete, the specifications must describe completely a specific embodiment of the process, machine, manufacture, composition of matter or improvement invented, and must explain the mode of operation or principle whenever applicable. The Patent Act requires three disclosure requirements:

(1) the descriptive requirement, (2) the best mode for carrying out her invention, and (3) the enablement requirement that the description is clear, full, and concise so that a person skilled in the art can make and use it. J. THOMAS MCCARTHY, ET. AL, MCCARTHY'S DESK ENCYCLOPEDIA OF INTELLECTUAL PROPERTY 183 (2004).

(4) Enablement & Best Mode

The claim must "enable" a person of ordinary skill in the relevant art or science to make and use the invention. An invention could be adequately described without being enabling, such as a chemical formula with no disclosed or apparent method of making, or be enabled without adequate description, such as a method of making a material without any specific formulation.

(5) Elements of a Design Patent Application

The elements of a design patent application should include the following: (1) Preamble, stating name of the applicant, title of the design, and a brief description of the nature and intended use of the article in which the design is embodied; (2) Cross-reference to related applications (unless included in the application data sheet); (3) Statement regarding federally sponsored research or development; (4) Description of the figure(s) of the drawing; (5) Feature description; (6) A single claim; (7) Drawings or photographs; and (8) Executed oath or declaration. As with other patent applications, the fee must accompany the application.

(L) PATENT INVALIDITY

The U.S. Patent Act provides that "[a] patent shall be presumed valid" and that "[t]he burden of establishing invalidity of a patent or any claim thereof shall rest on the party asserting such invalidity." 35 U.S.C. § 282. During prosecution, patent examiners give claims the broadest reasonable interpretation that is consistent with the specification. Section 132 requires that examiners give reasons for rejection and rights for reexamination.

(M) PATENT TERMS

The term of a utility patent filed prior to June 8, 1995 is the later of (1) 17 years from the date of issuance of the patent, or (2) 20 years from the first U.S. filing date for the patent. Internet-related patents are relatively recent and as recently as the 1980s, it was unclear whether software could be patented. Today software patents are primarily utility patents including compilers, application programs, and protection for "process or method performed by a computer game."

§ 13.2   Internet Related Patents

(A) SOFTWARE PATENTS

In the early software industry, lawyers used trade secrets or the law of copyright, assuming that software was not patentable. The U.S. Court of Appeals, Federal Circuit, however, in *In re Alappat* (1994), ruled that virtually all computer programs are patentable. Software patents have been granted for such diverse Internet related activities as hyperlinking, audio software, file formats, and search engines. A software patent application must clearly describe what the computer does when it performs the steps dictated by software code. Software patents have been slow to evolve outside of the U.S.

(B) E-BUSINESS METHODS

Business methods qualify as "patentable eligible subject matter" if they are a new and useful process. At a bare minimum, the process must produce a useful, concrete, and tangible result to qualify as a business method. Software was thought of as unpatentable subject matter until the 1980s because it incorporated algorithms. In *Akamai Technologies, Inc. v. Limelight Networks, Inc.*, 2008 WL 364401 (D. Mass. 2008), a jury found Limelight infringed an Internet content delivery patent asserted by Akamai Technologies, and handed down a verdict of $45.5 million. In *Akamai*, the patent claim covered software for delivering the embedded objects of a web page. Limelight argued that a reasonable jury could conclude the company believed it did not infringe or cause others to infringe Akamai's patents because of Akamai's prior history of suing infringers.

Courts accepted this business method exception for nearly a century until 1998 when the Federal Circuit reversed course in *State Street Bank & Trust Co. v. Signature Fin. Group, Inc.*, 149 F.3d 1368 (Fed. Cir. 1998). In State Street, Judge Giles Rich, writing for the panel, accepted a patent held by Signature Financial Group for a "hub and spoke" method of computing interest payments that made it possible for mutual fund managers to pool their assets into a partnership, allowing tax advantages and administrative savings. The mere presence of a mathematical algorithm does not preordain that USPTO will reject a patent claim. The Federal Circuit held a programmed computer using this mathematical algorithm was patentable so long as it produced a useful, concrete, and tangible result.

In *State Street*, the court found an algorithm or formula that produced a "concrete and tangible result," namely a final share price for each mutual fund within the partnership as determined by their contributions to the pool, was a practical application and thus patentable. The validation of business methods patents was extended in *AT&T Corp. v. Excel Communications, Inc.*, 172 F.3d 1352 (Fed. Cir. 1999) where the Federal Circuit approved a patent incorporating Boolean algebra to determine the long-distance carriers involved in a telephone call, creating a switching signal for billing purposes.

The *AT & T* Court reasoned that this was not an attempt to patent the Boolean principle, but rather a patent for the process to create the discrete switching signal. The method created a concrete and tangible result, and was therefore patentable. After State Street and AT&T, USPTO required business method patents to advance the technological arts.

Most E-Commerce, Internet, or data processing business methods are classified as Class 705. The number of Class 705 patents issuing skyrocketed from 120 to 1,191 from 1996 to 2006. Most E-Commerce methods, but not all, are related to financial and business data processing. The methods and apparatuses claimed in these applications are linked to financial and business data processing. Priceline, for example, holds a patent on an auction method for selling tickets. Netcraft filed suit against eBay and PayPal for infringing upon two related business method patents with variations on Internet Billing Methods. The USPTO has approved scores of business method patents for Internet purchasing, online advertising, and marketing. The USPTO was criticized for granting too many E-Business patents whose only novelty was that they were Internet-related.

(C) POST-STATE STREET CASES

Tens of thousands of business method patent applications have been filed since State Street opened the floodgates. In 2000, "Amazon.com was granted a patent on its affiliates' program, which allows "owners of other Websites to refer customers to Amazon in exchange for a fee." Geneva Sapp, *E-Businesses vie for Technology Ownership*, NETWORK WORLD (Mar. 6, 2000). Amazon.com's "one-click" technology for online shopping was issued a patent. Amazon.com's 1–Click, a "method, and system for placing a purchase order via a communications network" sparked one of the most famous Internet patent debates. The patent permitted customers to make online purchases with a single click, using a pre-defined address and credit card number.

A federal court granted Amazon an injunction, enjoining Barnes & Noble for using a single-click Express Checkout on their online store. The parties settled before a trial to determine the validity of the one-click method. Amazon and Barnes & Noble settled their patent infringement dispute in 2000, with Barnes & Noble licensing the 1–Click patent. See *Amazon.com, Inc. v. Barnesandnoble.com, Inc.*, 239 F.3d 1343 (Fed. Cir. 2001) (vacating preliminary injunction awarded in favor of Amazon.com in patent dispute over one-stop Internet shopping business method).

§ 13.3 Internet-Related Patent Litigation

(A) INFRINGEMENT LAWSUITS

Patent infringement occurs when the defendant has made, used, or sold products within the scope of the inventor's claims. In a patent infringement lawsuit, claim construction is an issue for the court. In March of 2012, Yahoo! filed a patent infringement lawsuit against Facebook just as the social media market leader was making its Initial Public Offering ("IPO"). Yahoo!'s patent lawsuit alleges that Facebook had infringed ten different Yahoo! patents that are fundamental to social media, such as "personalized advertising, customized portal pages and news feeds, recommendations to connect with other suggested users (and screen out spammers), social music and messaging applications, and authorizing some users (but not others) to see different sections of your content." Tim Carmody, *Yahoo! Sues Facebook in a Web Patent Showdown*, EPICENTER (Mar. 13, 2012).

Facebook filed a counterclaim, charging that Yahoo! infringed ten of its patents. Facebook agreed to pay Microsoft Corporation $550 million for hundreds of patents that it originally purchased from America Online. Companies like Facebook need a robust portfolio of software patents to stave off lawsuits by patent trolls and to protect their intellectual property. For example, Google purchased Motorola Mobility for $12.5 billion. Most of the company's value was in its patent portfolio. The Apple-Microsoft-Oracle-Nokia consortium bought Nortel's patent portfolio for $4.5 billion. Microsoft bought Novell's patent portfolio for $450 million and some of AOL's patents for $1 billion.

Critics of Internet-related patents contend that these innovations would develop more rapidly without the type of patent protection that dampens competition. All patents balance antitrust concerns against market dominance. Too much patent protection for Internet-related business method patents may not be desirable because it undermines competitiveness. The trend towards propertization of Internet infrastructure has led to a more complex online business environment.

(B) MARKMAN HEARINGS

Markman hearings are held the by the court to determine claim construction at the onset of patent infringement litigation. See *Markman v. Westview Instruments Inc.*, 517 U.S. 370 (U.S. 1996). The court construes claims by using intrinsic evidence (the language of the claim) and extrinsic evidence (treatises, dictionaries or expert testimony) in making its assessment.

(C) E-BUSINESS PATENT TROLLS

A patent troll is the owner of a patent that does not use its intellectual property to produce products, but rather to file suit against alleged infringers. Trolls do not produce goods or services but rather use their inventions to threaten patent litigation. Critics fear that outsized Internet-related business methods will result in companies paying high licensing fees in its online activities where they are not due. Patent law reformers call for Congress to act to thwart a litigation crisis created by abusive patent trolls. One of the problems with the concept of the patent troll is it is over inclusive, including many universities and research institutes that have patent portfolios but do not themselves use them in inventions. Patent reform has stalled in Congress because the major stakeholders cannot agree on a legislative solution.

(D) THE SUPREME COURT'S PATENT CASES

(1) MercExchange

The injunctive remedy is often more important than monetary damages in Internet-related patent cases. An injunction is classified as an equitable remedy routinely used to order defendants to refrain from infringing patents. In *eBay Inc. v. MercExchange L.L.C.*, 547 U.S. 388 (S.Ct. 2006), the

Supreme Court unanimously determined that a federal court should not automatically issue an injunction simply because it has found patent infringement. The case arose out of dispute between eBay, the Internet's largest auction site, and MercExchange, which owned U.S. Patent 5,845,265 that covers eBay's "Buy It Now" function. In 2000, eBay initiated negotiations with MercExchange to purchase its online auction patent portfolio.

When eBay abandoned the negotiations to purchase the patent, MercExchange filed suit against eBay for patent infringement. MercExchange prevailed in a 2003 Virginia jury trial that found eBay had willfully infringed the patent incorporated in its "Buy It Now" function. MercExchange sought an injunction to prevent eBay's continual use of the patent, but the federal trial court denied its request. The Federal Circuit Court of Appeals reversed the trial court, reasoning that its decision was consistent with its long-standing practice of issuing permanent injunctions against patent infringement absent exceptional circumstances.

The long-standing rule in the Federal Circuit was to issue injunctions liberally in patent infringement cases so long as the plaintiff could prove an ongoing infringement. To put it bluntly, the federal court of appeals did not require patent owners to demonstrate irreparable harm. In eBay, the lower court refused to enjoin the online auction house, finding that damages were adequate. The Federal Circuit Court of Appeals reversed, ruling that in patent infringement cases an injunction issues absent exceptional circumstances.

The *MercExchange* Court ruled that the Federal Circuit improperly applied a presumed irreparable injury test as opposed to the traditional four-factor test for the issuance of a permanent injunction. The Supreme Court reversed the Federal Circuit's traditional practice of liberally issuing injunctions in patent infringement cases. The *MercExchange* Court ruled that federal courts must now weigh four factors before issuing an injunction: (1) that the plaintiff has suffered an irreparable injury, (2) that remedies available at law are inadequate to compensate for that injury, (3) that considering the balance of hardships between the plaintiff and defendant, a remedy in equity is warranted, and (4) that the public interest would not be disserved by a permanent injunction. The Court's finding that permanent injunctions are subject to the ordinary rules governing equitable relief means that relief is discretionary, as opposed to issued routinely.

Injunctive relief is critically imperative in Internet-related patent litigation because of the rapidity with which online businesses can attain or lose market share. In the Internet based economy, the earliest mover has enormous advantages and patent law is sometimes employed strategically as a method for excluding potential rivals.

(2) Bilski v. Kapos

In *Bilski v. Kapos*, 130 S.Ct. 3218 (S.Ct. 2010), the U.S. Supreme Court unanimously upheld the

Federal Circuit's decision that the application for a method of hedging risk was "an unpatentable abstract idea" that was outside the scope of the U.S. Patent Act, § 101. The patent application in *In re Bilski* was for a procedure that helped buyers and sellers protect against price fluctuations in the volatile energy market by hedging against price changes. The patent examiner rejected the application, explaining that it was a mere manipulation of an abstract idea and solves a mathematical problem without sufficient practical application. The Board of Patent Appeals and Interferences affirmed, concluding that the application only involved mental steps that transformed physical matter and was directed to an abstract idea.

The Federal Circuit heard the case *en banc* and affirmed, reasoning that the machine-or-transformation test was the sole test for determining the patentability of a process under Section 101. The Federal Circuit's view was that an invention is a "process" only if (1) tied to a particular machine or apparatus, or (2) it transforms a particular article into a different state or thing. The U.S. Supreme Court granted certiorari to determine whether the process patent was excluded from patentable subject matter.

The Court held that the Federal Circuit incorrectly endorsed the machine-or-transformation test for a process as the only valid criteria. The Court reasoned that the Federal Circuit test was a useful tool but not the sole method of deciding whether an invention is a patent-eligible process.

The Court decided that the process patent for hedging was unpatentable as an abstract idea. In *Bilski*, the Court was concerned that to allow "petitioners to patent risk hedging would pre-empt use of this approach in all fields."

The Court upheld the Federal Circuit's denial of patent but disagreed with the appeals court in its assessment of process patents. The Court explained that "[i]f a high enough bar is not set" for process patents—which "raise special problems in terms of vagueness and suspect validity"—"patent examiners and courts could be flooded with claims that would put a chill on creative endeavor and dynamic change." The *Bilski* decision is expected to narrow business-related claims.

The Court explained that *Bilski*'s application essentially disclosed "the basic concept of hedging or protecting against risk" and that allowing him "to patent risk hedging would preempt use of this approach in all fields, and would effectively grant a monopoly over an abstract idea." The *Bilski* decision limits the availability of process patents. *Bilski* calls for a rigorous review of software, business method and many Internet-related process claims.

In *MySpace, Inc. v. Graphon Corp.*, 672 F.3d 1250 (Fed. Cir. 2012), the Federal Circuit ruled that a patent relating to the ability to create, modify, and store database records over a computer network was invalid as anticipated and obvious based on prior art. A dissenting judge would have applied *Bilski*, reasoning that Graphon's patents fell outside the ambit of section 101 "because they are too useful and too widely applied to possibly form the basis of any patentable invention."

CONCLUSION:

Patent law, like the other branches of the law, is constantly evolving in response to the Internet. Justice Holmes's classic essay on the path of the law drew upon six centuries of case reports and statutes. In less than twenty-five years, the Internet has created a huge number of new legal dilemmas and challenges in accommodating this new information technology. As this book has shown, the Internet transforms basic assumptions about the nature of communication, knowledge, invention, information, sovereignty, identity, commerce, human rights and community. Intellectual property law is being fundamentally reshaped because the Internet is shattering existing precedent by redefining distance, time, privacy and the meaning of territoriality. The phenomenal growth in traffic on the World Wide Web requires that established legal principles for all branches of the law be adapted to cyberspace.

Internet law must become a moving stream rather than a stagnant pool, evolving to meet the new risks and dangers in the twenty-first century's age of information. Further global coordination is essential to surmount the growing substantive and procedural barriers to cross-border Internet-related development. Travelers on the World Wide Web require uniform procedural and substantive remedies for cross-border civil rights and wrongs, a very difficult achievement because of national rivalries and cultural differences.

"Harmonization has proven difficult enough even in relatively uncontroversial areas like trademark law, however. It may well be impossible to harmonize laws where there is less agreement on principles among nations—laws relating to free speech...The prospect of being subject to litigation in a number of different countries is likely to be extremely daunting to individuals and even small and medium-sized businesses." MARK LEMLEY ET. AL., SOFTWARE & INTERNET LAW 617 (2003). My goal in writing this book is not only to show where Internet law is today, but also to explain the global conflicts over legal principles as a guide toward illuminating the path that this global harmonization needs to take.

INDEX

References are to Pages

CYBERSQUATTING

DAMAGES

DATA PROTECTION DIRECTIVE

INTERNET ARCHITECTURE BOARD

INTERNET-RELATED CONTRACT LAW

INTERNET CORPORATION FOR ASSIGNED NAMES AND NUMBERS (ICANN)